The Marijuana Smokers

THE MARIJUANA SMOKERS

ERICH GOODE

: :

Basic Books, Inc., Publishers

NEW YORK LONDON

TO MY WIFE

© 1970 by Basic Books, Inc.
Library of Congress Catalog Card Number: 78–126949
SBN 465–04381–x
Manufactured in the United States of America
DESIGNED BY VINCENT TORRE

FOREWORD

Alfred R. Lindesmith
Professor of Sociology, Indiana University

It seems clear today that our antimarijuana laws must and will be changed. Indeed, something like two-thirds of the states have already either reduced penalties or have such reductions under consideration. A similar trend has appeared on the national scene. In the meantime the great debate on the subject, which is so skillfully dissected and probed by Professor Goode, rages on. On the one hand, the use of marijuana seems to be spreading in ever-widening circles, while, on the other, the debate itself seems to be intensifying and regressing to lower levels. What began some decades ago as a fairly dignified intellectual argument among relatively small numbers of scholars, scientists, and public officials has degenerated into something like a huge barroom brawl with nearly everyone getting into the act. The fact that changes in the laws now seem to be in the offing probably has less connection with the debate than with the fact that pot is now being smoked by so many sons and daughters and some adults of the affluent and influential classes that wield political power.

The use of drugs constitutes intrinsically a personal habit, which, if it leads to any harm, directly and primarily injures the user himself rather than others. According to the doctrine of criminal law, acts ought ordinarily to be defined as crimes only when they threaten or injure others. Since our marijuana and other drug laws provide severe punishment for the mere possessor of the drug, regardless of whether there is any harm to others or even to self, they are correctly designated as morality legislation. Professor Goode has thus provided us with a superb account and analysis of the dilemmas, contradictions, and problems generated by the attempt to legislate morality.

Perhaps a central dilemma of the antimarijuana laws and of our drug laws in general is that the evil personal and social consequences of felony prosecutions are probably greater than are the effects of any drug, whether it be marijuana, heroin, or alcohol. Historical examples of the unhappy consequences that seem characteristically to follow from governmental attemps to suppress popular bad habits by exercising policy power are numerous. The current crisis with respect to heroin addiction in our biggest cities after a half century of severe repression is another example.

It is axiomatic in democratic societies that, to be effective and just, governing must be done with the consent of the governed. To be effectively enforced, laws must enlist popular support and be based on some reasonable societal consensus. Sheer majority rule is not the whole story either, for it entails the hazard of tyranny by the majority. On the majority principle alone the blacks in the United States would have no hope, since they could always be outvoted by the white majority. The drug problem, like that of race, involves fundamental principles that qualify and limit majority rule, such as those of minority rights, individual liberty, equality before the law, and the right of privacy. Official discussions of drug policy have in the past ordinarily ignored such matters and have, instead, focused almost exclusively on punishment, deterrence, and protection of society, with society so conceived as to exclude the user of illicit drugs.

To those who believe as I do that the present marijuana laws are unjust and divisive and that the pot debate is more dangerous to the society than pot itself, the current disposition on many questions to treat the whole subject as a joke suggests that basic change may be nearer than we think. As Goode effectively demonstrates, mere evidence, logical arguments, and the other standard devices that are used to persuade and produce consensus among reasonable men do not seem to work in this case—perhaps because the debate is not a real one but only an expression of underlying and unstated motivations, resentments, or political considerations. Perhaps the case for reform can best be made by jokes and laughter.

At any rate, it is evident that a great deal of public joking is being done and that the user of marijuana is not seriously regarded as a genuine criminal. Recent movies, for example, portray the use of pot as a gag, and at least one movie director has stated that real marijuana was smoked during the filming. Pot parties, involving the commission of what the statutes define as heinous crimes, have been presented on the television screen to entertain the viewing public. Various popular television programs regularly include pot jokes. In private conversations such jokes are even more common, and little or no stigma attaches in many circles to admitting in private that one has smoked or would like to smoke. Numerous stories float around about policemen, even naroctic agents, who smoke the weed or have at least tried it. The experiment with alcohol prohibition, it will be remembered, was also to some extent laughed out of court.

It, of course, is no laughing matter to be busted for a marijuana offense, as the police sometimes grimly remind us. Nevertheless, the statistical evidence demonstrates that criticism of the laws, widespread disregard and disrespect for the marijuana laws and their enforcers, and the sheer impossibilty and absurdity of trying to lock up any appreciable proportion of the users, especially of middle- and upper-class users, has begun seriously to undermine enforcement morale. In agreement with a large proportion of the public, enforcement and court officials probably intuitively believe that it is harm to others, not to self, that makes crime and consequently find it impossible or difficult to think of a marijuana user as a real criminal. The idea that such persons should be incarcerated in already overcrowded penal institutions in order to protect society and to cure them of a personal habit which harms no one else, and possibly not even them, is probably hard for officials to grasp also. At any rate, there is an enormous gap between the law as written and the law as actually enforced, and this fact further discredits the system and the establishment.

Professor Goode does not spell out precisely what changes ought to be made or what our drug policy ought to be. He is primarily concerned with depicting the way of life and points of view of the marijuana smoker and with analyzing the arguments and perspectives of those who are in one way or another concerned with marijuana policy. Information of the kind he presents so perceptively, honestly, and fully should play a vital and indispensable role in the eventual formulation of a wiser policy than the present one. Perhaps the implication of his book might best be described as procedural rather than substantive: that before we legislate we should know what we are doing and try to understand both the people whom we legislate against and those whom we think we are protecting. It is probable, for example, that if the drug laws were framed so as to provide protection from dangers which the young, users and nonusers alike, themselves perceive as dangers, they would support such laws. At present the law poses a greater threat than the drugs themselves. What is implied by these suggestions is not necessarily that marijuana be legalized, whatever that means, but that we return to the principle of government with the consent of the governed.

July 1970

ACKNOWLEDGMENTS

Styles of research are as varied as the researchers who practice them. At one pole we have the massively collective enterprise, located in a well-endowed bureau of research, often undertaken by no one in particular and completed by a dozen hands whose involvement bears no relation to the interests or passions of their lives; not uncommonly, the project is conducted for the simple reason that some organization will derive, or thinks it will derive, some practical utility therefrom, and is willing to pay for it. At the other pole, we have the efforts of a lone scholar, be he amateur or professional who imbues every aspect of his work with the stamp of his idiosyncrasies and concerns; with him, the project is undertaken and the research completed not because it was financially supported, but because he was determined to find out what the answers were.

In spite of the fact that this book belongs to the latter of these two types, the debts I have incurred in the effort are manifold. First and foremost among them is the thanks that is due my 204 respondents. It is their book, really, their story, and I hope that I have been faithful to their will and impulse. Certainly this book would not exist without their cooperation and their willingness to risk exposure by talking to me. It is their wish, naturally, to receive my thanks anonymously. Second, the cost of many of the more tedious details of research were covered by the National Institute of Mental Health whose grant (MH–15659) enabled me to pay a part-time research assistant for one year, a job which Miss Judith Rutberg performed with especial efficiency and good cheer. In addition, a Faculty Research Fellowship from the Research Foundation of the State University of New York relieved me of the burden of having to earn a living during the two summers of 1968 and 1969 that it took to write this book. To both granting agencies I am profoundly grateful. The sponsorship of neither indicates any agreement with my conclusions; in fact, insofar as it is possible to detect an official view, that of both agencies would be unfavorable to my own. It is a sign of a healthy society that support may be found for views which vary from the official perspective.

The third debt I owe is to the colleagues and friends who offered useful comments, criticisms, suggestions, and pieces of information. Some of the most helpful of these I received from Jerry Mandel, Eliot Freidson, Andrew Weil, Richard Evans Schultes, John Gagnon, Harvey Farberman, Bill French, Stephen Berger, James Hudson, Stephen Cole, John O'Donnell, Gilbert Geis, Robert Bagnall, Josephine Lopez, Richard Bogg, and David and Nanci Orlow. I was privileged to make use of a manuscript of a forthcoming book by Professor John Kaplan on marijuana use which proved to be extremely useful. Generally, our conclusions separately corroborate one another, but some cross-fertilization did take place. In writing style, my editor, William Gum, has done an heroic job of keeping my untidy prose in reasonably readable form. And finally, my wife, Alice, who tolerated a partial neglect during my productive months, deserves at least one hosanna.

A few sections of this book have appeared in print previously. Chapter 3, "Marijuana and the Politics of Reality," is a slightly revised version of an article of the same name which was published in the June 1969 issue of the *Journal of Health and Social Behavior*. Chapter 8, "Multiple Drug Use among Marijuana Smokers," is a revised and expanded version of a paper which first appeared in the Summer 1969 issue of *Social Problems* (published by The Society for the Study of Social Problems). Chapter 10, "Using, Selling, and Dealing Marijuana," appeared, in condensed form, in the *Columbia Forum*, Winter 1969 as "The Marijuana Market." The section in Chapter 7 on sexual behavior was published in the May 1969 issue of the *Evergreen Review*, as "Marijuana and Sex." I occasionally quote from my anthology, *Marijuana*, published by the Atherton Press, 1969. Permission to reprint these works is gratefully acknowledged.

E. G.

June 1970
Strong's Neck, New York

CONTENTS

The Marijuana Smokers

: *Chapter* 1 :

Overview

Social change during the decade of the 1960s has been phenomenal, especially in several dramatic sectors of society. Broadly based movements today characterized the position of only a few scattered individuals in 1960. Many ideas and forms of behavior practiced by those at the margins of society have been absorbed into groups that represent, if not the mainstream, then at least the growing edge, of American social life. In the less than half a generation from 1960 to 1970, fundamental changes have taken place that will permanently alter the shape of history. The most important of these changes have been cultural, not technological. That man has walked the surface of the moon, as this century lumbers into its last quarter, tells us very little about the texture of a single man's life; on the other hand, the fact that huge segments of American society are irretrievably disenchanted with legitimate political channels tells us a great deal about the quality of life in this society at this particular point in time.

The increased use of illegal drugs is one of the most dramatic of social changes in this decade. The use of marijuana in colleges in 1960 was almost unknown; in 1970, it is commonplace. Any activity that swelled to the same degree would attract a great deal of attention, whether it be wearing short skirts or engaging in premarital intercourse. The fact that marijuana use is subject to severe penalties makes it newsworthy indeed. That increasingly larger subcommunities cluster about it makes marijuana even better news. And because it powerfully ties in with dozens of other activities and institutions, study of its use has become vitally important.

Social change is the most troublesome and difficult of all areas of social life to analyze. The task of understanding a society at one point in time is formidable; to understand it in flux is overwhelming. Yet social scientists are expected to make predictions on demand. Like everyone else, they are often wrong. Fads and fashions wax and wane. Today's craze makes tomorrow's trash. Yet fluctuations are not Brownian bursts of random energy; some of what happens from year to year has a method and a design. The river that one steps into at one point in time is not wholly different at a later time. Many of the more trivial features of the social life of any society have no pattern; the core features of all societies make temporal sense.

One of the central theses of this book is that the immense increase in non-narcotic drug use in the past decade is an organic outgrowth of a newly evolving way of life whose precise features can now only be dimly perceived, even by its participants. Marijuana use today is not a fad, not a craze. It is not going to be wished away, and legal measures to eradicate it will be only partially successful. Whether we like it or not, potsmoking is here to stay. It might be wise to try to understand it.

Questions reveal biases. What we ask reflects what we think. The phenomenon of marijuana use is a bright, glittering jewel, each facet of which flashes a different color. Observers stand in one spot only, and see only one color. And each thinks he sees the whole. The questions of agents of social control are puzzled, anxious questions, revealing the incredulity that anyone would want to partake of such an activity. The question "Why?" indicates that the activity requires an explanation; "Why?" can often be transformed into, "Why would anyone want to do such a thing?"

Sociologists stand in a different spot, and therefore see a different reality. The "why" question takes many problematic questions for granted. Social scientists usually start with more basic questions: "What?" "How?" "Under what circumstances?" The "why" question assumes that many aspects of a phenomenon are already understood and, given these assumptions, those who ask it cannot conceive of the outcome which they observe. The sociologist urges us to take a first look at a poorly understood phenomenon—whether it be the family, the priesthood, or marijuana smoking.

His basic point of departure is the attempt to understand an activity, a belief, an institution, a way of life, in much the same manner as its participants. Each has its own peculiar, unique integrity and vibrancy, its own rules and logic. Each makes sense according to a set of principles often contradicted by, or irrelevant to, other activities, beliefs, institutions, or ways of life. To fully understand a social phenomenon, it is necessary to grasp it empathically, accepting it on its own terms and identifying emotionally with its central principles. Any social analysis missing this dimension is of limited value; as ethnography, it must be deemed worthless.

To understand is to condone, so the aphorism has it. In some sense or another, perhaps. But not to understand is to condemn without knowing why. As Peter Berger wrote, a spy ignorant of the enemy's strong points helps only the enemy. It is unfortunate that warfare analogies must be employed to illuminate the American drug scene, but we only reflect a scene where the battle lines have already been drawn. And whether we are propagandists for or against drugs, or whether we insist our stance is neutral (as all propagandists claim), we will be embroiled in controversy, and our statements will, inevitably, be used to defend or attack an argument. Whether we like it or not, we are participants in an ideological battle.

What does this do for our much vaunted objectivity? The mature sciences concern themselves not at all with their objectivity, never thinking of it as an issue; they know a fact when they see one. Social scientists are more defensive, almost self-righteous in their assertion of lack of bias. Like so many other issues, however, objectivity is a bugaboo. Of course, attempting an insider's view of a group or an activity is adopting a biased view. But so is adopting an outsider's view. In fact, there is no such thing as an "objective" view of reality. All views of reality are biased in one way or another. This does not mean that all are wrong, or even that all are right. It does mean that all rest on necessarily unprovable assumptions, all are underpinned by an ontology which transcends scientific technique. Scientific technique itself rests on faith. It demands that the real world be viewed in one manner, and that alternate versions of viewing the world be ignored. For certain purposes, this is very useful. For others, it is not. While the scientific version of reality offers the claim that it *is* the real world, as a sociologist, we must say that it is one particular version of the real world, true or false, according to certain assumptions. If we do not accept the rules of the game in the first place, then the whole scientific enterprise is meaningless.

Accepting cultural patterns as valid on their own level is a very useful bias for certain kinds of purposes. We do not, by doing so, attempt to prove, say, that the American government is riddled with Communists (if we are studying the John Birch Society), or that marijuana is harmless and beneficial (if we are studying pot-smokers). We do not mean that they are "true" in the traditional scientific sense of the word. We mean that they are true in that they are woven into the viscera of the people we are studying, and that they are extremely meaningful to them. They are true in the emotional sense. They represent valid belief-alternatives, and they spring from powerful social and psychological needs. They are part of an ideological and cultural whole, a fabric that is relatively consistent, a system that is eloquent testimony to personal and social locations. We say that the biggest slice of the most essential reality of each man is the reality as seen through his eyes. No matter that two versions of what is right and what wrong will be almost totally contradictory. Both represent authentic modes of living, ideological positions that are, on the affective level, inviolable and irrefutable. If we do not accept this principle, what we are doing cannot be called social science.

One of the reasons why the attempt to understand a deviant or criminal activity from the first-person point of view is seen as biased is that in the past, the "institutional" or "correctional" viewpoint has been dominant, that is, the conception that the legal and moral transgressor has in some measure erred and must be dealt with by agents of correction. Official agencies of social control have in the past been successful in defining the climate of right and wrong; their view (similar to and, supposedly, based on, the scientific point of view) was imperialistic in that they demanded the right to define right and wrong for all members of society. Any viewpoint which contravened their own was labelled biased. If deviance is viewed in correctional terms, we cannot but see the effort to understand the deviant from his own perspective as biased. But if we look at the agents of social control as one out of a multiplicity of definers of social reality, no more or less valid than any other, then the possibility is open for us to see the deviant through his own eyes. If, on the other hand, we adopt a condescending social worker point of view toward him, that is, the view that we must help him to adjust to society, we will be wholly incapable of understanding him.

We wish, therefore, to adopt a perspective which *decentralizes* sources of reality-definitions. We wish to throw open a dialogue with all participants in the activity that we are studying. No one definition of the situation will be allowed to impose itself on any and all participants. Each version of reality will glint a particle of the total (even though each version will almost invariably claim to tell the whole story). Each will be incomplete, although valid on its own level.

Another way of saying something similar is that we assume *intentionality* on the actor's part. Marijuana users are fully aware of what they are doing; they enter into the activity, from start to finish, with open eyes. They are not unwitting dupes, they have not been conned by a clever "slick," eager to make a profit from their naiveté. They have *chosen* to smoke marijuana. There is an active element in their choosing. They imagine themselves, prior to the act of becoming "turned on," actually smoking. They carry the actions through, in their minds, conceiving of what they would do "if." They have weighed alternatives. They have considered social costs. They operate on the basis of a value system; marijuana use is in part an outgrowth of that value system; using it is a realistic and a rational choice in that marijuana use will often be and obtain for them what they anticipate. The basic values may *themselves* be thought of as irrational by someone with a more positivistic and scientific-technological-economistic point of view, but this is largely a matter of definition. Let me illustrate: if I want to become high, smoking marijuana is a rational choice, but drinking a cup of coffee to attain that state is irrational. The value of becoming high might be viewed as irrational within the framework of certain values prevalent in America today, but many marijuana users question those very values.

This point of view holds that marijuana use grows out of many of the processes in society which we all take to be normal. It is convenient to label as pathological any phenomenon that we do not like. We attempt to legitimate our biases by claiming for an activity traits that we reject. Thus, marijuana use becomes a product of boredom—because boredom is a bad thing, and if marijuana use is produced by it, marijuana use must also be a bad thing. Or it is rebellion against the older generation or a result of a broken home or the wish to escape reality or to avoid meaningful attachments to other people.

My view is substantially different. It is quite conceivable that marijuana use grows out of these (socially defined) undesirable conditions, but we do not wish to force a premature closure. It could very well grow out of some characteristics which society holds are entirely desirable. By *defining* marijuana use as noxious, we are preordaining both cause and consequence. I feel that an important dimension is the definitions that users themselves bring to the drug and its use—and very often these definitions are wholly positive. The tack to take in attempting an understanding of marijuana use is not, they must be mistaken; why do they persist in being mistaken? But what slant on reality do these values have, and how can we attempt to understand them on their own terms?

In discussing with a psychiatrist some of the findings on sex—that two-thirds of the people interviewed said that they enjoyed sex more when high on marijuana—he remarked that it was obvious this was a wish-fantasy on their part. They needed something by which they *could* enjoy sex at all and therefore projected these qualities onto the drug. This psychiatrist discounted the users' self-expressed effects because of his preconceptions concerning the nature of and motives for marijuana use, as well as a theoretical tradition that makes such assumptions possible.

The sociologist, on the other hand, feels that he can uncover his respondent's actual feelings in a brief interview—that is, feelings on certain levels and about certain aspects of his life. The psychiatrist may feel that many months of deep psychoanalysis would begin to tap some unconscious feelings of which even the individual is not aware. Perhaps the two approaches should not be thought of as contradictory but merely different. The sociologist, at any rate, takes seriously the expressed meaning that an activity has for its actors. This does not necessarily mean that this is the only "true" approach, or even the approach that is "most true." But it is one layer of reality, and a layer very much worth knowing.

Another way of putting this is that we wish to examine the *mythological* level. This might appear to contradict our earlier principle. In fact, it is entirely consistent with it. We do not mean by "myth" that which is untrue. The question of truth and falsity is largely irrelevant—at least on the ethnographic level. That a rain dance does not really cause rain to fall is, in a sense, irrelevant. That is has a certain vibrancy in a tribal fabric is, on the other hand, of utmost relevancy. By treating a group or society's collective wisdom as tribal folklore is not to demean it; it is in fact an effort to elevate it to the status of the semisacred. Myth grows organically out of the visceral troubles of a people; any attempt to refute its validity is inevitably misplaced. The position of physicians or potsmokers, their elaborate descriptions of the effects of marijuana, its dangers or benefits, tells a great deal more about physicians and potsmokers than it does about marijuana.

An attorney declared to a California Senate committee that "marijuana is . . . less harmful than malted milk." A California lawman stated "That . . . marijuana is a harmful and destructive substance is not open to question or debate by reasonable individuals." The overwhelming fact concerning marijuana is that there is rabid debate about it, that disagreement concerning its essential reality is total, that opinions concerning what it is and what it does cover the entire spectrum from pernicious to wholly beneficial. The central problem about marijuana is not who uses it and why, or what does it do to the human body and mind, but how can such conflicting versions of its basic effects be maintained, and what sorts of arguments are invoked to justify its use or suppression?

My position is that myths are real—but not quite. Myths are one essential level of reality, one facet of the jewel, one layer of the elusive truths surrounding any phenomenon. Several competing myths may exist in the same society at the same time which are mutually exclusive. They cannot both be true in the traditional sense. The fact that marijuana is less harmful than malted milk and at the same time a harmful and destructive substance cannot, without quibbling, be both true. Yet they both tap an essential reality; they both answer certain kinds of sociocultural needs and correspond to certain values. (*In addition*, one *or* the other could be true in the more limited scientific or pharmacological sense.)

The most interesting thing about a drug to a sociologist is not what it *does*, but what it is *thought* to do. In fact, what it is thought to do often has a great impact on what it actually does. A sociology of drugs accepts as of only secondary importance a drug's strict pharmacological effects. In fact, the *concept*, the *category* "drug" is a social construct, not a pharmacological conception. This is the definition in the most popular pharmacology textbook, *The Pharmacological Basis of Therapeutics*: ". . . a drug is broadly defined as any chemical agent which affects living protoplasm. . . ." In an earlier edition the editors added, "Few substances would escape inclusion by this definition." Therefore, the roster of drugs elicited from a pharmacologist would look very different from one which a sociologist would make up. A corporation lawyer, too, would have his own conception of what a drug is—in fact, anything listed in a nation's pharmacopeia. A criminal lawyer, on the other hand, might think of drugs in terms of illicitly used substances. Society's definition would include various dangers of different substances as part of the definition, even though, pharmacologically, some substances which are included might very well be far less dangerous than some which are excluded; something "negatively valued," above and beyond an objective assessment of the "actual" dangers, is implied in the definition.

The notion of "drugs" as a single and "natural" entity is totally misleading. Some categories of drugs may form a relatively uniform family with similar pharmacologic properties. However, socially, they may be in totally different worlds. The interconnections between them may exist in a laboratory, may be expressed by a rat's responses, but they may have no connection in the real world, as to how they are used and why, what sorts of effects are imputed to them, who uses them, and indeed, what they actually do to the human mind and body.

This is self-evident to most of us. Yet, if it really were to most observers of the drug scene, many pages and many hours of pseudo debate could be avoided. For instance, take the question of whether marijuana is a dangerous drug. It is inconceivable that this question can be answered outside of a social context, in a social vacuum. *Dangerous under what set of circumstances?* As used by whom? While doing what? In what dosage? Combined with what life style? Given what national and cultural traditions? Used in conjunction with what other drugs? Dangerous *compared to what?* And what do we *mean* by "dangerous"? The definition of dangerous is a social definition. There will be some effects that all will agree are dangerous. But many effects will be thought dangerous by some, harmless by others, and beneficial by still others. None of the basic questions that are asked about marijuana can be answered outside a social setting; it is the social context that determines what sort of answer we give, not the intrinsic properties of the drug itself. The drug is an *element* in the equation, but only one among several.

These are obvious statements, but it would be mistaken to believe that most observers would accept them. Even experts blunder into one fatuous debate after another. It is as if general principles have nothing to do with specific issues.

We are told Oriental studies show, by the crude measures applied, that cannabis may have some long-term toxic effects on the human body. Yet we find that the marijuana or hashish smoked is (1) often smoked with opium and other substances with whose dangers we are more well acquainted; (2) is smoked very often by unemployed men who smoke eight, ten, or fifteen hours a day and who, almost literally, do nothing but smoke hashish; (3) that immense quantities are smoked of often potent substances, even 100 times as much as a daily marijuana smoker in America would be able to consume; (4) and that the level of caloric intake and health conditions in the countries described—India, Egypt, and North Africa—among all the poor inhabitants would be sufficient to induce many of the effects described without needing to consider the role of marijuana. Yet how easily we transfer the "effects" of this drug, whether American marijuana or the more potent Middle Eastern hashish, from one cultural and economic setting to the other. It is doubtful that the comparison is relevant at all, since none of the basic conditions are remotely similar.

The promarijuana lobby tells us that marijuana is a gentle herb, nothing more than pressed flowers and leaves, a peaceful and love-inducing substance. Both sides assume that there is some sort of property lodged within the drug itself that dictates to its users how to act under its influence. But whether it does, in fact, have this pacific property or not depends wholly on who uses it. If it is used by a social group that *thinks* marijuana is a pacific weed, whose members, when initiating a neophyte, preach a gospel of peace and love, discourage violent displays, and weave this peace motif into the things they do when high, then we should not be surprised that marijuana turns out to have a peace-inducing property. Only the most naive believes that marijuana creates a peaceful way of life out of whole cloth and induces it in those who are not peaceful. Both motorcycle gangs and hippies are prone to use marijuana but with very different results. Obviously, there is more to the picture than the laboratory properties of the drug.

I will attempt in this volume an overall study of the sociology of marijuana use. I will explore the myths clinging to it, the attitudes of the contestants in the marijuana debate, the question of who uses it, under what circumstances, and with what consequences. To answer many of the questions concerning marijuana use, it is necessary at times to leave the sociological level and deal with related issues. For instance, when discussing the effects of marijuana, I will reject the radically sociologistic approach—that the effects of the drug are wholly a function of its social definitions—and attempt an exposition on the objective properties of the drug's pharmacology. In other words, I have adopted a multidimensional approach; my perspective often shifts from one level to another. At the same time, we wish to understand the drug's nonsociological aspects more or less only insofar as they relate to, interpenetrate with, influence and are influenced by, the users' social life and the lives of those who interact with them. We court confusion with this kind of multifaceted perspective, but it is necessary if we are to understand the totality of marijuana's impact on the social life of any society.

Overview of Marijuana and Marijuana Use

Incidences of events connected with cannabis use, whether true or phantasmagoric, survive historically because they are useful ideologically. The history of marijuana use is, in itself, a study in creative mythology. This is as true of the history of the Assassins as it is of the Indian peace pipe. The Assassins killed out of fanatical religious devotion—hashish or no hashish—and the American Indian did not become peaceful as a result of smoking marijuana in his pipe, a myth which the procannabis side propagates to demonstrate the weed's pacific properties; the Indian had no marijuana to put in his pipe. "The American Indians never used it in their peace pipes," writes Richard Evans Schultes, one of the world's experts on ethnobotany; the "American Indian . . . did not anywhere have *Cannabis sativa* at his disposal in pre-Colombian times," agrees Michael Harner, an anthropologist who studies the use of psychoactive substances among Indians. Were Malayan tribesmen who ran amok high on marijuana? Were Patrice Lumumba's followers under the influence of cannabis when they displayed "orgiastic frenzy and homicidal ferocity" in battle? [1] Was Victor Licata intoxicated by marijuana when, on October 17, 1933, in Tampa, Florida, he hacked his entire family (father, mother, and three brothers) to death with an axe?[2] Have India's holy men been inspired by the cannabis high? Answers to these questions depend more on what we think of marijuana than what actually happened historically. Recorded history is largely myth-making, an effort to align supposed events with our own ideology.

Marijuana has played a medicinal role in every area in which it was grown, including the United States where from colonial days until well into the twentieth century it was used to cure a variety of ills: acute depression, tetanus, gonorrhea, insomnia, malaria, insanity, stuttering, migraine headaches, flatulence, epilepsy, delirium tremens, asthma, cancer, and chronic itching—with understandably mixed results. Until 1937, when federal law outlawed its possession and sale, marijuana was a staple in many patent medicine catalogues.[3] Today, of course, very few physicians take marijuana's therapeutic role seriously; in fact, physicians usually define drug abuse as the use of a drug outside a medical context. That marijuana use is invariably abuse is deduced from the fact that marijuana has no legitimate medical treatment function whatsoever; any use, in the medical view, is by definition misuse or abuse. Although the therapeutic argument for marijuana will occasionally be invoked by users and pro-pot propagandists, in general, most do not take it any more seriously than the physicians do; they are content with the argument that the drug is simply harmless and does not cause or compound any medical problems.

The use of marijuana, or Indian hemp, for medical purposes considerably predates its use for psychoactive purposes. Its origins as a medicinal herb are, of course, lost in primal obscurity. Norman Taylor, a botanist, writes that mention of hemp may be found in a pharmacy manual from 2737 B.C., supposedly written by a Chinese emperor, Shen Nung.[4] This story found its way into a vast number of essays on marijuana,[5] including my own.[6] Actually, the emperor turns out to be mythological; Shen is a component of Chinese folk religion, creator of agriculture, and one of the gods most widely worshipped in pre-Revolutionary China, with his own altar, *hsien-nung t'an*.[7] The *Treatise on Medicine* attributed to Shen was "compiled by an early Han dynasty writer, whose sources go back only as far as the fourth century B.C."[8] Marijuana's recorded history, then, stretches back at the very least two and a half millennia;

archaeological evidence of its cultivation and use may be placed something like five thousand years in the past. Its functions have been almost as diverse as the cultures which have employed it. It would be impossible to discuss its patterns of use in every country at all of its periods of history, even were such documentation available. This overview, then, will serve as a backdrop for our more detailed discussions of its use in contemporary America.

In the United States, the most common slang words for marijuana are pot, grass, tea, weed, and smoke, in decreasing order of frequency. The derivation of all of these terms is obvious, except for pot. One etymologist has claimed that the word pot comes from a South American drink which contained, among other things, marijuana seeds soaked in guava wine or brandy, known as *potacíon de guaya,* or *potaguaya.*[9] Marijuana is very occasionally called "shit" in America, a term usually reserved for heroin. The obvious import of this designation should delight the psychoanalytically inclined. It ties in with toilet training—especially in view of its conjunction with pot (i.e., the children's pottie or chamber pot)—as well as filth, in view of the disorganized, casual and even squalid way of life of a few conspicuous marijuana users, and its symbolization as a rebellion against traditional mores and most users' middle-class upbringing, and an effort to shock conventional relatives, neighbors, former friends, and other authority-figure observers.[10] The term "reefer" is often used among urban blacks to mean the marijuana itself; reefer can occasionally mean a marijuana cigarette, although this term is used much less today than it was a generation ago. The cigarette butt is known as a "roach," supposedly because it looks something like a small cockroach. (Such derivations are always problematic, often more fantasy than fact.) Also, conjecturally, because of the Mexican song, "La Cucaracha," in which a cockroach couldn't walk until it had its marijuana.[11]

Today's terms will probably go out of style, as have countless other terms used a decade or a generation ago. The word "viper," for instance, for marijuana smoker, has been replaced by the broader term "head," meaning the user (more or less regularly) of any drug, usually non-narcotic. Viper is used by no one today. Common terms for marijuana up until the late 1950s and early 1960s were gage, boo, Mary Jane; although used somewhat humorously today, they are rather obsolescent as simple descriptive names. Terms used more than twenty years ago (and less than that by older heads still using drugs), totally outdated, never used, and completely obsolete are mooters, mutah, mota, gates, greeters, griffo, griefo, giggle smoke, jive, mohasky, rope, mezz, goof-butts, Mary Warner, viper's weed, sweet Lucy, root and muggles. Many currently published glossaries will contain these terms, as if they were still used, or as if they might have a resurrection. An expert on criminal argot, for instance, claims: ". . . it is rare that a word can be labelled truly obsolete, for about the time that label is applied, it is almost certain to pop up in another area or among a different class of addicts; it has merely been kept alive in some obscure circles which have not been currently studied." [12] Although this process no doubt occurs, I think that it is safe to say that all of the above-mentioned terms are obsolete. Since no marijuana smokers to my knowledge know of these terms, it is highly unlikely that any of them will be revived. "Muggles" (the principal slang word for marijuana in Maurer and Vogel's classic book) would evoke uproarious laughter if a young user stumbled on it in a book today.[13]

Marijuana is a plant, *Cannabis sativa*. All marijuana plants are of one species, but there exists at least three varieties: *Cannabis sativa indica, americana,* and *mexicana,* whose names obviously denote the areas in which they characteristically grow. The Western Hemisphere varieties, however, are not indigenous; they were introduced by the coming of the European. In a reply to a request for information on this point, Richard Evans Schultes, director of Harvard's botanical museum, wrote: ". . . Cannabis . . . is Asiatic in origin, and . . . it ocurs in the New World only as an introduced species. . . . In the United States, it has spread from former hemp plantations and is now widely occurring as a spontaneous 'escape.' It apparently was brought to North America first by the Pilgrims . . . , and was grown for its fiber" (personal communication, July 8, 1969).

The marijuana plant today grows in the overwhelming majority of the countries of the world, including all those in the Western Hemisphere, Africa, the entire continent of Asia, Australia, and the Indonesian archipelago. A few scattered varieties may be found in Europe.[14] In spite of the botanical affinities between the various subspecies of *Cannabis sativa,* the psychoactive component of the plant is wildly variable from one plant to another. The strength of the drug in a given preparation may be determined by several factors:

1) Gender of the plant. Female plants are much more richly endowed with the active ingredient of the drug. The male plant, taller, weedier, and more fibrous—used in the last century and before for rope and cloth—contains some potency, but is considerably weaker than its mate.

2) Time of harvesting. Marijuana harvested too soon (before the resin appears) or too late (after the male plant fertilizes the female) will be considerably weaker and less active than plants harvested at the most favorable time (sometime in September, varying, however, from one region to another).

3) Method of harvesting. If the male is removed at harvesting time and only the female is harvested and processed, the impact of the substance is greater than if the two are harvested together. Since this is difficult and tedious, however, it is very rarely done.

4) Region in which the plant grows. Plants grown in hot, dry climates produce the strongest preparations. Temperate climates produce comparatively weak substances.

5) Proportion of resin. Hashish contains nothing but pressed resin or "flowering tops," of the Cannabis plant, and is about five times as strong as a preparation which contains mostly leaves, the substance most commonly designated as "marijuana." The higher the leaf grows on the plant, the more resin it contains and the stronger it is.

Some marijuana consumed in this country is grown here, usually on a small-scale basis and is reputed to be considerably weaker than imported varieties. The expert smoker will recognize at least a half-dozen or so varieties of marijuana, of which two, "Acapulco Gold," and "Panama Red," are especially potent. (Often any quality marijuana, "dynamite" grass in the jargon, will be labelled "Gold.") Hashish (hash in American slang, and *charas* in India and Pakistan) is imported into the United States from the Middle East (often Lebanon), North Africa (often Morocco), Afghanistan, and sometimes from the Indian subcontinent.

Harvesting hashish is a more delicate and time-consuming operation than harvesting simple marijuana. It is done by one of a variety of methods. In earlier times, the pollen was scraped off the sweaty bodies of laborers who had run through a cannabis field for this very purpose. Later, leather aprons were employed. I have heard of three contemporary techniques. An ex-hashish smuggler who operated in North Africa about 1965 explained to me that the stalk of the plant, pointing downward, is grasped in one hand, while the other hand, which is gloved, thrusts the flowering tops into a receptacle, simultaneously shaking off the resin. Sometimes the resin is removed from the plant by covering its top with a fabric much like cheesecloth in which the resin is collected. The third method is described in a book about Egypt published in the 1930s. At the appropriate season:

. . . the plant is harvested by means of scythes or sickles to ground level and is gathered into bundles and transported to the farm buildings. . . .

The stalks are now laid out side by side on especially made drying grounds of hard clay, exposed to the sun. . . . After two or three days the exposed surfaces of the plant begin to dry off. It is then turned over to the other side and this process is repeated every twenty-four hours for the next ten or twelve days. The plant is now carefully placed on large linen sheets . . . and is thus carried to a special shed or room which . . . must be clean and have smooth walls and be capable of being hermetically closed. The floor must be smooth and hard to avoid the introduction of any foreign matter. . . .

The plants are stacked in a heap in the middle of the room and workmen . . . shut themselves in and proceed to give the first beating by means of sticks or flails . . . to remove the useless twigs which are thrown aside, and to beat out from the plant the first and best qualities of hashish. Throughout this operation a cloud of fine powder rises from the heap and settles on the surrounding floor and walls. . . .[15]

Three sieves of varying degrees of fineness are now used. Little by little the heap of beaten debris is passed through the three sieves. The finest mesh is used for the extra quality. . . . The debris is now beaten again six or seven times, the sieving operation being carried out between each beating. Naturally, the quality of the powder deteriorates with each successive sieving. . . . The only real first class grades come from the first beating. . . .

The varying qualities of powder are classified and placed in bags . . . to await further preparation prior to being sent off to their destination.[16]

After collection, the resin is pressed into blocks, or cakes, ranging in color from a dull yellow to an almost-black deep chocolate-brown. In order to smoke hashish, small pieces of the hardened block will be flaked off, or sliced off with a sharp instrument, such as a razor blade, crumbled, and smoked. Hashish is much more often used in the Orient, especially the Middle East and North Africa, than substances containing leaves. Heavy hashish or charas users in the East would scorn such weak substances as are typically consumed by American smokers.

Smoking is by far the most popular method of consumption of marijuana in the United States and must account for well over 95 percent of the bulk consumed in this country. Ingesting the drug is still relatively rare and is practiced as a kind of treat, not as a regular routine. In the Orient, marijuana is brewed as tea and (also a practice in Jamaica) cooked or imbedded in food. In North Africa and in the Middle East, *majoon*,[17] a candy containing a product of the plant, is made. Such practices are becoming increasingly popular among marijuana habitués in the United States; an early cookbook listing cannabis as a recipe ingredient has been reissued,[18] and several new ones have appeared recently. One of the recent cookbooks using cannabis in the ingredients includes recipes for "High Tea," "Banana Bread," "Chili Pot," and "Boston Bean Pot," [19] all common American dishes, with marijuana added. Another recipe book, on the other hand, has exotic Oriental dishes, such as "Bhang Sherbet," "Moroccan Majoon," "Black Sabbath Salve," and "Nebuchadnezzar's Dream." [20]

A major reason why mixing marijuana into food ingredients is rare in America is that an immense quantity is required for any effect; smoking is a far more efficient method for getting the drug into the blood stream. In addition, it takes a much longer period of time for the drug to take effect orally, often an hour and a half. It is, therefore, a clumsy and lengthy (and expensive) route of consumption. However, it is more reliable. A small number of individuals seem unable to become high, even after smoking joint after joint, evening after evening. Eating is a more directly physiological method, and if enough marijuana is ingested in cooked food, an eventual high is almost inevitable, even in those most staunchly resistant to marijuana's effects by means of smoking. In fact, sometimes this is precisely the problem with ingesting. Since the effects are slow in coming, it is impossible to gauge intake to the desired level of one's high. The experienced user can "self-titrate" his high by smoking a quantity of marijuana and then, shortly thereafter, reach the level of intoxication he feels comfortable with. With eating, because of the time lag, this is impossible. A huge amount may be ingested with no immediate effect which, over the period of an hour or so, will produce unusual and extreme levels of intoxication. Because eating can take place within a few seconds while smoking takes many minutes cannabis, once ingested, cannot be retrieved. Thus, it is possible to become higher, for a longer period, by eating cannabis.

Contrary to a number of published accounts,[21] marijuana, unlike cocaine and heroin, seems almost never to be sniffed; at least I have never heard of it from a user and I have never seen it done. It is highly doubtful if this could achieve any effect at all. Since marijuana is water-insoluble, it is almost never injected. In addition, most users are "needle shy."

Although the cannabis plant grows naturally in most parts of the world, the bulk of the cannabis substances used illicitly in this country originates from relatively few countries. The specifically marijuana substances (i.e., those comprising mostly of the leaves of the plant) come largely from Mexico, possibly 90 percent, although the 1969 border blockade encouraged far more "home growing" of marijuana. When purchased in bulk, which is anything larger than a sixth of an ounce or so, the purchaser usually buys a mixture of leaves, twigs, stems, and seeds. When purchased in quantities of a kilogram, which is the standard packaging and shipping unit, the plants will have been chopped into fairly small pieces and pressed into bricks, or kilo blocks about five inches wide, eight inches long, and three inches high, which are then wrapped in rough paper. To smoke this, the user must strain the mixture through a medium or fine mesh tea strainer to remove the inert twigs, stems, and the seeds, which exude an unpleasant, oily smoke. (Often the seeds are saved for planting; we shall return to this topic when discussing the sale of marijuana.) The strained substance is then either smoked in joints or packed into a pipe. The joint is the most popular means of smoking. Rolling one takes skill and only an expert can produce a thin, tightly packed, smooth product; more often, the joint is sloppy and untidy. An ordinary pipe cannot be used without special preparation, since strained marijuana, much finer than tobacco, will be drawn through the stem. Sometimes aluminum pricked with holes is pressed into the bowl and the marijuana placed on the foil. Or a "toke pipe" will be used; especially constructed for marijuana or hashish (nearly always smoked in a pipe), some have extremely small bowls, slightly larger than a hollowed-out pea. Another common method of smoking marijuana in a pipe is to put a tiny screen especially constructed for cannabis use over the bowl of an ordinary pipe and then place the marijuana on the screen.

In America, hashish is typically smoked in a pipe, toke pipe, or some form of Oriental water pipe, such as the *hookah* (Arabic) or *narghile* (Turkish and Persian). Often a block of hashish will be broken into small bits and each piece will be placed onto the burning end of a tobacco cigarette; the fumes of the hashish will then be sucked through a straw or tube, such as the barrel of a dismembered ball-point pen. Often (especially in public) a small chunk of hashish will be placed inside the end of a partly hollowed out tobacco cigarette, and the paper twisted to keep it in place; it will then be smoked like a regular cigarette. Sometimes chunks of hashish will be sprinkled into cigarette paper, rolled into a marijuana joint, and then smoked just like a regular joint of marijuana. Occasionally, smokers will fabricate their own devices, such as a "flying saucer" or tin foil placed over a cup or small bowl.

In the past few years, far more hashish has been available to the American marijuana-smoking public than previously. (See Chapter 10 for more details.) In talking to users and dealers, my estimate is that, compared with the first few months of 1966, something like fifty to one hundred times the quantity of hashish had entered the country and was being smoked by the winter of 1970. (This might be partly attributable to the severe shortage—at least in New York—of Mexican marijuana available at the later period.) [22] Hashish is something like five times the strength of ordinary marijuana which usually means that less of the substance must be smoked to become high. One can get high with far less effort on hashish; it is impossible to become five times higher, even were it possible to calibrate the high with such accuracy. (Most users claim to become a good deal higher with hashish.) Some commentators fear that the introduction of more potent marijuana preparations, such as hashish, will produce use-patterns much like those of India and Egypt. This reasoning process assumes that if one element—the strength of the hashish—is present, then all the outcomes will be the same. But since all of the other preconditions are lacking, such an eventuality is highly improbable.

Another fear has been the introduction of the chemical which is probably the active principle in cannabis, tetrahydrocannabinol—actually a family of active and potent chemicals. Some observers feel that were this purified form of drug widely available, somewhat the same events as occurred with LSD would occur with cannabis.[28] Actually, a recently available substance called THC (the abbreviation for tetrahydrocannabinol), is not THC at all, but a mixture with varying ingredients—sometimes LSD, methedrine, and/or a barbiturate. Real THC has been used on an extremely limited basis on the street—or so some users claim. It seems to be agreed that the effect it might produce would be akin in many respects to an LSD trip. Strangely, many of marijuana's critics justify the present penalty structure with the argument that were marijuana itself to become more available, users would inevitably migrate to THC. Why this should be so is never explained, however. Because of the overwhelmingly sociable form that marijuana use takes, and its recreational character, it seems unlikely that a drug which requires so much of the user's attention as LSD would be used as frequently as marijuana is at present, although experimentation is a distinct possibility, indeed, a likelihood, for many users. This is, in any case, a matter for a later discussion.

Observations on the Social Context of Marijuana Use

Marijuana use is overwhelmingly a group activity; the drug, in other words, is highly "sociogenic"—or "cultogenic," as one commentator has labelled the psychedelic drugs.[24] Some deviant activities are conducted in relative isolation without group support. The heavy use of the barbiturates, tranquilizers, and the amphetamines by housewives does not form the basis for drug-related activities or groups; meperidine (demerol) addiction among physicians does not lend itself to friendships, interaction, and sentiments on the basis of being addicted. There is no bond of identity, no preference for interaction with other physician-addicts, no increment of prestige as a result of sharing the characteristic of drug taking. There is no subculture of physician-addicts. (This obviously has nothing to do with the physiological impact of the drug itself, since many street addicts use morphine, and there is a street subculture.)

What we mean when we say that marijuana, or LSD or heroin is sociogenic is that:

1) It is characteristically participated in a group setting.
2) The others with whom one smokes marijuana are usually intimates, intimates of intimates, or potential intimates, rather than strangers.
3) One generally has long-term continuing social relations with the others.
4) A certain degree of value-consensus will obtain within the group.
5) A value-convergence will occur as a result of progressive group involvement.

6) The activity maintains the circle's cohesion, reaffirms its social bonds by acting them out.

7) Participants view the activity as a legitimate basis for identity—defining themselves, as well as others, partly on the basis of whether they have participated in the activity.

We find that marijuana users form a kind of subcommunity. This does not mean that a powerful bond of identity holds all users together in a closely knit social group. But it does mean that users are more likely to identify and interact with other users than with someone who does not smoke marijuana. In a sense, they are part of a subculture. Crystallizing all of the possible meanings of this term, the following three are probably the most important:

1) *Sociologically:* the degree to which a given category of individuals form *associations* with one another, whether or not that category is a subcommunity; the degree of concentration of one's most intimate and frequently interacted-with friends and acquaintances within that social category

2) *Anthropologically* and *ethnographically:* the degree to which members of a given social category share a distinct way of life, whose patterns of social life and basic social outlook set them off to some degree from members of other social categories

3) *Social psychologically:* the degree to which identities revolve about the category; the degree to which both members and nonmembers define group membership as significant, binding, and strongly indicative of the "kind of person" who belongs to it

"Subculture-ness" must be seen as a continuum, not a dichotomy. Subcultures vary as to degree of institutionalization: the higher the "score" on one or all of these three dimensions, the more a given group may be called a subculture.

Group processes operate at the inception of the individual's marijuana-using experience. The neophyte marijuana smoker, at first exposure to the drug, is subject to group definitions of the desirability of the experience, as well as the nature of its reality. Marijuana use, even at its inception, *is simultaneously participation in a specific social group.* This generalization holds equally strong for the continued use of marijuana. Marijuana is characteristically smoked in groups, not in isolation. In the sample, only 5 percent claimed to smoke at least half of the time alone, and about half—45 percent—said they never smoked alone. Marijuana cannot be understood outside the web of social relations in which it is implicated.

Moreover, the nature of the group-character of marijuana use also significantly determines its impact. Marijuana is not merely smoked in groups, it is smoked in intimate groups. The others with whom one is smoking are overwhelmingly *significant* others. One rarely smokes with strangers, with individuals whom one does not care for, or is indifferent to, or whom one does not expect to like in the future. Even at large parties where marijuana is smoked, small cliques will form, oases of compatibles, wherein all share the same activity. Smoking marijuana is symbolic in ways that more accepted behavior is not; it resembles communal eating in civilizations for whom eating well is a rare or intermittent festivity. Brotherhood is an element in the marijuana ritual, as is the notion of sharing something treasured and esteemed. Emphasis is placed on passing a joint around to all present, completing a circle; this procedure is generally preferred to that of each participant lighting up his own joint and smoking it by himself, without any group continuity.[25] And, of course, the clandestine nature of the activity, illegal and underground, lends an air of excitement and collective intrigue to marijuana smoking that would be absent in a context of licitness, as with drinking.

All of these factors make marijuana use a highly significant and emotionally charged activity to the participants. These factors, some ideological and some inherent in the nature of the act itself, conspire to link marijuana smoking to group influences and to make those who participate in it highly susceptible to the group's definition of reality—right and wrong, good and bad, true and false.

The case is such that it is not too farfetched to view marijuana use in basically Durkheimian terms. That is, because of the cultural climate surrounding illicit drug use and the logistical problems involved (secrecy, the inability to be completely casual about use, the fact that the safest places to smoke are also the most intimate, etc.) and the fact that it is participated with those for whom one has some degree of friendship and emotion, the activity has strong elements of a tribal ritual: it reaffirms membership in the subcommunity of users, it recreates symbol and substance of the group, and it relives for its participants significant meaning, belonging, loyalty. There is even a vigorous mythology connected with use: tribal lore, a protohistory, an epistemology, a kind of marijuana *Weltanschauung*.

Marijuana is generally proffered with strong overtones of hospitality. When one person offers another a smoke of a marijuana cigarette, there is communication taking place between the two, as the person who offers consciously thinks of sharing and participating in a common activity. A kind of brotherhood is established in the act. Although most users are generally permissive about each individual acting out his own desires—"doing his own thing"—the refusal of a presented marijuana joint is felt as a rebuff, as is refusal of a gift in many societies. A refusal generally means some embarrassment, usually with both parties. It is not only the refusal of a gift, but the refusal of sharing a treasured activity, as well as possible condemnation of one's activities, which are part of one's life.

Although it might be something of a problem to "psyche out" the pot-smoking propensities of a potential friend with whom one has, at present, only a superficial acquaintance, the seriousness of the issue is dissipated once this barrier is cleared. Marijuana is usually an issue of any seriousness to regular users only in relation to the nonusing world. Use itself is a form of recreation, an enjoyable activity of the first order. It is treated as a "fun thing." It is a recreation like watching a film, going to the beach, or eating in a fine restaurant. It is, both in and of itself, a complete recreational experience, as well as an adjunct and a catalyst to other recreational experiences. *The recreational character of potsmoking is possibly its most outstanding feature.*

A typical intimate, informal (four to ten people) pot party will involve frequently and typically passing the joint from person to person and staring into space for long stretches of time, with nothing, apparently, actually going on. Often there is music and everyone will be intensely involved with the music, and seemingly not with one another. It will appear boring and vacuous to someone who is not high, especially since he has heard so much about wild, orgiastic pot parties and he expects something of that nature. It is not realized that the marijuana experience is, typically, thought of as *itself* a recreation—being high is thought of as fun, a state of pleasure. For one who is not high, and never has been, understanding its appeal, especially at such a party, would be like sitting in a concert hall and being deaf.

The typical user smokes pot for reasons relating to having fun, partaking in a form of recreation. The idea of being "hung up" on using marijuana is atypical. The most common level of use of more or less regular smokers is once or twice a week—mostly on weekends. A twenty-two-year-old law school student told me: "Pot is a form of entertainment for me—like going to the movies. I don't get any of that philosophical or mystical or religious stuff; it doesn't change my life. After six days of studying my balls off in law school, I plan on Saturday to blow my mind. But you're not leaving this world. For me, it's just fun, that's all."

N O T E S

1. Robert E. L. Masters and Jean Houston, *The Varieties of the Psychedelic Experience* (New York: Holt, Rinehart & Winston, 1966), p. 37.

2. A forthcoming book on marijuana by John Kaplan explores the Licata fable in some detail.

3. See Joseph E. Mayer, *The Herbalist* (Hammond, Ind.: Indiana Botanic Gardens, 1934).

4. Norman Taylor, *Narcotics: Nature's Dangerous Gifts* (New York: Delta, 1963), p. 12. This edition is a paperback version of the book published in 1949 as *Flight from Reality*.

5. David W. Maurer and Victor H. Vogel, *Narcotics and Narcotic Addiction*, 3rd ed. (Springfield, Ill.: Charles C Thomas, 1967), p. 116; Donald B. Louria, *The Drug Scene* (New York: McGraw-Hill, 1968), p. 113; Will Oursler, *Marijuana: The Facts, the Truth* (New York: Paul Eriksson, 1968), p. 70; Jerome Jaffe, "Cannabis (Marijuana)," in Louis S. Goodman and Alfred Gilman, eds., *The Pharmacological Basis of Therapeutics*, 3rd ed. (New York: Macmillan, 1965), p. 299; Joan S. Gimlin, "Legalization of Marijuana," *Editorial Research Reports* 2 (August 9, 1967): 587.

6. Erich Goode, "Introduction," *Marijuana* (New York: Atherton Press, 1969), pp. 6, 12.

7. C. K. Yang, *Religion in Chinese Society* (Berkeley and Los Angeles: University of California Press, 1961), p. 13.

8. Pierre Huard and Ming Wong, *Chinese Medicine* (New York: McGraw-Hill, 1968).

9. Maurer and Vogel, *op. cit.*, pp. 333–334, 380. See also David Maurer, "Marijuana Addicts and Their Lingo," *The American Mercury* 63 (November 1946): 571–575.

10. See Richard H. Blum et al., *Utopiates* (New York: Atherton Press, 1964), pp. 240–241; and Blum et al., *Society and Drugs* (San Francisco: Jossey-Bass, 1969), p. 337. It should be noted that Blum is not particularly Freudian in his analysis, although he does countenance somewhat these "shit" interpretations.

11. An illustration of how reality is selectively perceived through our ideological biases is provided by at least one (mis-)interpretation of the "La Cucaracha" song. Robert Gaffney, U.S. Deputy Commissioner of Narcotics, is quoted by a *New York Post* reporter, in a series of articles on marijuana, as saying that the song makes the point that "marijuana has a decidedly adverse effect, even on the lowly cockroach. He can't get anywhere because he's smoking marijuana." See John Garabedian, "Marijuana: The Narcotics Cops," *The New York Post*, October 19, 1967.

12. Maurer and Vogel, *op. cit.*, p. 334.

13. In fact, much of the content of this book is wholly out of date and even anachronistic today, at least for the marijuana scene. For instance, the authors claim that "a high proportion" of marijuana users "are devotees of various schools of swing music." Needless to say, users today would not even know what swing music is, let alone ever listen

to it (it died out in the middle 1950s, when the first edition of Maurer and Vogel's book appeared). Their preference is for "rock" music. See Maurer and Vogel, *op. cit.*, p. 282.

14. Gurbakhsh S. Chopra, "Man and Marijuana," *The International Journal of the Addictions* 4 (June 1969): 219–233.

15. Hemp workers, like all laborers who breathe fine dust, such as coal miners, are subject to various pulmonary diseases; see A. Barbero and R. Flores, "Dust Disease in Hemp Workers," *Archives of Environmental Health* 14 (April 1967): 529–532.

16. Baron Harry d'Erlanger, "Hashish, or the Gift of Nature," in *The Last Plague of Egypt* (London: Lovat, Pickson and Thompson, 1936), pp. 68–71.

17. For an account of this delicacy, see Ira Cohen, "The Goblet of Dreams," *Playboy,* April 1966, p. 125.

18. Alice B. Toklas, *The Alice B. Toklas Cookbook* (New York: Harper and Row, 1954). Hashish brownies seem to be the most popular item. A motion picture made in 1968, *I Love You, Alice B. Toklas,* had as its theme the cooking of marijuana brownies.

19. Anonymous, *Cooking With Pot* (Gamble Gulch, Col.: Sacred Mushroom Press, 1969).

20. Panama Rose, *The Hashish Cookbook* (Gnaoua Press, 1966).

21. For instance, Lloyd Shearer, "The Mystique of Marijuana: Why Students Smoke Pot," *Parade,* June 4, 1967, pp. 8, 10, 11; Robert Coles, *The Grass Pipe* (Boston: Little, Brown, 1969), p. 98; Richard Blum et al., *Students and Drugs* (San Francisco: Jossey-Bass, 1969), p. 134; Stanley F. Yolles, "Before Your Kid Tries Drugs," *The New York Times Magazine,* November 17, 1968, p. 129.

22. Steve Lerner, "Great Famine: 'I'd Love to Turn You On, But . . .' " *The Village Voice,* June 26, 1969, pp. 1, 32.

23. Roland H. Berg, "Warning: Steer Clear of THC," *Look,* April 15, 1969, p. 46.

24. Daniel X. Freedman, "Perspectives on the Use and Abuse of Psychedelic Drugs," in Daniel H. Efron et al., eds., *Ethnopharmacologic Search for Psychoactive Drugs* (Washington: U.S. Government Printing Office, 1967), pp. 88–89.

25. There may be logistic and economic reasons for this. Among some more affluent smokers, a sign of hospitality and the ownership of an abundance of marijuana, is to give each guest his own joint of marijuana. The brotherhood ritual does not prevail. The less deviant and criminal marijuana becomes, and the more easily obtainable it is, the less use becomes special and therefore significant. Under these circumstances, a detribalization occurs, and marijuana use loses its subcultural impact and its socializing power.

: *Chapter 2* :

A Profile of the Marijuana Smoker

Who is the marijuana smoker? The question might seem obvious and unnecessary: the marijuana smoker is one who smokes marijuana. But the question cannot be answered so facilely. How much marijuana? How often? With the heroin addict, we find a more or less built-in polarization. The syndrome of herion addiction is more clear-cut than with marijuana where we do not find the same compulsion to use. We will, of course, encounter the heroin experimenter, the nonaddicted weekend "joy-popper," the on-again-off-again-heroin user, a high percentage of whom eventually slide into outright addiction. But the proportion of addicts among the universe of heroin users is so enormous that we will be able to characterize the outstanding features of heroin addiction as a way of life, and capture the use-patterns of a significant segment of all heroin users. Our job is more difficult with marijuana use. There is not the same tendency to polarization. Instead, we must think of marijuana use in *dimensionalist* terms.

Again, who is the marijuana user? What of the college student who, on three occasions, puffed part of a passed-around joint, never became high, and never again used the drug? If we exclude him, what about the housewife who tried the drug ten times, got high twice, decided that her curiosity had been satisfied, and refused it thereafter? Or the Wall Street lawyer who happens upon a pot party once every two months and accepts opportunities to smoke every time they are offered? Is he a marijuana smoker? The solution has to be arbitrary. I have found there is no precise line that may be drawn which delineates the user from the nonuser. There is an unbroken continuum in use from the person who tried it once to the daily user, the mythical six-cigarettes-a-day smoker. (This is often cited as the "average" consumption of the "typical" smoker;[1] probably fewer than one out of a hundred individuals who have tried marijuana smokes that much.)

Although an exact line between the user and the nonuser is impossible to draw, some crude but useful categories of degrees of use might help to clarify the kinds of involvement with the drug that are likely to be encountered. We have the experimenter, the occasional user, the regular user, and the frequent user. Where we separate these categories is partly a matter of taste and cannot be decided with much rigor or with impelling logic. Further, it must be realized that there is no necessary progression from the least to the most involved category. A given user may float in and out of these categories over a period of time.* The experimenter may be the largest of these groups, and forms perhaps a half of the total universe of all individuals who have at least tried marijuana at least once. The experimenter may have obtained a high, but perhaps not. He has invariably not sought out the drug, but has been turned on by friends. He is curious about its effects, but, at this point, little more than that. It could be that his curiosity has been satisfied by his first few experiences, but it is as likely that his initial encounters have been either insufficiently conclusive or pleasurable, that is, he did not become as high as his expectations led him to believe to induce him to accept later offers.

In a sense, the experimenter is not really a drug user.[2] However, my analysis includes him. The one-time, two-time, or twelve-time marijuana "taster" will be, in many ways, half-way between the more regular user and the individual who has never had a puff of a marijuana cigarette. By including the experimenter, we capture this spectrum effect of drug use and users, rather than committing the error of reification in thinking in terms of natural airtight categories

---

* Actually, the way I have constructed these categories, it would be possible to move back and forth between the last three—from occasional to regular to frequent use and back again—but not in and out of being an experimenter. I look upon experimentation with marijuana as having used the drug less than a dozen times in one's lifetime, so that after that, one moves out of this category for good. Thus, this scheme is not a true typology.

of use. Moreover, an experimenter has a far higher likelihood of moving into the categories of regular use than does the complete abstainer, although we must not make the opposite mistake and assume that this progression is inevitable. It is neither inevitable nor is it typical. But it is more likely among experimenters, and for this reason, the experimenter is of great interest to us. In much of the description and analysis that follows, both here and throughout the book, I will be describing the user. It must be kept in mind that all social categories are abstractions, and our decision to use one or another must often be based on their usefulness. In most cases, I will term the marijuana user anyone who has tried the drug at least once. I do not claim that a consistent life-style will typify all of these individuals. Nor do I say that a radical disjunction will separate this group from the nonusing group. We have not trapped a distinct social animal by characterizing the marijuana user. But when we compare this gross category with the nonusing category, instructive and dramatic differences emerge. I will rely mainly on the vehicle of the molar comparison—the user versus the nonuser— in delineating the marijuana-smoker portrait. Whenever a different categorization is made, it will be explained.

Public stereotypes change more slowly than that which is being stereotyped. Often an activity or a group will never have its image catch up with itself. These images and stereotypes must be thought of as a kind of reality; they may not accurately describe the group they claim to apply to, but the fact that they are believed makes a great deal of difference, and to understand the social patterns of a given social group, we must often understand the myths that have purported to describe it. The media today transmit public images more rapidly and, possibly, more accurately, than they did a generation ago. The image of the marijuana user in the 1930s was not very different from that of the narcotics addict. The term "addict" as applied to the marijuana smoker was far from unusual; in fact, it was the rule. The milieu from which he came, the day-to-day activities in which he engaged, the dominance of the drug in his life, his involvement with crime, and the effects of the drug on his body and mind, were all thought to be continuous with the junkie's.

Although today many would recognize this typification as bizarre and anachronistic, there will be strong disagreement on even the bold outlines of a contemporary portrait of the marijuana smoker. How, then, can we characterize the potsmoker? What is distinctive about him? We could have our choice of various clichés. The most popular is that he conforms to the current stereotype of the hippie. He is unkempt, unemployed, politically radical (often apathetic), slightly mad, sexually promiscuous, and under the influence of the drug all of the time. Fading under the impact of mass media reports,[3] this image is gradually being replaced by one almost as absurd: the marijuana user is no different from the rest of us. There are the over-forty users, just as there are those under fifteen; there are bankers, executives and physicians, just as there are juvenile delinquents, hippies and criminals. There is the girl next door, and the girl "in the life." There are policemen and political demonstrators, clergymen and atheists, congressmen and the politically disaffected. In short, he could be anyone.[4] No one has ever studied a cross-section of marijuana users, of course, and it is not possible at the moment. Yet, in the absence of such definitive data, it is possible, from dozens of scattered surveys, to construct something like a reasonably accurate picture of what the social characteristics of a large proportion of users are likely to be.

Age

The marijuana user is more likely to be young than old. He is most likely to be in his late teens and early twenties; before, say, age thirteen, and after age thirty, the drop-off in the percentage who have ever used is sharp. Since very young users are extremely conspicuous, and since the fears of the older generation concerning the dangers of drug use are compounded when grade school children are involved, the opinion that use typically reaches down into the ten to thirteen age range has become widespread.[5] Actually, the average age for smoking marijuana is probably dropping, but it is far from typical for grade school children to smoke. In fact, the average high school or even college student has not tried marijuana, although in both milieu it is common among a big minority; however, in some schools, such as some in New York and California, a majority of high school students have tried marijuana. Moreover, among the very young, experimentation will be far more common than is true with older teenagers and young adults; frequent, daily use among early teenagers is extremely rare. In my survey, I interviewed an eight-year-old who smoked marijuana, but this does not mean that use among eight-year-olds, even in New York's East Village, is common.* The median age of my informants was twenty-two, with slightly over one-fifth in their teens (21 percent), and less than a tenth (7 percent) were thirty or over. At about the same time I was conducting my survey, *The East Village Other,* a New York underground newspaper whose 25,000 readers include a considerable percentage of drug users, did a study of its own. In the April 1967 issue, EVO included a fill-out, mail-in questionnaire on its readers' drug use. Keeping in mind the extraordinary possibilities for bias and distortion,[6] it should be noted, nonetheless, that the age range of my own study and that of the EVO study are remarkably similar (see Table 2–1).

TABLE 2–1

Age Range in Goode and EVO Studies
(percent)

Goode		EVO	
17 or under	5	16 or under	4
18 or 19	16	17 or 18	11
20 or 21	25	19, 20, 21	28
22, 23, 24, 25	30	22, 23, 24, 25	35
26, 27, 28, 29	18	26 to 30	12
30 or over	7	over 30	10

A third study, conducted by two sociologists at the New York Medical College in early 1969, interviewed seventy-four New York user respondents collected by "reputational" methods.[7] The age composition of this group was almost identical to mine and to EVO's (see Table 2–2).

Although none of these studies is random in its composition of users, or in its method of collection, the closeness in correspondence lends credence to the assertion that the age distribution of marijuana smokers in general (or at least in New York City) is very likely to be as described. More striking than its mere youth (since the median age of the American population in general is about

---

*In fact, I saw marijuana-using parents give a joint to their two-, three- and four-year-old children, much as a French mother might give her child a sip of wine to quiet him but this is, obviously, extremely rare.

TABLE 2-2

*Age Range in New York
Medical College
Study (percent)*

Teens	22
Twenties	70
Thirties	8

twenty-seven) is the high degree of concentration within the specific age range of about fifteen years, the middle teens upward to
about thirty. It is possible that use is spreading beyond these
boundaries, both upward and downward; perhaps in a few years, as
the present user population grows older, and, possibly, continues to
some extent in using marijuana, this overrepresentation among
those in their late teens and early twenties will no longer hold true.
In any case, this is, at the present time, the age breakdown of the
average user.

Sex

The user is more likely to be male than female. Or, to put it another
way, men are more likely to smoke, or to have smoked, marijuana
than women. The differences between men and women in their pot-
smoking participation are always fairly small, but distinct. For the
addicting drugs, especially heroin, the differences are massive. Only
about one-fifth of all known addicts turn out to be women. Men
have five times greater chance of becoming heroin addicts than
women.[8] The male dominance in marijuana use is never as great as
that. In the 1969 American Institute of Public Opinion study
(Gallup Poll) of a representative sample of college students,[9] 25
percent of the men and 18 percent of the women had tried marijuana
at least once. (The figure for the entire sample was 22 percent.) In the
EVO study, all of whom had used drugs, 98 percent of whom had
smoked marijuana, and 85 percent had used hashish at least once,
the sex distribution was 69/31, a remarkable overrepresentation of
males in New York's East Village drug-using community. In a study

of a sample of students at a small upstate New York college, about 20 percent of the women and 30 percent of the men had used marijuana at least once.[10] Regardless of the locus of the study in question, men were more likely than women to smoke pot.[11]

In our sample, there was a slight skew; 53 percent of our respondents were men, and 47 percent were women. However, since it is not representative, this figure, in and of itself, means very little. The simple population of all those who have had so much as a single puff of a marijuana cigarette is less relevant than *levels* of use and involvement. Not only are men far more likely to have had at least some minimal contact with drugs, the greater the degree of involvement and use, the greater the overrepresentation of men will be. Heavy and frequent marijuana use is a decidedly male-dominated activity. Men are more likely than women to use drugs, to use them often, to have tried and used more drugs, and to have participated in a greater variety of drug-related activities, such as buying and selling, turning others on, and, in short, to be far more involved in the drug subculture. These differences are more remarkable for their consistency and direction than for their strength. Of the 105 men in my study, 17 percent said that they smoked marijuana every day, while this figure was 7 percent for the 99 women; 17 percent of the men smoked less than once per month and 28 percent of the women were such infrequent smokers.

The men in my study were also more likely to have tried drugs other than marijuana, as we see clearly in the Table 2–3. Forty-two percent of the women had taken no other drug besides marijuana, while this was true of only 22 percent of the men. This male dominance was maintained for *every* drug. The proportion of men taking LSD more than a dozen times, as well as the proportion ever taking heroin was about three times that for women: 19 percent versus 7 percent in the first case, and 19 percent versus 6 percent in the second. Men were more likely to be involved in drug-using activities and in the drug-using community in a variety of ways. They were more likely to have drug-using friends than women were. They were also more likely to have bought and sold marijuana. Only one-sixth of the men said that they had never bought marijuana (16 percent), while this was true of between one-third and one-half of the women (42 percent). Typically, the woman is offered the marijuana cigarettes she smokes by a man, and if she buys, she usually buys it from a man. A majority of women have never sold marijuana (69 percent), while a majority of men (55 percent) have.

TABLE 2-3

Percentage by Sex Taking Different Drugs at Least Once

	LSD	Ampheta-mine	DMT or DET	Barbi-turates	Opium	Cocaine	Mescaline or Peyote	Heroin
Men	55	47	28	31	22	25	27	19
Women	41	37	25	14	18	12	8	6

One of the more striking differences in the entire study had to do with the number of people whom the respondent had turned on. A quarter of the men (26 percent) said that they had introduced ten or more people to marijuana for the first time, while only a tiny percentage of the women boasted of this degree of proselytization (3 percent). In part, all of these differences reflect general nondrug and nondeviant differences in gender. The man, after all, buys alcoholic drinks for his female companion, and he is more likely to introduce her to alcohol for the first time than she is to introduce him. These parallels should not be pushed too far, but the use of marijuana, as well as the hallucinogenic drugs, is a decidedly masculine activity. The male can be seen as somewhat "marijuano-genic"; he is more likely than the female to use the drug, to "progress" to other, more powerful, drugs, to buy and sell drugs, and to persuade others to use marijuana. It is from the male that use spreads. So much is this the case that I would speculate that in milieu in which drug use is high, as in colleges and universities, the women who interact most frequently and intimately with males are most likely to at least have tried marijuana, while the women who are least active and most isolated socially are the most likely to be "drug free."

Urbanness

The marijuana user is more likely to live in or near an urban environment than is true of the population at large. Large cities remain the centers of use; in rural areas, marijuana smoking is relatively rare. To be more precise, the larger the urban center, the greater the percentage of its inhabitants who will have smoked pot; the smaller the community, the lower is this likelihood. One of the few exceptions would be in colleges and universities located in rural or small-town areas, but this only confirms our point, since (1) students in these colleges who do smoke are far more likely to come from an urban area; (2) it is generally from the more urban-originated students that use spreads; and (3) in the more urban-located college, the greater the likelihood of use is anyway.

A very rough measure of the gross relative amount of use of various geographical areas may be gleaned from official arrest figures (though there is not space here for a critique of official crime data) and they confirm our impression. We would, of course, expect more marijuana arrests in urban areas, simply because of their larger numbers, but even on a per population basis, urban arrests are far more common with marijuana charges than rural arrests. (This is true of most crimes.) For instance, in California in 1967, half of all adult arrests on marijuana charges (13,000 out of a total of 26,000) as well as all juvenile arrests (5,000 out of 10,000) took place in Los Angeles county; the rest were in the remaining part of the state.[12] (However, it is possible that urban police are more diligent and observant, making use and possession more easily detected.) In a nationally representative survey of the sexual patterns of college youth, Simon and Gagnon found a high correlation between marijuana use and the size of the community in which the respondent had attended high school.[13] Only 3 percent of the college men and 1 percent of the college women from a small town or rural area had ever tried marijuana, whereas the figures were 21 percent and 13 percent of urban and suburban men and women.

Social Class

The class backgrounds of marijuana smokers, as opposed to those who have never smoked marijuana, are relatively higher. Probably the higher the income of one's family, the higher the education of one's parents, and the greater the prestige of one's father's occupation, the greater is the likelihood of smoking marijuana. Also, for the young adult who has begun working, and who has left his family of orientation, the higher is his education, income and occupational prestige, the greater are his chances of smoking marijuana. This might seem peculiar to someone with a narcotics-addict model of marijuana use. Heroin addicts, it is true, are more likely to stem from poorer areas, especially the urban slum. Yet not all social classes find drugs equally appealing. The picture is even stranger in view of the fact that it is possible that a few years ago (before 1960), the class background of the average marijuana user was different. A 1958 textbook on drug use attempted to explain the greater incidence of marijuana use among blacks by the "greater incidence of poverty, slum residence, and socioeconomic discrimination among Negroes," and the author claims that the marijuana-user's home is typically poverty stricken.[14] Possibly ten or more years ago, it might have been fair to say that there was something of a negative relationship between social class and potsmoking. Probably the only two groups that used with any frequency were residents of the urban slum ghetto, and bohemians and beats on the edges of the slum and the black culture—jazz enthusiasts especially.

Today this pattern has been reversed. Regardless of the specific measure of social class we wish to use—whether income, occupation, or education—the higher the social class, and the higher the social class of one's parents, the greater the likelihood the individual will smoke marijuana. There seems to be something like a *linear* relationship between social status and potsmoking. In a representative study of the high school youth of Michigan conducted in 1968, this relationship was empirically confirmed. * Using the father's education as an index of social status, a strong and stepwise correlation between the social class of the high school student and his chances of smoking pot reveals itself; moreover, the higher the student's father's education, the more likely it was that he would see marijuana as harmless or beneficial. (see Table 2–4).

A Gallup Poll, released in October 1969, verified this positive association between social class and the likelihood of marijuana smoking. About 4 percent of a nationally representative sample of adults said that they "ever happened to try marijuana." The per-

---

* The study was conducted by Richard Bogg of the School of Public Health, University of Michigan. This table was not tabulated in the study. I want to thank Professor Bogg for supplying me with the IBM cards on which the data are stored, so that I could make these tabulations myself.

centage of respondents with a grade school education who had done so was 1 percent; the figure for respondents with a college education was almost ten times as high, or 9 percent. Even in colleges, the same pattern holds. (College students are already a preselected group with regard to class, since their parents' occupation, income and education are generally significantly higher than that of their noncollege age peers.) The June 1969 Gallup Poll of college youth found that those students whose parents' family income was over $15,000 were considerably more likely to have smoked marijuana than those students whose family income was below $7,000.[15] One of the most complete studies of the drug-use patterns of college students, by Richard Blum and others, found that those from the wealthiest families were more likely to have tried marijuana—indeed, to have experimented with all drugs, except the opiates—than those from less affluent families.[16]

TABLE 2-4

*Marijuana Smoking and Evaluations of Marijuana
by Father's Education*

Father's Education	Ever Smoked Marijuana? (per cent "yes")	Believes Marijuana Is Harmful	Believes Marijuana Is Beneficial or Harmless
College graduate	22	52	48
Some college	11	62	38
High school graduate	12	69	31
Some high school	10	77	24
No high school	6	79	21

Not only is the youth with middle-class parents more likely to smoke marijuana than his working-class peer, but middle-class parents are more likely to be tolerant of their children smoking marijuana than working-class parents. Of course, parents of all social and economic levels overwhelmingly *oppose* marijuana use, especially by their children. But the higher the class level, the greater the chance that a parent will be part of that small minority which does not oppose its use. A Harris survey in 1968 documented this relationship. While 85 percent of the total sample of American parents of teenagers "would forbid" their children's smoking marijuana, this was true of 74 percent of the "affluent" parents. Not only were middle-status parents somewhat more likely to be tolerant of pot use, they also were more likely to know someone who smoked marijuana. While 5 percent of the total sample knew a youth who smokes marijuana, this was true of three times as many of the relatively affluent. Although this was true of every instance of "controversial" behavior questioned in the Harris poll, the edge was greater for marijuana smoking than for any other aspect. " . . . tolerance of controversial activities among teenagers is greater among the better educated and relatively wealthy [parents]." [17]

The "rebellion" and "rejection of authority" hypotheses of marijuana use and other socially illicit activities would predict that youngsters whose parents *most* oppose such activities would be most likely to participate in them. My view is that marijuana use, like many other forms of behavior that much of society condemns, is partly an extension of the social climate with which the individuals are involved. While most teenagers and young adults who smoke marijuana will find that their parents will condemn their behavior, it is the young adult whose parents are most tolerant toward marijuana use who will be most likely to try using it. Highly authoritarian parents discourage experimentation of all kinds. In part, the use of marijuana is an outcome of less authoritarian parents granting responsibility, initiative, and self-reliance to their children. Teenagers will move somewhat beyond parents' expectations; if those expectations lie close to the unconventional, the child will move into the arena of the unconventional. If the expectations are more severely restricted, the child will move a little beyond that. The potsmoking of young adults is partly an outgrowth and an extension of their parents' attitudes and expectations on marijuana, as well as related issues.

The classic view of class differences in freedom and authoritarianism, still believed today by many practicing psychiatrists, has been that the lower or working classes are freer, more unrestrained, less repressed, more natural and spontaneous, than is true of the middle classes. This point of view has been informed by the "noble savage" ideology, and, later, by many forms of romantic Marxism. Freud, in watching a performance of Bizet's *Carmen,* was struck by the differences between his own repressed middle-class upbringing and the free, willful, and savage outburst of emotion expressed by the crowds. This tradition influenced social research and theory until a generation ago, when careful surveys revealed that quite the reverse was true.

Working-class parents are far more likely to raise their children in an authoritarian manner; they are more likely to believe, for instance, that the most important thing a child can learn is obedience. The middle-class child is granted more autonomy, responsibility, and freedom, and allowed a freer expression of his emotions than the lower-class child. He is allowed to experiment more, to strike out on his own. It would be strange that these differences did not find their expression in such adolescent activities as marijuana use. (Of course, one problem in interpretation is that the historical trend has been from a predominantly working and lower-class clientele in marijuana use to a predominantly middle-class one.) In any case, the lower-class parent, as well as the lower-class child, is more conformist, tradition-oriented, conventional, restrictive, and more likely to stress obedience and a conformity to externally imposed standards. The middle-class person is more permissive, more likely to stress curiosity, exploration, self-satisfaction, self-direction and equalitarianism.[18] All of these attitudes have their impact on the readiness to use marijuana, to re-examine society's restrictions and decide for oneself what might be the most satisfying and interesting and fulfilling path.

College/Noncollege Differences

It is common knowledge that use has spread into the colleges and universities. Studies indicate that perhaps one-quarter of all college youth have smoked marijuana, and more will do so by the time they graduate.[19] This is a massive rise which has taken place only in the past few years. Studies conducted as recently as 1966 and 1967 showed that only something like 6 percent of all college students had tried pot.[20] At least part of this four to five times rise in the space of two or three years is actual. The Columbia Broadcasting System study, based on interviews conducted in April 1969 with about 1,300 nationally representative, randomly selected youths age seventeen to twenty-three, slightly more than half (723) in college and slightly less than half (617) not in college, showed the powerful difference between the average college and noncollege youth in their acceptance or rejection of the marijuana prohibition. College youths were far less likely to accept the prohibition, and far more likely to say that they reject it outright (see Table 2–5).[21]

TABLE 2–5

Columbia Broadcasting System Study

Marijuana Prohibition	College	Non-college
Accept easily	48	72
Accept reluctantly	20	11
Reject outright	31	17

It is, of course, conceivable that these differences do not translate into actual use patterns. Obviously, not all those who say that they reject outright the prohibition actually use pot, or have ever used pot. But equally obvious, those who say that they reject the prohibition are far more likely to smoke marijuana than those who say they accept it. It seems permissible to conclude from these figures that today's college student is more likely to use marijuana than is his noncollege age peer. But we must keep in mind the fact that the parents of college students are more likely to be middle class than the parents of youths who do not go to college, and by that factor alone, they would be more likely to try pot.

There are, in addition, systematic differences among different types of colleges, as well as different types of college students. We mentioned the urban factor: colleges in or near urban centers will have students who are more likely to smoke pot than rural schools. A second factor is geographical location: colleges and universities on the two coasts, especially in New York and California—especially California—will contain higher percentages of pot-smoking students than those in the South, Midwest, or Rocky Mountain areas. A third factor, interestingly enough, is the quality of the school: the higher the academic standing of a college or university, other things being equal, the greater is the likelihood that its students will smoke marijuana. A study conducted in 1966 demonstrated that a fifth of the students attending the "top ranking" institutions had ever smoked pot (or used "similar drugs or narcotics") while this was true of only 1 percent at the "not very selective" colleges.[22] Since 1966, of course, a rise in marijuana use has occurred in all schools regardless of quality.

Jewish/Gentile Differences

Perhaps because of their urban residence, or partly as a result of their almost exclusively middle-class socioeconomic status, Jews are far more likely to smoke marijuana than Gentiles, at least among young adults. About one-quarter of New York's population is Jewish, and by that factor alone, the Jewish youth is more likely to be exposed to opportunities for use than is the less urban Gentile population. My sample, although not representative, even of New York City's marijuana smokers, at least lends credence to Jewish overrepresentation among potsmokers; 44 percent of our respondents were Jewish in background. Although it is possible that this over-representation can be entirely explained by Jewish dominance in academic and quasi-academic milieu in New York City (the groups to which I had readiest access), there are indications that lead me to suspect that there are social and cultural factors linking the Jews to activities such as marijuana use.

Jews have historically been at the growing edge of every civilization where they have been a part. Many of the avant-garde political and artistic movements today are associated with marijuana smoking, and the Jews are strongly overrepresented in these movements. This does not mean that all Jews are so associated, or that all participants of these movements are Jewish. (Nor is it to say that only those actively involved with social change are likely to smoke marijuana.) But it is to say that Jews will be more likely to be found among the more progressive artists and writers, and among the more radical and revolutionary political activists in America today. And it is precisely the political and artistic avant-garde that is most likely to smoke marijuana. However, we need not even concern ourselves with society's most progressive and revolutionary members, since they form such a tiny percentage of any population. Even contrasting Jews in general (not merely the most liberal among them) with Gentiles in general, it is clear that in many ways, Jews grow up in a richer, more complex environment, in a family ambiance with a lower level of authoritarianism, greater tolerance, and a respect for intellectual experimentation. (The Jewish family is, however, much more rigid in many other ways, such as the closeness of family ties.) The average youth need not have participated in society's most radical and bohemian groups to have already developed certain attitudes toward innovation which make marijuana use more likely.

Whatever the reasons, Jewish youths do seem to experiment with drugs, particularly marijuana, more than Gentiles. A study was done by the Toronto Addiction Research Foundation, entitled *A Preliminary Report on the Attitudes and Behaviour of Toronto Students in Relation to Drugs.* Of the Catholic high school students, 7 percent had taken drugs (mainly marijuana), and 75 percent said that they would not take drugs. These figures were 9 percent and 74 percent for Protestants. Among the Jewish students, about 15 percent had taken drugs, and 64 percent said that they would not use them. The differences are not dramatic, but they are significant. And they are corroborated by a number of other studies in other locations.

Religious Observance and Belief

Even more dramatic than the Jewish-Gentile split in the likelihood of marijuana use is the difference between anyone who claims to have *no* religion as opposed to someone who claims *some* religious affiliation. A "no religion" is highly unconventional in many ways. Politically, he is at the far left of the ideological spectrum. In the CBS study on youth cited earlier, while only 8 percent of the total sample claimed to have "no religion," over 60 percent of the youths classified as "revolutionary" in political ideology said that they had no religion.[23] We would, therefore, expect a "no religion" to be unusual in many other ways. In Blum's college study, for all of the drugs on which a question was asked (except sedatives), "no religions" were by far the most likely of all religious groups to have experimented. (Jews were found to be second for all drugs).[24] The average potsmoker is highly unlikely to be religious in a traditional sense. He is less likely to claim religious affiliation, attend religious services, believe in traditional dogma, or participate in any way, with any of the formal religious bodies. In my study, only one-fifth of the respondents said that they ever attended formal religious services—that is, at least once a year. Slightly over a quarter said that they believed in God; 45 percent were atheists. (The rest had their own private version of God—pantheism, the human spirit as God, "God is love," etc.) In a study of the student body attending a New York City private high school, the New York Medical College team discovered a number of dramatic and striking differences between the drug users and the nonusers. The largest difference by far had to do with religion. Over half of the nonusers (54 percent) said that they attended religious services. *Not one* of the users said that they ever attended religious services.

The Simon-Gagnon college youth study corroborated these findings. Among men who had tried marijuana, 4 percent attended church frequently, while 36 percent of those who had not tried and did not wish to try marijuana, attended services frequently. Expressed differently, 2 percent of the frequent church attenders had tried pot, while 24 percent of those who said that they attended rarely or never had done so.

Political Orientation

One of the most empirically verified of all relationships with marijuana use is political ideology and activity. Marijuana users are far more likely to hold what are considered in America today liberal or radical views. The New York Medical College study of private school youths showed that the users (all but two had used marijuana) were far more active and radical politically. All but two of the thirteen users had joined a Vietnam march or demonstration, whereas just over one-third of the nonusers had done so; about two-thirds of the users agreed that the civil rights movement is not "militant enough," while only about one-fifth of the nonusers agreed.[25] In Blum's study of college drug use, a direct and linear relationship between political leftism and the use of any single illicit drug, including marijuana, was found. The more radical the student was, the greater the chance that he used any drug; the more conservative he was, the lower was this chance.[26] (The two Marxists in the study had not used marijuana, however; I will touch upon this point presently.) The CBS study, *Generations Apart,* also documented the powerful relationship between political ideology and the acceptance or rejection of the marijuana prohibition.[27] The more radical the student, the greater were his chances of rejecting the marijuana laws. (see Table 2–6).

TABLE 2–6

Political Ideology by Accepting or Rejecting the Marijuana Prohibition

Marijuana Prohibition	POLITICAL IDEOLOGY				
	Revolutionary	Radical Reformer	Moderate Reformer	Middle of the Road	Conservative
Accept easily	5	47	43	77	85
Accept reluctantly	3	8	25	10	8
Reject outright	92	45	32	13	7

The bulk of the most radical of these students (revolutionary) reject the marijuana prohibition, while the same is true of the most conservative wing accepting the prohibition, while the in-between ideological elements are also in-between on the pot issue. Marijuana, by and large, is part of the ideology and even, to a large degree, the politics, of the left wing in America today; at the very least, liberalism and radicalism increase one's chances of approving of pot and using it.

The 1969 Gallup Poll of college students also documented the linear relationship between potsmoking and political attitudes. Whereas about 10 percent of the students who classified themselves as conservatives had smoked marijuana at least once, about half (49 percent) of those who said that they were extremely liberal had done so. Only 15 percent of the students who had never participated in a political demonstration had ever smoked pot, but 40 percent of those who had demonstrated had tried marijuana. While over half of the whole sample felt that campus demonstrators who broke the law should be expelled from college, this was true of about a third of the marijuana smokers.[28] By any measure, then, the politics of the average college marijuana user runs at least somewhat to the left of his nonsmoking peers. Political leftists, in general, seem to smoke marijuana more than those who are considered to the right on the American political spectrum.

As a qualification to this massive and unambiguous relationship, it should be stated that there are a number of revolutionary leftist political parties and groups that implacably oppose marijuana use as a "tool" of the ruling classes. Marijuana, the reasoning goes, acts as a pacifier, tends to blunt the revolutionary fervor, one's activist drive.[29] This is, for instance, the position of the Progressive Labor Party, basically, a Maoist organization, which recently split off with the Students for a Democratic Society (SDS). In the film, *The Battle of Algiers,* the smoking of hashish was depicted as counterrevolutionary; certainly, internationally, communists vigorously oppose use of drugs of all kinds for the same puritanical reasons of many conservatives in America. Many Americans of the far right, however, believe that communists wish to impose drug use on Americans to corrupt them, make them peaceful, decadent and easily conquerable.[30] One of my interviewees, a twenty-one-year-old college student who described herself as a Marxist, revealed her political opposition to the use of marijuana. She said that she had not smoked marijuana for eight months. The following is a section of the interview I completed with her.

Q: Why don't you smoke marijuana more regularly?
A: I'm not letting the big boys take over my mind.
Q: What do you mean, the "big boys"?
A: President Johnson, all the political bosses. I feel powerless and inert if I smoke—I feel guilty. Some people think it's better for us to be stoned.
Q: What people?
A: The power structure. They want us stoned because we aren't as politically active then.

Sexual Permissiveness

Potsmokers are more liberal and unconventional in a variety of ways, not merely in political orientation. Sexually, they are more permissive. Or, expressed differently, sexually permissive people are more likely to try and to use marijuana than those who are more restrictive, conservative, or conventional. The more liberal in sexual matters the individual is, the greater is his chance of using marijuana once, a dozen times, or regularly. The two are part of the same basic thrust—freedom from some of the restraining mores of American society. Far more of the Simon-Gagnon college student study who were classified as liberal in sexual attitudes (24 percent of the men, and 14 percent of the women) had tried pot, than those whose attitudes were conservative on the sex-attitude scale (7 percent of the men, and 5 percent of the women). Sexual liberalism seems to increase considerably one's chance of taking marijuana. Sex is another area wherein the middle-class individual is more liberal and permissive—the age-old myths concerning the sexual aura of the lower and working classes notwithstanding. The middle-class sexual relationship is more equalitarian; the female expresses more satisfaction, and reports a higher frequency of orgasm; in intercourse, the couple is more likely to experiment with novel positions, ideas, and situations, and the couple prolongs having sex further into old age. The lower-class sexual pattern is more often characterized by "homosociality"—that is, conquest and exploitation of the female by the male for the purpose of approval from one's peers, rather than for its intrinsic satisfaction. It is characterized by the double standard, by the dichotomy between the good girl and the bad girl, by a narrower range of acceptable activities and a lower level of expressed satisfaction in the quality of the sex experienced, especially by the female, and an earlier discontinuation of sex relations in middle age.[31] (These are, remember, comparative statements.) All of these attitudes and forms of behavior have parallels in marijuana use. The more sexually permissive the person is, the greater the likelihood that the person will smoke marijuana, or try it at least once. The more equalitarian he envisions and acts out his sexual relationships, the greater the chances of potsmoking. The more he rejects many of conventional society's sexual restrictions and prohibitions, the more acceptable marijuana will seem. The more that he feels that the acceptability of a given sexual relationship is defined by the partners involved, rather than by some impersonal and absolute standard, the more "self-direction" he assigns to sexual partners, the less he will reject and condemn marijuana use, and the more willing he will be to actually try it himself. It should be realized, however, that these relationships are not directly dependent on sex itself, but on more fundamental underlying attitudes and behavior. Sexual permissiveness may merely be a manifestation of a general antiauthoritarian stance, a rejection of conventionality of all kinds. *Both* marijuana use and sexual permissiveness are dependent on the same basic factor, rather than one being dependent on the other.[32]

Authoritarianism

Many of these relationships can at least partially be captured by the notion of authoritarianism. Two decades ago, a massive study entitled *The Authoritarian Personality* was published. Although its authors assigned to the concept of authoritarianism an almost cosmic and all-embracing status, we need not be so ambitious in our use of it. Regardless of the generality of its applicability, the fact remains that some of us are more rigid in our thinking processes and in the way we act than others. Some seek comfort in rules, orders, and a strict hierarchy of power, in a black and white notion of right and wrong, an unambiguous morality; these people have an intolerance for ambiguity. Others are more comfortable with ambiguity. They do not need clear-cut rules, nor do they wish to follow a powerful leader. They do not find the need to divide the world up into good and bad, right and wrong; they recognize shades in between, and this does not distress them unduly. They do not ask, upon entering a new social situation, "Who's in charge here?" They seek the relevance of axes unrelated to power and authority, which are far less important to them. Some of us, in short, are highly authoritarian, while others are far less so. As we might expect, this conceptual scheme has relevance for marijuana use. Some are content to rest with society's prohibition: "No pot." Others, with a more flexible notion of right and wrong, do not accept this axiom. They have a more relativistic notion of right and wrong. Individuals with authoritarian attitudes are far less likely to smoke marijuana than those low in authoritarianism. In the Simon-Gagnon college survey, only 6 percent of the high-authoritarian men had tried marijuana, whereas 28 percent of the low-authoritarian men had; the figures for women were 3 percent and 15 percent, respectively.

NOTES

1. Six cigarettes a day figure was cited in the classic, *The Marihuana Problem in the City of New York* ("The LaGuardia Report"), and quoted thereafter as gospel. No one bothered to check its validity. It bears about as much correspondence to reality as does the statement that the typical drinker of liquor consumes a half a quart of Scotch a day.

2. Kenneth Keniston, "Heads and Seekers: Drugs on Campus; Counter-Cultures and American Society," *The American Scholar* 38 (Winter 1969): 99.

3. During the period of the interviews I conducted (July and August 1967), most of the mass magazines with the largest circulation, such as *Look, Life, Newsweek*, ran full-length articles on marijuana use, emphasizing the complexity of the users' characterstics. Many of the smokers I interviewed incorrectly took this as evidence of the immanence of the end of the marijuana laws.

4. John Rosevear, *Pot: A Handbook of Marijuana* (New Hyde Park, N. Y.: University Books, 1967), p. 118.

5. For a report expressing concern over the youth of recent smokers, "The Drug Generation: Growing Younger," *Newsweek*, April 21, 1969, pp. 107–108, 110.

6. Obviously, readers of EVO are not representative of drug users in general, even those living in New York's East Village. And those who had the six cent stamp to mail in the questionnaire will be somewhat different from those who did not; those who are willing to fill it out in the first place will be dissimilar in some ways from those who are not willing. And so on.

7. Richard Brotman and Frederic Suffet, "Marijuana Users' Views of Marijuana Use" (Paper presented at the American Psychopathological Association Annual Meeting, February 1969).

8. See Ernest Hamburger, "Contrasting the Hippie and Junkie," *The International Journal of the Addictions* 4 (March 1969): 123–126, for data on the sex ratios of drug addicts.

9. American Institute of Public Opinion, *Special Report on the Attitudes of College Students* no. 48 (Princeton, N. J., June 1969), p. 30.

10. Martin E. Rand, J. David Hammond, and Patricia Moscou, "A Survey of Drug Use at Ithaca College," *The Journal of the American College Health Association* 17 (October 1968): 43–51.

11. See also Richard Blum et al., *Students and Drugs* (San Francisco: Jossey-Bass, 1969), p. 64; Brotman and Suffet, *op. cit.*, p. 6.

12. State of California, Department of Justice, Bureau of Criminal Statistics, *Drug Arrests and Dispositions in California, 1967* (Sacramento: State of California, 1968), pp. 4, 5.

13. William Simon and John H. Gagnon, *The End of Adolescence: The College Experience* (New York: Harper & Row, 1970), forthcoming.

14. David P. Ausubel, *Drug Addiction* (New York: Random House, 1958), pp. 94, 95.

15. AIPO, *op. cit.*, p. 30.

16. Blum et al., *op. cit.*, p. 66.

17. Louis Harris, "Parents Draw the Line at Drug Use," *The Philadelphia Inquirer*, March 4, 1968.

18. Hundreds of articles, books, and studies have discussed and tested these relationships. See Albert K. Cohen and Harold M. Hodges, "Lower-Blue-Collar-Class Characteristics," *Social Problems* 10 (Spring 1963): 303–334; Melvin L. Kohn, *Class and Conformity* (Homewood, Ill.: Dorsey Press, 1969). See also the relevant papers in Rose Laub Coser ed., *Life Cycle and Achievement in America* (New York: Harper

Torchbooks, 1969), and Alan L. Grey, ed., *Class and Personality in Society* (New York: Atherton Press, 1969).

19. AIPO, *op. cit.*, p. 30.

20. American Institute of Public Opinion, "Views of College Students on Drug-Taking," unpublished manuscript (June 1967), and William J. Bowers, "A Study of Campus Misconduct," unpublished manuscript (Boston: Northeastern University, The Russell B. Stearns Study, 1968).

21. Columbia Broadcasting System News, *Generations Apart: A Study of the Generation Gap,* conducted for CBS by Daniel Yankelovitch, Inc., 1969, p. 18.

22. Bowers, *op. cit.*, table 3.

23. CBS, *op. cit.*, p. 82. The question of whether a "no religion" stance influences one's political orientation, or vice versa, is not relevent at this point.

24. Blum et al., *op. cit.*, p. 66.

25. Richard Brotman, Irving Silverman, and Frederic Suffet, "Some Social Correlates of Student Drug Use," unpublished manuscript (New York Medical College, Division of Community Mental Health), p. 13.

26. Blum et al., *op. cit.*, pp. 69–70.

27. CBS, *op. cit.*, p. 62.

28. AIPO, *op. cit.*, pp. 9–12, 21, 23, 24, 30.

29. For two Marxian analyses of the role of cannabis in the class struggle, see Allen Krebs, "Hashish, Avant Garde and Rearguard," *Streets* 1, no. 2 (May–June 1965): 17–22, and B. W. Sigg, *Le Cannabism Chronique, Fruit du Sous-developpement et du Capitalisme* (Marrakesch, 1960; Algiers, 1963). An exposition on the latter work, which is inaccessible (as is the former) may be found in Blum et al., *op. cit.*, pp. 73–76. For another article which emphasizes the political apathy-producing effects of marijuana, see Hunter Thompson, "The 'Hashbury' is the Capital of the Hippies," *The New York Times Magazine*, May 14, 1967, pp. 29, 123, 124.

30. See L. T. Frey, "Memorandum to All Marine Aircraft Group 11 Personnel," excerpts printed in *Avant Garde*, no. 4 (September 1968): p. 10, and Paul G. Rogers, "Transcript of Panel Discussion, Drug Abuse Control Amendments of 1965," in International Narcotic Enforcement Officers Association, *Sixth Annual Conference Report* (Miami Beach, Fla. September 26–October 1, 1965), pp. 20–21.

31. One of the most comprehensive of the many studies exploring this relationship is Lee Rainwater, "Some Aspects of Lower Class Sexual Behavior," *The Journal of Social Issues* 22, no. 2 (April 1966): 96–108.

32. The sociologist and the psychiatrist are likely to see different ranges of the sexual spectrum. While a sociologist, when he thinks of someone who is defined as "sexually permissive," is likely to think of the most permissive half, third, or quarter of the entire population, the huge majority of which are clinically healthy individuals, the psychiatrist will rather think of the tiny minority who are the most sexually active (comprising possibly 1 percent of the population) many of whom act on the basis of motives defined by much of the medical profession as neurotic. (The promiscuous girl, for instance.) Thus, he will take a dimmer view of sexual permissiveness. In fact, many of the most sexually active individuals, such as the promiscuous girl, actually reject the validity of their behavior, and could not, therefore, be called attitudinally permissive. In any case, if we were to adopt a broader view, and look at the most permissive half, third, or quarter of the population, we would find a much higher level of self-acceptance.

: *Chapter 3* :

Marijuana and the Politics of Reality

Introduction

One of the mysteries of recent social research is the seemingly contradictory conclusions about marijuana use. Perhaps no sector of social behavior is more disputed. Empirical questions concerning aspects of marijuana use arouse a hornet's nest of controversy. Even the fundamental question of the effects of the drug on the human mind and body is hotly disputed; two descriptions, both purporting to be equally "objective," often bear no relation to one another. Is marijuana a drug of psychic dependence? Or is it meaningless to speak of dependency in regard to marijuana? Does marijuana cause organic damage to the brain? Are its effects criminogenic? How does it influence the overall output of activity—in popular terms, does it produce lethargy and sloth? Does it precipitate "psychotic episodes"? What, specifically, is its impact on artistic creativity? What is the drug's influence on mechanical skills, such as the ability to drive an automobile? Does the use of marijuana lead to heroin addiction?

These questions can be answered within the scope of empirical sociological, psychological, and pharmacological scientific technique. Each query can be operationalized. Indices can be constructed and tests can be devised. Occasionally they are. Yet the zones of widespread agreement are narrow indeed. Surely this should puzzle the sociologist.

The Social Construction of Reality

All civilizations set rules concerning what is real and what is not, what is true and what is false. All societies select out of the data before them a world, one world, the world taken for granted, and declare *that* the real world. Each one of these artificially constructed worlds is to some degree idiosyncratic. No individual views reality directly, "in the raw," so to speak, but our perceptions are narrowly channelled through concepts and interpretations. What is commonly thought of as reality, that which exists, or simply is, is a set of concepts, assumptions, justifications, defenses, all generally collectively agreed-upon, which guide and channel each individual's perceptions in a specific direction. The specific rules governing the perception of the universe which man inhabits are more or less arbitrary, a matter of convention. Every society establishes a kind of epistemological methodology.

Meaning, then, does not automatically come about. Rather, it is read into every situation, event, entity, object, phenomenon. What one individual understands by a given phenomenon may be absolutely heterogenous to what another individual understands. In a sense, then, the reality itself is different. The only reality available to each individual consciousness is a subjective reality. Yet this insight poses a dilemma: we must see in a skewed manner or not at all. For, as Berger and Luckmann point out, "To include epistemological questions concerning the validity of sociological knowledge is like trying to push a bus in which one is riding."[1] Sociologists, too, are implicated in this same process. But unless we wish to remain huddled in the blind cave of solipsism, the problem should not paralyze us. We leave the problem of the validity of sociological knowledge to the metaphysical philosophers.

If we wish to grasp the articulation between ideology and what Westerners call science, we must look to fundamental cultural beliefs that stimulate or inhibit the growth of scientific-empirical ideas. One form of this selection process, the course of defining the nature of the universe, involves *the rules of validating reality*. A procedure is established for accepting inferential evidence; some forms of evidence will be ruled out as irrelevant, while others· will serve to negotiate and determine what is real. For instance, some religious systems have great faith in the validity of the message of the senses.[2] Other civilizations give greater weight to mystical insight, to the reality beyond empirical reality.[3]

The sociologist's task starts with this vast cultural canvas. While the "major mode" of the epistemological selection and validation process involves the decision to accept or rule out the data of our senses, within this tradition, minor modes of variation will be noticed. Clearly, even societies with powerful scientific and empirical traditions will contain subcultures which have less faith in the logic of the senses than others have. Moreover, all cultures have absorbed one or another mode of reasoning *differentially*, so that some institutions will typify the dominant mode more characteristically than others. Certainly, few in even the most empirical of civilizations will apply the same rules of evidence in the theater of their family as in their workaday world.

The more complex the society, the greater the number of competing versions concerning reality. The positivists were in error in assuming that greater knowledge would bring epistemological convergence. The arenas of controversy are more far-flung than they ever have been. Now, instead of societies differing as to how they view the real world, subsegments of the same society differ as well. This poses a serious problem for those members of society who have an emotional investment in stability and the legitimacy of their own special version of reality. The problem becomes, then, a matter of *moral hegemony*, of legitimating one distinctive view of the world and of discrediting competing views. These rules of validating reality, and society's faith in them, may serve as strategies in ideological struggles. Contending parties will wish to establish veracity by means of the dominant cultural mode.

All societies invest this selection process with an air of mystification. Using Peter Berger's phrase: "Let the institutional order be so interpreted as to hide, as much as possible, its constructed character. . . . [The] humanly constructed nomoi are given a cosmic status. . . ."[4] This process must not, above all, be seen as whimsical and arbitrary; it must be grounded in the nature of reality itself. The one selected view of the world must be seen as the only possible view of the world; it must be identified with the real world. All other versions of reality must be seen as whimsical and arbitrary and, above all, in error. At one time, this twin mystification process was religious in character: views in competition with the dominant one were heretical and displeasing to the gods—hence, Galileo's crime. Now, of course, the style is to cloak what Berger terms "fictitious necessities" with an aura of scientific validity. Nothing has greater discrediting power today than the demonstration that a given assertion has been "scientifically disproven." Our contemporary pawnbrokers of reality are scientists.

Value and Fact in Negotiating the Marijuana Reality

Probably no area of social life reflects this selective process more than drug use. Society has constructed the social concept "drug" in such a way that it excludes elements which are substantially identical to those it includes. What is seen as the essential reality of a given drug and its use is a highly contingent event. What society selects as crucial to perceive about drugs, and what it ignores, tells us a great deal about its cultural fabric.

The scientist makes a distinction between those questions that can be answered empirically and those wholly in the realm of sentiment. The question of whether marijuana causes crime is answerable, but the question of whether marijuana is *evil* or not is intrinsically unanswerable, within an empirical and scientific framework. It depends completely on one's perspective. However clear-cut this distinction is in the scientist's mind, as a tool for understanding the disputants' positions in this controversy, it is specious and misleading for a variety of reasons.

The strands of value and fact intersect with one another so luxuriantly that in numerous reasoning sequences they are inseparable. What one society or group or individual takes for granted as self-evidently harmful, others view as obviously beneficial, even necessary. In crucial ways, the issue of harm or danger to society as a result of the drug pivots on moot points, totally unanswerable questions, questions that science is unable to answer without the resolution of certain basic issues. And for many crucially debated marijuana questions, this modest requirement cannot be met. In other words, before we raise the question of whether marijuana has a desirable or a noxious effect, we must first establish the desirability or the noxiousness *to whom*. We must concern ourselves with the differential *evaluations* of the same objective consequences. Many of the drug's effects—agreed-upon by friend and foe alike—will be regarded as reprehensible by some individuals, desirable or neutral by others. Often antimarijuana forces will argue against the use of the drug, employing reasons which its supporters will also employ —in favor of its use. We have not a disagreement in what the effects are, but whether they are good or bad. This is probably the most transparently ideological of all of the platforms of debate about marijuana. Three illustrations of this orbit of disputation suffice.

Were marijuana use more prevalent than it is today, there would come the billowing of a distinct aesthetic. The state of marijuana intoxication seems to be associated with, and even to touch off, a unique and peculiar vision of the world. That the marijuana-induced vision is distinctive seems to be beyond dispute;[5] that it is rewarding or fatuous is a matter for endless disputation. Inexplicably, the drug seems to engender a mental state which is coming into vogue in today's art forms. An extraordinarily high proportion of today's young and avant-garde artists—filmmakers, poets, painters, musicians, novelists, photographers, mixed-media specialists—use the drug and are influenced by the marijuana high. Some of the results seem to be the increasing irrelevance of realism; the loss of interest in plot in films and novels; a glorification of the irrational and the seemingly nonsensical; an increased faith in the logic of the viscera, rather than in the intellect; a heightened sense for the absurd; an abandonment of traditional and "linear" reasoning sequences, and the substitution of "mosaic" and fragmentary lines of attack; bursts of insight rather than chains of thought; connectives relying on internal relevance, rather than a commonly understood and widely accepted succession of events and thoughts; love of the paradoxical, the perverse, the contradictory, the incongruous; an implosive inward thrust, rather than an explosive outward thrust; instantaneous totality rather than specialization; the dynamic rather than the static; the unique rather than the general and universal. The parallel between the mental processes associated with the marijuana high and the "tribal" mind typified by McLuhan is too close to escape mention.[6]

Those with conventional, traditional, and classic tastes in art will view these results in a dim light. A recent antimarijuana tract, for instance, comments on the highly unconventional and antitraditionalist novelist William Burroughs' approval of marijuana's influence on his creative powers: "The irony is that Burroughs meant his remark as an endorsement." [7] The sociologist of knowledge seeks to understand and explain the bases from which man's intellectual efforts spring. He will notice the prominent place in this debate the manner in which matters of taste, such as artistic aesthetics, are intimately and inseparably bound with views of the empirical reality of the drug. He who is opposed to the use of marijuana, and who believes that it is (empirically) harmful, is very likely to dislike contemporary art forms, and vice versa. The two are not, of course, necessarily causally related, but rather emerge out of the same matrix.

Marijuana's reputed impact on sexual behavior is all to the good to some who are comfortable with an unconventional view of sex. To the sexually traditional, the fact that marijuana could disrupt man's (and woman's) sexuality is an out-of-hand condemnation of the drug. While marijuana's opponents would label any imputed increase in sexual activity as a result of drug "promiscuity" [8] and would roundly condemn it, the drug's apostles would cheer society's resurgent interest in the organic, the earthy, the sensual. For instance, a 1967 court ruling in the Court of Massachusetts, held that sexual promiscuity was one of the undesirable consequences of marijuana use; Justice Tauro rejected the defendants' appeal. Strangely, *Time* magazine claimed that Tauro's ruling would be judged fair by even the staunchest of marijuana supporters.

Marijuana as a mind-altering drug has discrediting power to the one who thinks of the everyday workings of the mind as normal and desirable. But to the explorer of unusual and exotic mental realms, its mind-altering functions are in its favor. The ideologues of the psychedelic movement—and marijuana is considered by most commentators as the weakest of the psychedelic or hallucinogenic drugs —claim that every member of society is lied to, frustrated, cheated, duped and cajoled, and so grows up totally deceived. Barnacles of attitudes, values, beliefs, layer themselves upon the mind, making it impossible to see things as they truly are. This ideology maintains that far from offering an escape from reality, the psychedelic drugs thrust man more intensely into reality. By suspending society's illusions, the voyager is able to see reality in the raw, with greater verisimilitude. Aldous Huxley exclaimed, under the influence of mescaline, "This is how one ought to see, how things really are." [9]

The antipsychedelic stance will, of course, deny the validity of this process. What is real is the world as the undrugged person perceives it. Any alteration of the normal state of consciousness is destructive and inherently distorting. Drug use, it is claimed, is "a way to shut out the real world or enter a world of unreality"; the psychedelic drug user attempts to "take a trip away from the real world and to a society of his own making." [10] But what is astonishing about the controversy is that both sides presume to know precisely what *reality* is. Whatever version we choose to guide our senses, we should not fail to see the ideological character of the controversy. Both orientations are to a large degree arbitrary, conventional. Epistemological questions cannot be resolved by fiat or empirical test. Even the natural sciences rest on faith, an unprovable assumption that the senses convey valid information. Yet each side insists that it alone has a monopoly on knowing what is true and what false, what is real and what illusory. Both sides attempt to mask the capricious nature of their decision with an air of legitimacy and absolute validity. Taking a relativistic stance toward both perspectives, we are forced to regard both as statements of a distinctly political nature.

An essential component of dominant medical and psychological thinking about illicit drug use is that it is undesirable, that the user should be treated in such a manner that he discontinues use. The user is felt, rightly or wrongly, to threaten some of the more strongly held cultural values of American society:

In my opinion, psychopharmacologic agents may be divided into two major categories depending on the manner in which they either help or hinder the individual in his adaptation to society.

Drugs may be used in one of two ways to help relieve . . . tensions: by sufficiently diminishing emotional tension to permit the individual to function or by allowing the individual to totally escape from reality. Sedatives, tranquilizers, and antidepressants . . . often permit an individual to function more effectively. Psychedelic drugs . . . allow the individual to escape from reality so that he need not function at all. The first group of drugs is often useful to society; the second group would only destroy it.[11]

Given the basic premises on which statements such as these are based, it is difficult to understand just what the notion of detachment and objectivity toward the drug user might mean.

Another locus of unresolvable controversy, where value and fact interlock inseparably, is the question of a hierarchy of values. An impartial stance is claimed by combatants in a multitude of pseudo-scientific questions. Here, even the value issues may be resolved. Everyone agrees that marijuana may precipitate psychotic episodes, and that, further, psychotic episodes are a bad thing. The issue then becomes not, does it occur, or, is it good or bad, but does marijuana's claimed benefits outweigh its possible dangers? Should we restrict society's right of access to drugs so that we may minimize the potential harm to itself? How do one set of values stack up against another? One might, by donning a white coat, pretend to scientific objectivity in answering this question, but it might be wise to remember that even the emperor didn't succeed in the ruse.

The Logistics of Empirical Support

A second powerful reason why strictly empirical arguments seem to have exerted relatively little hold in the marijuana controversy, aside from the intricate intertwining of value and fact, seems to be basic panhuman psychic process that leads to the need for the confirmation of our strongly held biases; moreover, empirical reality, being staggeringly complex, permits and even demands factual selection. We characteristically seek support for our views: contrary opinions and facts are generally avoided. This opens the way for the maintenance of points of view which are contradicted by empirical evidence. And there is invariably a variety of facts to choose from. It is a comparatively simple matter to find what one is looking for in any moderately complex issue. Each individual facing an emotionally charged issue selects the facts which agree with his own opinions, supermarket-like. Individuals do not judge marijuana to be harmful or beneficial as a result of objective evidence, rationally weighed and judiciously considered. The process, rather, works in the opposite direction: the drug is considered harmful—as a result of customs that articulate or clash with the use and the effect of the drug, as a result of the kinds of people who use it, the nature of the "reading" process society applies to these individuals, and as a result of campaigns conducted by moral entrepreneurs, as well as innumerable other processes—and *then* positive and negative traits are attributed to the drug. The explanation for perceiving the drug in a specific manner follows the attitudes about it. A man is not opposed to the use or the legalization of marijuana because (he thinks) it leads to the use of more dangerous drugs, because it causes crime, because it produces insanity and brain damage, because it makes a person unsafe behind the wheel, because it creates an unwillingness to work. He believes these things because he thinks the drug is evil. The negative consequences of the use of marijuana are superadded to support a basically value position. But everyone, Pareto says, seeks to cloak his prejudices in the garb of reason, especially in an empirical age, so that evidence to support them is dragged in post hoc to provide rational and concrete proof. Clearly, not many interested participants in a given controversy are aware of the rules of the scientific method. They may feel that they are empirically proving a point by submitting concrete evidence, yet the mode of reasoning merely confirms their ideological biases. "Proof" by enumeration exemplifies this principle. The criminogenic effects of marijuana are demonstrated by listing individuals who smoke marijuana who also, either under the influence or not, committed a crime. Munch[12] and Anslinger and Tompkins[13] exemplify this line of reasoning. (We will elaborate on this point in the chapter on marijuana's supposed effects on crime.)

Conceptions of true and false are extravagantly refracted through social and cultural lenses to such an extent that the entire notion of empirical truth becomes irrelevant. True and false become, in fact, what dominant groups define as true and false; its very collectivity establishes legitimacy. A pro- or antimarijuana stance reflects a basic underlying attitudinal syndrome, ideological in character, that is consonant with its drug component. Prior to being exposed to attitudes or "facts" about marijuana, the individual has come to accept or reject fundamental points of view which already lead him to apprehend the reality of marijuana in a definite manner. These ideological slants are not merely correlates of related and parallel attitudes. They are also perceptual screens through which a person views empirically grounded facts. In other words, marijuana provides an occasion for ideological expression.

Perceptions of the very empirical reality of the drug are largely determined by prior ideological considerations. Almost everyone facing the issue already has an answer concerning its various aspects, because of his attitudes about related and prior issues. He finds facts to suit his predilections—whether supportive or hypercritical—and commandeers them to suit his biases. The essential meaning of the marijuana issue is the meaning which each individual brings to it. The marijuana "reality" going on before us is a vast turmoil of events which, like all realities, demands factual selection. Yet the selection of facts is never random. It is always systematic; it always obeys a specific logic. Any message can be read into the impact of the drug; anything you wish to see is there. We support our predilections by only seeing in the drug that which supports them. If the critic wants to see in the drug and its use violence, sadism, rape and murder, they are there, buried in the reality of marijuana. If the drug supporter wishes to see peace and serenity, they are not difficult to find either.

This is not to say, of course, that no research has ever been conducted which approaches scientific objectivity. (Scientific objectivity is, as we pointed out above, one form of bias, but since on most issues all participants in the dispute pay their respects to it, this axiom is apolitical in its import.) It is to say, however, that not all participants in the marijuana controversy have been trained as scientists, nor do they reason as scientists. *Interpretations* of the marijuana studies are more important to us here than the studies' findings themselves. Out of a multitude of findings a diversity of mutually exclusive conclusions can be reached. The multitude of results from the many marijuana reports forms a sea of ambiguity into which nearly any message may be read. The researcher's findings do not make themselves clear to the reader. Any opinion may be verified by the scientific literature on marijuana. Mayor LaGuardia's *Report* rivals the Bible in the diversity of the many conclusions that have been drawn from it.

Marijuana's proponents take heart in its conclusions,[14] and nearly all of the entire report has been reprinted in *The Marihuana Papers*, a decidedly promarijuana anthology. Yet at the same time antimarijuana forces find in the study solid evidence for the damaging effects of the drug.[15] Our point, then, is that drawing conclusions from even the most careful and parsimonious scientific study is itself a highly selective process. The welter of findings are subject to a systematic sifting process. Often the researcher finds it necessary to disassociate himself from the conclusions which others have drawn from his own work. For instance, a sensationalistic popular article on LSD was denounced as a distortion and an atrocity by the very scientists whose research it cited.[16] More attention ought to be paid, therefore, to the "reading" process of drawing conclusions from scientific work, rather than the findings themselves. In fact, specifically what might be meant by "the findings themselves" is unclear, since they can be made to say many different and contradictory things.

If a tactician were surveying the marijuana controversy, he would be struck by the ideological advantage of the antipot lobby in at least one respect: the single negative case is considerably more powerful than the single positive case—or, indeed, many positive cases. Harmfulness is far easier to prove than harmlessness. In order to demonstrate that marijuana is not damaging at all, it would be necessary to produce evidence that *all* cases of marijuana use did not result in damage—all individuals at all times—an obvious impossibility. Whereas to show that it is damaging in any degree, only a few scattered cases need be produced. (Even assuming that the "damage" can be traced to the marijuana, a question which is, itself, problematic.) Consequently, there is no *conceivable* evidence which can be presented to someone with a strong antimarijuana position which he will accept as a demonstration of the drug's comparative harmlessness.

Strategies of Discreditation

Labelling has political implications. By devising a linguistic category with specific connotations, one is designing armaments for a battle; by having it accepted and used, one has scored a major victory. For instance, the term "psychedelic" has a clear prodrug bias: it says that the mind works best when under the influence of this type of drug. (Moreover, one of the psychedelic drug proselytizers, in search of a term which would describe the impact of these drugs, rejected "psychodelic" as having negative overtones of psychosis.) The term "hallucinogen" is equally biased since an hallucination is, in our civilization at least, unreal, illusory, and therefore undesirable; the same holds for the term "psychotomimetic," capable of producing a madness-like state. The semantics and linguistics of the drug issue form an essential component of the ideological skirmishes.[17] As an example of how labelling influences

one's posture toward a phenomenon, note that the Bureau of Narcotics and Dangerous Drugs has jurisdiction over "addicting" drugs,
which supposedly includes marijuana, while the Food and Drug
Administration handles "habit-forming" drugs. Because of this juris-
dictional division, the Bureau is forced into the absurd position of
having to classify marijuana as an addicting drug, and to support
this contention, it supplies drug categorizations that follow jurisdic-
tional lines,[18] as if they had some sort of correspondence in the real
world. However, the Bureau seems not to take its own classifica-
tions seriously, since whenever the issue is discussed by its members, it is emphasized that marijuana is not addicting in the clas-
sical sense, but it produces a "psychological dependence." [19]

"Drug abuse" is such a linguistic device. It is often used by
physicians and by those in medically related fields. Encountering
the use of the term, one has the impression that something quite
measurable is being referred to, something very much like a disease, an undesirable condition which is in need of remedy. The
term, thus, simultaneously serves two functions: it claims clinical
objectivity and it discredits the action that it categorizes. In fact,
there is no such objectivity in the term; its use is baldly political.
Drug abuse is the use of a drug that influential persons with legitimacy condemn. Their objections are on moral, not medical,
grounds, although their argument will be cast in medical language.
Nonmedical drug use is, in the medical view, by definition abuse.

A linguistic category both crystallizes and influences responses to,
and postures toward, a phenomenon. The term "abuse" illustrates this
axiom. It announces that nonmedical drug-taking is undesirable,
that the benefits which the drug-using subculture proclaims for
drug use are outweighed by the hard rock of medical damage. Yet,
since the weighing of values is a moral, not a medical process, we
are full-face against an ideological resolution of the issue, yet one
couched in a scientific and empirical exoskeleton. Furthermore, the
linguistic category demands verification. By labelling a phenomenon "abuse," one is willy-nilly under pressure to prove that the label
is valid. The term so structures our perceptions of the phenomenon
that it is possible to see only abusive aspects in drug use. Therefore,
data must be collected to discredit the beneficial claims of drug use.

Another strategy of disconfirming the marijuanaists' claims to
legitimacy is the notion, closely interconnected with drug use as
abuse, that marijuana use is the manifestation of medical pathology.

This thrust bears two prongs: (1) the *etiology* of marijuana use as an expression of, or an "acting out" of, a personality disturbance; and (2) the effects of the drug as a precipitator of temporary but potent psychotic episodes. By assigning marijuana use to the twilight world of psychic pathology, its moral and willful character has been neutralized. The labelled behavior has been removed from the arena of free will; its compulsive character effectively denies that it can be a viable alternative, freely chosen. A recent discussion argues that assigning the status of medical pathology is an effective device for neutralizing the legitimacy of a political opponent's ideology.[20] An act reduced to both symptom and cause of pathology has had its claims to moral rectitude neutralized and discredited. As a manifestation of illness, it calls for treatment, not serious debate. In a sense, then, physicians and psychiatrists have partially replaced policemen as preservers of the social order, since attempts at internal controls have replaced external sanctions. Both presume to know for the subject how he "ought" to act. Yet the new sanctions, based on an ideology which the deviant partially believes in—scientific treatment of a medical illness—becomes a new and more powerful form of authoritarianism.

Generally, some sort of explanation, particularly one involving compulsion and pathology, is needed wherever it is not rationally understandable to the observer, that is, when it doesn't make sense. An anomalous and bizarre form of behavior demands an explanation. We can understand repeated dosages of poetry, because we all approve of poetry, so that no special examination is necessitated. It is only where the behavior violates our value biases that we feel it necessary to construct an interpretation. There is the built-in assumption that the individual *should* be able to do without recreational drugs, that their use is unnecessary, and a life without them is the normal state of affairs. Violation of our expectations requires an explanation. No explanation for abstinence from drugs is necessary, since our biases tell us that that is the way one ought to live.

Looking at all of the actions of which society disapproves—deviant behavior—we notice that they share fundamental similarities. However, these similarities inhere not so much in the acts themselves as in the way society reponds to them. One of the more interesting responses is the tendency to impute psychological abnormality to their authors. The issue of whether such judgments are "correct" or not is less relevant to us as is the nexus between the kinds of acts that attract such judgments, and the nature of the society in which they are made. It is said that Freud once had a patient who believed that the center of the earth was filled with jam. Freud was not concerned with the truth or falsity of that statement but with the kind of man who made it. Similarly, the sociologist of knowledge concerns himself with the kinds of explanations a society fabricates about behavior in its midst, and what those explanations reveal about that society. It should be regarded as extremely significant that deviant behavior seems to have attracted explanations which activate a principle of psychological abnormality. The sociologist legitimately raises the question as to what it is about American society which begets a personality abnormality explanation for marijuana smokers, as well as heroin addicts, homosexuals, unwed mothers, criminals, juvenile delinquents, and prostitutes, in addition to a host of other deviant groups and activities.[21] The fact that each of these social categories—and the activities associated with them—are severely condemned by American society makes the nature of the process of constructing pathology interpretations of deviance at least as interesting as the etiology of the deviant behavior itself. In all of these cases, adopting a medical approach to the deviant and his behavior effectively neutralizes his moral legitimacy, as well as the viability of his behavior. In this sense, the constructors of such theories serve to mirror the basic values of American society.

It is incredible that so many participants of this debate feel that the issues can be decided rationally—and in favor of their own side, naturally, which is, of course, how they decide what is rational. In reality, the marijuana debate is simply not an issue that permits rationality. Some questions are inherently unanswerable, while others, although ideally subject to empirical demonstration, are so heavily mired in sentiment that no amount of tugging is going to get them out. Only the naive think that "proof" proceeds in the manner of the scientific ideal. "Proof" involves gathering information, however dubious, which suits one's own biases, and suppressing that which threatens them. Actually, "facts" are instruments designed for the support of one's biases. These facts may actually be true, but truth is complex and elusive, and even seemingly contradictory facts may be "true." Anyone who thinks of marijuana use as *evil* wishes to attribute "evil" causes to it, as well as "evil" consequences (especially).

No one likes violence, crime, heroin addiction, or "psychological dependence," so marijuana is charged with generating them. Actually, these are all *code words*. The allegation that marijuana causes violence is code for "marijuana use is evil." Today's allegations have, of course, been retranslated into contemporary scientific metaphors, because religious imagery does not speak with much practical authority today, but their meaning is identical. Consider the following quotes (the emphasis is mine):

. . . marihuana is *addicting* in the sense that it is a *dangerous intoxicating drug.* . . .[22]

So far as I can see, I do not think it is irrational to legally define marihuana as a *"narcotic drug."* [23]

Although cannabism does not lead to an *addiction* in the classic sense of morphinism, the subjection to the drug is fairly serious. To a considerable extent, it decreases the *social value* of the individual and leads him to manifest physical and mental *decadence.* The tendency to an *unsocial conduct of relaxed morals,* of *listlessness,* with an *aversion to work* or the inclination to develop *psychotic phenomena,* is greatly intensified by marihuana.[24]

In each case, the reader thinks that he understands the distinction being made while, in fact, the writer is actually making a very different one: a logical sleight of hand, in a sense. Notice the transition; we think we know what addicting means, and we feel assured that marijuana is not addicting. But we know that addicting is bad, and such labels are useful for persuasion purposes. So, marijuana must be labelled addicting, making it bad. We know that narcotics are bad, and that narcotic refers to an analgesic, a pain-killer. By defining marijuana as a narcotic, one quality of the narcotic is isolated out (its image in the popular mind as evil), and its actual pharmacologic property (pain-killing), which marijuana doesn't share, is ignored. Thus, we have narcotic-evil-marijuana.

Although this procedure might seem strange to the logician, the methodologist, the scientist, it should come as no surprise to the student of primitive tribes. On such processes major elements of whole civilizations are built. Consider the uproar a generation ago in a tiny Indian village in Mexico following the discovery that an inoculation serum contained horse blood; no one wanted this substance injected into his body. Inoculation, as a consequence, had to be postponed until a more enlightened age and the population of the village exposed itself to the threat of lethal disease. What

Westerners consider the major characteristic of the serum (disease prevention) was ignored; the minor characteristic (horse blood) was emphasized. To the Indian, the attribution of importance was reversed. Such are the powers of conceptualization.

When the law, such as in New York State, defines marijuana as a narcotic, it is actually using the definition as a code—a kind of cryptograph—for unprovable assumptions about the drug's properties, the moral nature of its use, and the character of its clientele. The fact that in a pharmacological sense, the legal definition is erroneous and absurd, should not trouble us unduly. Actually, the pharmacological property of the drug has been suppressed in favor of a *moral* and *evaluative* properties. Narcotic is a code word for evil and (putatively) dangerous. The evaluation of marijuana as dangerous contains both moral and empirical judgments, as we pointed out earlier. It involves two processes: deciding what may be defined as dangerous, which is a value judgment, and how the evidence concerning marijuana's dangers may be evaluated. The law does not purport to make a scientific evaluation of the drug's characteristics; it is making a moral and conjectural judgment; by labelling the phenomenon it is criminalizing, the coupling is made powerful, and the elements are almost inseparable.

In fact, the entire marijuana controversy could be viewed as a series of semantic constructs. We could make generalizations about the position of one or another combatant on the basis of specific key words—even without examining his argument. These words could serve as linguistic devices or symbols for a whole line of reasoning. We know, for instance, that if Oriental studies are cited, the author thinks that marijuana is harmful. Or that if the alcohol-marijuana comparison is made, that the person presenting the argument feels that alcohol is more harmful than marijuana, and that pot should be legalized. Thus, the words, "India" or "alcohol" serve as a symbol for a position taken. Arguments are invoked; linguistic symbols are manipulated. It is a form of shorthand for an ideological position. Similarly, in many cultural forms, such as film, there are popularly understood and taken-for-granted summing-up devices which represent larger universes of discourse. At one time, in Westerns, the villan had to be dressed in black and ride a black horse: the hero was symbolized by white. We know today that sexual intercourse takes place when accompanied by the appropriate symbol referents, even without viewing the action; a musical crescendo and a fadeout tell us as much as an explicit rendition about what actually happened. (Sexual explicitness, however, is coming into style. All this means is that different cryptograms are utilized.) By examining the marijuana controversy as such a cultural fragment, we are able to see with crystal clarity the humanly fabricated nature of the issues and the ideological character of the arguments invoked.

Overview

It is the sociologist's job to discover and explicate patterns in social life. One side of a protracted and apparently insoluble controversy activates arguments that involve such putatively repugnant components as "socially irresponsible," "vagabond existence," "outlandish fashions," "long hair," "lack of cleanliness," and "disdain for conventional values." [25] The other side emphasizes factors that it deems beneficial: "discovery," "optical and aural aesthetic perceptions," "self-awareness," "insight," and "minute engagement." [26] So we are led to the conclusion that the controversy is a matter of taste and style of life, that it revolves about basically unanswerable issues, and its adjudication will take place on the basis of power and legitimacy, not on the basis of scientific truth. In fact, given the nature of the disputation, it is difficult to know exactly what is meant by scientific truth. The problem becomes one of getting support for one or another bias, rather than the empirical testing of specific propositions, whatever that might entail.

The American Medical Association urges educational programs as an effective "deterrent" to marijuana use. [27] It is not, however, the sheer accumulation of information about marijuana which the AMA is referring to, since the marijuana user knows more than the average nonuser about the effects of the drug. *Attitudes toward* the drug are referred to, not factual information:

. . . district officials are so fired up, they'd interrupt the routine of the whole district just to make sure our kids hear a good speaker or see a movie that will teach them the basic fact: *stay away from drugs.*

In order to know exactly what it is that they should stay away from, students must know the *nature* of drugs . . . they're provided with basic facts. These facts aren't given "objectively"—they're slanted, so there's not the slightest doubt that students understand just how dangerous drugs can be.

You can call it brainwashing if you want to. We don't care what you call it—as long as these youngsters get the point.[28]

Not only is the "meaning in the response," but both meaning and response are structured by power and legitimacy hierarchies. Society calls upon certain status occupants to verify what we wish to hear. These statuses are protective in nature, especially designated to respond to certain issues in a predetermined manner. Threats to society's security must be discredited. An elaborate charade is played out; debater's points are scored—with no acknowledgment from the other side—and no one is converted. Inexorably, American society undergoes massive social change, and the surface froth of marijuana use and the marijuana controversy changes with it.

N O T E S

1. Peter L. Berger and Thomas Luckmann, *The Social Construction of Reality* (Garden City, N. Y.: Doubleday, 1966), p. 13.

2. Robert K. Merton, "Puritanism, Pietism, and Science," in *Social Theory and Social Structure,* 3rd ed. (New York: Free Press, 1968), and Robert E. Kennedy, "The Protestant Ethic and the Parsis," *The American Journal of Sociology* 68 (July 1962): 11–20.

3. Joseph Needham, "Buddhism and Chinese Science," in *Science and Civilization in China* (Cambridge: Cambridge University Press, 1956), 2: 417–422, 430–431.

4. Peter L. Berger, *The Sacred Canopy* (Garden City, N. Y.: Doubleday, 1967), pp. 33, 36, 90–91, 203.

5. Peter Ludlow, "In Defence of Pot: Confessions of a Canadian Marijuana Smoker," *Saturday Night,* October 1965, pp. 28–32; Allen Ginsberg, "The Great Marijuana Hoax: First Manifesto to End the Bringdown," *Atlantic Monthly,* November 1966, pp. 106–112; Renata Adler, "The Screen: *Head,* Monkees Movie for a Turned-on Audience," *The New York Times,* November 7, 1968; Anonymous, "Thoughts on Marijuana and the Artist," in Erich Goode, ed., *Marijuana* (New York: Atherton Press, 1969), pp. 177–183.

6. Marshall McLuhan, *Understanding Media* (New York: McGraw-Hill, 1964).

7. Edward R. Bloomquist, *Marijuana* (Beverly Hills, Calif.: Glencoe Press, 1968), p. 189.

8. G. Joseph Tauro, "A Judicial Opinion: Commonwealth v. Joseph D. Leis and Ivan Weiss," *Suffolk University Law Review* 3 (Fall 1968): 23–41.

9. Aldous Huxley, *The Doors of Perception,* bound with *Heaven and Hell* (New York: Harper Colophon, 1963), p. 34.

10. American Medical Association, "The Crutch That Cripples: Drug Dependence," a leaflet (Chicago: AMA, 1968), pp. 1, 4.

11. Benjamin Kissin, "On Marijuana," Downstate Medical Center *Reporter* 7, no. 2 (April 1967): p. 2.

12. James Munch, "Marihuana and Crime," United Nations *Bulletin on Narcotics* 18 (April–June 1966): 15–22.

13. Harry J. Anslinger and W. G. Tomkins, *The Traffic in Narcotics* (New York: Funk and Wagnalls, 1953), pp. 23–35.

14. John Rosevear, *Pot: A Handbook of Marihuana* (New Hyde Park, N. Y.: University Books, 1967), pp. 111–112.

15. Bloomquist, *op. cit.*, p. 122–126; Henry Brill, "Why Not Pot Now? Some Questions and Answers About Marijuana," *Psychiatric Opinion* 5, no. 5 (October 1968): 20–21; Donald B. Louria, "The Great Marijuana Debate," in *The Drug Scene* (New York: McGraw-Hill, 1968), p. 105.

16. Bill Davidson, "The Hidden Evils of LSD," *The Saturday Evening Post*, August 12, 1967, pp. 19–23.

17. Joel Fort, "The Semantics and Logic of the Drug Scene," in Charles Hollander, ed., *Background Papers on Student Drug Involvement* (Washington: National Student Association, 1967), p. 88.

18. "A Schoolman's Guide to Illicit Drugs," *School Management*, June 1966, pp. 100–101.

19. Henry L. Giordano, "Marihuana—A Calling Card to Narcotic Addiction," *FBI Law Enforcement Bulletin* 37 (November 1968): 3.

20. Gregory P. Stone and Harvey A. Farberman, *Social Psychology Through Symbolic Interaction* (Waltham, Mass.: Blaisdell, 1970).

21. Isidore Chein et al., *The Road to H* (New York: Basic Books, 1964); Irving Bieber et al., *Homosexuality* (New York: Basic Books, 1962); New York Academy of Medicine, "Homosexuality," *Bulletin of the New York Academy of Medicine* 40 (July 1964): 576–580; Leontyne R. Young, *Out of Wedlock* (New York: McGraw-Hill, 1954), and "Personality Patterns in Unmarried Mothers," *The Family* 26 (December 1945): 296–303; David Abrahamsen, *The Psychology of Crime* (New York: Columbia University Press, 1960); Hyman Grossbard, "Ego Deficiency in Delinquents," *Social Casework* 43 (April 1962): 171–178; Harold Greenwald, *The Call Girl* (New York: Ballantine Books, 1960).

22. David W. Maurer and Victor H. Vogel, *Narcotics and Narcotic Addiction*, 3rd ed. (Springfield, Ill.: Charles C Thomas, 1967), p. 119.

23. Donald E. Miller, "What Policemen Should Know About the Marihuana Controversy," International Narcotic Enforcement Officers Association, *Eighth Annual Conference Report* (Louisville, Ky., October 22–26, 1967), p. 55.

24. Pablo Oswaldo Wolff, *Marihuana in Latin America: The Threat It Constitutes* (Washington: Linacre Press, 1949), p. 47.

25. Dana Farnsworth, "The Drug Problem Among Young People," *West Virginia Medical Journal* 63 (December 1967): 433–437.

26. Ginsberg, *op. cit.*

27. American Medical Association, "Marihuana and Society," *Journal of the American Medical Association* 204 (June 24, 1968): 1181–1182.

28. "How One District Combats the Drug Problem," *School Management*, June 1966, p. 103. The interview is with Dr. Sidney Birnbach, director of school health, physical education, and safety, in the Yonkers, New York, school system.

: *Chapter 4* :

The Smoker's View
of Marijuana

Marijuana's supporters are almost as varied in their advocacy of its benefical qualities as are its opponents in their allegation of its dangers. We will encounter expressions ranging from the simple and vague, "Pot's groovy," to complex, subtle, and abstruse philosophical systems requiring volumes far weightier than this to characterize. Yet, throughout the broad spectrum of opinions for the drug, some more or less consistent ideological threads may be detected. To begin with, users and supporters are generally eager to neutralize arguments asserting the drug's harm; there is an almost complete uniformity on the promarijuana side in regard to the absence of damaging effects of cannabis. Users who feel that the drug is harmful almost invariably discontinue its use. Now, we might expect this to be true by definition: he who uses something is not likely to assert that it is dangerous. Not necessarily so, however. It is possible for a weighing process to have taken place, for the user to say that it is somewhat dangerous, but on the whole it's not all bad. Or we might encounter someone who recognizes the compulsive aspects of an activity and who wishes he could stop, but feels that he cannot, for instance, the alcoholic. The chronic amphetamine user will readily grant the harmfulness of his drug, admitting, wistfully, that his body is slowly being destroyed. This does not deter him from using the drug; he is still rhapsodic in praising it.

It is significant, therefore, that the marijuana supporter invariably denies that the drug has any significant dangers associated with its use. He further asserts that were he to discover some hidden danger associated with the use of pot, he would stop using it.

Both sides of the dispute claim to be positivistic in their stance. Each believes that facts will vindicate its position. With regard to marijuana, the American Medical Association writes: "An informed citizenry . . . is the most effective deterrent of all," [1] and the New York State Narcotics Addiction Control Commission designed as a drug prevention organization, in its official publication, asks: "Will Facts Put Lid on Pot at Ithaca?" [2] The procannabis side, too, assumes that an impartial, unbiased survey on marijuana use will inevitably uphold its claims. The two purposes of LEMAR stated in its constitution were "to disseminate information about marijuana and the anti-marijuana laws" and to promote "the re-legalization of marijuana use, possession and sale in the United States" and are held to be causally related; if more people knew about the true nature of pot, the laws outlawing it would be abolished. The only reason that Congress and the Federal Bureau of Narcotics were able to push the 1937 statute through was public ignorance about the harmlessness of the drug; LEMAR hopes to correct that ignorance. In any case, the bedrock of the promarijuana position is that the drug is essentially harmless. Thus, marijuana propaganda will nearly always include a point-for-point refutation of the anti-marijuana demonology. [3]

Generally, the issue is whether or not marijuana may properly be labelled a "dangerous drug." Not all cannabis advocates will agree on this question, but the range of opinion will be relatively narrow, at least as compared with the other side. The radical position is that the drug is *completely* innocuous, harmless in every conceivable way: ". . . marijuana . . . is in *all* respects socially useful, and absolutely *non*addictive. We defy anyone to produce a shred of evidence that marijuana . . . produces at *any* time any adverse, depressive, or toxic effect." [4] (The "completely innocuous" position is not to be taken absolutely literally, since an "overdose" of *water* may prove to be fatal; what is meant is that cannabis presents no dangers beyond such commonly accepted substances as coffee, tea, aspirin, wine, and food.) The most conservative pro-pot position is that the drug may, given an unfavorable setting or taken by an unstable personality, precipitate a temporary state which could, by some definition, conceivably be labelled as something potentially dangerous. In general, users do not take the propagandized "dangers" of the drug seriously, since they have spent hundreds and thousands of hours high, and have seen dozens of others high, with little or no ill effect.

There is more-or-less complete agreement on the *relative* harm of the drug: that marijuana is, for instance, far less dangerous than liquor.[5] Another comparison often made is that marijuana is less (or no more) dangerous than driving an automobile. Both of these arguments are open to empirical test and could, conceivably, be supported or refuted with data.

The alcohol-marijuana comparison carries a great deal of weight among potheads. They feel that they have a solid case for the irrationality of the marijuana prohibition if liquor is, in fact, more dangerous than their own choice of drug. They contend that drinking carries with it very real dangers (although a high proportion of marijuana smokers also drink, very few do so heavily), whereas marijuana is, at worst, no more dangerous, and at best, completely innocuous. ". . . alcohol is frequently productive of a hangover, cirrhosis of the liver, violence, Dylan Thomas scenes, and the creeping quivers . . ." declaims *The Marijuana Newsletter,* a one-time organ of LEMAR, in a vigorous effort to urge defiance of the marijuana statutes.

A marijuana user, in fact, feels a sense of superiority to the liquor drinker, a feeling that can be labelled moral, ideological and cultural snobbery. There is the faint hint of religious zeal in claiming a convert, of winning proselyte from "lush." The fact that so many young Americans once involved with alcohol are becoming "heads" is confirmation to the potsmoker that his intoxicating agent is spiritually preferrable. The marijuana user will refer to the liquor drinker in condescending terms as lacking in style, sophistication, imagination, polish, subtlety, and taste. He is gross, obnoxious, boisterous, boring, fatuous, inane, and often violent. A twenty-two-year-old college graduate, a "dealer," explains: "I go out in the drinking world, sorta. . . . A lotta my friends in school aren't hip to drugs, and they don't think I am. It's really strange. When I'm stoned, I find it real hard, 'cuz, I don't know, their ways, you know, the jokes and slapping around and loud tones, really gets to you after a while. But when I'm straight I can sorta take it. But not high." It might be hypothesized that this sense of superiority grows out of real or imagined criticism for partaking in a condemned activity. Regardless of the origin of the feeling, it is genuine, and it forms an element in the marijuana subculture.

One of the more damaging antimarijuana arguments that users wish to demolish revolves around the notion of the drug being capable of producing psychological dependency. This item in the opposition's propaganda baggage is emphatically rejected; users assert it simply does not happen. "I can take it or leave it," is an almost universal response. Heroin addicts contrast sharply: they often can pinpoint the exact day they realized they were hooked, and, at the more extended stages of use at least, almost never deny their dependency, except insofar as it may be tactically advantageous. Anyone who asserts that marijuana is as dependency-producing as heroin ("At this point the [marijuana] user is just as 'hooked' as are the persons we used to call addicts") [6] must explain the vast difference between the claims of the two groups; true or false, we assume that they tap some kind of underlying reality.

The following affidavit submitted by a former user in defense of a friend who was arrested for marijuana possession illustrates the claim to the complete lack of power of dependency in the chemical agent, cannabis; tobacco, the argument runs, in contrast, has this power:

Marijuana is not harmful to my knowledge, because I have been using it since 1949, almost daily, with only beneficial results. It has a relaxing effect when tenseness is present. My depth of perceptions has been increased; this carries over into times when I am not under the influence of marijuana. Teaching children is my profession. I have been a teacher for thirty years and at present am the teacher-principal of a public school. During school I never feel the need of using cannabis sativa, however, each recess is eagerly awaited for smoking cigarettes. I do not consider marijuana a habit-forming drug, but to me nicotine is.[7]

After the furor which followed this public testament (given to a judge), its author wrote: ". . . my house is 'clean.' I have had no marijuana in the house [since then], nor have I smoked it. This way I am able to prove that marijuana is not addictive or habit-forming, any more than brushing one's teeth or listening to music is addictive." [8]

In an unpublished study of 131 marijuana smokers (24 percent were daily smokers and 6 percent smoked marijuana less than weekly) two law school students, Lloyd Haines and Warren Green, asked the users' subjective views on the dangers of several commonly used drugs. Ratings of one (least harmful) to five (most harmful) were given to each substance. About 80 percent rated marijuana one, or least harmful, in terms of physical damage; none rated marijuana four or five. On the other hand, a majority rated the other drugs very harmful, physically. Two-thirds rated cigarettes (63 percent) and stimulants (68 percent) four or five on the physical damage scale, and over half rated alcohol (55 percent) and LSD (56 percent) either four or five. In terms of psychological harm, only two respondents rated marijuana either four or five, and about 90 percent rated it one or two. Cigarettes were not seen as a particularly great psychological threat; only 24 percent considered it four or five in this category of harm. However, stimulants (amphetamines), LSD and, to some extent, alcohol, were seen as capable of harming the individual psychologically. Two-thirds for the stimulants and LSD (66 percent for both) and not quite half for alcohol (46 percent) were rated in the two most harmful categories.

These data point to two clear facts: marijuana users vigorously deny that the drug is harmful in any significant degree, and smokers are capable of making clear-cut distinctions among various drugs as to danger. Overall, amphetamines (speed) of all the drugs on the Haines and Green list were seen as the most dangerous, with alcohol and LSD contending for second place.

Often explanations for a somewhat puzzling activity are unduly complex; subterranean and insidious interpretations are presented where the participant explains it more simply: "I like it." It seems that we find it necessary to search deeper when we cannot identify with the reason supplied. If it does not seem conceivable that anyone would actually "like it," whatever the activity or substance, then a more plausible theory, often invoking a pathology, must be summoned from the deep. To the critically inclined, "I like it" is insufficient, merely a rationalization.

Yet marijuana's severest critic must recognize the fact that users overwhelmingly describe the effects of the drug in positive terms. (See the chapter on "Effects.") The fact that the high is thought of as largely favorable cannot be ignored in understanding the justification that smokers use. "It's fun" and "I like it" are organic fixtures of the rhetoric for marijuana use. Yet, so elastic is the real world that this very trait, often cited by users themselves, is actually wielded by the cannabis critics to condemn the drug. Donald Louria, in summing up his critique of the question of legalization, writes:

"The arguments for legalization of marijuana are based on pure hedonism—the proponents want the legal right to use the drug because it gives them pleasure." [9] Another physician-educator, typifying the marijuana smoker's psychological characteristics, writes: "The marijuana user . . . is . . . actively concerned with experiencing the sensuous and hedonistic components of drug-induced euphoria." [10] Translated, these statements merely mean that pot is fun to smoke; its users like it because it is fun. It is a telling comment on the nature of a civilization that fun—even "pure" hedonism —is taken as a criticism. Indeed, most potheads would say, it is precisely hedonism that the drug resurrects in a work-oriented Puritan society. Pot ideologues would assert that a whiff of pure hedonism would be a refreshing tonic to "up tight" Americans.

Thus, one of the key weapons in the armory of the marijuana worldview is that pot is fun and pleasurable to smoke—that sheer hedonism is part of the cannabis scene. Marijuana is seen as one of the primal joyous activities of man, like making love, dancing and eating—all of which often accompany a pot high. Whoever tries to understand the drug, its users and their mentality, has to contend with their assertion that marijuana smoking is fun. It is used as an adjunct and stimulus to the gratification of the senses. He who takes a dim view of the gratification of the senses will certainly be a critic of the drug. The fact that cannabis is densely woven into sensual and gratifying activities and is, moreover, seen as being, in and of itself, sensual and gratifying, is perhaps its most essential and powerful appeal.

Marijuana's ideologues attribute to the drug a favorable impact on their aesthetic impulse. The most commonly voiced such effect is, of course, on the quality of perceived sounds: marijuana, it is claimed, has the power to make music sound better. In a study conducted by the New York Medical College, 85 percent of all marijuana users in the survey agreed with this contention. [11] Among my own interviewees, nine-tenths of those who had listened to music high preferred it to listening "straight." Further, there were specific qualities attributed to the music while high that made the experience unique and exciting. One of these qualities is the ability to concentrate selectively on a single sound or instrument, to hear that one in bold relief, while the rest of the music behind it seemed flat.

Another music-enhancing power attributed to the drug is associated with its synesthesia characteristics. [12] Of all of the descriptions of this phenomenon I encountered, perhaps nine out of ten involved music. Sounds under the influence of pot, it is often said, are more than sounds; music is more than simply music. Somehow a multiplicity of the senses seemed to be stimulated by music. Each sound reverberates to the other senses and is translated into seeing or feeling. An exquisite example of this phenomenon may be found in a short story by a contemporary hip writer, Terry Southern. A listener, high on hashish, describes the effect on him of jazz being played by a musician, who is also high:

. . . every note and nuance came straight to him . . . as though he were wearing earphones wired to the piano. He heard subtleties he had missed before, intricate structures of sound, each supporting the next, first from one side, then from another, and all being skillfully laced together with a dreamlike fabric of comment and insinuation; the runs did not sound either vertical or horizontal, but circular ascensions, darting arabesques and figurines; and it was clear . . . that the player was constructing something there on the stand . . . something splendid and grandiose. . . . It seemed, in the beginning, that what was being erected before him was a castle, a marvelous castle of sound . . . but then, with one dramatic minor—just as the master builder might at last reveal the nature of his edifice in adding a single stone—[he] saw it was not a castle being built, but a cathedral. . . . A cathedral—and, at the same time, around it the builder was weaving a strange and beautiful tapestry, covering the entire structure. At first the image was too bizarre, but then . . . he saw that the tapestry was, of course, woven *inside* the cathedral, over its interior surface, only it was so rich and strong that it sometimes seemed to come right through the walls. And then [he] suddenly realized . . . that the fantastic tapestry was being woven, quite deliberately, face against the wall.[13]

Often the notes of the music will themselves become transformed into physical objects; one of our interviewees saw the notes played by an organ playfully bouncing off his ceiling while listening, high, to rock music. Or, often while listening to records, the musicians will be envisioned—metamorphosed into their subjective musical equivalent—playing the music. A college student describes a common experience with the drug:

Very often I can place myself inside a concert hall when I'm listening to records. I can see the performance taking place in front of me. This happened the first time I got high. I saw the band, and they were dancing, and the drummer's feet, and all the performer's heads, came to a sharp point, because the music was very shrill, and the notes were sharp and pointed. And during the solo, I remember the drummer got up and danced around his drums while he was playing them—on his points, the points of his toes.[14]

Although laboratory tests have underplayed the role of marijuana in stimulating musical "ability," [15] certainly the increase in subjective appreciation of music is difficult to deny. It is part of the appeal of the drug, is a fixture of the ideology and mythology of the user, and is one important scoring point for the pot proselytizer. Users all the time and everywhere cite marijuana's impact on listening enjoyment as a positive attribute of the drug, and any critic of the drug's effect must wrestle with this trait in attempting to understand its fascinations.

In dispute are marijuana's reputed effects on the visual sense. While clinicians busy themselves recording the drug's hallucinogenic temperament, its power to distort reality, the users themselves utilize this to attract potential converts. About one-tenth of our respondents reported that colors were brighter and more vivid under the drug's influence; in a laboratory study, subjects reported that, under the influence of THC, they perceived keener visual and auditory impulses, indicating to researchers (along with other effects) that the drug is psychotomimetic in nature.[16]

But far beyond the simple claim that colors seem more vivid is the impression that one's aesthetic sense is heightened, that art works are understood better; the fine points once lurking only in the artist's mind become wondrously evident to the high viewer. Allen Ginsberg describes this enhancement effect on his own understanding of a number of paintings:[17]

I first discovered how to see Klee's Magic Squares as the painter intended them (as optically three-dimensional space structures) while high on marijuana. I perceived ("dug") for the first time Cezanne's "petit sensation" of space achieved on a two-dimensional canvas (by means of advancing & receding colors, organization of triangles, cubes, etc., as the painter describes in his letters) while looking at *The Bathers* high on marijuana. And I saw anew many of nature's panoramas & landscapes that I'd stared at blindly without even noticing before; thru the use of marijuana, awe and detail were made conscious. These perceptions are permanent—any deep aesthetic experience leaves a trace, and an idea of what to look for can be checked back later. I developed a taste for Crivelli's symmetry; and I saw Rembrandt's *Polish Rider* as a sublime Youth on a

Deathly horse for the first time—saw myself in the rider's face, one might say—while walking around the Frick Museum high on pot.[18]

Many of our interviewees who were practicing artists agreed that marijuana had a decided impact on the execution of their works. A successful commercial artist told me:

My color sense is more vital and more flexible. I see and use colors I don't normally. This isn't a fantastic increase in enlightment, but a slightly greater sensitivity to color and form. Marijuana makes me think more about the work, rather than just plunge right in, without thinking. It heightens my conceptual powers. I am able to trespass on a greater variety of media. I think of structures and concepts I might not think about normally. But the results are somewhat experimental. I'm usually satisfied with the experiment, although not always satisfied with the actual physical painting.

This process—the heightening of the aesthetic sensibility—is said to occur not only with music and the plastic arts, but with all of the art forms. It occurs not merely because of a physiological change in one or another specific sense, but is said to receive its principal thrust from a change in thinking process, an impact on the mind, on one's mentality, one's outlook on the world.[19] Leslie Fiedler said at the 1969 "New Worlds" drug conference at Buffalo, "The end of both drugs and the arts is exaltation and ecstasy." Psychedelicists assert that marijuana, as the mildest of the psychedelics, allows the individual to transcend his background limitations, free himself from the encrustation of lies in his past and unhook himself from a socialization of ignorance and error. Pot allows the individual to communicate with his primal being, blocked so long by a repressive civilization. Reality, high, may be viewed "as it really is," without the aid of artificial props and distorting social lenses. In fact, the very meaning of being high is said to be encapsuled in the term "ecstasy," from the Greek, meaning to get out of a fixed, inert state, and to become one with the shimmering, pulsating cosmos.[20]

. . . we know much more than we think we know, and grass is one way of tapping that rich field of knowledge, insight and revelation. Each of us has stored up in the mind and in the body a mine of awareness. . . . But by adulthood our pattern of thinking, of bringing out these thoughts, have become pretty rigid. Old patterns of thought are repeated, and the same conclusions are reached. But the unconscious has other answers locked away; marijuana may be seen as a key to that attic. It breaks down this pattern by forming new associations between previously unrelated material . . . perhaps grass, by temporarily altering the chemistry of the brain, stimulates new connections, linking up memories and information in unusual ways. By this synthesis, fresh concepts are formed. . . . Whereas my thinking is normally structured along traditional lines of linear thought, reasoning, building from particulars to generalities, and vice versa, and drawing associations, corollaries, various conclusions based on other ideas, when I think behind grass, I frequently think in flashes of insight, which may be related to what had previously just passed through my mind, or which may not necessarily be related to anything that went through my mind as much as 30 seconds before that. So thought is not so architectural and not so "linear," but more "mosaic." The pot smoker sometimes makes conceptual *leaps* that are difficult for others to follow.

In the McLuhan age, the important aspect of art is the experience of the audience. The depth of the art is contingent on the number of responsive chords struck in each individual; this indicates a kind of art that is nonspecific and suggestive, rather than explicit and denotative. The images produced by marijuana and the other mind-expanding drugs lend themselves to this form of art. When I'm stoned, my mind leaves the linear plane and moves into new dimensions. Montage and synthesis are the media of perception and expression. The images are symbolic and mosaic, rather than logical and linear. The new art requires participation. You have to get into it for it to work fully. Pot puts the artist in touch with his unconscious, permitting him to explore truths about himself which his ego has kept hidden. Even the audience is expanding its conscious by becoming more involved in the art. Marijuana is an important catalyst in this evolutionary change.[21]

Many of the drug's critics, particularly the psychiatrically oriented, discount its "mind expanding" qualities and its favorable impact on the artistic imagination.

. . . marihuana . . . allegedly augments creativity, but there are no valid data in support of this contention. On a substantial number of occasions creative people have deliberately been given marihuana and asked to carry out and interpret their artistic activity under the drug's influence. In the majority of cases, during the actual period of marihuana intoxication they felt that their creative activities were enhanced. However, almost uniformly, when the effects of the marihuana had disspitated and they again viewed their creative activities, they found that in actuality they had done very badly, a judgment substantiated by impartial observers. . . . for most people there is no true increase in aesthetic sensitivity under the influence of the drug and that in general such effects, if valid, would be limited to those who would ordinarily score high on tests designed to measure aesthetic appreciation. . . .[22]

Most artist-users view this assertion as being overly literal-minded; few would expect any artist, in a laboratory situation, high on the drug, to produce a work of art of high quality. Aside from being misleading because it is artificial and mechanical, the experimental situation cited above is deficient in that it does not account for working while high as being one of number of possible methods. Few artists actually do all of their work under the influence of the drug. Many, however, use it as an adjunct to their work. Some, for instance, use the high experience as a resource for insight and imagination drawn upon at a later time. One of our respondents, a twenty-year-old painter, said: "I can't paint when I'm high—too many things are happening in my head; I can't make a brush stroke because I can't make a decision." Yet, at the same time, he felt that having been exposed to the thought processes associated with the drug experience had enriched his artistic work.

Another style is to do some work while high, refine and revise when "normal." The argument goes, one is able to take advantage of the greater flow of ideas in the intoxicated state, and to correct any incoherence, irrelevancies, inconsistencies, momentary stylistic lapses and errors in judgment while straight. It is not that the high mentality is simply superior, its defenders would assert—but it is undeniably different. The high and the straight mentalities "somewhere have their field of application and adaptation," to use William James' phrase. Why not incorporate the best of both worlds, each whenever it is appropriate? Our anonymous informant, cited earlier, tells us:

When I write I generally turn on, do a first draft, and then re-write when I'm straight. I find that my style is fresher and more original than it was before. As an amateur playwright, I've found that what I write high is freer and more honest. It is occasionally somewhat incoherent, but I can correct that when I'm straight. The point is that, freed from conventional processes, the mind can produce more vivid, more original images and thoughts.

Whatever the process, marijuana and contemporary art are inextricably linked. Few knowledgeable observers of today's artists and art forms would deny that the overwhelming majority has smoked marijuana at least once, and possibly close to a majority do so regularly. Allen Ginsberg tells us:

. . . most of the major (best and most famous, too) poets, painters, musicians, cineasts, sculptors, actors, singers and publishers in America and England have been smoking marijuana for years and years. I have gotten high with the majority of the dozens of contributors of the Don Allen *Anthology of New American Poetry 1945–1960;* and in years subsequent to its publication have sat down to coffee and a marijuana cigarette with not a few of the more academic poets of the rival Hall-Pack-Simpson anthology. No art opening in Paris, London, New York, or Wichita at which one may not sniff the incense fumes of marijuana issuing from the ladies' room.[23]

Obviously marijuana's reputed ability to release man's creative impulses need not be restricted to the aesthetic realm. The effects of the drug, supposedly, are liberating and freedom-inspiring. New associations pop into the head's mind. The arbitrary "mind-forged manacles" are shattered. Conventional linkages enforced and reinforced from birth appear as only one among a vast series of equally viable alternatives. The marijuana user questions the ultimate rightness and wrongness of society's mores. His world, it is said, expands. He is suddenly in awe of the multiplicity of new possibilities. He emerges from a tunnel into a teeming jungle dense with potential. Blinders are removed. He finds himself doing and feeling what he had once rejected, and scorning what he had never even questioned before. His mind is overwhelmed by demons, strumpets, and wizards previously altogether excluded from his workaday world. His ability to take on new roles, consider fresh alternatives, and carry out novel ideas, seems inexplicably expanded. *Or so the claim goes.*

Is this a consequence of the drug? Or the subculture of marijuana smokers? Is it something that occurs because its participants *think* that it occurs? Does it occur at all? Is it, like many other beliefs about marijuana, pure myth? Myth or not, it is believed; it is part of the smoker's folklore.

There is, moreover, an ancient lineage; one of the most engaging statements of marijuana's powers comes not from a contemporary figure, but from the American poet, John Greenleaf Whittier, whose wholesome non-head life spanned almost the entire last century. In a poem, "The Haschish," Whittier dramatized the capacity of cannabis to allow—even force—man to step out of the habitual into the novel:

The Mollah and the Christian dog,
Change places in mad metempsychosis;
The Muezzin climbs the synagogue;
The Rabbi shakes his beard at Moses!

. . .

The robber offers alms, the saint
Drinks Tokay and blasphemes the Prophet.

. . .

The preacher eats, and straight appears
His Bible in a new translation.[24]

What was suggested a hundred years ago is today a dominant theme.

Yet we must underscore the ideological nature of this claim. If, indeed, such a process occurs at all, our reading of it is totally determined by our present political position. To a conservative, any agent which causes its users to question the foundations of society as it is presently constituted is pernicious, undesirable, and should be banned. To the critically minded radical who wishes to reform society, such an agent is for the good. It is impossible to settle the dispute rationally, since the values on which it is based are totally within the zone of the nonrational. Since most marijuana smokers are either politically liberal or radical, they naturally would see this property of the drug as being wholly desirable. And since most of marijuana's staunchest opponents could be labelled politically conservative, their opposition to this is predictable.

The smokers themselves look at this effect in more positive terms. Although no mention was made of using marijuana because it had the effect of releasing one's inhibitions, it was nonetheless seen as a beneficial result of smoking the weed. One of our interviewees describe this aspect of the marijuana high:

I'm more honest, open, more willing to let go, and admit to others my feelings that they might interpret negatively. Time, the phenomenon, the feeling of time passing, of growing old, disappears, and I feel less depressed. Worrying about time and me getting older, disappears. Time becomes more relative; I'm not as worried about time. I feel as if I control my universe. I feel as if every beautiful thing I want is right here in my room, and I don't have to go outside to get it. I see beauty in myself, how sensitive I am. I can become a fantastic creature, like a fairy. I can see into truths and look for and find the answer to them. Marijuana takes away fear and shyness. You can say what you think and not worry about how the other person will respond. I can see causes of my problems and can decide how to change things. There's nothing to fear. This is what you learn on pot.

Twenty-eight-year-old songwriter, female

What can we make of the claim that marijuana releases inhibitions? In part, it depends on our image of man. If it is basically demono-Freudian, we will fear the uninhibited man, for we will see the superego protecting man and society from man's savage, destructive, animalistic inner being. This model, as we saw, guided so many marijuana horror stories from the 1930s. "An eighteen-year-old boy, from a respected family in a Midwestern city, smoked two reefers and an hour later choked his sweetheart to death because she refused his shocking, lustful advances born in a marijuana-crazed brain." [25] Needless to say, although this floridly paranoid version of the effect of marijuana is not taken as seriously as it was in the 1930s, some residue of fear as to the outcome of releasing man's inhibitions remains. If we look upon society's restraining institutions as necessary, beneficial, and for the commonweal, then any agent which weakens man's grasp on them is suspect. If, on the other hand, we see civilization as repressive of man's true instincts —healthy, robust, vital, thick with wholesome sweat and whoops of unrestrained desire—we can only applaud an agent that is reputed to liberate man from his social bonds.

My position fits neither of these assumptions. Civilization cannot be equated with repression—or protection. Man *is* civilization, his inner being included. One layer stripped off reveals only other layers, onion-like, into infinity. No one layer is any more basic or genuine than any other. If man really wishes to sleep with his mother—or his sister—it is something that he has learned. If, under the influence of marijuana, his sense of sexual urgency is unbearably importunate, we must point out that sexual desire, too, is a learned response.[26] Our feeling about the "possibility increase" effect of cannabis is that what man may do when under the influence of this drug will be neither outstandingly destructive nor noble. It will be much like what he does normally. Their essential character may change somewhat—more whimsical, less practical, perhaps more sensuous, but not a world apart. If man will be somewhat more likely to do what he wants to do—whatever that may mean—we need have no fear that he is going to destroy civilization. At least, not any more so than normally; man may very well do that without the aid of drugs.

In contemporary existentialist terms, "bad faith" is the illusion that the possibilities presented to the individual by society are necessities. It is falling dupe to the lie that the restrictions placed upon each person are real, legitimate, and binding. By accepting a role which involves only one degree of freedom, man denies the full circle of 360 degrees that is available to him. Most men become "one-dimensional" men, thinking that they cannot possibly act out all of the other dimensions that represent their full human potential. They accept the "fictitious necessity" of restricted possibilities. In a sense, they become alienated from the multiplicity of selves that they might become; they deny the possibility of the many human forms which are actually available to them. They cut themselves off from themselves—the selves they might be, if they were to reject society's restrictions. As Peter Berger once said, sociology studies not only what is, but also what might be. The existentialist philosophers and sociologists, then, wish to explore the limits of human freedom, what man might be.[27]

One such fictitious necessity is the ban on drug use. Society presents a single dimension: no use of recreational drugs. The existentialists would say that this is an unnecessary and artificial restriction; man may become a fuller, richer, and multidimensional being by exploring the drug phenomenon. By trying drugs, man probes a fuller set of human possibilities. Taking drugs becomes a philosophical choice, and might be seen as growing out of the same earth as avant-garde art forms, radical politics, unconventional sex, and uncompromising antimilitarism; in each case, a more complex alternative is substituted for the relatively simplistic one that society proffers.

Another positive quality attributed to the drug by many of its users and supporters is the claim that marijuana has an effect on human empathy. The drug supposedly acts as a kind of catalyst in generating emotional identification with others. This is said to occur both on the microcosmic level—with those whom one is smoking with —as well as on a more panhuman level. It is easier to see how this process might occur within the context of a small, intimate gathering of smokers. The physical act of passing a joint around from one person to another (in contrast, say, to each individual drinking his own glass of liquor), sharing in an activity and a substance that all agree is beneficial, will probably create bonds of identity and affection, even if the drug itself had no effect whatsoever.

This rapport assumes numerous guises. One form is the assumption that it is possible, under the influence of marijuana, to both identify with and to understand one's alter better. Communication is facilitated. One of our respondents, twenty-eight-year-old female songwriter and ex-schoolteacher, described it: "You can get into the other person's head, identify with his position. You learn to see the other side. Your mental vision becomes super-vision—extrasensory. You pick up 'waves' from the other person."

Other users will ascribe to the drug a simple positive role in gregariousness. A recent study of seventy-four New York users concerned with the described effect of marijuana, showed that a high proportion (two-thirds) claimed that marijuana "helps a person feel more sociable at a party." [28] Still others will maintain that not only are the barriers to socializing removed, but that "it also suddenly became much more *fun.*" The magic spark of the joy of human companionship seemed spontaneously ignited. Through an inexplicable chemical, psychological or social process, or perhaps as a result of social definitions of this process, marijuana somehow touches off a kind of rapport in individuals that may have been absent before the high. Truman Capote, the novelist, puts it: "Pot makes the most stupid sound amusing—that's the best thing about it. They never turn mean, they laugh at everything, and they turn charming even if they are dull." [29]

This principle sometimes takes on international overtones:

The American hemp connoisseur can travel to the mountains of Mexico, the deserts of Egypt, and the bush country of Australia. There he can sit down with the natives, and by sharing the pot experience, can establish warm and human communications with them. Certainly anything which so enables human beings to overcome differences . . . and communicate as fellow members of the human race cannot be without positive moral value.[30]

On several weekends during the summer of 1967, several "smoke-ins" took place at Tompkins Square Park in New York's East Village, where marijuana smoking took place in public on a large scale in front of the police. (There were no arrests at these times.) I was present at two of the smoke-ins, interviewing several of the participants, one of whom described his reactions to the events.

There was, like, a kind of community that developed between everybody there who was smoking, an identity among everybody. I was just standing there, digging the scene, and a cat laid a joint on me. I took a drag and gave it to a PR [Puerto Rican] next to me. He says, "Solid," takes it and hands me a bottle of beer. I mean, you don't get that kind of scene without pot, man; it pulls us together.

The events generated several eulogies in the underground press, and some optimistic predictions of an expanded and widespread public violation of the laws, along with a tolerance by the agencies of formal control, such as the police, who made no arrests. ("By next year will the Good Humor man be selling potsickles?" [31])

A fantastic extrapolation of this attribution of empathy by the drug's proponents is the claim that it has a kind of pacific effect on users. (Evidence is sometimes presented that marijuana was an ingredient of the Indian peace pipe, which turns out to be historically erroneous.) Since it enhances emotive communication with one's fellow man, the reasoning goes, it must therefore decrease his aggressive tendencies and increase the inhibitions against harming others. The war in Vietnam is said to corroborate this assertion:

The real beauty of pot, as every head knows, is that it turns hostility into friendship, and hate into love, not only between individuals, but even between nations.

I have seen it with my own eyes at Rest and Recreation centers where both the NLF and the Americans send their boys. . . . [We] inadvertently ran into our [Viet-Cong] counterparts one evening . . . and as both parties were stoned, some curious and warm friendships were formed . . . . While this melange shared a couple of joints, the Americans were instructed in some of the fine points of Viet-Cong pot use, and in return, the Vietnamese were told about American innovations. . . . Conversation was warm, the war was not discussed and the friends left each other in an atmosphere of good fellowship.

When the two sides sit down at the conference table . . . let's be sure the top brass is serving marijuana tea.[32]

Whether it actually occurs or not, whether a result of the marijuana itself, or social definitions of the drug, peace and love form essential components of the mythology of marijuana users and their supporters, and are often used to support the argument that the drug is not only harmless, but actually is of benefit to society.

Some users—certainly a minority, albeit a highly vocal one— claim that marijuana has a contrary revolution-inspiring role. The powerful socializing influence of parents and early peers is said to weaken, and many of the rights and wrongs of childhood are questioned. American politics suddenly sounds sour and badly out of tune. Pot supposedly puts one's mind into a broader ideological arena and, somehow, engenders sympathy for the mistreated, the downtrodden, the suffering, and those contemptuous of the oppressors:

The right-wing connects psychedelic drugs and radical politics: they know where it's at. When the government outlaws dope, it's like the government outlawing fun. Especially in a country where the biggest barrier to building a revolutionary movement is supermarkets.

Drugs are an inspiration to creativity, and creativity is revolutionary in a plastic, commercial society. Drugs free you from the prison of your mind. Drugs break down conceptual and linear molds, and break down past conditioning. When past conditioning breaks down, personal liberation becomes possible, and the process of personal liberation is the basis of a political revolutionary movement.[33]

Smoking pot is a political act, and every smoker is an outlaw. The drug culture is a revolutionary threat to plasticwasp9-5america.[34]

Pot is central to the Revolution. It weakens social conditioning and helps create a whole new state of mind. The slogans of the Revolution are going to be: "POT, FREEDOM, LICENCE." The Bolsheviks of the Revolution will be long-haired pot smokers.[35]

All of these activities and perspectives that marijuana supposedly enhances may be summed up, paradoxically, by one of the antipot arguments which seems to score more points than any of the other weapons in the arsenal: smoking marijuana is an escape from reality. By refuting this argument, potsmokers feel that they have not only neutralized a damaging contention, but have even scored a few points in the drug's favor. Far from seeing the use of marijuana as an escape from reality, the apologists in fact look upon it as one possible means of *embracing* reality, even more dramatically and soulfully than is possible normally. Art, sex, fun, freedom, human companionship—all form slices of life, and the point is, to make them even larger and more emotionally involving. The argument is that marijuana drives the user into life more intensely, magnifying the emotional significance and enjoyment of the best things that life has to offer. "Pot," says Allen Ginsberg, "is a reality kick."

It is only a specific kind of reality the antipots accept: marijuana offers an escape from the mechanical, sterile, senseless striving of a nine-to-five world, basically antilife in its steely thrust. Marijuana, thankfully, helps to obliterate *that* version of reality. Potsmokers see this attribute entirely in the drug's favor. In their basically romantic revolt, the ideologists of the marijuana movement wish to glorify one particular mode of living, discrediting another. The fact that the success-oriented, materialistic, middle-class, over-forty generation has labelled its special way of life the total compass of "reality" is of no concern to the members of the drug movement. Their version of reality is very different, a world populated with denizens of a divergent phylum. If *The Green Berets* is reality, does that make the *Yellow Submarine* any less real?

The civil libertarian position on freedom parallels the pot-smoking prolegalization faction's.[36] If, indeed, the argument runs, the medical profession knows relatively little about the effects of marijuana,[37] then what is really being said is that there is no case for the drug's dangers. A case has to be made for the deprivation of liberties.[38] It is impermissible to incarcerate anyone before there is definitive evidence concerning the dangers of a drug. The federal and state statutes were passed long before anything was known about the effects of the drug. From a civil libertarian point of view, a solid case has to be make before an activity is illegalized. And no irrefutable causal connection has been established between the ingestion of marijuana and potential or actual danger to oneself or others, and until that connection has been established, the marijuana statutes are unconstitutional and in violation of essential rights and liberties. The cry that more research is needed before its hazards are known is a transparent admission of the deprivation of fundamental human rights.

The marijuana user is subject to society's definition of marijuana (since it is illegal, he may be arrested for possessing and using it), but society can safely ignore his definition of the drug. For the user, the law, and society's evaluation of the drug, lack legitimacy. That is, he feels that the law is wrong; he feels that what he is doing is right, and in no way immoral or rightfully subject to control and penalty. Users generally support legalization of marijuana use; 95 percent of my informants supported some form of legalization, and 80 percent wanted to see legalization without any restriction. This lack of legitimacy for the law among its broachers does not, of course, demonstrate that the law is wrong, but when a society's legal apparatus meets widespread opposition, then the basis of the law ought to be re-examined if that society claims to be a just and rational one. It is possible, in fact, that much of what the older generation sees as "lack of respect" for the law among the young and dissident stems from this feeling of outrage that such a harmless (in their eyes) activity should be made criminal. It is an irrefutable fact that among huge segments of the young, the pot laws simply do not make sense. Now, that attitude may be argued, the dangers of pot may be argued, the necessity for the laws may be argued, but the fact that many feel this way cannot be argued.

In the Oakland study by Blumer and others, this attitude was taken into account at the outset; exhortation against drug use was seen as silly by the user. The original aim of the project was to act as a brake on drug use of the young adults they encountered; this goal was abandoned because of their informants' attitude toward their efforts. They saw them as absurd.

. . . we found rather early that we were not having any success in developing a form of collective abstinence. It became clear that the youths were well anchored in their drug use and well fortified in their beliefs against all the "dangers" of drug use. From their own experiences and observations they could refute the declaration that the use of harmful drugs usually led to personal or health deterioration; they viewed with contempt the use of opiates and rejected with evidence the claim that the use of harmful drugs led naturally to opiate use. They pointed out that the break-up of home life, with which many of them were very familiar, was due to other factors than the use of drugs; they were able to show that the limitation of their career opportunities came from other conditions than the use of drugs, as such. They met the fear of arrest by developing greater skill and precautions against detection in the use of drugs. Added to these stances was a set of collective beliefs that justified their use of drugs, so that such use resulted in harmless pleasure, increased conviviality, did not lead to violence, could be regulated, did not lead to addiction, and was much less harmful than the use of alcohol, which is socially and openly sanctioned in our society. Parenthetically, we would invite any group of educators, scientists, welfare workers or police officials to try to meet effectively the well-buttressed arguments, based on personal experience and observation, that our youthful drug users present in frank, open, and uncowed discussion. In sum, we learned that youthful drug users are just not interested in abstaining from drug use.[39]

This finding—and I encountered it in my own survey—has not only practical but theoretical interest. Some deviants differ from each other as much as they differ from conventional society. It must be remembered that deviance and deviant are nonevaluative terms from our point of view. Society condemns the deviant, but we are only taking note of society's condemnation, not approving of it—nor disapproving of it. (We may *also*, as a person, humanist, civil libertarian, conservative, or anything else, approve or disapprove; but for the moment, we are merely observing. Unless we know what is happening, we are not in a position to condemn or praise.) However, many participants in deviant and criminal acts disapprove of what they do. A child molester, for instance, agrees with society's judgment of his act as depraved and immoral—so much that he denies having committed the act for which he was sentenced while condemning other child molesters as depraved and immoral.[40] Thus, an extremely important distinction among various kinds of deviance and crime has to do with the attitudes of the authors of the prohibited activity toward its moral rectitude. Marijuana smokers do not look upon themselves as deviants. Most realize that society at large sees their acts in negative terms. But they do not feel that what they are doing is wrong. They do not agree with society's judgment.

Many deviant activities generate a mythology that reflects society's condemnation—the *fall from grace* motif. As Goffman points out, we find it among inmates of mental institutions.[41] Prostitutes explain to the customer how she became corrupted, and took to "the life." I did some interviewing on the Bowery and the same stereotyped themes emerged. Homosexuals who are uneasy about their status will sometimes relate their version of the fall from grace. The essential elements include a normal, or even idyllic, past, an accidental occurrence which, linked with the deviant's fatal flaw, produced the downfall, along with some superficial genuflections at warning the population at large not to tread the same path. There is a need to construct rationales for their failure to live up to society's expectations. These tales are streamlined and simplified; the dissonant elements of the deviant's actual past are eliminated. In fact, the story need not even be true in any respect; what is important about them is that they respond to an expectation by society or the deviant, or both, that there be some sort of rationally understood explanation for the downfall. No one would actually choose to live the life of a moral outcast; myths must be put forth to fill that void of puzzlement. The fabrication need not even be conscious; it is not simply a lie. It is a myth, a folk tale which helps members of a society to adhere to a specific version of the moral universe. It may, in fact, be believed by all participants. These myths are interesting because of the social forces that brought them about.

During the 1930s, myths about marijuana use abounded. They detailed the downfall of innocent, unsuspecting youths, and their subsequent life of debauchery, a consequence of curiosity about the evil weed. They are propagated even today. However, what is interesting about them—and this marks the crucial difference between marijuana smokers and the deviants just mentioned—is that present users, unlike prostitutes, or winos, never find the need to construct and disseminate the fall from grace. It is attributed to them by antimarijuana crusaders. Since marijuana users do not regard their life as evil, nor the activity as an expression or instrument of their corruption, they do not accept the mythology; its absence reveals the lack of self-condemnation among users. Their view is that either smoking marijuana is a trivial and irrelevant leisure activity, to be enjoyed much like watching the movies, or it is part of a larger, richer, more complex and exciting universe of activities which, thankfully, they were priviliged to be initiated into. Very few smokers look upon use of the drug as corruption, a downfall, or a fall from grace.

Heresy, as we know, is worse than merely sinning. The sinner who is repentant may be forgiven; he who persists in proclaiming that what he has done is not a sin—indeed, who puts forth the claim that it is virtuous—must be consigned to the flames of eternal damnation. If the public and the moral enterpreneurs perceive that a group does not accept the evil of its way, then a corrollary or compensatory explanation must be put forth. As Richard Blum, a social psychologist studying drug use, has put it:

For . . . legislators, responsibility for self-indulgence in drugs must be punished. Others . . . sometimes speak of the abominable degradation of the addict who, paradoxically a victim of his habit, resists all efforts to correct him. These people deserve, so the lobbyists say, the harshest penalties. The drug "addict" . . . in their view has succumbed to temptation, has embraced the evil power in drugs, and refuses correction. . . . The only recourse is further punishment for his wickedness, his demon and himself now being one. Death itself is not ruled out as too high a price for scourging demons—and death is the penalty for drug sales under some statutes. On the other hand, the repentant junkie or acid head is the most welcome of guests.[42]

This lack of repentance, however, is far more common among potheads than among junkies—and the repentant junkie far more common than the repentant pothead. Part of society's wrath (and outright puzzlement) stems from the lack of willingness on the part of the marijuana subculture to see the other side, from their lack of shame and even their feeling of superiority to the rest of society.

NOTES

1. AMA, Council on Mental Health, "Marihuana and Society," *The Journal of the American Medical Association* 204, No. 13 (June 24, 1968): 1182.

2. The title of an article published in *The Attack*, July 1968, p. 13.

3. This term was invented by Joel Fort to describe the irrational nature of the anti-pot propaganda. See, for instance, "A World View of Marijuana: Has the World Gone to Pot?," *Journal of Psychedelic Drugs* 2, No. 1 (Fall 1968): 5. Dr. Fort also writes of the marijuana "mythogenesis."

4. Editors of the *Marijuana Newsletter* 1, No. 2 (March 15, 1965): 9.

5. Many of the drug's opponents agree, but rule that it is irrelevant: Donald B. Louria, *The Drug Scene* (New York: McGraw-Hill, 1968), p. 115:

. . . marihuana's dangers . . . seem no greater than the documented deleterious effects of alcohol. If the questions before us were a national referendum to decide whether we would use . . . either alcohol or marihuana, I might personally vote for marihuana— but that is not the question. The question is simply whether we are to add to our alcohol burden another toxicant.

6. Edward R. Bloomquist, "Marijuana: Social Benefit or Social Detriment?" *California Medicine* 106 (May 1967): 352.

7. Garnet E. Brennan, "Marijuana Witchhunt," *Evergreen Review*, June 1968, p. 55.

8. *Ibid.*, p. 56.

9. Donald B. Louria, "Cool Talk About Hot Drugs," *New York Times Magazine*, August 6, 1967, p. 51. In his book, *The Drug Scene*, Louria makes the same point; cf. p. 112.

10. David P. Ausubel, *Drug Addiction* (New York: Random House, 1958), pp. 99–100.

11. Richard Brotman and Frederic Suffet, "Marijuana Users' Views of Marijuana Use" (Paper presented at the American Psychopathological Association Annual Meeting, February 1969), p. 13.

12. Synesthesia is more common with the more potent psychedelics (hallucinogens). For a technical discussion, see Heinrich Klüver, *Mescal and Mechanisms of Hallucination* (Chicago: University of Chicago Press, 1966; originally published in 1928), pp. 49–50, 72, 93–94.

13. Terry Southern, "You're too Hip, Baby," included in the collection of stories, *Red-Dirt Marijuana and Other Tastes* (New York: Signet, 1968), pp. 76–77.

14. The quote is taken from a transcript of a taped interview of one of my respondents; this interview was included as a selection in my reader, *Marijuana* (New York: Atherton Press, 1969), pp. 52–55, in the chapter on the "Physiological Effects of Marijuana."

15. C. Knight Aldrich, "The Effects of a Synthetic Marihuana-like Compound on

Musical Talent as Measured by the Seashore Test," *Public Health Reports* 59 (March 31, 1944):431–433.

16. Harris Isbell et al., "Effects of (–)△⁹ Trans-Tetrahydrocannibinol in Man," *Psychopharmacologia* 11 (1967): 184–188.

17. "The Great Marijuana Hoax: First Manifesto to End the Bringdown," *Atlantic Monthly*, November 1966, pp. 106–112.

18. *Ibid.*, pp. 109–110. The tie-in between aesthetic appreciation and human empathy explored a few pages below is evident in the claim that cannabis enables one to understand the artist's intentions.

19. A detailed exploration of the interpenetration of the psychedelic drug thought processes and artistic creativity may be found in Robert E. L. Masters and Jean Houston, *Psychedelic Art* (New York: Grove Press, 1968). Of special interest is the essay by Stanley Krippner, "The Psychedelic Artist," pp. 164–182.

20. Timothy Leary has been one of the most prolific proponents of this particular ideological stance. See his collection of essays, *The Politics of Ecstasy* (New York: Putnam's Sons, 1968), and his "autobiography," *High Priest* (New York: World, 1968). See also the book of essays edited by his colleague, Ralph Metzner, *The Ecstatic Adventure* (New York: Macmillan, 1968).

21. Statement prepared by an actor, filmmaker, and writer, at the request of the author. Published in Goode, *op. cit.*, pp. 180–183. The writer of this statement wishes, of course, to remain anonymous.

22. Donald B. Louria, *The Drug Scene*, pp. 112–113.

23. Ginsberg, *op. cit.*, p. 110.

24. From the collection of poems, *Snowbound and Other Poems*, any edition.

25. Elmer James Rollings, "Marijuana—The Weed of Woe," leaflet (Wichita, Kans.: Defender Tract Club, n.d. [circa 1938]), p. 5. See also Lionel Calhoun Moise, "Marijuana: Sex-crazing Drug Menace," *Physical Culture* 77 (February 1937): 18–19, 87–89.

26. To debate this point—an essential difference between sociologists and Freudian psychologists—would require an entire volume-length study. For an example of the sociological position on the origin of sexual desire, see William Simon and John H. Gagnon, "Psychosexual Development," *Trans-action* 6, No. 5 (March 1969): 9–17. Needless to say, this position is anathema to orthodox Freudian psychologists.

27. Marx's work on alienation, particularly in the *Economic and Philosophical Manuscripts of 1844*, provides the cornerstone to this line of reasoning; nearly all of Sartre's writings are also relevant to these concepts. For some more sociological discussions, see Peter L. Berger, *Invitation to Sociology* (Garden City, N. Y.: Doubleday, 1963); Berger and Luckmann, *The Social Construction of Reality* (Garden City, N. Y.: Doubleday, 1966); Berger, *The Sacred Canopy* (Garden City, N. Y.: Doubleday, 1967); Herbert Marcuse, *One-Dimensional Man* (Boston: Beacon, 1964); Ernest Becker, *The Birth and Death of Meaning* (New York: Free Press, 1962).

28. Brotman and Suffet, *op. cit.*, p. 10.

29. C. Robert Jennings, "Truman Capote Talks, Talks, Talks," *New York*, May 13, 1968, p. 55.

30. Randolfe Wicker, "Odds and Ends," *The Marijuana Newsletter* 1, No. 2 (March 15, 1965): 9.

31. Howard Smith, "Scenes," *The Village Voice*, August 3, 1967.

32. "Stephen Nemo," Letter to the editor, *Avant-Garde* no. 2 (March 1968): pp. 9–10. Often the same individuals who report the drug's pacifist-inducing properties will also relate, with sadness, the fact that it does not always work. A recently returned veteran of the Vietnam conflict, a confirmed pothead, describes several "head" colleagues in his company's tank crew: "These guys would start at one end of a village and run over the roofs all the way down to the other end, and crush every man, woman, child, chicken, cat, dog, everything. Dead. Then they'd cross the street and go down over the roofs on the other side. . . . And when everything stopped moving, they'd take the machine gun. . . . These cats are, you know different. . . . These guys turn on, but they've got war in their hearts." See Ken Weaver, "Viper Vision Vietnam" (an anonymous interview), *The East Village Other*, November 1, 1968, p. 17.

33. Jerry Rubin, "The Yippies Are Going to Chicago," *The Realist*, September 1968, p. 22.

34. Rubin, "An Emergency Letter to My Brothers and Sisters in the Movement," *The New York Review*, February 13, 1969, p. 27.

35. Jerry Rubin, quoted in Peter Schjeldahl, "Thoughts of Chairman Jerry," *Avant-Garde*, No. 7 (March 1969): p. 33.

36. The following remarks are based on Prof. J. W. Spellman's talk given at the "New Worlds" Drug Symposium at the State University of New York at Buffalo, February 28, 1969; Spellman is a Canadian professor of Asian Studies.

37. See, for instance, Sylvan Fox, "Marijuana Still a Mystery to Scientists," *The New York Times*, February 2, 1969, pp. 1, 58, for an exploration of the extent of disagreement and lack of knowledge among scientists concerning marijuana's effects, both long- and short-term.

38. Michael Town, a law student, has argued precisely along these lines: the state must "show a compelling interest" in the "infringement of the individual's rights" regarding marijuana possession. The burden of proof as to the drug's dangers rests with the state, and as yet no adequate defense of the deprivation of liberties has been submitted. See Michael A. Town, "The California Marijuana Possession Statute: An Infringement on the Right of Privacy or Other Peripheral Constitutional Rights?" *The Hastings Law Journal* 19, No. 3 (March 1968): 758–782. See also, Joseph S. Oteri and Harvey A. Silverglate, "The Pursuit of Pleasure: Constitutional Dimensions of the Marihuana Problem," *Suffolk University Law Review* 3, No. 1 (Fall 1968): 55–80; John R. Phillips, "Free Exercise: Religion Goes to Pot," *California Law Review* 56, No. 1 (January 1968): 100–115.

39. Herbert Blumer et al., *The World of Youthful Drug Use* (Berkeley: University of California, School of Criminology, January 1967), p. ii.

40. Charles H. McCaghy, "Child Molesters: A Study of their Careers as Deviants," in Marshall B. Clinard and Richard Quinney, eds., *Criminal Behavior Systems: A Typology* (New York: Holt, Rinehart & Winston, 1967), pp. 75–88.

41. Erving Goffman, *Asylums* (Garden City, N. Y.: Doubleday, 1961), pp. 150–151.

42. Richard Blum et al., *Society and Drugs* (San Francisco: Jossey-Bass, 1969), p. 328.

: *Chapter 5* :

Physicians on Marijuana Use

Introductory Remarks

A sociologist of knowledge seeks to explicate whether and to what extent man's social surroundings influence his intellectual efforts. Adopting this perspective toward the sentiments of the various disputants in the marijuana controversy, we are alerted to the possibility that attitudes about, and orientations toward, the use of marijuana, as well as what effects it has, and whether these effects are good or bad, may be at least in part traceable to a specific kind of role one plays, or status one has, in society. It would seem highly peculiar if, somehow, doctors were exempt from the generalization that ideas have a powerful existential referent, that individuals are compellingly influenced by their social locations and interactions. We expect, therefore, that the ideas of physicians in the sphere of marijuana use are influenced by, and can be traced partly to, their social contexts. (This is a testable proposition, not an axiom beyond the reach of empirical investigation.) The question which remains, therefore, is what is the nature of the social expectations, demands, and sentiments related to the position of physician in American society, and what is their articulation with regard to marijuana use.

Physicians act not only as individuals; they also act as representatives. Unlike intellectuals, writers, and professors, their clients comprise everyone, all classes and groups in society. In their hands is entrusted the health of the social body. They are burdened (or blessed, depending on one's point of view) with the responsibility of protecting the well-being of society at large, and therefore are under a pressure to act in a manner that society defines as responsible and mature. The physician knows that when he speaks, many listen. His favored position disinclines him to a radical direction.[1] His prestige and power are a mixed blessing, because whatever he says will be taken seriously. He is highly visible, and he is expected to make sober and responsible pronouncements. The physician and the intellectual, although equally well educated, informed, and occupying roughly the same social class position, differ markedly in their accountability to a constituency, and thus usually differ radically on crucial issues. The question, therefore, becomes not so much: "What is the opinion of the medical profession, trained in the scientific technique and objective about anything affecting the human body, on the dangers of this drug, marijuana?" It is, rather: "What sorts of responses toward marijuana use might be expected from a group of individuals who are highly respected and affluent members of their community, geared to social functions of a distinctly protective nature, and responsible to a public?" I would predict that the responses of doctors regarding marijuana use would not be much different from individuals in positions much like theirs: bankers, politicians, attorneys, executives, judges. Their attitudes, I maintain, stem less from their medical knowledge than from their social position in society.

The position of medical men is a conservative posture, if we understand that as having the implication of "conserving" the status quo—protecting society from any possible danger. The basic thrust of such a position is that any substance has potential dangers that have to be thoroughly examined before it can be released to the unsuspecting public. It is far better, this line of reasoning goes, to restrict access to an innocuous drug than to permit access to one which is truly dangerous. The parallel between marijuana and thalidomide—inadequately tested and prematurely marketed—is obvious and sobering. The physician's stance, then, is paternalistic; certain decisions have to be made for the public, who, without expertise, cannot possibly decide on the danger or safety of a drug, unaided by those whose responsibility it is to perform that very task. As Henry Brill, physician, professor of medicine and hospital director, wrote: "All drugs are guilty until proven innocent." [2]

A guiding principle in this analysis is the specialness of the physician's orientation toward marijuana and its use.[3] I intend "specialness" to bear two distinct but interrelated meanings. First, that physicians' attitudes toward marijuana, as with everyone else, are largely "nonrational," not simply untrue or false in a scientific sense, but that their stance is a possible one out of several competing versions, and that all of these versions "surpass experience," that is, are based on attitudes that are sentiments and values which cannot be either supported or refuted scientifically. It follows from these expectations of society that the physician will act in a manner society defines as "responsible," that is, he will make essentially *protective* pronouncements.

Let us assume something true that is false, namely that it has been established scientifically that the statistical chance of experiencing a "psychotic episode" while under the influence of marijuana is one in a thousand—or even one in a million. This is, we will assume, a fact on which all observers agree. (It is not, of course.) The manner in which the physician makes his decision, that is, to be "responsible," will lead him to decide that this is too great a price for society to pay for the luxury of allowing a small freedom, and therefore marijuana use ought to be prohibited. Someone with a different set of values would make the decision in a very different way. The civil libertarian would say that the incidence of danger is sufficiently small to offset the larger threat to society's freedom to smoke marijuana. Both may agree on the facts, but it is the sentiments, even among the physicians, that ultimately decide.

The ideas of physicians are "special" in a second sense as well: doctors have been successful in defining the nature of reality for the rest of society in a vast number of areas. They have been successful in claiming that they alone are competent to interpret the reality of marijuana, and that their version of the drug's actions is the only legitimate, valid, and objective one. They have managed, that is, to establish epistemological hegemony. Their position enables their special version of the nature of the drug and its use to be regarded by others as neutral, impartial, and objectively true, and all other versions to be biased and based on special interest pleading. The physician is seen as transcending the accidental and irrational prejudices that blind others. In the area of drug use, physicians are "instant experts," knowledgeable and unbiased.

Since most members of society are not aware of professional and scientific distinctions, they will make little effort to seek out the word of those physicians who are most qualified to speak and write on marijuana, that is, those physicians who have actually done studies themselves, or who have closely read such studies. In fact, it might very well be disadvantageous to publicize the views of those physicians who are best-informed on the effects of marijuana, because they will present a more complex view, one which does not square with official morality. The contrary, in fact, will be true: the public will encourage those physicians whose views are most hostile to marijuana use which, almost inevitably, will be those physicians who are *least* informed on the subject. As a general rule, doctors whose writings on marijuana indicate dubiousness concerning its dangers are more likely to have done original research. Those physicians who are most stalwartly against its use, and whose writings indicate a strong feeling that clear dangers attend its use, are more likely to be without any systematic research experience on the drug's use, have no real contact at all with users, or be acquainted with them only as patients. (Patients who smoke pot and who visit doctors, especially psychiatrists, in connection with their drug use are, as we might expect, radically different from the average user—as are individuals who visit psychiatrists for any reason.)

It is not only the characteristics of the physician that would enable us to predict the role he would take vis-à-vis marijuana use. We must also look to the tie-in between the doctor's role and the cultural values of American society that generate his concern. It has become a cliche that American civilization still retains many strong traces of a Puritan ethic. Not all cliches are completely wrong; this one has at least a grain of truth. One axiom in the Puritan ideology is that pleasure must not be achieved without suffering. In fact, much of the machinery of Calvinist culture was devoted to making that axiom a self-fulfilling prophecy. Through guilt, ridicule, and punishment, the pleasure-seeker was *made* to suffer. We consider our age more enlightened. We have lost faith in many of the stigmata that once indicated sin. We no longer believe that it is possible, by outward sign, to "tell" if a girl has been deflowered, and we no longer counsel the adolescent boy against masturbation for fear of insanity or pimples. Yet we have not entirely moved away from this form of reasoning. With regard to marijuana use, we still take seriously the notion that the user must pay for his evil deed. No one is permitted to experience great pleasure without suffering a corresponding pain—a kind of moral Newton's Third Law. This is

97

one of the reasons why alcohol is such a perfect American intoxicating beverage: getting drunk has its price. (There are, of course, historical reasons as well for liquor's acceptance.) It is, however, puzzling to the American cultural mainstream that anyone could enjoy cannabis without suffering any misery. It is necessary, therefore, for the cultural apparatus to construct a *pathology* explanation on marijuana use. A search must be made for signs of mental and bodily suffering that the marijuana smoker experiences as a consequence of his use. In the vastness and diversity of the many experiences that users have, at least some pathological traces may be dredged up. By searching for and emphasizing these traces, we have satisfied our need for discrediting marijuana use, and have done so in a manner that specifically calls forth the efforts of physicians to verify our cultural sentiments.

It follows that marijuana use will be viewed as a medical matter. And that it is a matter for physicians' attention. It might be presumed that physicians' word is sought on marijuana use because it is a medical matter. The sociologist looks at the issue differently. That marijuana use is a medical matter is an imputation, not a fact. It is because society has already adopted the pathology or "disease" model on marijuana use that it seems reasonable to infer that marijuana use, therefore, is a medical matter. But the prior imputation was necessary to see it that way in the first place.

The central point of this book, explained in detail in the chapter on "the politics of reality," is that we all view reality selectively. We notice that which verifies our own point of view, and ignore that which does not. We accept a "world taken for granted," and an exposure to contrary worlds does little to shake our faith in our own. Moreover, when our version of what is real and true is threatened, we marshall pseudoevidence to support this version. Facts used in arguments are *rhetorical* rather than experimental. Societies whose values do or would oppose a given activity face a tactical problem: how to make a condemnation of that activity seem reasonable and rational? A rationale must be provided, and a personnel whose word is respected must provide that rationale. Thus, by generating statements from physicians, society is utilizing a valuable ideological resource. The antimarijuana lobby will therefore court and win the sympathies of doctors whose word on cannabis is largely negative. Society is searching for verification of an already held ideological position, not for some abstract notion which idealistic philosophers once called "truth." (We all assume that we have truth on our side.) So that the pathology position will be crystallized out of the magma of society's needs and expectations, out of the social and cultural position of physicians, their self-conception —partly growing out of society's conception of them—as preservers of society's psychic and bodily equilibrium, and as experts on anything having to do with what is defined as a health matter. It is these pressures that generate the concern of physicians regarding marijuana, and not any particular expertise they might have.[4]

In lieu of actually doing a survey, it is necessary to examine the writings of physicians on marijuana. However, to use these written statements to characterize the dominant medical view on cannabis use it would be necessary to resolve at least one difficulty first. There is the question of the typicality of published and widely disseminated statements, as opposed to the actual sentiments and actions of the vast bulk of doctors who do not write on marijuana. Those who wish to spread their views by publishing them might, for instance, be those who feel most strongly involved—both for and against; they might be "moral entrepreneurs," to use Howard Becker's phrase. Yet, in spite of the possibly nonrandom sentiment expressed in physicians' printed statements on marijuana, we must also remember that these are the views that tend to have the greatest impact. The American Medical Association makes an official pronouncement, reported by major newspapers and magazines, which means that a position is congealed and more easily utilized in the continuing debate. Published statements take on a life of their own. Although the question of whether or not physicians' published statements are typical is an empirical question, and not one on which we have an answer, nonetheless, the basic thrust of these statements is overwhelmingly negative, largely cast in the form of a pathology model,[5] and used by the antipot lobby to verify its own position. Thus, although we will encounter some diversity of orientations regarding drug and drug use, it is possible to discern a relatively consistent ideology, both in "official" and in working day-to-day terms. In the remainder of this chapter I intend to elaborate on the mainstream medical position on marijuana use. This position is made up of a number of separate elements. Let us examine each element.

Drug Abuse

In the typical medical view, marijuana use is by defintion "abuse." Drugs are taken for therapeutic purposes, to alleviate pain, to aid adjustment, to cure a disease, and must be prescribed by a physician. Marijuana has no known or recognized, professionally legitimated role whatsoever. The human body operates best, in the absence of a pathology, without drugs. Drugs are unnecessary without illness. The purpose of getting high is seen by this view as illegitimate. *All* use of marijuana is abuse; all use of drugs outside of a medical context is in and of itself the misuse of the purposes for which drugs were designed. The AMA writes: ". . . drug abuse [is] taking drugs without professional advice or direction." [6]

Marijuana is hallucinogenic and has *no* medical use or indication. . . . Feelings of being "high" or "down" may be experienced. Thought processes may be disturbed. Time, space, distance and sound may be distorted. Confusion and disorientation can result from its use. Reflexes are slowed. Marijuana does not produce physical addiction, but it does produce significant dependence. And it has been known to produce psychosis. With this description of the effects of its use and the total lack of any medical indication for its use, medically it must be stated that any use of marijuana is the *misuse* of a drug.[7]

The damning constituent of marijuana, like all "recreational" drugs, is that it is used to get high; the normal state is seen as desirable—the state of intoxication, pathological. The use of a drug to get high is abuse of that drug: "There is no such thing as use without abuse in intoxicating substances." [8]

In an essay in what is widely considered the bible of clinical pharmacology, the following is a definition of drug abuse (of which marijuana abuse is discussed as an instance; a distinction is made between obsolete "Therapeutic Uses" and current "Patterns of Abuse"):

In this chapter, the term "drug abuse" will be used in its broadest sense, to refer to use, usually by self-administration, of any drug in a manner that deviates from the approved medical or social patterns within a given culture. So defined, the term rightfully includes the "misuse" of a wide spectrum of drugs. . . . However, attention will be directed to the abuse of drugs that produce changes in mood and behavior.[9]

Etiology of Drug Use

In terms of the etiology of marijuana use, physicians may generally be found within the orbit of the personality theory of causality. Now, no psychologist or psychiatrist would dispute the contention that sociological factors play a decisive role in marijuana use. Clearly, a milieu wherein marijuana is totally lacking, or in which its use is savagely condemned, is not likely to generate many marijuana smokers, regardless of the psychological predisposition of the individuals within that ambiance. Yet, at the same time, a theory of marijuana use set forth by a psychologist, psychiatrist, or physician, will look and sound very different from one delineated by a sociologist. Doctors will tend to emphasize individual and motivational factors in the etiology of marijuana use. It is necessary, therefore, according to this perspective, to understand the individual's life history, particularly his early family relations, if we are to understand why an individual does as he does, particularly if he challenges the established social order—as, to some degree, his use of marijuana does. An individual of a certain family background will be predisposed to specific certain kinds of behavior.

More than merely being generated to a considerable degree by personality factors, physicians (following psychologists and psychiatrists) often see marijuana use as being at least to some degree generated by pathological or abnormal motives. Sometimes this is seen as a general process; marijuana use, like all illicit, deviant, and illegal drug use, represents a form of neurosis, however mild: "The willingness of a person to take drugs may represent a defect of a superego functioning *in itself*." [10] It is, of course, necessary to specify the degree of drug involvement. Most physicians will not view occasional or experimental use in the same light as frequent, habitual, or "chronic" marijuana use. Probably we can make a safe generalization about the relative role of the factors we are discussing: the heavier and the more frequent the use of marijuana, the greater the likelihood that most doctors (as well as psychiatrists and personality oriented psychologists) will view its etiology as personality-based, as well as pathological in nature, and its user to some degree neurotic; the less frequent and regular the use of marijuana, the greater the likelihood that the cause will be located in accidental and sociological factors, and the lower the likelihood of being able to draw any inferences about the functioning of the user's psyche. This qualification is essential.

Probably the commonest view of marijuana use within the medical profession is that it is a clumsy and misplaced effort to cope with many of one's most pressing and seemingly insoluble problems. Drug use is not, of course, logically or meaningfully related to the problem, but is, rather, a kind of symbolic buffer serving to mitigate it by avoiding it, or by substituting new and sometimes more serious ones. Feelings of inadequacy, for instance, are said to be powerful forces in precipitating drug use.

An individual who feels inadequate or perhaps perverted sees in drugs a way out of himself and into a totally new body and mind. For some a drug does give temporary surcease from feelings of inferiority, but for most it provides only numbness and moderate relief from anxiety, with no true or constant feeling of strength or superiority. Often this search for a new self is what leads to escalation and a frantic search for new drugs which may lead to addiction.[11]

Occasionally, this notion of inadequacy is further pinpointed to sexual inadequacy. One prominent physician, analyzing a case history, writes: "Tom began to smoke marijuana and to gamble. He also suffered from impotence. Tom's need for marijuana and gambling was to help him overcompensate for his physical and mental inferiorities. He was underweight, had only a grade school education and suffered from the fear of organ-inferiority, called a 'small penis complex.'"[12] Another physician concurs: "I know of several cases where males would use marijuana to overcome feelings of sexual inadequacy. Their marijuana use ceased after psychiatric treatment."[13]

Sexual failure may be seen as a manifestation of a general inadequacy; marijuana use is seen as a kind of smoke-screen for the real issues. It becomes a means of avoiding responsibility, of concealing one's failures and inadequacies, of "copping out" of life:

Individuals who have a significant dependency on marijuana and use it chronically report a decrease of sexual drive and interest. A reduction in frequency of intercourse and increased difficulty becoming sexually aroused occurs with the chronic user. However, there is usually a concomitant decrease in aggressive strivings and motivation and an impoverishment of emotional involvement. These changes are generally true for the chronic alcoholic, the chronic amphetamine or barbiturate user. Marijuana dependency is a symptom and the person who avoids experiencing parts of himself through the chronic use of drugs, is usually lonely and frightened of impersonal contact prior to drug use. Some of the diminished sexual activity of the marijuana dependent individual is part of his general withdrawal from emotional contacts with other human beings. The temporary gratification of drug-induced feelings are preferred to the gratification of interpersonal closeness which involves the risks and vicissitudes of real emotional intimacy.[14]

Rebellion is another common component in many medical conceptions of marijuana use, especially as applied to high school and college students. Some doctors feel that the use of the drug represents a symbolic rejection of parental values, a desire to shock one's elders, to aggress against them for real or imagined hurts, to use the drug as a weapon in the parent-child struggle:

The reason why drugs have so strong an appeal to the adolescent are several. The reason most commonly cited is rebellion, and this probably is a factor of importance in most instances. Children begin at fourteen to gain satisfaction from doing the opposite of what is expected. This is a way of retaliating against parents for years of what is now felt to have been unjustified subjugation. . . . Anything that is disapproved of by adults begins to have a certain allure. . . . Drugs are clearly beyond the pale in the eyes of both parents and legal authorities, and thus have a particularly strong appeal. A lot of the mystique that is part of the drug taking experience is directly related to the satisfaction the participants gain from realizing how horrified their parents would be to know what was going on. The secrecy surrounding meetings, the colorful slang words, the underworld affiliations make it all seem very naughty.[15]

The intrinsic appeals of the drug itself, its specific effects, the nature of the marijuana high, are overshadowed by its symbolic appeal as both indication of and further cause of rebellion:

Smoking marijuana has become almost an emblem of alienation. The alienated student realizes that the use of "pot" mortifies his parents and enrages authorities. . . . [Marijuana] has become a rallying cause for students, a challenge to adults and a potent catalyst for widening the gap between generations.[16]

Marijuana as a Dangerous Drug

The doctors feel that the drug is prohibited for a reason. It is a dangerous drug, and *because* it is a dangerous drug, it is (and should be) prohibited: "Certain drugs because of known characteristics are classified as dangerous drugs."[17] They take, in other words, a "rationalist" position that men who make such decisions for society respond rationally and logically to a real and present danger. Medical bodies (like the legal structure of societies as a whole) do not authorize marijuana use; they disapprove of its use because there is enough evidence to be able to decide on the drug's dangers—or there is enough indication that it might be thought of as dangerous. ". . . those of us who oppose legalization are . . . implacable in insisting that all cannabis preparations are potentially dangerous. The potential dangers, to our minds, are severe."[18] As a result, ". . . there is overwhelming consensus that this drug [marijuana] should not be legalized, and no responsible medical body in the world supports such action."[19]

Marijuana, then, according to the medical profession, is a "dangerous drug." The question, therefore, is: In what specific ways does the medical profession see its use as dangerous? Opinion is not unanimous on the questions of what, precisely, the effects are, whether certain effects represent, in fact, a clear danger, and to what extent the danger appears. Nonetheless, the differences within the profession should not be exaggerated.

PSYCHOLOGICAL DEPENDENCY

Without question the danger most commonly seen by physicians and psychiatrists in marijuana is its power to engender a kind of psychological dependence in the user. No observer of the drug scene attributes to marijuana the power of physiological addiction; instead, psychological dependence is imputed. "Drug dependence is a state of psychic dependence or physical dependence, or both, on a drug, arising in a person following administration of that drug on a periodic or continued basis."[20] Each drug has its characteristic syndrome, and each must be designated with its own specific title;

we are interested in "drug dependence of the cannabis type." Marijuana, then, produces a psychic dependency in the user which impels him to the continued and frequent use of that specific drug—a dependency that is similar in important respects to actual physical addiction.

Marijuana smokers hold the lack of physiological addiction of their drug of choice to be a powerful scoring point in its favor; many physicians, on the other hand, see this point as trivial in view of the parallels between addiction and dependency. The dimension of interest to us is not whether the impelling force is chemical or psychological, but whether the user persists in his use of a substance which physicians have defined as noxious, whose use constitutes "abuse." Thus, a person is defined as being dependent on the basis of whether use of a drug is continued over a period of time, and is ruled undesirable by drug experts. The imputation of undesirability is necessary to the definition, since the repeated administration of crepe suzette[21] is not labelled "dependency"—even though it can occur with the same frequency and with the same degree of disruption in one's life. The fact that a withdrawal syndrome does not appear upon abstinence is outside the focus of this definition; the telling point is that the drug is capable of producing dependency.

It has . . . been customary to distinguish between drugs that are habit-forming and drugs that are addicting . . . the present writer, however, fails to perceive any value at all in this distinction. . . . Hence, it would be quite correct to use the terms habit-forming and addicting synonymously and to refer to common habit-forming drugs as addictive in nature.[22]

The troika of abuse, pathological etiology, and dependence combine forces to pull in the same direction. He who tries marijuana is impelled by the same motivational syndrome which may lead to abuse and, ultimately, dependence; the three concepts are seen as part of the same pattern.

The chronic user develops a psychological dependence which in view of today's knowledge, is the prime detrimental factor. This dependence soon causes him to lose control of his use of the drug because the psychological factors which drew him to try it in the first place now precipitate a pattern of chronic, compulsive abuse. At this point the user is just as "hooked" as are the persons we used to call addicts.[23]

The fact that, supposedly, marijuana use enlarges the sphere of one's freedom, by broadening the field of the choice of one's actions, can, ironically, have the opposite long-range effect, according to dominant medical views. Dependency limits one's possibilities for acting; by being dependent on a drug, one has severely limited his freedom, although to have taken that drug in the first place meant greater freedom. No physician has presented this dilemma more strikingly than a nonphysician, Seymour Fiddle, a social worker who coined the term "existentialist drugs" to capture this contradiction. Existentialist drugs are those a man takes to enact his fullest human potential, to test the limits of his ability to act, just to see how much he can do and be and still retain his essential humanness—but ends by so severely shrinking his possibilities that he is able ultimately to act out only a single role, virtually identical for everyone: that of street junkie.[24] Thus, we chance upon a paradox: man takes drugs to be free, only to discover that he is enslaved by them. The Fiddle argument, then, would hold the freedom issue to be irrelevant, since drugs are a dead-end trap which ultimately kill off all freedom of action. Drugs produce, in the end, even more narrowly restricted one-dimensional men. As to whether marijuana properly belongs in this category is an empirical question, and cannot be assumed in the first place, but the fact that physicians commonly hold it to be a drug of dependence demonstrates that they do believe that it can in fact act in this manner.

PANIC STATES AND PSYCHOTIC EPISODES

Cannabis opponents consider the psychotomimetic quality of the drug another potential danger. Physicians and psychiatrists, especially, feel that marijuana is capable of precipitating powerful, though temporary, psychotic episodes—or, more generally, disturbing psychic adverse reactions. There are, of course, problems with this view; to mention only three: (1) What constitutes such a reaction and how do we define an "adverse effect" of marijuana? (2) How extensively does it occur? (3) Under what conditions does it occur?

The smoker, under the influence of the drug, is held to be subject at times to confusion, panic, disorientation, fear, and hallucinations —a schizophrenic break with reality. This point of view holds that this state—ranging from a simple amused befuddlement all the way to a full-blown outbreak of transient psychosis—"can" happen and "does" happen. The fact that it has occurred with at least some modest degree of frequency is, in the eyes of many health figures, powerful damaging evidence that the drug is, or can be, dangerous and harmful.

While physicians are adamant about the existence of these episodes and their attendant dangers, smokers are equally as vociferous in denying to the drug such diabolical powers. Donald Louria writes: "The evidence on panic seems so clear that to deny its existence indicates either abysmal ignorance of the facts or intentional intellectual dishonesty." [25] Yet, writers supporting use of the weed minimize and often dismiss outright its madness-inducing potential. Their claim is that if marijuana can induce psychosis, then the causal sequence posited has nothing intrinsically to do with the effects of the drug itself. Rosevear, for instance, writes: ". . . a broken shoelace may also be used as a parallel for precipitating psychosis." [26]

Those who seek psychiatric and medical help as a result of an untoward reaction to marijuana are far from typical of potheads, or the mental state of the characteristic marijuana intoxication. The average smoker has probably never seen any evidence of an untoward reaction of any seriousness—so that he denies its existence completely. It is difficult to deny that marijuana *can* potentiate panic or a psychotomimetic experience, given the "right" person and setting. To assert, however, that such reactions are typical, widespread, common, or even more than merely occasional is, I think, entirely incorrect, since, by all accounts, extreme psychosis-like reactions to the drug are extremely rare. Even the staunchest opponents of the drug are careful to point out that they are of relatively infrequent occurrence. The Medical Society of the County of New York informs us that cannabis "is an unpredictable drug and is potentially harmful even in its mildest form. Even occasional use can produce (*although rarely*) acute panic, severe intoxication, or an acute toxic psychosis." [27] A pair of physicians, reporting on panic reactions in Vietnam, inform us that at the extreme of the continuum, cannabis is capable of touching off in some individuals "a frank schizophrenic-like psychosis," but, at the same time, are careful to point out that "smoking marijuana for most persons is a pleasant, nonthreatening, and ego-syntonic experience." [28]

Work by physicians on cannabis psychosis breaks down into clinical [29] and laboratory [30] research. In general, clinical work must, of necessity, be unsystematic since it is impossible to detect the degree to which the patients who come to a physician for problems connected (or unconnected) with their drug use are in any way representative of users in general. It is impossible to know just what it means when a number of marijuana-using patients show up in a physician's office. How typical are their experiences? What universe of individuals are they supposed to represent? How widespread are their complaints? What role does marijuana play in their problems? Clinical work can answer none of these troublesome but central questions. But clinical reports do have the advantage that they describe people in real-life situations. Laboratory work suffers from the opposite problem. Although it is systematic, the laboratory situation is artificial and outside the marijuana-using situation in which the smoker actually conducts his activities. Although this qualification in no way invalidates either form of research, it should be kept in mind when generalizations from clinical and laboratory situations are made to the use-patterns of the typical marijuana smoker in real-life situations.

The complexity of the issue increases when we consider the relative potency of the various cannabis preparations. Hashish, as we know, is more powerful than the varieties of marijuana commonly available in the United States. Although heavily used in the Orient, it is less commonly, but increasingly, consumed in America.[31] Many of the differences between the gloominess of the findings of many studies conducted on hashish and charas users in North Africa, the Middle East, India, and Greece, and the relative lack of mental pathology associated with use in the United States, can be attributed to the strength of the drugs available. Marijuana grown in the United States is weak; and even Mexican varieties generally lack the strength of their Oriental sisters. The fear, therefore, is that were marijuana to be legalized, it would be impossible and irrational to disallow hashish. "If all controls on marijuana were eliminated, potent preparations probably would dominate the legal market, even as they are now beginning to appear on the illicit market. If the potency of the drug were legally controlled, predictably there would be a market for the more powerful illegal forms." [32] Thus, could it be that hashish, were it freely available to Americans, would produce many of the symptoms described in the Eastern studies?

. . . no amount of qualification can obscure the fact that marijuana can produce psychotic reactions (this is a simple medical fact) and that a psychotic state can release violence and precipitate criminal behavior. This is not to say that it will in every case but that it can and has. Because of the relative mildness of Mexican and American varieties of cannabis we have seen very little of this kind of cannabis-induced reaction. But with the coming of hashish, we can look for more instances of psychosis and violence as a result of a cannabis use.[33]

MOTOR INCOORDINATION

A third reason why physicians consider marijuana dangerous and not to be legalized or made freely available is that it supposedly deteriorates one's motor coordination, rendering the handling of a machine, particularly an automobile, hazardous. The fear is that the current slaughter on the highways of America—partly due to drunken driving—will increase dramatically with the increase in marijuana use. The assumptions underlying this supposition are that marijuana use characteristically leads to intoxication; that intoxicated marijuana smokers are likely to drive; and that one's ability to drive is, in fact, impaired by the use of marijuana. These are all, of course, empirically verifiable (or refutable) propositions, and cannot be assumed. But whether true or false, this line of reasoning will be encountered frequently in antimarijuana arguments: "The muscular incoordination and the distortion of space and time perception commonly associated with marijuana use are potentially hazardous since the drug adversely affects one's ability to drive an automobile or perform other skilled tasks." [34] More dramatically, the marijuana smoker, intoxicated, "may enter a motor vehicle and with "teashades (dark glasses worn because of the dilated pupils) over his handicapped eyes and with impaired reflexes he may plow through a crowd of pedestrians." [35]

Not only is there the fear that widespread use of cannabis will increase the highway death toll, but since there is no reliable or valid test at the moment for determining whether the driver is high on marijuana, there are, therefore, no possible social control mechanisms for preventing an accident before it happens. Since effective tests exist for alcohol, physicians hold that this makes marijuana a more dangerous drug than liquor, at least in this respect. "With marijuana, there are currently no adequate methods for measuring the drug either in the blood or urine. . . . Under such conditions, the thought of legalizing the drug and inflicting marijuana-intoxi-cated drivers on the public seems abhorrent." [36]

LOSS OF AMBITION AND PRODUCTIVITY

A common concern among members of the medical profession is that marijuana—particularly at the heavier levels of use—will pro-duce lethargy, leading to a loss of goals and a draining off of poten-tial adolescent talent into frivolous and shiftless activities. One physician speculates whether marijuana might be America's "new brain drain." [37] The AMA states that frequent use "has a marked effect of reducing the social productivity of a significant number of persons," [38] and that as use increases, "nonproductivity" becomes "more pronounced and widespread." [39]

As the abuse pattern grows, the chronic user develops inertia, lethargy and indifference. Even if he does not have psychotic or pseudopsychotic epi-sodes or begin a criminal or violent existence, he becomes a blight to society. He "indulges" in self-neglect. And even though he may give the excuse that he uses the drug because it enlarges his understanding of him-self, it is the drug experience, not his personal development, which is his principal interest.[40]

Physicians with academic responsibilities particularly see a nega-tive impact of marijuana use on achievement and motivation. Dana Farnsworth, director of Harvard's health services, writes: ". . . the use of marijuana does entail risk. In fact, we find it to be harmful in many ways and to lack counterbalancing beneficial effects. Many students continue to think it is beneficial even when their grades go down and while other signs of decrease in responsible and effective behavior become apparent." [41] Harvard's class of 1970 was issued a leaflet which contained a warning by the Dean of the College, which read, in part: ". . . if a student is stupid enough to misuse his time here fooling around with illegal and dangerous drugs, our view is that he should leave college and make room for people prepared to take good advantage of the college opportunity." [42] The message was that learning and drug use are incompatible. However, the amount of marijuana smoking and the degree of involvement with the marijuana subculture are not specified. Since possibly close to a majority of all individuals who have smoked marijuana at least once do so no more than a dozen times in all, there is no reason to suppose that marijuana smoking should have any effect on the ambition of the average smoker. The problem, as the doctors realize, is with the frequent user. It is entirely possible that heavy involvement in marijuana use (as with nearly any non-academic activity, from heroin addiction to athletics) leads to academic nonproductivity. It is difficult to say whether or not this is due directly to the action of the drug itself. Involvement with a subculture whose values include a disdain for work probably contributes more to the putative "nonproductivity" than the soporific effect of the drug.

THE EFFECT ON THE ADOLESCENT PERSONALITY

It would be naive of marijuana legalization enthusiasts to think that the average age of first smoking the weed would not drop if their demands were somehow realized, in spite of any potential age restrictions—think of the facility with which adolescents obtain cigarettes and liquor. I suspect that if the antimarijuana arguments carry any weight at all, the noxious effects of the drug will be aggravated among the very young. And even if the promarijuana arguments turn out to substantially sound, that is, that the effects on a well-integrated, fully developed adult personality are either beneficial (within agreed-upon definitions) or negligible, the impact on adolescent and pre-adolescent children (taking eighteen as a rough demarcation line) is a matter to be investigated separately. It is a legitimate question to raise as to the influence of marijuana on the young. The following questions might present themselves as heretofore unanswered requests for much-needed information:

1) Are adolescents able to assimilate and integrate the insights of a novel and offbeat perspective into a rewarding day-to-day existence in society?
2) Will they be able to avoid making the drug the focus of their lives, a complete raison d'etre?
3) How aware will adolescents be of the distinction between situations in which marijuana is relatively harmless (such as with friends, or watching a film), and those where it may be dangerous (such as, perhaps, in stressful situations)?

Physicians are acutely aware of the potential damaging effects of the drug on the adolescent personality. (In fact, even many non-medical observers who take a relatively tolerant view of marijuana use in general are concerned about its possible impact on the young.) [43] The Director of the National Institute of Mental Health, a physician, writes:

One needs to be particularly concerned about the potential effect of a reality distorting agent on the future psychological development of the adolescent user. We know that normal adolescence is a time of great psy-, chological turmoil. Patterns of coping with reality developed during the teenage period are significant in determining adult behavior. Persistent use of an agent which serves to ward off reality during this critical development period is likely to compromise seriously the future ability of the individual to make an adequate adjustment to a complex society.[44]

THE USE OF MORE POTENT DRUGS

Finally, some physicians oppose marijuana use on the sequential grounds that it leads to the use of more powerful, truly dangerous and addicting drugs. At one time, heroin was the primary concern of society, but within the past six years, it has had to share society's concern with LSD. Physicians have absorbed a good deal of sociological thinking and generally deny that there is an actual pharmacological link between marijuana use and the use of LSD and heroin. Being high does not make one crave another, progressively more potent, drug. As Dr. Brill says, there is no connection between marijuana and other drugs "in the laboratory," but the association "in the street" is undoubtedly marked.[45] The pusher line of reasoning as to progressive drug use is sometimes cited: ". . . marijuana is frequently the precursor to the taking of truly addictive drugs. Those who traffic in it often push other more dangerous substances." [46]

Another argument is that the reason for the progression from marijuana to either heroin or LSD is experiential: marijuana use leads one into patterns of behavior which make more serious involvement likely. The less potent drug acts as a kind of "decompression chamber" gradually allowing the user to get used to increasingly more serious drug use, getting used to it bit by bit.

There is nothing about marijuana which compels an individual to become involved with other more potent drugs. Marijuana use, however, is often an individual's initiation into the world of illicit drug use. Having entered that world—having broken the law—he may become immersed in the drug subculture and in sequential form progress to abuse of a variety of other drugs, including amphetamines LSD, amphetamines, and heroin.

. . . Marijuana does not in any way mandate use of other drugs, but it may be the beginning of the road at the end of which lies either LSD or heroin. . . . [If] certain individuals . . . did not begin with marijuana, they would never get around to using the more potent and dangerous drugs.[47]

THE ALCOHOL-MARIJUANA COMPARISON

As we stated earlier, marijuana's supporters take seriously the argument concerning the relative dangers inherent in marijuana and alcohol usage; physicians, on the whole, are not so impressed, and tend to dismiss it as irrelevant.

As we said in the last chapter, potheads draw the conclusion from a comparison of marijuana with alcohol that marijuana is unfairly discriminated against; the laws represent a double standard, just as if there were laws permitting one social group to do something and prohibiting another from doing the same thing. If alcohol (which is toxic, lethal, and dangerous) is legal—then why not pot? Marijuana is certainly no more dangerous than alcohol. Why aren't both allowed?

The medical answer to this argument is basically that it is irrelevant. Physicians rarely attribute marijuana with a more dangerous temperament than alcohol. The disagreement is far less on the facts than on the conclusion to be drawn from the facts. Potheads will say that alcohol is far more dangerous than pot, which is relatively innocuous, while doctors will say that pot is no more dangerous than alcohol—both of which are dangerous drugs. Yet this is a matter of emphasis only. Even were marijuana smokers to grant the medical argument, the disagreement concerning the implications of this position would still be rampant. Dr. Bloomquist, author of an antimarijuana book, in testimony before the California Senate Public Health and Safety Committee, when asked a question on the relative dangers of the two drugs, replied: "I would almost have to equate the two of them." [48] And Donald Louria wrote: "Surely alcohol itself is a dangerous drug. Indeed, marijuana's dangers . . . seem no greater than the documented deleterious effects of alcohol. If the question before us were a national referendum to decide whether we would use . . . either alcohol or marijuana, I might personally vote for marijuana—but that is not the question" [49] Physicians say that the damage to society following the legalization and widespread usage of marijuana would only be additive to the harm inflicted by alcohol. Whatever thousand deaths traceable to alcohol we actually experience now would be increased by a considerable number if marijuana restrictions were removed.

. . . the existence of alcoholism and skid rows is not an argument in favor of cannabis but one against it. If alcohol has ruined six million lives in this country, how can it possibly be an argument for permitting cannabis to do the same, or worse? Logic compels those who argue against alcohol to excuse cannabis to take another stand: they should be arguing for the control of alcohol and the elimination of its evils, not for the extension of those or similar evils to a wider segment of society.

The attack on alcohol implicitly acknowledges the evils of cannabis and goes on to urge that we let two wrongs make a right. . . . legalization of cannabis will in no way alleviate the problems of alcoholism but is very likely to add problems of another sort. . . . one drug is *as* socially and personally disruptive as the other. The question is whether we, as a nation, can afford a second drug catastrophe.[50]

A Minority Opinion

Although mainstream medical opinion holds marijuana to be damaging, potentially dangerous and, on the whole undesirable, a minority of doctors demure. We have claimed that the dominant view of physicians is that marijuana is a dangerous drug, capable of causing adverse psychic reactions and psychotic episodes. Yet David E. Smith, physician, toxicologist, pharmacologist, and director of the Haight-Ashbury Medical Clinic in the midst of a heavy drug-using population, writes that he has never seen a "primary psychosis" among his 30,000 patients, and, outside the clinic, he says that he has witnessed only three cases of marijuana-induced psychosis—"extreme paranoid reactions characterized by fear of arrest and discovery." [51]

I have stated that most physicians dismiss the pothead's point that marijuana is less dangerous than alcohol as irrelevant. Yet, Joel Fort, a physician, claims that alcohol is the most dangerous of all drugs currently available in America, whether legally or illegally. He has developed a scheme characterizing dimensions of drug "hardness," i.e., dangerousness. Fort's feeling is that any impartial observer will arrive at at least the following list of dimensions of hardness: addiction (or psychic dependency), insanity, tissue damage, violence, and death. Thus, some drugs may be hard in one way, but not in other ways. Fort claims that alcohol scores high on all of these dimensions; barbiturates and the amphetamines are also extremely hard as well. Marijuana, says Fort, is probably the least hard of the drugs available in today's pharmacopoeia. The fact that a truly dangerous drug (alcohol) is legal and freely available, while the possession of a far less dangerous drug (marijuana) is severely penalized, is patently absurd, according to Fort.[52]

Andrew T. Weil and Norman E. Zinberg, both physicians, after detailed controlled tests on subjects high on marijuana, concluded that the drug is relatively safe, and its effects, mild.[53] James M. Dille and Martin D. Haykin—pharmacologist and psychiatrist respectively, and both physicians—along with several nonphysicians, minimize the drug's deleterious effects on simulated driving performance.[54] And Tod H. Mikuriya, director of the San Francisco Psychiatric Medical Clinic, in a pamphlet entitled "Thinking About Using Pot," refuses to persuade readers not to use marijuana; he rejects the contention that marijuana leads to heroin and states, with regard to psychosis, that "marijuana is exceedingly safe." [55] His advice to those who "choose to turn on" concerns understanding how to use marijuana wisely. What is more, Mikuriya employs marijuana in his therapy. In treating alcoholics, one of his recommendations is that they give up alcohol, in his view the more destructive drug, for pot, which is far less damaging. It is obvious that this doctor disagrees with the majority view on at least two points: (1) marijuana no longer has any therapeutic value, and its use constitutes "abuse," and (2) it is a dangerous drug whose use should be avoided.

Another medical figure, Dr. Eugene Schoenfeld, writes a column syndicated by a number of "underground" (and invariably pro-pot) newspapers, such as *The East Village Other*. His stance is usually skeptical concerning the putative dangers of marijuana. One piece attacked the AMA's June 1968 statements condemning marijuana use, "Marihuana and Society." The critique is replete with such phrases as "the AMA . . . has chosen . . . to ignore . . . ," "casting itself into the role of prophet the Council demonstrates its lack of familiarity with the current American marihuana situation by the following statement . . . ," "contrary to all known evidence, the AMA statement denies. . . ." The review concludes with the claims: ". . . the scientific judgment of the AMA will now be looked upon with some suspicion by the millions of American marijuana users . . . the AMA would certainly be surprised by the great numbers of medical students and young residents who chronically use marijuana with no observable detriment to their physical or mental well-being." [56]

It is clear, then, that *some* physicians do not accept the dominant current medical views concerning marijuana. They underplay its dangers and hold that smoking pot is less a medical matter than a social and political question. Medically, they say, there is relatively little problem with marijuana. It is important to recognize that this is a minority opinion. Yet it is also interesting to speculate on some of the roots of this "different drummer" opinion. Probably the safest bet on the characteristics of the minority physicians has to do with age: the younger the doctor, the greater the likelihood that he will minimize its dangers; the older the doctor, the more danger he will see in pot smoking. Because of this generational difference, it is entirely possible that a tolerant attitude in the medical profession toward cannabis use will become increasingly common and may, in time, become the reigning sentiment. That day, in any case, will be a long time in coming.

It is also possible that doctors engaged in research will be more tolerant than those who have more extensive patient responsibilities. Issues of welfare and security will become predominant when others are in one's care, and decisions will be inclined in a conservative and protective direction. Risk will be minimized. Moreover, when one's actions and decisions are constantly scrutinized by one's clients, one feels pressure to conform to the stereotype of the responsible, judicious, reliable physician. The greater the accountability to a public, the more that the physician will perceive dangers in marijuana. (It may also be that doctors who decide to do client-oriented work are more conservative and cautious to begin with than the research-oriented physician.) The more independent the physician is—"safe" from retaliation and free of accountability—the less danger he will see in marijuana use.

Third, the possibility exists that the positive correlation between the quality of one's college and tolerance for marijuana use also applies to medical schools. We found this relationship with students in general; it seems natural to assume that it would hold up for physicians specifically. What is distinctive about the more highly rated schools, whether medical or otherwise, is that the student lives in an ambiance of experimentation, of greater tolerance for diversity and deviance and ambiguity. The better schools offer a richer, more complex view of the universe. It is not that better medical schools offer a more advanced technical training. It is that the more highly rated the school, the more daring the intellectual environment, the greater the willingness to diverge from conventional opinion, the more attuned both faculty and students will be to avant-garde cultural themes which presage later dominant modes of thinking and acting. Whatever the virtues or drawbacks of marijuana, it is clear that it shares a place with other developments which are thought to be fashionable among those who consider themselves (and who are also so considered by others),[57] progressive, knowledgeable, and ahead of their time. This is, in any case, speculation. Yet is capable of being tested empirically. Anyone interested in the appeal of marijuana has to consider this side of its attraction.

As a qualification, it must be stated that the attitudes of many physicians are in flux, in large part moving in the direction of a decreased severity of criticism of marijuana. Many doctors are becoming aware of the vastness of the phenomenon of use, as well as the predominance of relatively infrequent users in the ranks of potsmokers. Data on the effects of use are beginning to refute many of the classic antimarijuana arguments, and physicians sufficiently respect the empirical tradition to be influenced by this. Many influential medical figures have shifted their position from the "pathology" model outlined in this chapter to one which minimizes pot's actual or potential danger. Dr. Stanley Yolles, for instance, Director of the National Institute of Mental Health, cited earlier in this chapter as typifying some aspects of the antipot pathology argument, has made recent statements to the Senate Judiciary Subcommittee on Juvenile Delinquency which minimized marijuana's medical dangers; his statements were summarized in an article written by himself entitled: "Pot Is Painted Too Black." [58] It may very well be, then, that the medical profession is moving in the direction of a more "soft" stand on the dangers represented by marijuana.

If polled, the vast majority of physicians in America would certainly oppose the relegalization of marijuana possession.[59] However, nearly all medical commentators admit that the marijuana laws are unnecessarily harsh. Very few will support the present legal structure. Although nonmedical figures who do—principally the police—invoke medical opinion on pot to shore up their own position, utilizing the pathology argument in regard to use, they do not mention the doctors' opposition to the laws as they are presently written. Their conclusions on the justness of the present legal structure is made contrary to medical opposition to it.

NOTES

1. The prestige of physicians is higher than that of any other widely held occupation. See Robert W. Hodge, Paul M. Seigel, and Peter H. Rossi, "Occupational Prestige in the United States," in Reinhard Bendix and Seymour Martin Lipset, eds., *Class, Status and Power,* 2nd ed. (New York: Free Press, 1966), pp. 322–334.

2. Henry Brill, "Drugs and Drug Users: Some Perspectives," in *Drugs on the Campus: An Assessment,* The Saratoga Springs Conference of Colleges and Universities of New York State (Sponsored by the New York State Narcotics Addiction Control Commission, Saratoga Springs, New York, October 25 to 27, 1967), p. 49.

3. The literature on the "specialness" of the medical view of reality—as the term is defined here—particularly regarding psychosis, is among the most impressive and exciting in the entire field of sociology. For examples of sociological lines of attack on the medical view see Thomas Scheff, *Being Mentally Ill* (Chicago: Aldine, 1966); R. D. Laing, *The Politics of Experience* (New York: Ballantine, 1968); Thomas Szasz, *The Myth of Mental Illness* (London: Secker and Warburg, 1962). (It should be noted that both Laing and Szasz are themselves physicians.) For the process of the dynamics of constructing this reality in the patient relationship, see Thomas Scheff, "Negotiating Reality: Notes on Power in the Assessment of Responsibility," *Social Problems* 16 (Summer 1968): 3–17.

4. The sword cuts two ways, however. Physicians who have conducted research on marijuana use may also be employed as rhetorical devices by the pro-pot lobby. In fact, the scientific method may be employed as a rhetorical device for the purpose of convincing the opposition. As many of the arguments of the antimarijuana side fail to be substantiated empirically, the scientific rhetoric will tend to be invoked correspondingly less, but will become increasingly emphasized by the opposition.

5. This concept of the disease or pathology model is precisely equivalent to what Dr. Norman Zinberg independently calls a "medical model" on marijuana use.

6. American Medical Association, Committee on Alcoholism and Drug Dependence, Council on Mental Health, "The Crutch That Cripples: Drug Dependence," pamphlet (Chicago: AMA, 1968), p. 2. For some reason, a small but vigorous contingent of marijuana supporters maintain that the drug may actually be therapeutic. For instance, in the vast and decidedly promarijuana anthology, *The Marihuana Papers,* edited by David Solomon, several articles were included which dealt specifically with marijuana's healing powers in some regard or another. A physician-psychiatrist, Harry Chramoy Hermon, is licensed to employ cannabis in his therapy. See Hermon, "Preliminary Observations on the Use of Marihuana in Psychotherapy," *The Marijuana Review* 1, no. 3 (June–August 1969), 14–17.

7. E. D. Mattmiller, "Social Values, American Youth, and Drug Use" (Paper presented to COTA, January 22, 1968), p. 5 (my emphasis, in part).

8. Brill, *op. cit.,* p. 52.

9. Jerome H. Jaffe, "Drug Addiction and Drug Abuse," in Louis S. Goodman and Alfred Gilman, eds. *The Pharmacological Basis of Therapeutics,* 3rd ed. (New York: Macmillan, 1965), p. 285.

10. Paul Jay Fink, Morris J. Goldman, and Irwin Lyons, "Recent Trends in Substance Abuse," *The International Journal of the Addictions,* 2 (Spring 1967): 150.

11. Graham B. Blaine, Jr., *Youth and the Hazards of Affluence* (New York: Harper Colophon, 1967), p. 68.

12. Frank S. Caprio, *Variations in Lovemaking* (New York: Richlee Publications, 1968), p. 166.

13. Duke Fisher, "Marijuana and Sex" (Paper presented to the National Symposium on Psychedelic Drugs and Marijuana, April 11, 1968), p. 3.

14. *Ibid.*

15. Blaine, *op. cit.,* pp. 67–68. Blaine qualifies his assertion by distinguishing the "hard core" user, who would be impelled to drugs in the absence of the rebellion motive, and the "experimenter," for whom parental rejection is a strong impetus to sporadic and eventually discontinued use of drugs.

16. Seymour L. Halleck, "Psychiatric Treatment of the Alienated College Student," *American Journal of Psychiatry* 124 (November 1967): 642–650.

17. Mattmiller, *op. cit.*

18. Donald B. Louria, *The Drug Scene* (New York: McGraw-Hill, 1968), p. 101.

19. Henry Brill, "Why Not Pot Now? Some Questions and Answers About Marijuana," *Psychiatric Opinion* 5, no. 5 (October 1968): 19.

20. Nathan B. Eddy et al., "Drug Dependence: Its Significance and Characteristics," *Bulletin of the World Health Organization* 32 (1965): 721.

21. The parallel with agents of which society approves was made by Eliot Freidson, in "Ending Campus Incidents," Letter to the Editor, *Trans-action* 5, no. 8 (July-August 1968): 75. Freidson writes, with regard to the terms psychic addiction and habituation: "What does this term mean? It means that the drug is pleasurable, as is wine, smoked sturgeon, poetry, comfortable chairs, and *Trans-action.* Once people use it and like it, they will tend to continue to do so *if they can.* But they can get along without it if they must, which is why it cannot be called physically addictive."

22. David Ausubel, *Drug Addiction* (New York: Random House, 1958), pp. 9–10.

23. Edward R. Bloomquist, "Marijuana: Social Benefit or Social Detriment?" *California Medicine* 106 (May 1967): 352.

24. Seymour Fiddle, *Portraits From a Shooting Gallery* (New York: Harper & Row, 1967), pp. 3–20.

25. Louria, *op. cit.,* p. 103.

26. John Rosevear, *Pot: A Handbook of Marihuana* (New Hyde Park, N. Y.: University Books, 1967), p. 90.

27. The Medical Society of the County of New York, "The Dangerous Drug Problem —II," *New York Medicine* 24 (January 1968), p. 4 (my emphasis).

28. John A. Talbott and James W. Teague, "Marihuana Psychosis: Acute Toxic Psychosis Associated with Cannabis Derivatives," *The Journal of the American Medical Association* 210 (October 13, 1969): 299.

29. For some representative clinical work by physicians on the use of marijuana, see Martin H. Keeler, "Adverse Reaction to Marihuana," *The American Journal of Psychiatry* 124 (November 1967): 674–677; Doris H. Milman, "The Role of Marihuana in Patterns of Drug Abuse by Adolescents," *The Journal of Pediatrics* 74 (February 1969): 283–290; Aaron H. Esman et al., "Drug Use by Adolescents: Some Valuative and Technical Implications," *The Psychoanalytic Forum* 2 (Winter 1967): 339–353, Leon Wurmser, Leon Levin, and Arlene Lewis, "Chronic Paranoid Symptoms and Thought Disorders in Users of Marihuana and LSD as Observed in Psychotherapy," unpublished manuscript (Baltimore: Sinai Hospital, 1969).

30. The most well-known of the cannabis laboratory experiments are those conducted in the Addiction Research Center in Lexington, Kentucky. (Actually, THC is used, not natural marijuana.) See Harris Isbell et al., "Effects of (-)$\triangle$⁹-Trans-Tetrahydrocannabinol in Man," *Psychopharmacologia* 11 (1967): 184–188, and Harris Isbell and

D. R. Jasinski, "A Comparison of LSD-25 with (-)$\triangle$⁹-Trans-Tetrahydrocannabinol (THC) and Attempted Cross Tolerance between LSD and THC," *Psychopharmacologia* 14 (1969): 115–123. See also Reese T. Jones and George C. Stone, "Psychological Studies of Marijuana and Alcohol in Man" (Paper presented at the 125th Annual Meeting of the American Psychiatric Association, Bal Harbour, Fla., May 1969).

31. The use of hashish in America is, as we stated earlier, increasing rapidly, certainly much faster than the use of the less potent cannabis preparations. As a rough indication of this trend, consider the fact that more hashish was seized by the United States Customs in the year 1967–1968 than in the previous *twenty* years combined. See *The New York Times*, September 19, 1968. The California police in 1968 seized over seven thousand grams of hashish, whereas none was recorded as having been seized in 1967. (In neither year was a category for hashish provided on the official police forms.) See State of California, Department of Justice, Bureau of Criminal Statistics, *Drug Arrests and Dispositions in California, 1968* (Sacramento, 1969), pp. 40–41. In 1969, this tendency was further accelerated by the "Great Marijuana Drought" caused by increased federal vigilance in reducing the quantity of Mexican marijuana entering the country. Thus, hashish, which comes from Asia, was more in demand and imported in far greater volume than previously. And, of course, used with greater frequency.

32. American Medical Association, Council on Mental Health, "Marihuana and Society," *The Journal of the American Medical Association* 204, no. 13 (June 24, 1968): 1181.

33. Edward R. Bloomquist, *Marijuana* (Beverly Hills, Calif.: Glencoe Press, 1968), p. 102. For some of the Oriental studies on marijuana use referred to, see Ahmed Benabud, "Psycho-Pathological Aspects of the Cannabis Situation in Morocco: Statistical Data for 1956," United Nations *Bulletin on Narcotics* 9, no. 4 (October–December 1957): 1–16; Ram Nath Chopra, Gurbakhsh Singh Chopra, and Ismir C. Chopra, "Cannabis Sativa in Relation to Mental Diseases and Crime in India," *Indian Journal of Medical Research* 30 (January 1942): 155–171; Ram Nath Chopra and Gurbakhsh Singh Chopra, *The Present Position of Hemp-Drug Addiction in India*, Indian research Memoirs, no. 31 (July 1939); Constandinos J. Miras, "Report of the U. C. L. A. Seminar," in Kenneth Eells, ed., *Pot* (Pasadena, Calif.: California Institute of Technology, October 1968), pp. 69–77.
It should be made clear that the validity of many of these studies has been severely called into question. For instance, in the Leis-Weiss trials in Boston during 1967, conducted by Joseph Oteri, it was revealed that the Benabud data were collected at a time when there was not a single certified psychiatrist in the entire nation of Morocco; the admitting diagnosis cards were filled out by French clerks, who recorded the opinions of the police who brought in the suspect. The transcript of the court proceedings in which Oteri reveals these facts is to be published in book form by Bobbs-Merrill.

34. Stanley F. Yolles, "Recent Research on LSD, Marihuana and Other Dangerous Drugs" (Statement Before the Subcommittee on Juvenile Delinquency of the Committee on the Judiciary, United States Senate, March 6, 1968). Statement published in pamphlet form by the National Clearinghouse for Mental Health Information, United States Department of Health, Education and Welfare, National Institute of Mental Health.

35. Bloomquist, "Marijuana: Social Benefit or Social Detriment?" p. 348. It should be noted that dark glasses may be worn because the user *thinks* that his pupils are dilated, but not "because of the dilated pupils," because, as we shall see in the chapter on the effects of marijuana, the pupils do not become dilated.

36. Louria, *op. cit.*, pp. 107, 108.

37. Brill, "Why Not Pot Now?" p. 21.

38. American Medical Association, "Marihuana and Society," p. 1181.

39. AMA, "Marihuana Thing," Editorial, *Journal of the American Medical Association* 204, no. 13 (June 24, 1968).

40. Bloomquist, "Marijuana: Social Benefit or Social Detriment?" p. 352.

41. Dana Farnsworth, "The Drug Problem Among Young People," *The West Virginia Medical Journal* 63 (December 1967): 434.

42. J. U. Monro, unpublished memorandum to the Harvard class of 1970, April 13, 1967.

43. William Simon and John H. Gagnon, "Children of the Drug Age," *Saturday Review*, September 21, 1968, pp. 76–78.

44. Yolles, *op. cit.*

45. Brill, "Why Not Pot Now?" and "Drugs and Drug Users."

46. Blaine, *op. cit.*, p. 74.

47. Louria, *op. cit.*, pp. 110–111.

48. Edward R. Bloomquist, Testimony, in *Hearings on Marijuana Laws Before the California Public Health and Safety Committee* (Los Angeles, October 18, 1967, afternoon session), transcript, p. 43.

49. Louria, *op. cit.*, p. 115.

50. Actually, Bloomquist misses the point here somewhat. Potheads do not say that marijuana is *as* dangerous as alcohol—and that both are dangerous—and therefore marijuana ought to be legalized. They say that alcohol is dangerous and legal, while pot is *not* dangerous, but illegal, and legalizing marijuana would *reduce* the seriousness of the drug problem, because more pot and less alcohol would be consumed. See Bloomquist, *Marijuana*, pp. 85, 86.

51. David E. Smith, "Acute and Chronic Toxicity of Marijuana," *Journal of Psychedelic Drugs* 2, no. 1 (Fall 1968): 41.

52. Of Fort's many publications, perhaps the most relevant to these points is "A World View of Marijuana: Has the World Gone to Pot?" *Journal of Psychedelic Drugs* 2, no. 1 (Fall 1968): 1–14. See also "Pot: A Rational Approach," *Playboy*, October 1969, pp. 131, 154, 216, et seq., in which Fort argues for the legalization of marijuana. See also *The Pleasure Seekers* (Indianapolis: Bobbs-Merrill, 1969).

53. Andrew T. Weil, Norman E. Zinberg, and Judith M. Nelsen, "Clinical and Psychological Effects of Marihuana in Man," *Science* 162, no. 3859 (December 13, 1968): 1234-1242; Zinberg and Weil, "Cannabis: The First Controlled Experiment," *New Society* (January 19, 1969): 84–86; Zinberg and Weil, "The Effects of Marijuana on Human Beings," *The New York Times Magazine*, May 11, 1969, pp. 28–29, 79, et seq.; Weil, "Marihuana," Letter to the Editor, *Science* 163, no. 3872 (March 14, 1969): 1145

54. Alfred Crancer, Jr., James M. Dille, Jack Delay, Jean E. Wallace, and Martin D. Haykin, "A Comparison of the Effects of Marihuana and Alcohol on Simulated Driving Performance," *Science* 164, no. 3881 (May 16, 1969): 851–854.

55. Tod H. Mikuriya and Kathleen E. Goss, "Thinking About Using Pot" (San Francisco: The San Francisco Psychiatric Mental Clinic, 1969), p. 24.

56. Eugene Schoenfeld, "Hip-pocrates," *The East Village Other* 3, no. 36 (August 9, 1968): pp. 6, 16.

57. I am not making the claim that marijuana is *inherently* part of an intellectual avant-garde movement. At certain times and places, it may be looked upon as reactionary. It is just that today, in America, it is so considered. We also do not say that it is *only* among those who consider themselves in the historical vanguard that marijuana will appeal; it is just that those who do think this way will be *more likely* to try marijuana than those who do not.

58. Stanley F. Yolles, "Pot Is Painted too Black," *The Washington Post*, September 21, 1969, p. C4. Compare this later statement with those made in the National Clearinghouse for Mental Health Information, NIMH pamphlet, published in part in the March 7, 1968 issue of *The New York Times*, p. 26, and the article "Before Your Kid Tries Drugs," *The New York Times Magazine*, November 17, 1968, pp. 124, et seq.

59. In an actual mail-in questionnaire study by a physician of the attitudes of psychiatrists and physicians in the New York area on the legalization of marijuana, it was found that the large majority (about 60 percent) said that they were against legalization. Only a quarter were for it. See Wolfram Keup, "The Legal Status of Marihuana (A Psychiatric Poll)," *Diseases of the Nervous System* 30 (August 1969): 517–523. (Another way of looking at these figures, however, is that there is far from unanimous agreement within the medical and psychiatric professions on the status of marijuana.)

: *Chapter* 6 :

Turning On: Becoming a Marijuana User

The verb "to turn on" has many meanings within the drug-using community. It is a rich and magical term, encompassing an enormous variety of situations and activities. Its imagery is borrowed from the instantaneous processes of the electrical age, which McLuhan has described with perverse brilliance. An electric light is turned on, and one's inept fumbling about a once-dark room ceases; a machine is turned on, and one can do what previously was impossible; the television is turned on, and a naked glass eye becomes a teeming, glittering illusion. The most general meaning of the verb to turn on is to make knowledgeable, to make aware, to open the senses, to sensitize, to make appreciative, excited. Thus someone may turn on someone to another person, a recording artist, an author worth knowing. A certain woman may turn on a man sexually. Reading a book may turn on its reader to an area of knowledge—or onto himself. A teacher may turn on his students. Someone may simply be turned on to the excitement of the world. Turning on is an enlargement of one's universe.

The specific meaning of the word is using drugs. Within the drug context, "to turn on" has at least three interrelated connotations: (1) to give or have one's first drug experience—usually with marijuana; (2) to become high for the first time—with marijuana; (3) to use a drug—usually marijuana. "Let's go to my place and turn on," would nearly always mean to smoke marijauna and become high. A significant element in the marijuana subculture is that marijuana use *is* a turning on, an enlargement of one's awareness, an opening up of the receptivity of one's senses and emotions. To turn on with marijuana is, at least to its users, a part of living life as fully as possible.

We will now use the term in its first meaning: using marijuana for the first time—the process of "becoming a marijuana user." [1] Our guiding concern will be the dynamic transition between being a nonuser to trying the drug initially. It is the story of the initiate, the neophyte's first drug exposure. What are the factors which make for such a transition? What sorts of experiences does the convert go through, and why? What are the appeals of this drug to the young, to the drug-naive, to the inexperienced, that make this transition so widespread? It should be kept in mind that we are describing an event that took place in the past. The smoker today was turned on previously, not today, perhaps a few days ago, perhaps a few years ago. Thus, there exists the possibility for distortion in our respondents' reports of their turn on. They may make their past consistent with present sentiment or events. The past may be shaped to tell an interesting story based on how they feel today. We have no idea how this tendency distorts the respondents' stories about their initial use of marijuana, but we ought to be attuned to the possibility of such a distortion.

Every marijuana user passes through the process of being turned on. Not all experiences will be the same, of course, but a hard core of common experiences will prevail among most users. Certain features will parallel *any* new experience, while some will be unique to marijuana use. Nearly all human activities at least indirectly involve other people, and being introduced to marijuana offers no exception to this rule; in fact, marijuana use in general is exquisitely a group phenomenon. Only six of our interviewees (3 percent) turned themselves on, that is, the first time that they ever smoked marijuana, they were alone. (They all had, of course, obtained their marijuana from someone else.) Eight individuals (4 percent) were turned on exclusively in the company of other neophytes. At their initial exposure to the drug, the user-to-be is subject to the tribal lore of the marijuana-using subculture, a distinctive and idiosyncratic group in society; his experience with the drug is, in a sense, predefined, channelled, already structured. He is told how to get high, what to do when he is high, how to recognize the high, what to expect, how he will react, what is approved high behavior, and what is disapproved, what experiences are enriched by the high, and which are not. The nature of the experience itself is defined for the initiate. Although these definitions in no way substitute for the experience itself, they are a variable which goes into its making. They do not determine the nature of the high experience, totally irrespective of any and all other variables, but they are crucial. It is necessary, therefore, to examine the impact of group structure in the experience of turning on.

Not only is the initiate turned on by experienced marijuana users rich in the collective wisdom of their group, but these proselytizers are also *intimates*.[2] In *no* case did a peddler turn on the respondent —unless he was a friend. The profit motive in these conversions was simply and frankly absent. Friends were involved in every stage of the process—supplying information about marijuana, or supplying the opportunity, or the drug. But equally as important is that a friend or group of friends supplied a kind of legitimation. They were an "example." Prior to any first or second hand acquaintance with the drug, many users have a stereotype in their minds about the kinds of people who use marijuana. They might have been convinced that smoking pot is an undesirable thing to do because, in their minds, only undesirable people used it. Even more important than any knowledge about the effects of the drug in convincing them that turning on might have merit was their association with and attitudes toward people who endorsed and used marijuana. At the point where the individual realizes that it isn't only undesirable (in his eyes) people who use it, but many poised, sophisticated ones as well, his defenses against using it have been weakened, possibly more than by any other single factor. "I didn't want to smoke it because that added you to a collection of people who were undesirable," said one nineteen-year-old ex-coed. "The times when I could have turned on, I didn't want to try it with the people I was with—they were depressing people to be around," added another young woman. The disillusionment came with the awareness that "people I respected smoked it. I gradually began to realize the fakery about it," in the words of a thirty-year-old executive. "People I like smoked it." "Friends I knew and respected smoked it and like it." "A guy I admired was smoking, and I asked him if I could smoke." This theme ran through our interviews. "At first I looked down on it—it's dope, it's habit forming, it leads to heroin, it's demoralizing. But once, when I was staying over at my cousin's house, I thought, if my cousin, whom I dig, is doing it—she's a great kid—it can't be too bad," a twenty-year-old clerk explained. "I was apprehensive, a little excited, scared, and ignorant, but I trusted the guy I was with," a twenty-nine-year-old commercial artist told me, describing his turn-on ten years ago.

It is necessary that the proselytizer be someone whom the potential initiate trusts; he is generally unwilling to put his fate in the hands of a stranger. If he accepts society's generally negative judgment of the drug, there must be some powerful contrary forces neutralizing that judgment before he will try marijuana. Peer influences are just such powerful forces. Society's evaluation, even if taken seriously, is a vague and impersonal influence. The testimony of one or several friends will weigh far more heavily in the balance than even parental disapproval. If an intimate friend vouches for the positive qualities of cannabis, the ground has been cleared for a potential convert.

More specifically, the relationship between the neophyte and his marijuana initiator is crucial. The lack of association in the naif's mind of marijuana with a specific unsavory "scene" is, of course, important, but it lacks the immediacy and impact of his feelings for those who actually hand him a glowing joint. Although sexual parallels should not be pushed too far, something of the same significance is imputed to one's first sex partner as to the person one has decided to be turned on by. With women, the conjunction is closer than for men, since women are usually turned on by men, whereas men are more often turned on by other men.

Looking at smokers through the eyes of the potential convert, it is clear that, on the whole, a high proportion are respectable. More than that, many are at the center of the youth culture—the most highly respected of the younger half of the population are known as users. Known users are generally brighter, more creative, socially active, and knowledgeable in those aspects of the youth culture that the young take most seriously. A young black man, president of his sophomore class at Andover, was quoted by *The New York Times* as saying, "No matter what parents instill in their sons, they lose a lot of it here. Everybody wants to be identified with the 'in' crowd, and the 'in' crowd is now on the left." He might have added that the left is into pot. It is not merely that marijuana is fashionable to youngsters today, its users are seen as role models; they are, in many ways, a reference group for slightly younger nonusers. It is from the using population that many of the dominant values of today's youth spring—in music and fashion, to mention two of the most obvious examples—and from whom standards of prestige and desirability flow. One of the appeals of the drug, and why its use has spread with such facility, is that endorsers and users are seen by their peers as socially acceptable and even highly desirable human beings. As Alan Sutter, one of the researchers on the Blumer study[3] of drug use in the Oakland area, wrote: "Drug use, especially marijuana use, is a function of a socializing movement into a major stream of adolescent life."[4]

Another reason why marijuana spreads with such rapidity is that users project relatively unambiguously favorable endorsements. Not only are they interested in making converts to a degree unequal to that of any other drug culture, but they advertise their drug better. Their propaganda is more effective, because they present more of its favorable qualities and fewer of its negative traits. The chronic amphetamine user or the heroin addict are ambivalent about their drug of choice and rarely portray it in unambiguously positive terms. They are willing to admit its dangers, its damages to their body, the hazards of use. Asked if their drug of choice is harmless, the amphetamine and heroin users are unlikely to agree, while the pothead is likely to do so. An indication of the relativity in images of the various drugs, what they do to the body, and their users, may be gleaned from the jargon for users of these drugs. The term "head" implies no negative connotation; it is a purely discriptive term. Thus, a "pothead" is simply one who uses marijuana heavily. But the terms "fiend" and "freak" are predominantly negative. Freak and fiend are never used in reference to marijuana users, whereas they are frequently applied to methedrine and heroin users—"meth freak," "speed freak," "scag fiend," and so forth. A linguistic projection of these differential images does not prove our point, but it does lend it support.

The image of potential and present potsmokers as "wild thrill seekers" has no basis. Most of the users interviewed were cautious and apprehensive about trying marijuana, and would not have made the leap unless they had been convinced that it would not harm them. The lure of cannabis is not that it represents danger; it is almost the reverse. It represents no obstacle to the future user when he is led to believe that it is safe. He rarely tries it himself to determine whether it is safe, but accepts testimony about its safety from those whose judgment he trusts. If it were depicted by his intimates as a dangerous drug or a narcotic (as defined by law), the overwhelming majority would never have tried it.

Americans generally pride themselves on being objective, hardheaded, empirical, and tough-minded. This is the show-me country, where the challenge to prove it calls for scientific demonstration. "I'll try anything once" is an open-minded attitude toward experience. Yet, for some reason, these injunctions are highly selective; they apply to some spheres of experience and not to others. There are, presumably, many activities and experiences that need no testing and are rightfully condemned out of hand. But the younger generation is taking the pragmatism of the American civilization literally, at face value. If it applies to technology, to the business world, to foods and fads, then why not pot? "Don't knock it unless you've tried it," was a theme running throughout my interviews. The firsthand experience is respected by America's young, and he who condemns without having "been there" will be ignored. And the reason why the pull to the promarijuana side is especially powerful is that positive personal testimony is more common than negative personal testimony, negative testimony being largely nonexperiential. Physicians who give talks designed to discourage marijuana use are invariably asked by young audiences whether they have tried the drug they condemn. Although the reply—you don't have to *have* a disease to recognize its symptoms—satisfies the middle-aged physician, it is insufficient for the experience-oriented high school or college student.

We are struck by the dominant role of at least five factors in this process:

1) The initiate's perception of *danger* (or the lack thereof) in marijuana use
2) His perception of its benefits
3) His attitude toward users
4) His closeness to marijuana's endorsers
5) His closeness to the individual trying to turn him on*

Of course, these five variables are only theoretically independent —in actual cases, they interpenetrate and influence one another.

---

* This discussion assumes that the potential user has been provided with an opportunity to try marijuana; this is, itself, a variable and not a constant. We are concentrating on the characteristics of the individual himself in this discussion.

For instance, the neophyte is more likely to believe that marijuana is harmless if he is told this by intimates—less likely if told the same thing by strangers; therefore, (1) and (2) are partly determined by (4) and (5). Each of these factors should be thought of as a variable that is neither necessary nor sufficient; the only absolutely necessary precondition for turning on is the presence of the pot. Thus, the individual can come into a turn-on situation with almost any conceivable attitude toward trying marijuana—although, obviously, if the turn-on is to be successful, certain kinds of attitudes on the potential convert's part are more likely than others. However, what is necessary is that certain combinations of these variables exist.

To understand how the process of a typical turn-on might work, let us play a game by assigning each factor an imaginary (probably unrealistic) weight of twenty, and each individual a score ranging from zero to twenty, depending on the degree of favorableness; in his case, each factor is for a turn-on. Let us further claim that a turn-on occurs when our candidate—who has just been given an opportunity to turn on—is assigned a total score of fifty. Let us look at the following actual cases:

I had notions that marijuana was harmful, that I might commit suicide, that it was a real drug; pot wasn't separated from the other drugs in my mind. Then, I had a neighbor in Berkeley who was a pothead. He explained what it was like to me. He told me not to be frightened about it. He described the high as a very sensual experience. It was as if I was a virgin. He talked to me for about two months before I tried it.
                    Twenty-two-year-old public school art teacher, female

I knew almost nothing about pot. I had no attitude about it one way or another. I was in high school, and a friend took me to a bar, he made a connection—I didn't know it until after—and then we drove off. In the car, he asked if I wanted some. I asked him a few questions about it, and then I tried it.
                    Twenty-seven-year-old graduate student in sociology

I didn't believe in it. I felt as if I was above it. I didn't need a thing like that. Others seemed to take it when they have problems, and not when they were happy.

It seemed to be a miserable type of drug. I was visiting friends who were marijuana smokers, who were talking about it constantly, but I didn't want to smoke, and everybody else did. They said at first that it was okay if I didn't smoke and everybody else did, but I felt awkward not smoking when everybody else was, and I felt pressured into it. They all tried to teach me how to do it.

> Twenty-two-year-old writer, female

I can remember thinking, if I were offered marijuana, I would try it. I knew it wasn't dangerous. I was offered it coming back from skiing with somebody I'd just met. We were riding home in a car.

> Twenty-one-year-old advertising specialist, female

I didn't want to go along with everyone else. It was the hip thing to do in my high school in the tenth grade. I just didn't want to be a part of the drug scene. I was against it, but I knew I would eventually try it. I felt as if I might really like it. I just didn't happen to like those kids I knew that smoked. One day, two of us were sitting in a coffee house, and a friend dropped in and said, let's try it. We went into the back, into the ladies' room, and smoked it.

> Eighteen-year-old college freshman, female

I was sixteen years old, in the Air Force. Near the base, in a bar, a whore picked me up, and we went to her place. She turned me on. My attitudes were hostile concerning pot. I thought it was dope, I thought it was addicting. I took it because I'm a chump for a broad. Anything she suggested was okay.

> Twenty-eight-year-old carpenter

I knew it would be groovy two years before I turned on. I didn't have any opportunities before then. I would have snatched them up if I had. I studied up on drugs before I took it. I knew what the hygiene course we had in high school was teaching were lies.

> Twenty-year-old bookstore clerk

At first, I thought, it's a terrible drug, and it leads to heroin. But my brother demolished all the fallacies. It sounded good. There was nothing wrong with it but I was still afraid of it. My brother turned me on.

> Nineteen-year-old clerk in a bookstore, female

My feelings about pot were nonexistent, though I was vaguely favorably disposed to it. I discounted the negative jazz as hoopla and propaganda; I couldn't see, after reading about it, any harm from it. I didn't accept the first few opportunities I had, because I didn't like the people I was with. Finally, I visited some friends, and they offered me some.

> Twenty-seven-year-old dishwasher

129

Before, I didn't want to—I didn't see any reason for it. I wasn't around people who smoked it. But at the job I have now, people at the office talked about it. I got interested. I mentioned to someone in the office I'd like to try it: Could you get me some? So, one night my husband and I had guests. No one had ever had the stuff before. Three of us turned on with the pot I got from the office. My husband didn't try it.

Twenty-five-year-old assistant research analyst, market research firm

I knew it was harmless, and I was curious about it. I was sitting in the park, and a guy came to me and asked if I wanted to buy some, and I bought a nickel bag, and went over to a friend's place, and we turned on.

Nineteen-year-old college student

I was against the idea of marijuana. I was ignorant. I knew it was a drug, and I thought it was addictive. But my closest friend smoked—I was close friends with this guy for four years. He asked me several times to turn on and I said no. Finally, I decided, what the hell—give it a try.

Twenty-four-year-old market research study director

My older brother gave it to me. He told me not to turn on out of social pressure; I should be turned on by someone I trusted—himself. He got it for me, and then I went up to the attic and turned on alone. I came down and talked to my parents. Only my brother knew I was high. Before that, I didn't know people well enough, or trust them, to turn on.

Twenty-five-year-old artist-performer

I knew almost nothing about pot, but I was completely confident that nothing would happen, since my brother turned me on.

Twenty-one-year-old unemployed college drop-out

I felt safe with good friends, and I felt it would be all right.

Twenty-year-old coder, female

Thus, someone who is extremely close to both the endorser and the individual turning him on (forty points), and who has an ambivalent attitude about users (ten points), sees no benefits in use (zero points), and is unsure about its safeness (ten points), is a potential candidate for being turned on, when the occasion arises. Another person who thinks of the stories about its dangers as myths, thinks that it would be fun, and has at least a moderately favorable image of smokers, is likely to be turned on, even by a stranger. One indication that our scheme reflects something of the actual situation is the fact that many marijuana users (46 percent of our respondents) report having *refused* opportunities to turn on prior to their eventual conversion because one or another circumstance at that time was not favorable. Any one of these factors could have been the reason, but the two most often mentioned were the fears about the drug's danger and a lack of closeness with the person or persons offering the opportunity to try it. With this scheme in mind as a very rough model, it is possible to see how someone could accept an offer to smoke even though he is still fearful of the drug's effects, although this is empirically infrequent.

It is relatively rare for the initiate to try to simulate prior drug experience, although it does occur. The majority going through the initiation ceremony are known to be novitiates by all present (70 percent of our interviewees), while occasionally some present at the turning on ceremony will know, while others do not (6 percent)— at a large party, for instance. It is not uncommon for the respondent to be unaware of what others know of his prior drug experience (15 percent), and sometimes none present at his turn-on knew that he was marijuana-naive (9 percent). Typically, both initiate and initiator regard the turn-on as a highly significant event in the novice's roster of life experiences. It is a kind of milestone, a *rite de passage*; it is often seen as a part of "growing up" for many adolescents.[5] Even when others are not in the know, the subject is nervous and excited at the prospect. Its importance in one's life is overshadowed only by (and is similar to) losing one's virginity. Although the following account is atypical because it is so extreme, it captures much of the flavor of the ritual-like nature of the characteristic turn-on; I present the verbatim transcript of a portion of the interview of a twenty-three-year-old dramatics graduate student. (I am asking the questions.)

Q: Do you remember how you got it for the first time?
A: It was given to me. I smoked it with a friend of mine, and a friend of his, and another amiable person.
Q: Do you remember what the occasion was?
A: There was no occasion; the occasion was the turning on.
Q: You got together for the purpose of turning on?
A: Yes.
Q: All the others present—did they know you were smoking for the first time?
A: Yes. And if the party was the celebration of anything, it was the celebration of a new person coming to turn on, and that was a big

deal. And everyone was very nice, you know, and brought all sorts of great things to eat. And taste, and wild things, and put on a *whole show,* you know, it was a *great, marvelous* experience: just absolutely marvelous.

Q: Did you get high?

A: Yes, I got very, very high. Had an enormously good time. The first time I got high, I think we were listening to jazz, and the notes became visual, and turned different colors, and became propellers. And jazz became kind of formalized in a great color and motion thing that I created from my own imagination—wonderful things like this happened. And the room was tilted slightly up, you know, turned on its side; it was like a rocket ship taking off for somewhere, you know, way out in the vastness of outer space.

A significant element in the marijuana subculture's tribal lore is the technique involved in smoking the weed. For those who do not smoke tobacco cigarettes, the whole procedure might seem particularly strange. But even for those who do smoke, much of the tabacco cigarette agendum is inapplicable to smoking marijuana cigarettes; if pot is smoked exactly like an ordinary cigarette, the novice probably cannot become high—it is difficult enough in the beginning when done correctly—although it is possible with practice. The initiate, to become high, must inhale the marijuana smoke deeply into his lungs; take some air in with the smoke; hold it there for a few seconds; and let it out slowly.[6] These procedures require observation and instruction. They are part of the technology of marijuana use that must be mastered. Although they do not compare in complexity with heroin technology, they are necessary for attaining the desired state of intoxication.

By itself, without becoming high, marijuana smoking is not pleasurable. All users smoke marijuana to become high—in traditional language, "intoxicated." They see no point to smoking it for its own sake. There is no pleasure to be derived from inhaling the fumes of the burning marijuana plant (although the same could be said for the leaves of the tobacco plant), and there is, moreover, no ideology which claims that mere smoking, without intoxication, is pleasurable or good, or relaxing—or anything—as there is with regular tobacco cigarettes. (Pot, in addition, lacks the physiological compulsion-imperative built into nicotine.)

We may take it as an axiom that everywhere and at all times, marijuana is smoked in order to attain the high. It might seem surprising that at this point we encounter another learning process. No activity, bodily state, or condition is *inherently* pleasurable. Physiological manifestations of human sexuality, for instance, experienced by the completely untutored are apt to be interpreted as disturbing and puzzling, not necessarily pleasurable. We are prepared for and instructed in the pleasures of sex; sufficient negative tutoring will generally yield disgust and a desire for avoidance in the individual. Now, it should be mentioned that some bodily states have greater potential for being defined as pleasurable: sex, for instance, or the marijuana high. But the social-defining and learning process must be there. It seems a paradox to say that one must learn how to have fun, especially as the Freudians tell us that culture is primarily repressive, not liberative, but it is difficult to avoid such a conclusion.

The unprepared individual is unlikely to think of the marijuana intoxication as pleasurable. The pleasures or discomforts of the high are interpreted, defined, sifted by group definitions. One is, in a sense, programmed beforehand for the experience, for feeling a pleasurable response. Even as one is in the very process of becoming high and beginning to experience the effects of the drug, a dialectical relationship exists between the high and the user's moral and epistemological ambiance. Group definitions constantly interpret and reinterpret the experience, so that subsequent feelings and events are continually tailored to fit the expectations of the group. Although when a marijuana circle has a novice on its hands, the instruction is generally verbal and calculated, much of the learning process is preverbal. It need not be consciously didactic: one may be taught by example, tone of voice, movements, laughter, a state of apparent ecstasy. Merely by looking around him, the novice senses that this is a group preparing to have fun, this is the type of situation in which people enjoy themselves. Thus, even when turning on for the first time, the neophyte will rarely experience something which is wildly out of line with group expectations. If he does, the initiate is "talked out" of them. The statistically few events that do occur contrary to the group's expectations are noteworthy for their rarity.

Since users most generally think of marijuana use as normal, healthy, appealing, and sybaritic, the novitiate absorbs mostly favorable definitions and expectations of what he is about to experience. Interpretations concerning the high emanating from the group become assimilated into the beginner's moral outlook, and most commonly his experiences are a reflection of these definitions. If use were condemned by users who saw themselves acting out of "compulsive" and "sick" motives, and who thought of smoking in morbid, self-flagellating terms, not only would the novice be unlikely to try the drug, but even if he ever did, his high would be experienced as unpleasant, distasteful, repellent and even psychotomimetic. This is not generally the case because each new user is insulated from negative experiences with the high by favorable definitions; it is the "legacy" which the marijuana subculture passes down to succeeding generations.

Curiosity is the dominant emotion of the neophyte at the time of his turn-on;[7] this is often mixed with excitement, apprehension, joy, or fear. It should be stated at the outset that I do not endorse the "forbidden fruit" argument. If marijuana use were not considered improper or immoral by the bulk of society, there is no doubt whatsoever that it would be more common. Social condemnation, particularly among one's peers, keeps down the condemned activity, although, obviously, the less significant the condemning individual or group is felt to be, the less effective the condemnation will be; it is even possible to find "negative reference groups." I would hold that one of the appeals of marijuana is *not* that it is abhorred by adult society; it does not represent rebellion or a rejection of adult values. Yet, its mystery, its underground character, the fact that it is clandestine and morally suspect—all lend an air of excitement and importance that would be absent otherwise. For the neophyte, the maintenance of a matter-of-fact attitude is almost impossible. Although use is not greater because it is forbidden, its contraband nature, at least in the beginning, make it special and outside the orbit of the everyday. The excitement is manufactured: it is a social artifact. Inexperienced users perceive its socially imputed gravity through cues ranging from the voice tone of marijuana participants to the reactions of the police to the discovery of marijuana possession. The more contact the user has with the drug and other users, the less "special" use becomes.

Users often draw parallels with sex; being turned on is seen as equivalent to losing one's virginity. Feelings of the specialness of one's activities and uniqueness dissolve with the growing awareness that many seemingly respectable individuals also smoke marijuana: "After being turned on, I realized that many straight types smoke, too. It's sort of like when a virgin has just been deflowered; she realizes that others must also be nonvirgins, too, after having experienced it herself," said a twenty-two-year-old law school student, a weekly smoker. In fact, there is often a certain degree of *disappointment* in the experience. The experience has been billed as bizarre, beautiful, frightening, orgiastic, but either pro or con, the descriptions are invariably *unusual*. "At first I thought it would be the passageway into heaven," a young man of Catholic parentage told me, somewhat disenchanted that it wasn't. "I expected a fantastic change," said a twenty-three-year-old woman writer about her experience of being turned on in a cafe in Tangiers; "I was disappointed," she added. "I was scared shit," a student in pharmacy told me about an experience six years earlier.

Aside from the expectation that the high would be much more spectacular, some of the disappointment stems from the fact that many initiates do not become high the first time that they smoke, or at least do not recognize it. Marijuana's effect is subtle, and is, as I have stated, quite dependent on the learning process. In Becker's words,

. . . the new user may not get high and thus not form a conception of the drug as something which can be used for pleasure. . . .

. . . being high consists of . . . the presence of symptoms caused by marijuana use and the recognition of these symptoms and their connection by the user with his use of the drug. It is not enough, that is, that the effects alone be present; alone, they do not automatically provide the experience of being high. The user must be able to point them out to himself and consciously connect them with having smoked marihuana before he can have this experience. Otherwise, no matter what actual effects are produced, he considers that the drug has had no effect on him.[8]

It is possible that the drug sometimes does not take effect on an individual who has smoked once or even a dozen times. A small proportion of individuals seem almost incapable of attaining a high, at least using conventional smoking techniques. Whether this is physiological or psychological, it is impossible at this point to determine. Many of these individuals have been socialized into the subculture, know the proper techniques and what to expect from them, have seen others enjoying pot, and yet never seem to cross the threshold of becoming high. More commonly, however, the reason for the lack of attainment of the high is inexperience. Among our respondents, 41 percent said that they did not become high the first time and 13 percent said that they weren't sure whether or not they were high. The attainment of the high, however, usually comes with experience. Twelve percent of our respondents said that they became high on their second attempt, 9 percent on their third, 8 percent on their fourth, and so on. Only seven individuals in our sample claimed never to have been high, and all but one had tried only half a dozen times or fewer. The completely resistant individual, although he does exist, is a relative rarity.

Of the various reasons offered for their lack of becoming high on the first attempt, the most common (twenty-seven individuals) was improper technique; fear and nervousness accounted for a dozen or so responses. Again, the sexual analogy seems relevant. Becoming high smoking marijuana is similar in many respects to the attainment of sexual orgasm, at least for the woman, in that:

1) It is more likely to occur when emotion is part of the relationship; the differential is greater, obviously, with sex than with pot.
2) It often does not occur with the first attempt.
3) With experience, its likelihood increases.
4) Some individuals seem especially invulnerable to it ever occurring; they seem to resist it, possibly for fear of losing control, or, for some reason, their bodies seem peculiarly incapable of attaining that blissful state.
5) Nervousness and fear reduce the likelihood.
6) Simple technique has a great deal to do with its attainment.
7) Some individuals (with sex, always women) wonder whether they have ever reached that state, since the line between attainment and "normalcy" is tenuous and the symptoms of attainment have to be learned.
8) Its importance is exaggerated to such a degree that the neophyte will often be puzzled as to what all the fuss is about.

It is only after repeated interaction and involvement with the marijuana subculture that some of these initial disappointments begin to evaporate, just as the recently deflowered girl gradually learns that the delights of sex blossom with time and nurturance. There is a progressive accretion of sensitivity to the subtle and not so easily discerned marijuana high; it takes time to learn how to enjoy marijuana, to absorb the prevailing group definition on the drug's pleasures and virtues. By interacting repeatedly with more experienced users, the neophyte takes their definitions of what the drug does to his body and mind as his own and eventually comes to experience those effects.

Among individuals acquainted with marijuana over a period of time—individuals who have used it on many occasions, who have seen others high, and who have participated in a variety of activities high—the drug becomes demythologized. Much of the excitement and awe of the new adventure gradually drains out of its use. It becomes taken for granted. At this point the propagandists step in and inform us that a jaded palate inevitably generates the desire for increasingly greater thrills and kicks. No one has successfully explained why this should be so; for some reason it appeals to common sense. The truth is the drug need not retain that mixture of fear, awe, and excitement in use to retain its appeal. Experienced users become comfortable with the marijuana high, much as they might enjoy making love with a spouse of long duration. By losing much of its subterranean character, marijuana does not necessarily lose its appeal. In fact, whatever uncomfortable or even psychotomimetic effects the drug might have had earlier, with limited experience, become dissipated with increased use. In general, experienced users describe their high in more favorable terms than the inexperienced. (Although individuals who do experience discomfort in use tend to discontinue smoking.) Simultaneously, the experience becomes increasingly less and less "apart" from the everyday, less and less discontinuous with it, and increasingly a normal and taken-for-granted element in one's day to day existence.

Among the more experienced users, marijuana comes to be regarded as an ordinary item in one's life—it becomes "no big deal." In fact, users of long duration have a difficult time switching back and forth from their taken-for-granted attitude toward pot to society's fearful and punitive stance. Many users do not regard marijuana as a drug—i.e., in a special and distinct and harmful category —just as few liquor drinkers will claim to be users of any drug, so unaccustomed are they to thinking of their drug of choice as anything of particular note. During the research, I went into a psychedelic book store in New York's East Village and asked the salesman, wearing long hair, beads, and bells and sandals, if they had any books on drugs. "What kind of drugs?" he asked. When I said marijuana, he replied, "Marijuana's not a drug." This theme emerged in the interviews. A twenty-three-year-old woman, a daily smoker of marijuana, told me, "I can't think of marijuana as being a drug—it's just pleasurable."

NOTES

1. Howard S. Becker, "Becoming A Marihuana User," *American Journal of Sociology* 59 (November 1953): 235–243.

2. In a study of the drug use of 432 "Yippies" in Chicago's Lincoln Park at the time of the 1968 Democratic National Convention, Zaks, Hughes, Jaffe, and Dolkart found that the most common reason claimed by the respondents for "starting on drugs" (i. e., for turning on)—marijuana was by far not only the most popular drug, but was most likely to have been the first drug used—was that he was *turned on by friends;* almost two-thirds of the sample (63 percent) gave that as their reason. (Cf. Table 6, p. 24.) Without an understanding of this process, this answer might seem a nonsequitur. But the fact that a friend (whose judgment we trust) gives us an opportunity to try a drug has a great deal to do with whether we ever turn on or not. An additional fifth of the sample (22 percent) gave "associaton with users" as a reason for turning on. See Misha S. Zaks, Patrick Hughes, Jerome Jaffe, and Marjorie B. Dolkart, "Young People in the Park: Survey of Socio-Cultural and Drug Use Patterns of Yippies in Lincoln Park, Chicago Democratic Convention, 1968" (Presented at the American Orthopsychiatric Association, 46th Annual Meeting, New York, March 30, to April 2, 1969), unpublished manuscript, 28 pp.

3. Herbert Blumer et al., *The World of Youthful Drug Use* (Berkeley: University of California, School of Criminology, January 1967).

4. Alan G. Sutter, "Worlds of Drug Use on the Street Scene," in Donald R. Cressey and David A. Ward, eds., *Delinquency, Crime, and Social Process* (New York: Harper & Row, 1969), p. 827.

5. John Kifner, "The Drug Scene: Many Students Now Regard Marijuana as a Part of Growing Up," *The New York Times,* January 11, 1968, p. 18.

6. A recent film, *Easy Rider,* released in 1969, in which marijuana is smoked nearly throughout, depicted a turning-on scene which contained the neophyte's fears: that he would become hooked on marijuana and that it would lead to harder stuff. This was laughed at by his initiators. The initiate was provided with instructions on how to smoke the joint. According to an interview with the film's director, actual marijuana was used in the smoking scenes. Hopper said, in the *Times* interview, "This is my 17th grass-smoking year. Sure, print it, why not? You can also say that that was real pot we smoked in *Easy Rider.*" See Tom Burke, "Will 'Easy' Do It for Dennis Hopper?" *The New York Times,* Sunday, July 20, 1969, D11, D16.

7. The Zaks et al., study found that curiosity was the second most often cited reason for turning on; over a third of their sample (37 percent) said that the reason for starting on drugs was curiosity, *op. cit.,* Table 6, p. 24.

8. Becker, *Outsiders* (New York: Free Press, 1963), pp. 48—49.

: *Chapter 7* :

The Effects of Marijuana

Introductory Considerations

As with other aspects of the drug, describing the marijuana high
has political implications. Both sides of the debate wish confirmation of their prejudices, and most facts presented will be distorted
to fit them. The postulate, accepted on faith, not fact, that marijuana is a "crutch" and an "escape from reality," and that man
ought to be able to live completely without recreational drugs naturally approaches the drug's effects in a negative way. Even if
harmless, the effects, whatever they may be, are *defined* as undesirable.

This aprioristic thinking dominates both sides of the dispute. The
pro side engages in the same mental gymnastics by deciding beforehand that marijuana can do no harm. It is easy to say that what we
need is less bias and more fact; more fundamental than facts themselves is the powerful tendency to read facts selectively. At least
two processes operate here: the likelihood of *accepting* one or
another fact as *true* depends on one's prior attitudes toward the
drug; and facts may be *interpreted* to mean many things since what
is a positive event to one person may be seen as supremely damaging to another. The description of being high by a user illustrates
this axiom: "I felt omnipotent and completely free. I'm a free soul,
a free person, and I often feel bigger and better than I am now."

The marijuana defender would see this as strong evidence for marijuana's beneficial effects. The antimarijuana forces would interpret the description as evidence of the fact that the drug is used as an ego-booster by spineless personalities; a person should be able to "face life" without the aid of artificial props. The goodness or badness of the events themselves clearly depends on how they are viewed.

Descriptions of the marijuana high run the gamut from pernicious to beatific; one's conceptions of the drug's impact are highly structured by ideological considerations. In the 1930s, widely believed stories were circulated, detailing massacres, rapes, widespread insanity, debauchery, and feeblemindedness as inevitable consequences of the use of the insidious weed.[1] One account, publicized nationwide, had a young man chopping his family to bits after a few puffs of marijuana. The blood has disappeared, but the controversy remains, and a novel element in the debate has been introduced. Whereas marijuana's adherents in the 1930s saw the drug's effects as being confined within a fairly limited scope, largely hedonistic and artistic in nature, today's smokers often extrapolate into philosophical and sociopolitical realms as well. Although it strains one's credulity to accept the notion that a marijuana "turn-on" of contemporary political, military and business figures will result in "everlasting peace and brotherhood," [2] this utopian fantasy is as much a fixture of the ideology of many of the drug's most committed propagandists as were the scare stories for the marijuana prohibitionists of the 1930s. Yet the question remains: What are the effects of marijuana?

This seemingly simple question is answerable only with major qualifications, specifications, and prefatory explanations. To pry into the subject, it might be fruitful to structure our thinking around a series of interlocking issues. To begin with, the question of *dosage* is crucial. Generally, other things being equal, the heavier the dosage of a given drug, the more extreme the effects, with some variations. Marijuana grown in different locations, under varying climatic and soil conditions, will differ in strength, which we explained earlier. Also, in general, hashish will produce more striking and noticeable effects than marijuana containing mostly leaves. It has been determined that the principle active chemical in marijuana is *tetrahydrocannabinol* (abbreviated THC). Thus, the most powerful effects may be obtained by administering the pure chemical to subjects. It is, therefore, meaningless to ask simply, "What is the effect of marijuana?" without specifying dosage.

A second qualification before detailing the effects of the drug involves prior marijuana experiences of the subject. A significant proportion of marijuana users did not become high the first time that they smoked the drug,[3] as pointed out in our chapter on "Becoming a Marijuana User." In part, much of this may be attributed to improper and inefficient technique. However, even with the most careful instruction and technique, some fail to become intoxicated. But when the neophyte does attain a high, an interesting phenomenon occurs. The effect of the drug on the newly initiated marijuana smoker appears to be highly dramatic and almost baroque in its lavishness. His laughter approachs hysteria. Insights are greeted with elaborate appreciation. His coordination might rival a spastic's. The experienced marijuana smoker, on the other hand, learns to handle his intoxication so that the noticeability to an outsider is almost nonexistent. He compensates for the effects of the drug, so that his coordination is no different from "normal." This is a learning process, not attributable to the direct pharmacological properties of the drug (which, however, sets limits on the compensatability of the subject). It is simply a characteristic that experienced users share and neophytes lack. Yet it is an important qualifying element in the marijuana picture.

In addition, many of the effects of the drug vary with the attitudes, personality, expectations, fears, and mood of the user; this is generally referred to as "set." One experience might be euphoric and wholly pleasurable; another might be uncomfortable and frightening, for the same drug, the same dosage, and the same person. No one has adequate explanation for this variation. Although the vast majority of all users report pleasant effects much of the time, a proportion will occasionally have an experience significantly different from the usual one. A very few users—who do not, for this reason, become regular users—report more or less consistently unpleasant experiences with the drug. Here, personality factors may be the controlling factor.

Some observers say that marijuana imposes behavior on the user, that the drug has effects that can be measured, that whatever happens to the human mind and body during a marijuana intoxication is a function of the drug so that the individual is said to be under its influence. To some degree, we have to admit that the drug is an "objective facticity." It is difficult to deny a certain degree of factorness of the drug's effect: the drug is not a zero or a cipher. There are neophytes who smoke oregano imagining their responses are due to the powers of marijuana. However, suggestibility has limits. Were all of the world's cannabis magically substituted for an inert substance that looked the same, it would become known at once. It would be foolish to deny that the drug has its effects. Now, this observation might seem blatantly obvious. Not so. Because the drug's pharmacology exists only as a potentiality, within which forms of behavior are possible as an "effect" of the drug. The effects of any drug are apprehended as subjective experience and experiencing a drug's effects must be learned. The subculture translates and anticipates the experience for the neophyte, powerfully shaping the experiences he is to have. The same bodily response will be subjectively apprehended in many different ways, and, in a sense, the "effect" is different. The important dimension is not simply, "What does it do?" This cannot be anwered until we know the answer to the question, "What does it mean?" What does it mean to the participant? How do the meanings of individuals relevant to him impinge on his conceptions of the experience? By itself, the simple physiological question is meaningless, since prior experiences and learning substantially alter what a drug does.

Another fundamental question connected with, and prior to, the effects of this drug is, "is the subject *high*?" The same quantity of marijuana administered to two subjects will produce a "bombed out of his mind" reaction in one and no response in the other. Although objective tests may be applied to determine this state, many users who report being high do not react very differently from their normal state. Many inexperienced users, of course, are not really sure whether they are high or not, and, as stated earlier, some users seem unusually resistant to becoming high. The point is, then, that whether the person is high or not is problematic, and if we want to know the impact of the drug, we must know this beforehand. The police make an issue of this point; they feel that *if* the promarijuana argument on the relative harmlessness of marijuana bears any authority at all, it is merely because the varieties of cannabis available in America are far weaker than varieties available elsewhere. The drug may be innocuous, but only because it is the very weakest varieties to which the American user is exposed. Were the drug legalized, we would be flooded with extremely potent varieties, causing some of the same kinds of debilitating and disastrous effects reported in the East:

American-grown cannabis is likely to be a fraud on the hopeful hippie in that its cannabinol content, in certain seasons and places, may approach what would be near-beer to the boozer. This marihuana is almost harmless except for asphyxiation from air pollution. The hippie's kick is a psychic kick. Chemically speaking, the victim often is not smoking marihuana, but burning underbrush. He is not the victim of a drug, but is the sucker of a hoax. There is enough of this gyp going on to help support the notion that marihuana is innocuous.[4]

(There is some cross-fertilization in regard to the language going on here; Donald Miller, Chief Counsel, Bureau of Narcotics and Dangerous drugs, in an article which justifies the present legal structure on marijuana, writes: ". . . many persons report they obtain no effects whatever when they use marihuana. They are not the victims of a drug, but merely have been deceived with a hoax. There is so much gyping going on that it helps support the notion that marihuana is innocuous. Chemically speaking, many . . . 'triers' of marihuana really have . . . become partially asphyxiated from polluted air.")[5]

The reader is seriously asked to believe that a great percentage of all marijuana users, even some experienced ones ("the hopeful hippie"), have never really been high, and that they are experiencing a placebo reaction. Actually, this point serves propaganda purposes: if anyone who has smoked marijuana has not been damaged in any way, he must not have gotten high. Thus protected, the antipot lobbyist is better able to defend the position that the drug is really dangerous. Actually, the position itself is something of a fraud. The placebo reaction occurs, of course, with no mean frequency, but the greater the amount of experience with the drug, the less likely it is that the subject has experienced either no reaction or nothing but a placebo reaction. In fact, the likelihood that a given person who has smoked marijuana more than, say, a dozen times, thinks that he has been high without actually experiencing what a truly experienced user would call a high, is practically nil. The experience has been described in such florid detail by so many more experienced users that he who has not attained it is eventually aware of it, and knows when he finally does attain it.

Throughout any discussion of the effects of marijuana, we must alert ourselves to the complexity of the equation. The simple question, "What are the effects of marijuana?" is meaningless. The answer to this query would have to be a series of further questions: Under what circumstances? At what dosage level? Engaged in what kinds of activities? Given what kind of legal and moral climate regarding marijuana use? All of these factors influence the nature, quality, and degree of response to the drug.

Yet, at the same time, we must not exaggerate the variability of marijuana's effects. Responses are to some degree systematic. We do not wish to suggest that individuals react randomly to the drug. The police will often make this assertion, in support of the dangers of marijuana: "Medical experts agree on the *complete unpredictability* of the effect of marijuana on different individuals." [6] The reason why this statement is nonsensical is that, of course, the effects of marijuana cannot be predicted with absolute certainty, though there will be a reasonably high degree of predictability. It is extremely important as to the kind of effect we wish to describe or predict. *Some* of the many effects of marijuana will be experienced by *nearly all* smokers who become high. Many other effects will be experienced by only a few users.

The Marijuana High: Experiments and Descriptions

Of the thousands of works describing the psychic and bodily effects of marijuana, the first to meet fairly strict standards of the application of scientific controls—that is, (1) standardized dosages were administered, (2) of actual marijuana[7] (3) in a "double blind" situation, (4) with sytematic measures used to study the effects, (5) to groups with varying degrees of experience with the drug (naive and experienced), (6) in a uniform environment—was published in December, 1968.[8] (Also, significantly, the drug was administered to a nonincarcerated population.) All of the previous studies were lacking in some of these respects, or were primarily anecdotal, informal, literary, or were based on the literal descriptions of the high by smokers, without checking the accuracy of their descriptions.

Conducted in Boston by pharmacologist-physician Andrew Weil

and psychiatrist, physician, and social psychologist, Norman Zinberg, this study established beyond question the generation of a few strictly biological effects of smoking marijuana and suggested the likelihood of others. It did, however, totally negate the possibility of some effects commonly associated with pot. The strictly physiological consequences of marijuana, the study found, were, first of all, highly limited, and second, extremely superficial in their impact. Most of the multifarious effects described in the literature are too ephemeral to be studied under rigid clinical controls, or simply turned out to be myths. The only positive effects which the Boston team could establish beyond dispute were a slight increase in the rate of heart beat, distinct reddening of the eyes, and probable dryness of the mouth.

This descriptive clinical study documented a few positive effects; it also demonstrated some negative ones as well. Not only is the public deluded into believing many myths about marijuana, but experienced marijuana smokers themselves accept a few. For instance, it is standard marijuana lore that, when high, one's pupils dilate. Yet careful measurement under the influence of the drug produced no such result; pupils remained the same size after administration.[9] How could such a myth be believed by individuals with countless hours of experience in the presence of others while smoking marijuana? The Weil-Zinberg team suggests the answer: marijuana smokers customarily consume the drug under conditions of subdued light, which would, in the absence of marijuana, produce dilated pupils anyway. This finding strongly underscores the need for controlled experimentation, with each of the suspected causal factors being isolated successively to test their impact. It also addresses itself to the possibility of empirically false beliefs having widespread currency among even the most knowledgeable of individuals.

This research team also turned up a negative finding with regard to marijuana's impairment of various skill and coordination functions among experienced users, an area in which it was thought to have substantial impact. Marijuana, it is said, impairs the ability to perform manual tasks and manipulations. For instance, it is claimed that the widespread use of the drug represents a massive danger to society because of its obvious deterioration of driving ability, thus increasing the likelihood of fatalities on the road.[10] "I ask the kids," a journalist intones, in a series of articles attempting to avert marijuana use in her readers, "If you have to fly someplace, which would you rather see your pilot take, a martini or smoke a marijuana cigarette?" [11] Aside from the inaptness of the comparison (since very few drinkers can become intoxicated on one martini, while most marijuana smokers do become high on one "joint"), the striking thing about the verbal gauntlet is that the author assumes that the answer is a foregone conclusion. In fact, *do* we know the answer? Which is, as a result of actual tests, the safer, and which is the more dangerous? Curiously, the assertion that it is far more dangerous to drive under the influence of marijuana has never been documented; it is assumed. After all, the role of alcohol in driving fatalities is only too well known; something like twenty-five thousand deaths every year from automobile accidents can more or less be directly attributed to the overindulgence of liquor. The reasoning is that if alcohol is dangerous, marijuana must, of necessity, be worse, because it is legally prohibited; moreover, the results of the two together can only be additive.

The only tests done on driving skills was completed a few months after the Boston experiments in the state of Washington. A team of researchers, including Alfred Crancer of the Washington State Department of Motor Vehicles, and James Dille, Chairman of University of Washington's Department of Pharmacology, conducted an experiment on simulated driving skills.[12] (Tests on actual driving conditions are planned.) The various driving functions were accelerator, signal, brake, speedometer, steering, and total test score; a total of 405 checks were made throughout the course of the entire experiment, so that a subject's total number of errors could range, theoretically, from zero to 405. Subjects were experienced marijuana users who were also acquainted with the liquor intoxication. They were administered the test (1) high on marijuana—they smoked two joints, or 1.7 grams of marijuana (as a comparison, Weil and Zinberg's subjects were given half a gram as a low dosage and two grams as a high dosage); (2) intoxicated on alcohol (two drinks were administered, and a Breathalyzer reading taken); and (3) in a "normal" state of no intoxication. What were the results of this driving test? The overall findings were that marijuana did *not* impair motor skills, that there were almost *no* differences driving high on marijuana and normal. The total number of driving errors for the normal control conditions was 84.46; the total number of errors while driving high on marijuana was 84.49, a trivial difference, well within random fluctuation. (The only significant difference between the marijuana-high subjects and the same subjects "normally" was that high users, on the Crancer test, had to check their speedometers more.)

The same could not be said for alcohol. Being intoxicated on liquor significantly diminished one's ability to take the driving test without error. The total number of errors for the subjects under the influence of alcohol was 97.44. Crancer, the principal investigator in this experiment, concludes from it that the drunk driver is a distinctly greater threat than the high marijuana smoker. He is quoted, "I, personally, would rather drive in a car where the chauffeur is high on pot than drive in a car where the chauffeur is high on alcohol." [13] However, it is difficult to extrapolate from this test, done in an artificial setting, to actual road conditions; Crancer himself designed the test, and found an extremely close correlation between test scores and actual driving skills. But only real-life driving experiments will answer these points definitively; in any case, at the very least the Washington State driving tests certainly cast doubt on the fears of many propagandists that widespread marijuana use will result in an even greater salughter on the nation's highways than prevails today. It is even conceivable that were pot substituted for alcohol in many drivers, the death toll would actually drop, not rise.

Certainly no one would argue that driving under the influence of marijuana is preferable to being without the influence of any drug. But Crancer speculated beyond the test-driving scores in saying that his "feelings and observations, and that's all they are—they are not scientific conclusions—lead me to believe that marijuana has a submissive effect on users." [14] The effects of the drug subjectively exaggerate the sensation of speed, and the high driver often thinks that he is going much faster than he actually is. Some of my own informants report driving to the side of the road because they thought they were traveling at a frighteningly rapid speed, when, in fact, they were driving well under the speed limit. But it is difficult to see how marijuana could possibly *improve* driving performance. However, there is incomplete evidence that high on marijuana, drivers often drive more slowly than normally, out of fear. The proposition that the high driver is no worse than normal is definitely worth exploring; it is conceivable that further tests will reveal little or no deterioration in driving ability when high on marijuana. But the hypothesis that the marijuana high deteriorates motor skills far less than alcohol is, it may safely be said, firmly established. There is no doubt that, in the typical case, marijuana affects the ability to drive much less than alcohol.

The Crancer test results, by extension, would seem compatible with the Boston team's research. Various tests by Weil and Zinberg were administered to both inexperienced and experienced subjects under normal and marijuana-intoxicated conditions. These tests were "pursuit rotor" test, measuring muscular coordination and attention; the "continuous performance" test, measuring ability at sustained attention; and the "digit symbol substitution" test, measuring cognitive functioning. Most generally, the results consistently showed that among experienced marijuana smokers, no impairment whatsoever was discerned in the ability to perform cognitive and muscular tasks, whereas impairment was significant among inexperienced subjects. Experienced users were fully as able to perform motor skills and cognitive functions while under the influence of the drug as in a normal state. Although further research is needed in the *kinds* of motor skills in question, this finding powerfully illustrates the need to support one's prejudices with empirical facts. To justify marijuana's present legal status, it is necessary to use damaging "facts" about marijuana, such as its impairment of driving skills, even though they are imaginary in character. Recent research shows the argument that increased marijuana use would contribute considerably to automobile fatalities to be largely specious. Nonetheless, it will continue to be invoked for years to come, because of the need for such an argument. The belief that marijuana makes one a far more dangerous driver is believed, and will continue to be believed, even though the chances are great that it is scientifically false. Yet, scientifically false beliefs can exert a powerful hold on men's minds.

The Boston research points to the clear presence of almost complete compensation in the case of marijuana. The ability of the intoxicated marijuana user to compensate for his state in pursuing motor tasks is 100 percent. With alcohol, there is partial compensation. The alcoholic will be able to perform better than the drunk man once he has had a little experience with alcohol, but the experienced drinker, sober, always performs better than the experienced drinker, intoxicated. With marijuana, on the other hand, there seems to be complete compensation. However, the inexperienced user, with little or no experience with the drug's effects, will suffer a distinct loss in motor skills and coordination, and will be unable to compensate. (The Crancer driving tests, on the other hand, found no difference between inexperienced and experienced subjects; subjects who had never smoked marijuana before the test performed just as well when high on pot as the experienced users did.) It is a relevant question as to how quickly compensation takes place for both marijuana and alcohol. I suspect that after a very small number of experiences with marijuana—perhaps a half-dozen—full compensation takes place, whereas with alcohol, even partial compensation takes place only after long conditioning with its effects. The question of the dose-relatedness of marijuana's impact on coordination is relevant, although not fully answered. The Weil research team supplied its subjects with low and high dosages, the former two cigarettes of a quarter of a gram each, and the latter two cigarettes of one gram each. Not too surprisingly, with the inexperienced subjects, impairment was distinctly dose-related, i.e., the stronger the marijuana administered, the more of a negative impact the drug had on their coordination. However, with the experienced marijuana smokers, a higher dosage of the drug had no additional impact on their skills and coordination; they were able to perform equally well normally, slightly high, and very high.

Because of obvious possibilities for distortions, as with the pupil dilation myth, pharmacologists are uncomfortable leaving the sphere of the directly observable, the experimentally verifiable, the clearly empirically demonstrable. The sociologist, being somewhat more detached from the scientific tradition, is less careful about what he accepts as a "fact." He usually bases his data on *reported* statements, rather than direct observation. Now, this has both advantages and drawbacks. A competent pharmacologist, performing a carefully controlled experiment, is far more certain that what he says is true; it is less necessary to repeat the same experiment, but if it is repeated, he has more confidence than a sociologist that the results will be confirmed. Although a sociologist will more often be wrong than a scientist working within a firm experimental tradition, he will be able to cover a wider field. By including within his purview the verbal reports of the individuals whose behavior he is studying, he includes a range of data which may be highly significant, and which may tell us a great deal about human behavior. Since I am a sociologist, verbalized reports by my respondents

forms a rich lode of information for me. Keeping in mind the realization of large possibilities for distortion, we should nonetheless be
able to piece together a more complete picture of the effects of the
drug than a pharmacologist is able to do, although one which is
more open to question since it is less tightly tied down by unques-
tionable, demonstrable fact.

We should keep in mind the *level of meaning* at which we are
aiming. With some phenomena, we may look at the marijuana
smoker as a kind of scientist, reporting on the accuracy of an observation, which we can check. We have an independent means of
measuring, for instance, reddening of the eyes. Aside from asking
the user, we can simply look at his eyes. Then, we can check our
observations, which we are sure are correct, against the descriptions
of the marijuana user, which may be subject to error. If there is a
discrepancy, as with pupil dilation, we should supply an explanation for the discrepancy. However, there are vast realms wherein
the ultimate validating device is the experience of the user, where
the subjective grasp of the experience *is* the experience, where external verification is not only impossible but meaningless. It is a
level of meaning complete within itself. And it is here that we must
part company with the more careful pharmacologist.

Psychologists tell us that there are two analytically distinct processes involved in sense perception. We have, first, the primary functions, whereby the sense organs are stimulated directly. Certain
sounds are measurably louder than others and, other things being
equal, the mind will apprehend the louder sound as being louder.
However, the directly perceived sense must, in order to be actually
felt, be transmitted to the brain. Thus, there exists a secondary
function associated with sense perception, and that is how the brain
receives the message. The mind might *feel* differently about one
sound as another; perceptions, then, might also stem from secondary functions, or what a brain decides to do with the sense impression it receives. The mind can deal with similar sense impres-
sions in very different ways, according to their subjective significance. It can, for instance, subjectively exaggerate the significance
of a "quiet" sound, while minimizing that of a "loud" sound.

This distinction comes extravagantly into play with the psychoactive effects of marijuana. For the overwhelming majority of all of
the effects described by marijuana smokers are those involved with
subjective experience. The directly observable consequences of the

drug are few, minimal in importance, and superficial in impact. Those effects which can only be gotten at by asking the user to describe them are extravagant, elaborate, and extremely significant. These effects are wholly subjective and beyond the reach of scientific tools and instruments. We are in the area of "thinking makes it so." The experience is defined in its totality by the subject himself. The mind assimilates and, in a sense, becomes the experience. The subject apprehends a reality, explores a subjective realm which reverberates in his own psyche, accepts the total reality of a given phenomenon without regard to external validation, and in a sense defines the configurations of the experience completely.

For this level of meaning we must, of course, ask the marijuana user what are the effects of the drug. We must rely on his descriptions of the high to know anything about the subjective lineaments of the experience. In our interview we included the question:

I want you in as much detail as you can, describe to me everything that happens to you when you get high: the high and everything else. Try to describe it to a person who has never been high before; please include everything that you feel, think, perceive, etc., whatever it is.

Of our 204 respondents, seven said that they had never been high, and six said that they had, but claimed not to be able to describe it in any way, holding that its reality was too subjective and elusive for description. Our information, therefore, is based on the 191 individuals who said that they had been high and offered to describe their experience. It must be remembered that this was an open-ended question, with no attempt to structure the responses in any way. This has both virtues and flaws. On the one hand, we did not force any responses on the interviewees. On the other hand, their answers might, by their own admission, be incomplete; they did not necessarily think of all the effects of the drug in an artificial interview situation, to a stranger. However, we assume that the ones they mentioned will be most salient to them, a not unreasonable assumption, although one not in every instance correct. A structured question will also yield a far higher overall response rate. If we had asked our interviewees directly whether or not marijuana had an impact on, say, their conception of time, more than one-quarter would have agreed that it did. Every effect would have drawn greater agreement, but the rank-order of effects should be roughly the same with the two techniques. This contention is born out when our data are compared with studies wherein a direct closed-choice question is asked for each effect. For instance, in an informal study of seventy-four marijuana users in New York, 91 percent agreed that marijuana made them feel more relaxed, 85 percent said that being high makes music sound better, 66 percent said that the drug helps a person feel more sociable at a party, and 35 percent claimed that it helps a person understand himself better (62 percent disagreed with the last effect).[15] The structured question, however, was unworkable for my study, due to the diversity of responses; we could not have offered every possible effect as an alternative, for we would have had no time for any other questions. If and only if we remember two methodological qualifications will our analysis of the responses be meaningful:

1) The *form* of the study instrument—open-ended or forced choice—gives us results that are superficially different (the magnitude of the responses, for instance), but fundamentally the same (the order of the responses).

2) Individuals who do not mention a given effect on our open-ended question are not thereby automatically agreeing that marijuana does not have that effect on them—they just did not think of it at that moment in that situation (although we do have a certain amount of confidence that those who did not mention the effect were *less* likely to experience it than those who did mention it).

Overviewing the responses elicited, we see that there are over 200 totally distinct effects described. (We have presented only those which ten or more subjects mentioned; there are almost 150 effects each of which was mentioned by fewer than ten respondents.) Sixty-four of these were proffered by single individuals, completely idiosyncratic responses that could not in any way be classified with other responses which were somewhat similar. For instance, one individual said that she had the feeling of "being sucked into a vortex." Another reported more regular bowel movements while intoxicated. A third said that she could feel her brains dripping out of her ears. In addition to the sixty-four unique and therefore totally unclassifiable responses, there were twenty-eight where only two respondents agreed that marijuana had that effect on them. However valid these responses might be to the individual himself, they are not useable to us, since they are still quite idiosyncratic.

Although the diversity of the responses was in itself an interesting finding, the picture was not totally chaotic. Each individual offered an average of roughly ten different effects of the drug as a description of the high. Some of these effects were offered independently by a large percentage of the interviewees although, curiously, none attracted a majority; every effect described was given by a minority of the sample. That is, in spite of the huge diversity in the responses, some agreement prevailed.

Marijuana users seem to describe the effects of the drug in overwhelmingly favorable terms. Certainly the vast majority of the effects mentioned would be thought positive if the judge did not know that marijuana touched off the state in question. Let us suppose that we have been told that the list characterizes how some people react to a warm spring day; our sense would be that they think well of its effects. Thus, most of the characteristics of the marijuana high, as described by its users, would be looked at as beneficial. Yet with the knowledge that the triggering agent was marijuana, the judge reinterprets his favorable opinion and decides that the effect is in actuality insidious and damaging; the question then becomes a moral rather than a scientific one, with the judge being thrown back on his second line of defense—'Why should anyone need an artificial stimulus anyway; isn't reality sufficient?' But in spite of one's ideological stance, marijuana's effects remains to be described.

TABLE 7-1

Effects of Marijuana: Responses by Users

	N	Percent
More relaxed, peaceful, calmer; marijuana acts as a tranquilizer	88	46
Senses in general are more sensitive, perceptive	69	36
Think deeper, have more profound thoughts	60	31
Laugh much more; everything seems funny	55	29
Exaggeration of mood; greater subjective impact, emotional significance	48	25
Time seems slowed down, stretched out, think more time has passed	44	23
Become more withdrawn, introverted, privatistic	42	22
Generally, feels nice, pleasant, enjoyable, fun, good, groovy	40	21
Mind wanders, free-associates, stream of consciousness	40	21
Feel dizzy, giddy, lightheaded	39	20
Become tired, lazy, lethargic, don't want to move	37	19
Feel light, airy, floating, elevated	35	18
Feel "happy"	35	18
Forget easily, have memory gaps, can't remember things	34	18
Feel freer, unrestrained, uninhibited	34	18
Stimulation of senses more enjoyable	34	18

Table 7–1 (*cont'd.*)

	N	Percent
Become hungry, want to eat more	32	17
Hear music better, musical ear sharper, more sensitive, accurate	32	17
Enjoy music more, greater pleasure from listening to music	30	16
Feel paranoid	28	15
Have hallucinations	28	15
Feel sleepy	26	14
Care less about everything, worry less, don't give a damn	25	13
Become erotically aroused, marijuana acts as an aphrodisiac	25	13
Mouth and throat feel dry	24	13
Concentrate better, become more involved in anything	24	13
Selective concentration: concentrate on one thing, shut out all else	23	12
Can communicate with others better	22	12
Euphoria, ecstasy, exhiliration	22	12
Sense of depersonalization: being cut off from myself	22	12
Food tastes better	20	10
Tend to fixate on trivial things	20	10
Feel secure, self-confident, get a sense of well-being	20	10
Able to understand others better, their meaning and being	20	10
The pleasure of touching is greater, touch more sensuous	19	10
Feel depressed	19	10
Tend to talk a lot more	19	10
Hear better, auditory sense more acute, hearing more sensitive	18	9
Colors appear to be brighter, more vivid	17	9
More uncoordinated, clumsier, motor skills impaired	17	9
Sex is more enjoyable	16	8
Become pensive, introspective, meditative	16	8
Senses become numb; marijuana acts as an anesthetizer	15	8
Body feels warm	15	8
Other people annoy me more, find fault in others	15	8
My vision is clearer, sight improved, see more, see more detail	15	8
Enjoy dancing more	14	7
Subconscious comes out; the real you emerges, one's truer self	14	7
Feel a sense of unity in the universe, a sense of oneness	14	7
Asthetic impulse greater, enjoy art works more	14	7
Feel more nervous	14	7
I feel thirsty	14	7
Skin feels tingly	14	7
Become outgoing, gregarious, convivial, extroverted	13	7
Eyes become hot, heavy, bloodshot, puffy	12	6
Body feels heavy	12	6
Sense of touch improved, more sensitive, can feel things sharply	12	6
Mind works more quickly, mind races	11	6
Experience synesthesia phenomena	11	6
Become more active, want to move around more	11	6
Feel a sense of unreality of everything around me	10	5

There is an abundance of striking contradictions in the effects described. The drug, it would appear, is associated with opposite effects on different individuals—and even on the same individual at different times. Yet these dualities are specifically located with certain effects and not others. Only one individual said that music sounded worse high, another that it sounded dimmer, and a third that it sounded strange; these responses are obviously negligible next to those who reported greater acuteness and appreciation of music while high. Yet many characteristics attracted mutually exclusive responses. Table 7–2 lists some of the more arresting paradoxes.

TABLE 7–2

Contradictions in Effects Described (percent)

More sensitive (36)	vs. numb, de-sensitizer (8)
Introverted (22)	vs. extroverted (7)
Emotion exaggerated (25)	vs. care less about everything (13)
Feel happy (18), things seem funny (29)	vs. feel depressed (10)
Mind wanders (21)	vs. greater concentration (13)
Feel paranoid (15)	vs. feel more secure (10)
More relaxed (46)	vs. feel more nervous (7)
Talk a lot (10)	vs. difficulty talking (8)
Time slowed down (23)	vs. time speeded up (4)
Feel light, floating (18)	vs. feel heavy (6)
Feel warm (8)	vs. feel cold (3)
Feel lethargic (19)	vs. feel more active (6)
Depersonalization (12)	vs. your true self emerges (7)
Touch more acute (6), fun (10)	vs. numb, de-sensitizer (8)
Mind more profound (31)	vs. fixate on trivia (10)
Selective concentration (12)	vs. synesthesia (6)

Many of these responses were highly conditional. The impact of marijuana seems to vary by mood and setting, as we mentioned, and our interviewees made it clear that the drug affected them in different ways at different times. For instance, nearly all of the descriptions including "feel depressed" as an effect of marijuana were prefaced by the qualification that only if I feel depressed beforehand does marijuana make me feel *more* depressed. The drug is often tagged with the power to heighten one's present mood, so that a pre-high mood of elation will yield to an even more exquisite feeling of elation, while a depression beforehand will become an even deeper depression.

We must bear in mind the fact that such an investigation can inherently yield only limited and selective information. However, this is also true of laboratory reports, which only display one facet of the drug crystal. Yet, piecing together several incomplete stories might very well give us a more comprehensive one. In asking the marijuana smoker the effects of the drug on himself, we tap only the subjective vein, a valuable but fragmentary source. This information should properly complement clinical findings, not contradict them. Thus, since we have asked for the effect of the drug on the person taking it, we have largely sidestepped the objective-subjective dilemma which is so often a source of confusion. We do not ask the smoker to be a scientist, reporting objectively on drug effects, but to re-create the drug experience itself, to convey the expressive character of the marijuana high.

One-third of the responses to the open-ended question reported that their senses were more receptive, more sensitive. We straddle two realms here. Tests can be constructed to measure the ability of the subject to discern stimuli. But for the subjective impact of sense-stimulation, we have to abandon the laboratory approach, because it does not tell us anything; we must ask the subject himself. Most responses have this dual character. And the subjective meaning of phenomena and sense-impressions forms a vast and uncharted territory, with a logic and integrity of its own—yet one of immense significance.

Why should music be so often singled out as a locus wherein marijuana is said to have such a pronounced impact? There are, after all, five senses, thousands of sources of sound, an infinitude of possible changes in thinking, doing things, feeling; why music? There are at least three explanations:

1) The physiological and psychological explanation. There actually is something about the effects of marijuana that relates specifically to music, to rhythm, movement, sound, and pitch.
2) The culture explanation. Marijuana smokers happen to be people who enjoy music and merely project onto marijuana, which they also enjoy, the positive effects of *any* activity toward which they feel positively.
3) The logistical and ecological explanation. It just happens that, given the personnel and the setting (in one's living room for the most part), it is highly likely that music is one of the activities in which marijuana users will be engaged while high.

There is no doubt that reasons (2) and (3) operate powerfully; the question is, do they account for *all* of the variance? Is there any pharmacological thrust at all?

A quarter of a century ago, an objective test of musical talent was done on incarcerated individuals, experienced with marijuana's effects, who had been administered parahexyl, a marijuana-like compound.[16] The study found that the drug did not increase musical ability. The typical test result (except for rhythm) was to improve very slightly without the drug as a practice effect, and then to drop back to the original, pre-practice level when high. Although the magnitude of the differences was extremely small, this was a consistent pattern.

However, the Seashore test measures neither musical talent nor ability. What it does measure is the ability to discern differences in pitch, loudness, rhythm, time, and timbre in a laboratory setting. We have to guess as to the effect of the drug in an actual music-playing situation. In any case, this objective test has nothing to do with the subjective impact of music on the high listener. And in this realm, the evidence is overwhelming that marijuana stimulates a much more powerful identification, appreciation, and feeling for the music. The music means more when high, musical ability or not. "My most intense highs are when I listen to music," I was told by a twenty-seven-year-old mother. "I hear more. I hear five different levels at the same time. I can see the vibrations of the strings. I can identify exactly with what the composer was feeling and thinking when he composed the music. I am *in* the music, engulfed by it. It's happening *through* me." Another respondent, a twenty-year-old salesman, specifically mentioned the synaesthesia phenomenon as a catalyst for enjoying music more:

Once, listening to Wagner, I had three visions. I was a Pegasus horse, flying through the air, with hundreds of smaller-type horses spanning out behind me, all colors, like a peacock. I was also a spirit, soaring through space. The third one was, I envisioned myself, I was crawling on the ground, watching flowers bloom and little animals crawling around. I've always enjoyed music more high than straight. Music has a visual correspondent.

In the interview, I asked a specific question on music (as well as sex and food): "What is music like when you are high?" If this question failed to elicit a meaningful response, I then asked the interviewee to compare the experience of listening to music high on marijuana with listening to it "straight." About 85 percent said they had actually listened to music while high, partly a testimony to the fact that music is a fixture in the marijuana mythology—everyone knows that listening to music while high is *the* thing to do—and partly a simple matter of the logistic fact that marijuana is smoked in one's living room. But is there a physiological component as well? Out of this music-listening contingent, 173 individuals, 10 percent felt that music was more or less the same, high or straight; it sounded no better and no worse. Two individuals thought that music sounded worse high, and preferred to listen to it while not under the influence of marijuana. All of the rest thought that music sounded better, that the high experience improved the listening experience.

Their reasons varied, however. As for the dominant and first mentioned reason for this, 40 percent said that their ability to become subjectively involved in the music, their emotional identification with it and appreciation of it, was heightened. They could "get into" the music better and became, in a sense, *part* of the music. About one quarter (23 percent) claimed that they could separate out the various instruments, sounds, and levels of sound, better appreciating the elaborate interweaving of sounds occurring in a musical composition. Some even likened listening high to having a built-in stereo set. The sounds actually seemed physically separated; one respondent felt that he could hear the notes of an organ bouncing off the ceiling, while the other sounds of the piece were off somewhere else in the room. Related to this perception was the sensation that they could hear one sound only, while all of the other sounds seemed subdued; there appeared to be some sort of ability to concentrate selectively on a single instrument, tune, sound, or level. Ten individuals, or 6 percent of the high music listeners, claimed that this was the first and most dominant characteristic of listening to music while smoking marijuana. Seventeen percent said merely that their hearing was more acute, that being high improved their listening ability. And 6 percent mentioned the synesthesia phenomenon, claiming that listening had a visual correspondent. They could see the music while listening to it.

Another of the more puzzling and intriguing products of the marijuana high that our interviews tapped remains its impact on the subject's perception of the passage of time. About a quarter of our respondents claimed that under the drug's influence they sensed much more time had passed than actually had. Time, in other words, seems to move extraordinarily slowly. Now, the positivistically inclined clinician will see this as a "distortion." It might, however, be more fruitful to look at time in a more relativistic sense. The division of the day into minutes and hours of standard length is only one of many possible ways of looking at the passage of time. Time also has a subjective element, a kind of organic flow. Under certain circumstances, a visceral grasp of time might coincide with a mechanistic one where, in laboratory terms, the subject will be able to judge time "correctly." Under other conditions, the two will be at variance with one another. Yet it is too narrow to view the mechanical measurement of time as its one true measurement; this may be expressed in many ways, for different purposes. The subject's "erroneous" estimation of time may have a powerful internal validity. We are reminded of Hans Castorp's words in Mann's *Magic Mountain*: "But after all, time *isn't* actual. When it seems long, then it is long; when it seems short, why, then it is short. But how long, or how short, it actually is, that nobody knows."

In the Boston experiments, three out of the nine inexperienced users overestimated the passage of time under the influence of a low dosage, while four did so with a high dosage. (No report was given for the experienced users, who may have learned to compensate for the time-altering effect of the drug.) In this case, our informal reports and the laboratory findings to some extent corroborate one another. It is impossible at this point to locate the source of this phenomenon, but it is possible that the exaggeration of mood described by my informants might have a good deal to do with it. Somehow, the drug is attributed with the power to crowd more "seeming" activity into a short period of time. Often nothing will appear to be happening to the outside observer, aside from a few individuals slowly smoking marijuana, staring into space and, occasionally, giggling at nothing in particular, yet each mind will be crowded with past or imagined events and emotions, and significance of massive proportions will be attributed to the scene, so that activity will be imagined where there is none. Each minute will be imputed with greater significance; a great deal will be thought to have occurred in a short space of time. More time will be conceived of as having taken place. Time, therefore, will be seen as being more drawn-out. One of our respondents, a twenty-six-year-old secretary, expressed it this way: "Time is different. You think it may take like *five years* to pick up a cigarette."

Marijuana's reported effect on memory is one of the more fascinating aspects of the drug's impact; almost one-fifth of the respondents said that, while high, they tended to forget simple things, that their memory seemed to be impaired by the drug. Psychologists divide memory into three zones, corresponding functionally to three areas of the brain; these are immediate, recent, and long-term memory. The marijuana smoker never forgets who he is, who his friends are, or where he is, but he may forget what he has been saying just ten seconds before. Weil and Zinberg pinpoint this speech impairment to marijuana's selective impact on the various memory functions in the brain:

If this effect can be demonstrated, it is likely that it is, itself, a manifestation of a more general acute effect of marihuana on a specific mental function: namely, an interference with ultra-short (or immediate) memory. By immediate memory we mean memory over the past few seconds. To be more precise, the interference seems to be with retrieval of information while it is an immediate memory storage; once it passes into the next (recent-memory) storage, it again seems to be easily accessible to consciousness.[17]

Whatever the physiological foundation of the effect, my informants commonly report it occurring. One user told me: "I can't remember what I said two seconds after I said it. I'm unaware of whether I actually said anything or not, even just after I've said it." In fact, most of the activities which involve forgetfulness while high take place when the subject is *talking*. This is an event which is both *likely* to occur and is relatively *short-term*. Thus the concentration on talking as a memory-impaired locus.

Let us consider hunger. It is an important component of the marijuana subculture that the drug makes you hungry. There seems, however, to be no physiological basis for the hunger. Some of the descriptions were so pungent that it is difficult to believe that some sort of physiological mechanism does not back them up: "I get a ravenous hunger high. When I start eating, my hunger is frightening. I could eat my finger if it got in the way." *Hyperphagia*, simply eating more, is common among high marijuana users, but the physiological basis for it is obscure. Yet it would be a mistake to throw out the observation, merely because it is not grounded in biochemical fact.

Pot's impact on taste was almost as influential. In fact, since there is no pharmacological reason for the hunger, it may perhaps be accounted for by the fact that the subject wishes to eat more because he knows that the food will taste much better. The idea of food suddenly seems much more attractive. Taste was reported as fabulously improved, almost a wild and orgasmic adventure. One of our respondents said that he rolled on the floor in ecstasy after eating some raspberries, so exquisite did they taste. Another respondent, a twenty-eight-year-old woman artist and art teacher, clearly delineated this distinction between the simple desire to eat more and a true, physiologically-based hunger, a hunger in the stomach rather than in the mind: "I love to eat when I'm high. I'm more interested in food. I don't think it's a matter of appetite; it's not hunger, it's mostly interest. Food tastes more interesting." Some of our most interesting and dramatic interview descriptions of the marijuana high were located in this impact on the subject's hunger and taste. The following account is presented by an eighteen-year-old college coed who was high for the first time two weeks before the interview. She smoked in her dormitory room with her roommate, who was a regular smoker:

Throughout the whole thing, every time we'd go to the cupboard, we'd see this big bottle of Cremora, and we just had to find a use for it; it was like an obsession. And finally (laughs) we got some tuna fish, and we found a use for it. We mixed up the Cremora and water to make tuna fish stew—we didn't have any mayonnaise—and we used it like mayonnaise. And we thought it was delicious (laughs). And we kept making more, and we devoured it, and then we realized what we were eating. Except at the same time, we felt, I felt, natural, except, you know, this is, like, stupid, we're eating Cremora and tuna fish, and it's horrible, and everybody will think we're absolutely nuts. But meanwhile, it was delicious (laughs). And the whole time, I felt, like, the things I was doing might be silly, but they felt very natural.

Hunger and taste was another question which I singled out specifically; 150 respondents, or about 75 percent of the sample, said that they had eaten food while they were high. Of this 150, six said that there was no difference between eating high and eating straight, that marijuana had no effect on the nature of the eating experience. Eight percent said that the experience was worse in some way; they had less of an appetite, or the food tasted worse, and that they did not enjoy the experience of eating food when they were high. Thirty-eight percent said that the most dominant characteristic about being high and eating was that one's appetite was stimulated; one had a tremendous appetite while high. Thirty-one percent said that the food tasted more delicious high than ordinarily, that eating was a more enjoyable experience. Eleven percent said, merely, that they were more acutely aware of taste, that they could discern the various tastes more accurately while high. The remaining respondents said that they were more aware, above all, of the *texture* of the food while high, that the most important thing was that they suddenly desired unusual combinations of foods, that they wanted to eat weird foods they had never considered before, and that they had a special craving for *sweet* things.

We should also expect sexual activity to be closely intertwined with, and powerfully influenced by, smoking marijuana, and in this, our expectations are well supported. Three-quarters of our interviewees said that they had experienced sex while high on marijuana. We asked several specific questions on the difference between sex high on marijuana and sex normally.

First I asked, "Do you think being high on marijuana stimulates your sex interest, or not?" More than a third of the respondents said that marijuana had no effect on their sexual desire. Five percent said that marijuana had a negative effect, that it turned them off sexually. Thirteen percent said that the effect depends on their mood or on their sexual partner. In this group, a common response among the women was that marijuana acts as a sexual stimulant when they're with someone with whom they're already intimate, but when they smoke with a stranger, the prospect of sex becomes even more distasteful than ordinarily. For these women, marijuana seems to polarize sexual desire. But 44 percent, a strong plurality, replied that marijuana definitely increased their sexual desire.

Next, I asked, "Is your enjoyment of sex any different high?" The respondents were less divided on this question. An overwhelming majority, 68 percent, replied that marijuana increased their sexual enjoyment, that their orgasmic pleasure was heightened by the drug. Yet most scientists claim that in physiological terms marijuana lacks an aphrodisiac effect. If anything, it tends to reduce desire and to dull the sexual areas. Norman Taylor, a botanist, writes, "As to being a sex-excitant, marijuana appears to be just the opposite." [18] Constantinos Miras, a Greek pharmacologist and one of the drug's severest critics, disclosed to a seminar at the UCLA Department of Pharmacology that marijuana actually impairs sexuality, and when administered to rats, their rate of "reproductive activity" declined 90 percent.[19] If, physiologically, marijuana is neutral—or even negative—to sexuality, why are so many people sexually turned on by it? Why, after smoking the faddish banana, don't its users descend from a trial high to discover that it is neutral to sex desire and enjoyment?

Consider the mythology. Its use has traditionally been associated with the dramatic loss of sexual inhibition, and with what were thought to be the inevitable consequences: depravity, degradation, shame. Marijuana, according to an historic description, completely inflames the erotic impulses and leads to revolting sex crimes. For years, propaganda from the press assisted the Federal Bureau of Narcotics' campaign to nurture an evil image. An account written in the 1930s chronicles the degradation of a young girl lured into smoking:

Her will power dropped away from her like a rent garment, leaving her a tractable, pliant creature, as exposed to chance suggestion as if her soul had been naked to the wind.[20]

The unfortunate girl so discarded her inhibitions that she accepted proposals from strangers. When she came to her senses, she was so mortified that she committed suicide. $B.S.!$

The sex-loaded invectives of the antimarijuana campaign may have been a tactical blunder. They seem to have attracted more recruits than they discouraged. Sociologists and psychologists stress the power of mood, expectation, social conditioning, setting, and myth in shaping the nature of the drug experience. And our mood, expectations, social conditioning, setting and myths have long associated marijuana with sex. We have learned to associate it with sensuousness and carnality, with hedonism and physical gratification. And so it stimulates those very reactions which are called debauchery by its critics and rapture by its adherents.

The human, unlike the caged rat, has a broad latitude in shaping the nature of his environment, even of his own body chemistry. Man's somatic responses are often influenced more by what he thinks than by biological and chemical imperatives; in fact, it can happen that what he thinks actually becomes his biological and chemical imperative. Thus the user's attitude toward marijuana may determine what happens to his body when he smokes it. It is only in the narrowest sense that the drug is not a sexual stimulant; that is, in the sense that it will not excite mindless, laboratory-located animal tissue. But many human marijuana users report an actual increase in sexual desire and sexual pleasure. Part of the reality may be analyzed as a "self-fulfilling prophecy." With marijuana's reputation, even a placebo could carry a sexual stimulus.

Women seem to respond more strongly than men to pot as an aphrodisiac. Exactly half the women said that the drug increased their sexual desire, as opposed to only 39 percent of the men. Two related explanations come to mind: (1) marijuana is an aphrodisiac for women because of its cultural association with sex: women are more likely to think themselves into becoming excited; and (2) women need an excuse to justify their desire. However, almost three-fourths (74 percent) of the men said that they enjoyed sex more high, but less than two-thirds (62 percent) of the women felt the same. The explanation for this discrepancy probably lies not in the properties of the drug, but in the characteristic sexual attitudes of men and women in our society. A woman is concerned with the ritual of sex and with what the textbooks refer to as "foreplay." For her, these aspects of the sexual act are often more meaningful than the immediate physical gratification it gives her. Because a woman is more preoccupied than a man with the path to sex, marijuana is more active for her during the overture. For a man, on the other hand, seduction (the overture) is often only instrumental. He is much more localized in both body and temperament; his concentration is on the orgasm. So more often he receives the most pleasure from marijuana during the act itself. But it should be noted that this is only a difference of relative emphasis: for both sexes, marijuana is more stimulating during the act itself than as an aphrodisiac.

The answers to my questions also indicated that both sexual stimulation and sexual enjoyment were directly correlated with frequency of smoking. The heavier smokers were the ones who most often answered "yes" to my two basic questions. I divided the sample into frequent users (at least three times a week) and infrequent users (less than once a week). Over half (52 percent) of the frequent users said that marijuana stimulates their sexual desire. Less than a third (30 percent) of the infrequent users agreed. Likewise, more than three-quarters (77 percent) of the frequent users claimed that marijuana increased their sexual enjoyment, while less than half (49 percent) of the infrequent users agreed.

Do the frequent users smoke more often because smoking makes them sexual, or does smoking make them sexual because they smoke more frequently? Do some people have minds and bodies that are naturally more receptive to the marijuana high, and therefore smoke more frequently? Or have those who smoke more already explored the psychic and bodily experiences available to them? Have they had more exposure to the sex-enhancing properties of the drug?

Another variable, of course, is strength of dosage: both the quality of the marijuana and the number of cigarettes smoked. But these are almost impossible to calculate. I don't know, and neither do my subjects, how potent their marijuana was. Most agree, however, that when they get very high, marijuana becomes soporific. After two or three "good" joints, the only erotic experience the pot head will have will be in his dreams.

To many marijuana users, the question of whether pot is a sexual excitant misses the point. Sex is just one example—though the example *par excellence*—of the kind of activity the drug enhances. But they were discriminate in their praise of the drug's power. Whereas it was recommended as an adjunct, collaborator, and stimulus to physical and sensual activity, it was found to be an impediment to cerebral activity. Only about a third of the sample had read anything during their high and, of these, about two-thirds said that reading was actually impaired by the high. Most material, particularly if it was logical, rational, traditional, and "linear," was rendered stuffy, incomprehensible, and impenetrable.

Marijuana seems to allow detours from the customary channels of experience and permit transcendence of some of our peculiar social inhibitions. The middle-class American is taught to be uncomfortable about his body and its gratification. The process of toilet training has made him uneasy about defecation. The taboos surrounding sex and sex education continue to cling to him. He has learned to respect the ritual surrounding food. He may not simply fill his stomach: he must not become too fat, nor stay too thin, nor eat at the wrong time or under inappropriate circumstances. He is warned against belching, flatulating, sweating. Every one of his bodily functions is stigmatized by prohibitions and restrictions. Marijuana may diffuse some of the rigid associations acquired from a culture ambivalent about bodily things. "Sex-evil," "sex-dirty," "sex-forbidden" is a class of linkages which, under the influence of the drug, is sometimes replaced by "sex-fun," "sex-nice." Consequently, users often claim that their involvement in sex is more total while high.

The attitude of play, of novel and unusual roles and activities, is also part of the sex-marijuana calculus. A twenty-year-old waitress said, "You do a lot of weird things in bed." A graduate student in psychology said, "I come up with new sex ideas." Alexander Trocchi, novelist and drug addict, puts it this way:

Experts agree that marijuana has no aphrodisiac effect, and in this as in a large percentage of their judgments they are entirely wrong. If one is sexually bent, if it occurs to one that it would be pleasant to make love, the judicious use of the drug will stimulate the desire and heighten the pleasure immeasurably, for it is perhaps the principal effect of marijuana to take one more intensely into whatever the experience. I should recommend its use in schools to make the pleasures of poetry, art and music available to pupils who . . . are . . . insensitive to symbolic expression. It provokes a more sensual (or aesthetic) kind of concentration, a detailed articulation of minute areas, an ability to adopt play postures. What can be more relevant in the act of love? [21]

Marijuana cannot create a new mentality, a conscienceless, superego-free psyche. It does seem to endorse some of our more whimsical and carnal tendencies. The person who condemns marijuana because of its bestial and violent effects probably does so because in his subterranean self he actually regards sex itself as bestial and violent. The person who claims that marijuana's liberating effects will ultimately cause destruction and brutality probably has a destructive and brutal image of man's inner being. He who in his inner self condemns sex will, under the influence of marijuana, have basically antisexual experiences. Marijuana does not create anew, it only activates what is latent.

A young woman described it this way:

A boy smoked it with me so that I'd enjoy the sex more, but it backfired! Every time he touched me, I'd get an electric shock, but if he would move away, I'd get very cold. At another time, it made me aware of the sex so that I'd become self-conscious of my sexual aggressiveness and realize that I wasn't worthy of sex. Often it would be like a psychodrama: I'd act out my problems, and become aware of what was bothering me—and become upset by it. I often became aware that I didn't want to have sex, and my body would freeze up. It brings out what your subconscious holds at the time . . .

Marijuana is much more than a mere chemical. The nature of its social reality, how it is defined, regarded, and treated, how its users shape their lives around it, will determine how it will treat them. A twenty-seven-year-old divorcée, was able to achieve orgasm only under the influence of marijuana. An eighteen-year-old coed chimed in, explaining how sex on marijuana was better, "Well, 'cuz, like you're all, you know, loose, free, and wild, and abandoned, and reckless and freaky. But, like, when I'm straight, I'm inhibited, you know, and cold, I guess, but when I'm, you know, on grass, I dig it." However, another girl experienced her only unpleasant sexual episodes when she was high. In the midst of being seduced, she saw little green men coming through the windows to attack her.

Another of the most popular of responses describing marijuana's effects dealt with laughter; there was widespread agreement that many more things seemed to be funny when high than normally. Even what we would consider quite ordinary in a normal state seemed extraordinarily droll, peculiar, incongruous, and even ludicrous. This is often pointed out by nonsmokers and critics as documentation of the distorting mechanism of the drug. The fact that someone laughs at something that is not really funny seems to prove pot's ability to take the user's mind out of reality, that the drug has the power to distort what is real, putting a "false conception" in its place. However, the user would say that the fact that something which appeared banal "straight" suddenly took on titanically comic proportions means that the experience itself was heightened—that the response *was* the experience; analyzing the reasons for the laughter destroys its validity and richness. Who is to say what is really funny and what is banal? (The user's reasoning parallels perfectly the symbolic-interactionist perspective's axiom, "The meaning is in the response.") If something is funny when high then it is funny—at that moment and under those circumstances. Whether something is funny or not is not a quality inherent in the thing, but in the field which is generated between the thing and the audience. The laughter evoked is the act of funniness.

In any case, this aspect of the extreme sense of amusement while high dominates our interviews and strikes the reader with dramatic force:

The slightest little thing that's not right, it'll crack you up. You'd break your sides laughing. I was high in school once, and the teacher wrote a word on the board—this was in economics—and I forget what word it was, but to me it seemed funny. In fact, anything anybody does seems, like, it'll seem funny.

Nineteen-year-old high school student

167

I get silly. . . . So all kinds of things, like, can crack you up, you know, that aren't really that funny, I guess, in regular life. But they can be really, really funny out of proportion. You can laugh for 20 minutes.

Twenty-six-year-old secretary

A friend told a joke, and I couldn't even listen to it, and yet, I recall laughing at it, you know—I thought it was a riot, a very old joke which I probably heard before.

Twenty-six-year-old social worker

Many of the responses reported can be summarized under the general category that Matza calls a "sensibility to banality." [22] Many of the things we take for granted somehow are seen in a new light; the everyday is viewed with virginal eyes. Often the straight nonsmoker cannot understand the response of astonishment of a circle of marijuana smokers at a party at what appears to be nothing at all. Cries of "Oh, wow!" will greet the normal observer, and he will attribute them to mere stupidity or silliness. But what is actually going on is an appreciation of something that the detached nonuser has long ago taken for granted, something which to him seems quite devoid of any special meaning. According to Matza, and to most of our respondents, marijuana touches off this new look at the objects and events around us which we have ceased to wonder about.

For something to become ordinary it must be taken for granted. . . . To take . . . for granted . . . is to render . . . empty of human meaning . . . it will not be an object for reflection. . . . Belief suspended, an aesthetic of the ordinary may appear. The unappreciable may be appreciated . . . the ordinary becomes extraordinary.[23]

Many of the effects attributed to the drug and described by our informants fall within the orbit of the sensitization to the normally banal. We do not ordinarily reflect on the food we eat, unless it somehow seems extraordinary; marijuana is attributed with the power to make our commonest meals, meals we would never remark upon while "straight," seem uncommon and unbelievably delicious. Laughter is evoked by seeming banality. We are struck by the incongruity of the congruous, by the ludicrousness of the ordinarily serious, by the absurdity of the everyday. Paradoxes crowd in on us where we saw none before. A sense of wonderment animates the high, whether it be in sex, food, jokes, music, life in general, or, seemingly, nothing at all. (Everything is not reduced to the same basic level; there can be *degrees* of wonderment.) A twenty-three-year-old graduate drama student describes his sense of wonderment at snow:

The way I'm using pot now is to try out everything new again. Like, there was a huge snow about a month ago and I went down to Riverside Park, completely stoned out of my mind. And the sky was full of snow, and the snow was eighteen inches deep in the park. And I went through the whole thing rediscovering snow, you know, sort of kicking my way through it and saying, "What's that, daddy?" You know, and sort of re-creating that experience of, you know, snow before snow meant slush and taxicabs, and blech, and inconvenience, and all of the other things that it means now. To go back and find the child-like snow. Pot is trying things out over again.

Of course, the effect need not involve such a conscious pursuit of the new in the guise of the banal. Most of our respondents felt the dramatization of the everyday without having to search for it, without even stepping outside their living room where they were sitting, smoking. Even the very act of smoking took on, sometimes, a new semblance. "When I'm high, I get hung up on little things that I wouldn't even notice straight," an eighteen-year-old coed told me. "Like, oh, wow, a cigarette. You start thinking about the cigarette and you think, you know, you're drawing in the smoke, and it's just going into your lungs, and you think about what's happening."

The issue of the generation of panic states, or psychotic episodes, by this drug marijuana is extremely thorny. There is no doubt that some individuals at some time while taking the drug have had some psychotomimetic experience. This is, however, a flabby, imprecise, and not very useful statement, for a number of reasons. First of all, it has never been established that these occurrences with marijuana are any more common than under any other exciting and possibly stressful situation, such as during a seduction, in an examination, or in athletic competition. There is no clear indication that the effects described as adverse effects of marijuana are due directly to the drug or to an unusual and novel situation, to social pressures and expectations—worrying about not becoming high, for example, or becoming too high, about having a good time—or possibly fears about the drug, about being arrested. One thing is clear, at least from anecdotal material: the factors of "set" and "setting" described earlier make a great deal of difference in the generation of "adverse reactions" to the drug, in fact, in the effects in general which the drug has.

A healthy psyche, taking the drug in a supportive, familiar and enjoyable environment, is highly unlikely to experience a psychosis-like episode. The presence of stress, hostility, strangeness, and a past with psychiatric difficulties, all make it more likely. As with virtually any psychoactive drug, marijuana can induce acute anxiety with some feelings of panic in the user. This type of reaction is uncommon and is often related to an improper set or attitude by the user, or pre-existing personality problems. The perceptual alterations produced by moderately high doses of marijuana occasionally produce a feeling of depersonalization in the user, and his fear that this effect may last produces fear and anxiety. Individuals who are insecure or threatened by circumstances surrounding the drug experience, such as arrest, are more prone to this type of reaction. Prolonged reactions have been reported, but almost always are related to high dose use in individuals with unstable predrug personalities or individuals who have had experiences with more potent psychoactive drugs such as LSD.

I have seen three cases of marijuana-induced psychoses . . . all . . . were using marijuana for the first time in "far out" environments. All had extreme paranoid reactions characterized by fear of arrest and discovery . . .

The . . . psychotic reactions represented the users' attitude toward experimenting with an illegal drug and their rigid personality structure rather than an indictment of the pharmacological properties of marijuana, and demonstrates only that "upright" Americans committed to the current dominant value system should not experiment with illegal drugs even though they might be quite capable of handling accepted intoxicants such as alcohol. Were the illegality of the drugs reversed, then their experiences would also be reversed.[24]

Clearly, a factor making for variability in potentiality for adverse reactions is the setting. The user may find himself in surroundings which are unpleasant to him, in the company of strangers or others whom he does not like, or in danger of some kind. These circumstances will influence his response to the drug. The fact that he is on the street, in public, or in his own house or apartment, will influence what he feels, sees, and does. Marijuana smokers often report paranoia as one of the effects of the drug on their psychic state while high. Many, however, qualify this with the reservation that it is only because of the legal climate, because of the drug's illegality, their fears of being arrested, the fact that a friend may have been arrested, that this mood is engendered. In other words, part of the setting of all users is the fact that the outside world punishes the act, and this realization is often woven into the experience itself, in the form of fear. Yet to say that this effect is a direct product of the drug, and not the legal setting in which the user consumes the drug, is to distort the reality of the situation. As Kenneth Keniston said in a drug symposium, given February 28, 1969 at the "New Worlds" Drug Symposium, at the State University of New York at Buffalo, "The only thing that we know *for sure* about marijuana is that you can get arrested." The smoker knows this, and sometimes responds, while high, accordingly. Those who charge the drug with generating panic states are often the very same ones who themselves produce them. Allen Ginsberg attributes his sometimes-feeling of paranoia to the prevailing legal climate:

I myself experience . . . paranoia when I smoke marijuana and for that reason smoke it in America more rarely than I did in countries where it is legal. I noticed a profound difference of effect. The anxiety was directly traceable to fear of being apprehended and treated as a deviant criminal and put through the hassle of social disapproval, ignominious Kafkian tremblings in vast court buildings coming to be judged, the helplessness of being overwhelmed by force or threat of deadly force and put in brick and iron cell.

From my own experience and the experience of others I have concluded that most of the horrific effects and disorders described as characteristic of marijuana "intoxication" by the US Federal Treasury Department's Bureau of Narcotics are, quite the reverse, precisely traceable back to the effects on consciousness not of the narcotic but of the law and threatening activities of the US Federal Treasury Department . . . Bureau of Narcotics itself.[25]

Another difficulty with the contention that marijuana is psychotomimetic is that it is never clearly defined what constitutes a psychotic episode. Thus, at one end of the spectrum of adverse reactions, we might find various vague and superficial sequelae, such as nervousness after drinking coffee, which are easily dispelled. It is possible to place any effect on the Procrustian bed of value judgments; hysterical laughter, for instance: "I laughed for hours at 'Please pass the potato chips.'" Certainly laughing for hours at such a straightforward request is not normal. Yet the respondent reported the event in positive terms; a clinician might see it in a different light.

In fact, the conceptual difficulties which plague the advocates of the psychotomimetic position are even more fundamental than this. The charge is not simply that cannabis generates psychosis-like states. It is that being high on marijuana *is* a psychosis-like state. The very nature of the experience is abnormal, according to many medical observers. For instance, the Lexington studies'[26] assertion that cannabis has psychotomimetic properties relies on a questionnaire, a battery of questions which purport to measure the degree to which the subject is suffering a psychosis-like state. Yet, when the items in the questionnaire are examined, they contain almost nothing that would qualify as a true clinical psychosis, or anything like it. The general psychotomimetic questions include: "Is your skin sensitive?" "Are you happy?" "Are colors brighter?" "Time passes slowly." "Are you having a lot of thoughts?" "Do you feel silly?" "Is your hearing keener?" The statements specifically related to marijuana (actually THC) include: "My thoughts seem to come and go." "My appetite is increased." "I notice things around me which I have not noticed before."

In other words, what is labelled a psychotomimetic experience is nothing more than the characteristics associated with the marijuana high. The fact that any of these items were actually used to measure a state labelled a psychosis is nothing more than a display of the researchers' prejudices, a display of an archaic epistemological ethnocentrism which rejects any and all experience which does not fit the narrow positivistic mold. This form of reasoning clearly illustrates the interpenetration of science and ideology—ideology parading as science. The marijuana experience is, of course, different from "normal." Marijuana is a psychoactive drug; it influences the mind, influences perceptions. This is, in fact, precisely one of the main reasons why it has the appeal it has to some. Some people may like this state, and others may not. But is it madness? How frail are the facts in the path of the mighty concept!

Thus, the attribution to marijuana of psychotomimetic properties is an ideological and political act. It involves a definitional process of deciding that certain psychic manifestations subsequent to smoking marijuana in fact (1) may properly be characterized as psychotomimetic in nature; (2) are generated by the drug; and (3) are not typical of, or generated by, substances of which society approves. There is a tacit assumption in descriptions of adverse reactions to pot that the laws prohibiting this substance are legitimate, and that one of the reasons *why* it is outlawed (and should continue to be outlawed) is that it is capable of producing a psychotic episode. Yet there is a mirror process at work; not only must we ascribe to marijuana a causal nexus with temporary psychoses, we must also ignore the role of other substances equally as capable of producing the same or even more extreme states. It was found, as a parallel example, that numerous household substances had the same chromosome-breaking properties as LSD—aspirin, nicotine, caffeine, tranquilizers, and so forth. The fact that no hue and cry was raised concerning these findings demonstrates the political character of the controversy.

The firmer root which a marijuana subculture would take in American society as a result of its legality is another change that must be considered. Many of the values that marijuana users pass on to neophytes are a contextual feature of its underground status. Elements of paranoia (for instance, fear that one's phone is being tapped by the police, apprehensiveness that someone who wants to do harm is following when one is high on the street) are part of the culture and are only partially a matter of personality configurations. The cultural beliefs evolving subsequent to legalization would not include these elements of paranoia, at least in the same degree.

As Becker has pointed out,[27] the more solid and fully developed that a psychedelic drug culture is, the more it cushions the subject from untoward or psychotic reactions by giving them an approved and fully explained status. Where the high neophyte—or the individual who is not part of a drug culture, or is taking a drug for which there has developed as yet no subculture—senses reactions which he did not expect, or which his companions did not expect, they rely on the interpretation which a positivist society passes on to them about anything novel or strange or fantastic: he's crazy. If he says, "I'm Jesus," or "I just saw infinity," or "I want to make love to this flower," where no subculture which has handled such eccentricities exists, the conclusion is obvious: he's crazy. And the message flashes back to the subject; eventually this becomes: *I'm crazy!* With this lack of cultural and interpersonal support, the individual, high on a strange drug, loosened from his traditional moorings, heavily influenced by the interpretations of his behavior by his equally naive companions, comes to look on his behavior and himself as insane. In this situation, psychotic episodes are highly likely. But if his statement "I'm Jesus" is met with "Groovy, baby; just groove on it," a psychotic self-image is not likely to be engendered. The fully developed drug subculture acts as interpretative "decompression chamber" for bizarre feeling and behavior, which are alien to a rational civilization. By finding such feelings and behavior acceptable, even admirable, by setting them into a more or less commonplace universal and to-be-expected context, and by providing some sort of explanation for their occurrence, they are experienced by the individual as a normal part of his drug adventure, an inevitable unfolding of his destiny and psyche. According to this thesis, with an elaborate and ramified drug subculture, few users of the drug will experience psychotic reactions as a result of such a definition by their peers; in fact, few psychotic reactions will occur at all.

It is Becker's thesis that this process has in fact happened with marijuana historically. Prior to the development of a society of marijuana users with a distinct view of the world, and especially with its own version of the effects of the drug, panic reactions were common; nowadays they are rare. Extending Becker's argument one step further, we would predict that they would be even rarer in the absence of legal sanctions against its possession. The paranoid elements would fall away. There would be less of a need to set oneself off from the nonsmokers—the squares—since there would be less need to play at being straight when one is high. The "bad vibrations" which marijuana users often feel from uncertain situations and individuals—often nonsmokers—would lose much of their force. And a richer and firmer and more supportive subculture would protect the high user from any potentially untoward reactions, from incipient feelings which, in the absence of a justification, might bring on panic.

In the approximately two and a half thousand man-hours of observing marijuana smoking taking place, I did not encounter any response that could qualify as a psychotic episode, even by the most generous definition. The closest manifestation of such a state was when a girl left a party because she felt uncomfortable. However, the descriptions of the marijuana high brought out a small amount of material; two girls experienced more or less consistent adverse and even psychotomimetic episodes while under marijuana's influence. And reactions which would be judged adverse by anyone were sprinkled throughout the descriptions of the high. Some were more commonly reported than others; as we saw, 15 percent of the whole sample said that they sometimes felt paranoid while smoking, a not unreasonable reaction given the present legal setting. However, considering the number of respondents and the frequency with which they had been high, acute panic states while under the influence of the drug seemed to be extremely rare.

This generalization is corroborated by research done in a San Francisco clinic associated with a heavily drug-oriented hippie population. Summarizing his observations in the clinic, David E. Smith, a toxicologist, writes:

In fifteen months of operation the Haight-Ashbury Clinic has seen approximately 30,000 patients. . . . Our research indicated that at least 95 percent of the patients had used marijuana one or more times, and yet no case of primary psychosis was seen. There is no question that such an acute effect is theoretically possible, but its occurrence is very rare.[28]

We would expect that powerful differences in the nature of their answers should obtain among different kinds of marijuana smokers. For instance, do men and women react to the drug, or report acting to the drug, in the same way, or are there systematic differences between the sexes? Curiously, our data suggest small and not very enlightening differences between men and women in their descriptions of the marijuana high. They both give the same average number of characteristics describing the high—about ten per person. And for each effect, the proportion of men and women who proffered it is about 54/46—the ratio of men to women respondents answering this question. The only pattern that significantly departs from this is in the realm of adverse reactions. Although for both men and women the effects which the subject and an outside observer of any idiological persuasion would describe as pleasant heavily outweigh the unpleasant, women seem to be more likely to mention unpleasant characteristics in their description of the high.

This pattern holds true, for instance, with feeling paranoid; less than 10 percent of the men included paranoia as one description of their drug experience, while this was true of 21 percent of the women. Women were also more likely to report sometimes feeling depressed (6 percent for men, 15 percent for women), introverted

(16 percent vs. 30 percent), or a sense of depersonalization, being cut off from themselves (8 percent vs. 16 percent). In short, women seemed to dominate the negative responses.

Differential involvement with the drug might also be expected to yield differential responses. Strangely, the heavy marijuana smoker (who used the drug at least three times per week) gave the same number of average characteristics describing the high as did the more infrequent user (smoking less than once per week). Adverse reactions were slightly higher for the infrequent user, but the differences were small, although consistent. Contrariwise, the more the respondent smoked, the greater was his attribution of favorable characteristics to the marijuana high.

Aside from three effects—the feeling that everything seems funnier while high, the sense that time is moving slowly, and the impairment of memory, as well as the sex findings which we mentioned—no strong differences of any kind emerged from the interviews outside of the pleasant-unpleasant orbit. In these three, the less frequent smoker gave them more emphasis as a valid description of the high; yet for even these, the differences were never over 10 or 12 percent. What is so striking about these descriptions, then, is the relative consistency of descriptions, the sameness in the qualities chosen to describe the marijuana experience; the variations are always minimal in comparison with the uniformity.

It is possible that our differentiation between the less than weekly smokers and those who used the drug at least three times per week is not sufficiently sharp to capture differences among levels of use. As mentioned above, compensation with marijuana probably develops fairly quickly and easily. Thus, most of our less than weekly smokers were experienced users: they had had sufficient experience with the subjective effects of the drug as to be aware of how to control the high. Thus, the most striking point of difference in the descriptions of the drug's effects would lie between the complete neophyte, who had just been turned on and had experienced the drug's effects once or twice, and the experienced user, who had been high more than a few times. Our differentiation, at any rate, did not yield any interesting contrasts in level of use.

It is often asserted that "nothing is known" about the effects of marijuana, and it is, for this reason alone, a dangerous drug. In the narrow sense that even supposed experts disagree fundamentally about most of the basic issues, this is true. But a great deal of evidence has been collected, and if read critically, a reasonably consistent picture emerges. The one thing that we do know about the effects of marijuana is that many of the components of the classic diatribes from an earlier age turn out to be hoaxes. It is peculiar that "nothing is known" should become a rallying anti-marijuana argument today, since what was asserted previously was that we do, indeed, know the effects of marijuana—and they are all bad. However, what is not known, above all, are the effects of long-term usage, particularly long-term heavy usage. And unfortunately, even the most tentative and exploratory answer to this question lies quite distant in the future.

NOTES

1. If one were to do a social history of marijuana use, it would be necessary to grapple with the question of the events so hysterically described. There are several possibilities: (1) events were fabricated, utterly and totally, by the Federal Bureau of Narcotics, to initiate and justify the statute outlawing marijuana possession; (2) marijuana use was unconsciously "read" into events that actually took place; some murders, for instance, may have taken place by someone who smoked marijuana, may have smoked marijuana, would have been the kind of person who could have smoked marijuana, etc.; (3) the events actually occurred, but were due to the unfamiliarity of the populace with a new drug, and disappeared with the accretion of a subculture of users who have learned, and who initiate the neophyte into learning, what to expect of the drug, how to handle its effects, what to do in case of unusual events or panic. For an imaginative presentation of the third argument, and its extension to LSD use in the early and middle 1960s, see Howard S. Becker, "History, Culture and Subjective Experiences," *Journal of Health and Social Behavior* 8 (September 1967): 163–176.

2. In regard to the "peace" component of this equation, it must be remembered that an extraordinarily high proportion of the American soldiers in Vietnam (and the Viet Cong as well, according to returning veterans' stories) have smoked marijuana; some estimates put the figure at 60 percent.

3. Two complications muddy this simple statement: (1) the excitement of smoking marijuana for the first time—the *idea* of smoking—often produces many symptoms which are similar to an actual high, for instance, an increase in the heartbeat rate; (2) many initiates do not recognize the actual effects, thinking them to be much more extreme than they are, and may be high without realizing it.

4. Malachi L. Harney, "Discussion on Marihuana: Moderator's Remarks," in the International Narcotic Enforcement Officers Association, *Eighth Annual Conference Report* (Louisville, Ky., October 22–26, 1967), p. 50.

5. Donald E. Miller, "Marihuana: The Law and its Enforcement," *Suffolk University Law Review* 3 (Fall 1968): 83.

6. Harry J. Anslinger and W. G. Tompkins, *The Traffic in Narcotics* (New York: Funk and Wagnalls, 1953), p. 21.

7. Although researchers often complain of the unstandardizability of the natural

marijuana, it is, nonetheless, the substance actually used illicitly, so that synthetic products will produce misleading results.

8. Andrew T. Weil, Norman E. Zinberg, and Judith M. Nelson, "Clinical and Psychological Effects of Marihuana in Man," *Science* 162, no. 3859 (December 13, 1968): 1234–1242.

9. An earlier research study, Harris Isbell et al., "Effects of (−) △ 9 Trans-Tetrahydrocannabinol in Man," *Psychopharmacologia* 11 (1967): 185, also turned up the negative finding on dilation of the pupils.

10. Donald B. Louria, *Nightmare Drugs* (New York: Pocket Books, 1966), p. 36, and *The Drug Scene* (New York: McGraw-Hill, 1968), pp. 107–108; Edward R. Bloomquist, *Marijuana* (Beverly Hills, Calif.: The Glencoe Press, 1968), pp. 195–198; Pablo Osvaldo Wolff, *Marihuana in Latin America* (Washington, D.C.: Linacre Press, 1949), p. 31; United Nations Document E/CN 7/481, "Effects of the Use and Abuse of Narcotic Drugs on Accidents in General and on Road Accidents in Particular," September 14, 1965. Louria correctly writes that "there are no statistical data linking marijuana to automobile accidents." Cf. *Drug Scene*, p. 107. This does not appear to dim the fervor of Louria's argument, however.

11. Myra MacPherson, "Parents Need Facts on Pot," *The Washington Post*, July 10, 1969, p. K3. The stated purpose of the article is something of an admission of defeat of the antipot argument. The marijuana-using youngster is well equipped to demolish the other side's arguments with facts of his own, which, in its inexperience and ignorance, the older generation is often unable to refute. The MacPherson article, then, attempted to fill this void. Needless to say, what was provided was not facts, but propaganda—as is true of the facts wielded by the opposition.

12. Alfred Crancer, Jr., James M. Dille, Jack C. Delay, Jean E. Wallace, and Martin D. Haykin, "Comparison of the Effects of Marihuana and Alcohol on Simulated Driving Performance," *Science* 164, no. 3881 (May 16, 1969): 851–854. Significantly, *The Journal of the American Medical Association* rejected publication of this important research report.

13. Lloyd Shearer, "Marijuana vs. Alcohol," *Parade*, July 6, 1969.

14. Shearer, *op. cit.*

15. See Richard Brotman and Frederic Suffet, "Marijuana Users' Views of Marijuana Use" (Paper presented to the American Psychopathological Association, February 1969), p. 10.

16. C. Knight Aldrich, "The Effect of a Synthetic Marihuana-Like Compound on Musical Talent as Measured by the Seashore Test," *Public Health Reports* 59 (March 31, 1944): 431–433.

17. Andrew T. Weil and Norman E. Zinberg, "Acute Effects of Marihuana on Speech," *Nature* 22 (May 3, 1969): 437.

18. Norman Taylor, "The Pleasant Assassin: The Story of Marihuana," *Narcotics: Nature's Dangerous Gifts* (New York: Delta, 1963), p. 21.

19. Constandinos J. Miras, "Report of UCLA Seminar," in Kenneth Eells, ed., *Pot* (Pasadena: California Institute of Technology, October 1968), pp. 69–77.

20. Lionel Calhoun Moise, "Marijuana: Sex-Crazing Drug Menace," *Physical Culture* 77 (1937): 19.

21. Alexander Trocchi, *Cain's Book* (New York: Grove Press, 1961), p. 123.

22. David Matza, *Becoming Deviant* (Englewood Cliffs, N.J.: Prentice-Hall, 1969), p. 136 et seq.

23. Matza, *op. cit.*, pp. 138, 139.

24. David E. Smith, "Acute and Chronic Toxicity of Marijuana," *Journal of Psychedelic Drugs* 2, no. 1 (Fall 1968): 41.

25. Allen Ginsberg, "The Great Marijuana Hoax," *Atlantic Monthly*, November 1966, pp. 108, 109.

26. Isbell et al., *op. cit.*, and Harris Isbell and D. R. Jasinski, "A Comparison of LSD-25 with (−)△9 Trans-Tetrahydrocannabinol (THC) and Attempted Cross Tolerance between LSD and THC," *Psychopharmacologia* 14 (1969), 115–123. The items of the questionnaire are not included in the published articles, but are available from the

senior author on request. One piece of clinical evidence on the psychotomimetic properties of THC was offered in passing: two subjects withdrew from the experiments because of their experience with psychotic reactions. It need hardly be stressed that these experiments have an extremely limited applicability to marijuana use. Pure THC is considerably more potent than the cannabis substances typically consumed, so that the reactions of subjects will be considerably different for the two substances. In addition, different reactions can be expected in a laboratory as opposed to one's own living room.

27. Howard S. Becker, "History, Culture and Subjective Experience: An Exploration of the Social Bases of Drug-Induced Experiences," *Journal of Health and Social Behavior* 8 (September 1967): 163–176.

28. Smith, *op. cit.*, p. 41.

Chapter 8

Multiple Drug Use among Marijuana Smokers

The Premise

The antimarijuana argument most widely encountered and taken seriously is that marijuana is a "threshold" drug; its use, it is said, "precipitates," "predisposes," or "potentiates" the user to the more potent and dangerous drugs, particularly heroin. It is the empirical and logical basis of this argument that we will now examine.

It is interesting that the Federal Bureau of Narcotics did not take this argument seriously during the period of the richest and most virulent diatribes against the drug. In 1937, the year of the passage of the Marihuana Tax Act, Harry Anslinger, in testimony before a congressional committee, said that the marijuana user specifically did *not* progress to heroin: "I have not heard of a case of that kind. . . . The marihuana addict does not go in that direction." With the post-World War II wave of heroin use and addiction, the connection was suddenly perceived by Anslinger. No studies were done in the interim which demonstrated the connection, or even hinted at it. (Some observers claim that the shift in the association, if it has occurred, is evidence that it is the laws and the law enforcement officers which have created the marijuana-heroin link.) In any case, beginning in the late 1940s and early 1950s, asserting the marijuana-heroin link was part of official FBN policy.

Other observers in the 1930s, however, were affirming the association that Anslinger denied. In fact, an even more elaborate association was constructed for marijuana. One of the most widely circulated and widely quoted works of the 1930s, *On the Trail of Marihuana: The Weed of Madness,* written by Earle Albert Rowell and Robert Rowell, asserted that cigarettes lead to marijuana, and marijuana, eventually, to heroin.

This argument emphasizes progressive moral decay as the dynamic thrust generating this movement from one drug to another, a kind of "greased toboggan to hell" approach to activities that society condemns. In a sense, one sin begets another greater sin. By getting away with one sinful activity, one is emboldened to try a more serious one. The only way of avoiding this descent into total corruption is to avoid all contact with evil. Since cigarette smoking is clearly an evil activity, one can avoid being sucked into the maws of marijuana use—and subsequently, narcotics addiction—by never smoking at all:

Marijuana is especially dangerous because it comes in cigarette form. The great tobacco companies have prepared the way for the Devil's parade of death; they have popularized the use of cigarettes . . . until today in America, men, women, boys and girls think nothing of lighting up their choice tobaccos. . . . It is easy now, for a young man or woman planted by the peddler, to pass out this new cigarette and American youth, always looking for adventure, will fall an easy prey. The step from Marijuana to . . . morphine is a short one.[1]

Today's observers would consider this portrait absurd, even amusing. As pointed out in the chapters on selling marijuana and on becoming a marijuana user, the neophyte is turned on and supplied by friends; the peddler does not supply cigarettes to get his customers hooked on narcotics. The percentage who go from tobacco cigarettes to marijuana and from marijuana to heroin is miniscule so that no peddler could possibly afford to spend the necessary time to recruit customers.

In spite of its late entry into the pot-to-heroin debate, the FBN (now the Bureau of Narcotics and Dangerous Drugs, a subunit of the Justice Department) is presently the most vigorous proponent of the progression theory (although the Bureau, now under John Ingersoll, may eventually represent a departure from its earlier stand of the Anslinger-Giordano years).

. . . it cannot be too strongly emphasized that the smoking of the marihuana cigarette is a dangerous first step on the road which usually leads to
enslavement by heroin. . . .

Ordinarily, a person is tempted first with marihuana cigarettes. He may
not even know they are dope. Then, someone already addicted makes it
easy to try some heroin. *Most* teenage addicts started by smoking marihuana cigarettes. *Never let anyone persuade you to smoke even one marihuana cigarette. It is pure poison.*[2]

One particularly grave danger of habitual marihuana use is that there is
often a clear pattern of gradation from marihuana to the stronger addictive opiates.[3]

Often antidrug and narcotics associations, as well as educational
and parents' organizations, will sponsor lectures by ex-addicts who
describe the horrors of addiction, along with the inevitability of the
transition from smoking pot to leading the life of a junkie. One of the
most dramatic and effective of such talks, at Miami Beach, is ex-
cerpted below:

I am a drug addict. . . . For twenty-three years of my life I was a junkie.
I spent seventeen years . . . in jails. . . .

I come from a very nice Jewish family, a middle-to-upper income family.
I was the baby and they loved me. They educated me; I got a degree in
anthropology at the University of Wisconsin.

And what did I do to them? I have had forty-seven arrests. For using
narcotics. Felonious possession of narcotics. Selling narcotics. For being a
whore. For being the madam of a whorehouse. For running a con game.

I'm not a thief . . . , but when you have a $185-a-day habit of cocaine
and heroin, no legitimate job can support it.

Look at me. . . . I'm a fifty-year-old hippie. Every vein is collapsed. I
must carry my stigma all my life, a card that warns the doctor he must
never try to give me a shot of anything, that only the vein in my neck can
be used to take blood out if necessary. . . .

I was finishing six months as an habitual user in New York. I gave an
"honest" cop $10 to slip a letter out to my connection, Porkchop, in East
Harlem. I told Porkchop to meet me when I got out, to have a fix ready, I
couldn't go out on the street without it.

He was waiting for me. I went into a phone booth and right through my
clothing I gave myself a shot. Just then a police matron came in to make a
call, and she busted me. Another six months—a year, back to back. And I
started to get scared.

I was forty-six years old. I couldn't go out and hustle. There are twenty-
year-olds doing that. I couldn't shoplift; my mug is known in every store

from Klein's to De Pinna. I was a five-time loser, I could get fifteen to thirty years. I didn't get smart. I got scared. . . .

Here I am. I loused up a complete lifetime. I'm starting a new life and I'm forty-nine.

The revelation of this talk was not simply that someone could become a junkie and live a life of degradation and infamy; it was that pot was the front door to this downfall. "All I did was start with pot," the ex-addict explained. "At the university I fell in love and married a musician . . . . My husband smoked pot, and what my love did, I did." When asked by a sophisticated student about the "statistics on marijuana leading to drug addiction," she replied:

Will you believe me if I tell you that I know junkies after twenty-three years of living in the gutter with them? Will you believe me when I tell you that I don't know any junkie that started on horse, that they all started on pot?

I don't know statistics, but I know a thousand junkies, and I tell you that they all started on marijuana. Using drugs is sheer stupidity. . . .[4]

The question before us, then, is what do the studies on multiple drug use tell us about the likelihood of "progressing" from marijuana to more potent drugs, such as heroin?

Multiple Drug Use among 200 Marijuana Smokers

In my questionnaire, I asked interviewees what drugs other than marijuana they had taken at least once to become high. With two specific drugs, heroin and LSD, I also asked how often they had ever taken them. I excluded those drugs taken for strictly utilitarian purposes, such as amphetamine pills taken for dietary reasons or for studying. Needless to say, the fact that a given individual, or a certain percentage of the sample, *ever* took one or another drug at least once does not imply continued or even occasional usage of that drug. In fact, most individuals who try any given drug to become high do so a small number of times; the majority of all drug users are experimenters, and the regular users, although numerous for many drugs, are usually in the minority.

TABLE 8-1

Multiple Drug Use among Marijuana Smokers: Two Studies
(percent)

	Goode	EVO	
LSD	49 ✓	77	LSD
Amphetamine	43 ✓	70	Methedrine
		55	"Diet pills"
		4	Darvon
DMT or DET	26	50	DMT
		14	DET
Barbiturate or tranquilizer	24 ✓	18	Barbiturate or tranquilizer
Opium	20	11	Opium or morphine
Cocaine	19 ✓	31	Cocaine
Peyote or mescaline	19 ✓	41	Peyote
Heroin	13	21	Heroin
Amyl nitrite	8		
Codeine	5	5	Codeine
		4	Cough medicine
Morning-glory seeds	5	10	Morning-glory seeds
Psilocybin	4	12	Psilocybin
Romilar	3		

About the same time I was interviewing respondents, *The East Village Other* conducted the survey on drug use cited in Chapter 2, which made inquiries about the age of first turning on, arrests for drugs, feelings of paranoia, selling marijuana, and so forth. One question asked the respondent to enumerate all the drugs he had taken at least once. While this study, like my own, had problems of interpretation,[5] I will examine parellels between the two studies, showing that, although the percentage using nearly every drug is higher for the EVO respondents, the rank-order (i.e. degree of popularity) of the drug used was surprisingly similar.

Among the 204 respondents, the use of drugs in addition to marijuana was more characteristic than it was exceptional. About two-thirds of the respondents (68 percent) had taken at least one drug other than marijuana or hashish once or more. (Some of the interviewees, I found out later, did not distinguish between marijuana and hashish.) The median number of drugs taken by the interviewees was two and the mean was 3.4. More important than the sheer number of drugs taken is both the kind of drug taken, as well as the frequency. In spite of the commonly stated belief that involvement with marijuana will lead to the use, and eventual addiction to heroin, this potentially dangerous narcotic was used by only a small minority of the sample. Twenty-seven respondents, or 13 percent of the sample, had used heroin at least once, with extremely limited use predominating.

The picture that LSD presents is different in the extent of its use among marijuana smokers, but similar in the characteristic infrequency. Half had taken the drug at least once and of these, a quarter, or 12 percent of the whole sample, tried LSD only once; nineteen took it twice. Only fourteen respondents took the drug twenty-five times or more, and of these, four had taken it one hundred or more times. Thus, LSD typically is not a drug of frequent use. It is most often taken for curiosity, exploring unusual psychic states, affirming one's status in, and experiencing some of the bases of, a distinctive subculture. Probably more than any other drug in use, the drop-off after the first drug experience is precipitous. There was usually little desire to continue use. Of course, the frequent LSD user may be found (Timothy Leary has claimed to have taken more than 400 "trips"), but relatively rarely. And, of course, fear of chromosome damage temporarily brought the widespread use of LSD almost to a halt, sometime after the interviews, by the fall of 1967. However, after the initial scare, many drug users gradually discounted the findings on the damage to the chromosomes, partly as a result of contrary propaganda, and the extent of LSD usage climbed back up to its former level, accompanied by the use of other psychedelics, such as mescaline.

Since our sample is not representative, we have no idea whether the percentage taking each of these drugs can be applied to the larger marijuana-using population; it is a safe guess that our respondents are much more heavily involved with other drugs than is the average group of cannabis smokers, including everyone who has sampled the drug at least once up to the daily smoker. What we want to know are the factors that are related to multiple-drug use; what is there in the social life of some users that contributes to the use of drugs other than marijuana? What is it that helps a marijuana user go on to other drugs?

We found that the most potent variable, by far, in determining a user's use of drugs other than marijuana was how much he smoked marijuana. For instance, nearly all of the *daily* smokers had tried at least three drugs other than cannabis (92 percent), while almost none of the less than monthly smokers did so (9 percent). Each of the categories of use in between formed a step-wise pattern of multiple-drug use; there was a perfect relationship between how much the person smoked marijuana and the likelihood of trying other drugs. (This relationship is presented in Table 8–2).

In fact, the concatenance of many factors relating to marijuana use, conceptions of identity, and marijuana-related activity, was remarkable. The more that the respondent used marijuana, the greater the likelihood of conceiving of others in marijuana-relevant terms, conceiving oneself in terms of being a marijuana user, and of desiring that others around oneself smoke marijuana.

TABLE 8–2

Frequency of Marijuana Use and Involvement with Drug Activities (percent)

Marijuana Use	Ever Tried at Least Three Drugs Aside from Marijuana	Ever Took LSD at Least Once	Ever Sold Marijuana	Ever Bought Marijuana
Daily	92	82	92	96
3 to 6 times per week	69	71	80	93
1 or 2 times per week	29	49	40	84
1 to 4 times monthly	19	25	14	67
Less than monthly	9	22	11	29

With extended, frequent use and its invariable concomitant, sub-cultural association, attitudinal shifts generally take place relative to drug use and drug-associated identities. The more that one smokes, the greater the likelihood that he will see himself as a marijuana smoker and the higher that drug-connected identities will rank on his "who am I?" responses. The more that one will look for drug cues in others, the more he will think of others in drug-associated terms; also the more one will think it necessary that others with whom he associates smoke. The more that one smokes, the greater the *salience* that marijuana has in his life. (The evidence for this assertion is presented in Table 8–3.)

It is impossible at this point to draw causal arrows. We must, rather, think of the relationship between our variables in dialectical terms. One variable, the amount of marijuana smoked, influences a person's conception of himself as a smoker which, in turn, also influences how much he smokes. The simple cause and effect model is inadequate here. All of the factors form a kind of configuration. The amount a person smokes is easily quantifiable, but it is itself a partial consequence of other factors. To attempt to separate a strand does violence to the whole.

Moreover, the more an individual smokes marijuana, the greater is the likelihood that he will also be involved in drug-related activities which further strengthen his social ties to the drug-using group. For instance, the more he smokes, the greater the chances of his having bought and/or sold marijuana. The more he smokes, the greater the need to purchase marijuana; the more he smokes, the

TABLE 8-3

Salience of Marijuana by Amount of Use

Percent saying "yes" to the following questions:
"When you meet a person for the first time, is the fact that he smokes marijuana one of the first half-dozen things you think about?"
"Is it preferable that your friends smoke marijuana, or not?"
"Do you think that you would turn on your younger brother or sister, if you had one?"

Marijuana Use	First Half-dozen Things	Preferable if Friends	Turn on Sibling
Daily	81	56	88
3 to 6 times per week	69	53	73
1 or 2 times per week	45	37	65
1 to 4 times monthly	39	33	57
Less than monthly	16	31	41

greater is the chance of being able to take advantage of the economy in large purchases, and the greater the likelihood of having a surplus to sell; the more he smokes, the more he associates with others who smoke, especially heavily, and thus the more centrally located he is in the marijuana distribution system, and the more knowledge he has about buying and selling.

But the arrows move in both directions. The more he buys and sells, the greater the number and the intensity of his personal acquaintances in the marijuana network, and the more reinforced will be his marijuana-related activities, including smoking; the more that he buys and sells, the more marijuana there will be around— the greater the likelihood of his keeping a supply—to smoke, and the greater the likelihood of having marijuana to offer to friends when they visit. Simultaneously, both use and sale can be seen as

TABLE 8–4

Nonmarijuana Drug Use by Buying and Selling Marijuana
(percent)

		Taken Marijuana Only	Taken One or Two Other Drugs	Taken Three or More Other Drugs	N
Bought Marijuana	Yes	27	27	49	147
	No	49	37	14	57
Sold Marijuana	Yes	13	22	64	89
	No	45	35	20	115

indices of the degree of involvement in the marijuana subcommunity (see Table 8–4).

The greater the proportion of one's friends who are regular marijuana smokers, the greater is the likelihood that one has taken drugs other than marijuana, and the more extensive one's experience with other drugs is likely to be. Likewise, buying and selling push the individual into social relations that alter his conception of himself regarding drug use and provide opportunities for involvement with other kinds of drugs. The fact that the individual has bought and sold marijuana means that he has had contact with other individuals who are likely to be heavily involved in drug use and who define drug use in favorable terms. This clearly means that other drugs are more available to him (friendships and drug use are empirically related in Tables 8–5 and 8–6).

Heavy marijuana use, then, implicates the individual in intense and extensive social interaction with other marijuana users, involves him with numerous marijuana users and in numerous marijuana-

TABLE 8–5

Nonmarijuana Drug Use by Marijuana-Smoking Friends
(percent)

Percent of Friends Who Are Regular Marijuana Smokers	Taken Marijuana Only	Taken One or Two Other Drugs	Taken Three or More Other Drugs	N
60-100%	16	25	59	73
30-59%	23	30	46	56
0-29%	53	32	15	72

TABLE 8-6

*Taking LSD by Marijuana-
Smoking Friends*

	Percent	N
60–100%	64	73
30–59%	57	56
0-29%	26	72

related activities, alters the role of marijuana as a relevant criterion
in his conceptions of others, and changes his conception of himself
as a drug user. Moreover, it increases the likelihood of his taking
drugs, in addition to marijuana, of which the subculture approves.

The higher the proportion of friends who were also regular marijuana smokers, the greater were the individual's chances of taking
LSD. The fact that he bought or sold marijuana also increased his
chances of having taken LSD. It can be seen in Table 8–7 that since

TABLE 8-7

*Taking LSD by Buying and
Selling Marijuana
(percent)*

		LSD		
		Yes	No	N
Bought Marijuana	Yes	59	41	147
	No	23	77	57

		LSD		
		Yes	No	N
Sold Marijuana	Yes	72	28	69
	No	30	70	115

marijuana selling is a more intense commitment than mere buying
—selling takes one further into the core of the drug-using subculture, particularly the psychedelic drug community—it serves as a
more effective predictor in differentiating whether a person will
have taken LSD. (Thirteen percent more of the sellers of marijuana
have taken LSD than the buyers, and 7 percent fewer of the non-
buyers have taken it than the nonsellers.)

For every drug that we computed, the daily marijuana smoker was far more likely to have tried it than was the less than monthly marijuana smoker. For instance, only a tiny proportion of the least involved smokers (4 percent) had tried heroin at least once, while slightly over a third of the daily smokers had. A quarter of the less than monthly smokers had taken one of the amphetamines to get high, while four-fifths of the daily smokers had. So the greater the amount of marijuana use, the greater the chance of having taken nearly any drug. Intense and continuing involvement with marijuana use implies involvement in a drug-using subculture. But it must be recognized that this is a highly conditional statement; it refers specifically to heavy use and intense involvement. At the lowest levels of use, the use of drugs considered dangerous is highly unlikely.

By smoking marijuana, one does not automatically hurl oneself into an LSD miasma. But by smoking marijuana regularly, one makes friends who also smoke. By making friends who smoke, one's attitudes about not only marijuana use, but also the use of the hallucinogens may change as well. The more that one smokes, the more likely it is that one will make friends who approve of LSD use, and who offer opportunities for the use of the LSD-type drugs. We must think of this process in dynamic, as well as in dimensionalist, terms. This is a time-bound process. And it is a process that is a matter of degree. A single puff of marijuana will do practically nothing in the way of "potentiating" one to LSD use. But daily use over the process of several months, within a milieu of heavy marijuana use, with friends who smoke regularly—the greater the number of friends, and the more intimate the relationship—the greater is the likelihood that this will occur.

Logic and Fact in Multiple Drug Use Studies

Unfortunately, no adequate cross-section of marijuana users has ever been studied. Every work done in this area, including my own, suffers from sampling bias. What holds up for one segment of marijuana users may have no relevance for another. Probably no study reveals this problem more than a recent paper from the New York State Narcotic Addiction Control Commission, by Glaser, Inciardi, and Babst.[6] A five and ten year follow-up study was conducted of about 700 males who were, in 1957 and 1962, referred to the New York City Youth Council Bureau, "an agency established for handling juvenile and youthful persons alleged to be delinquent or criminal and not deemed sufficiently advanced in their misbehavior to be adjudicated and committed by the courts" for the following three offenses: marijuana use, heroin use, and nondrug offenses.

The study then checked the appearance of the names of the members of its sample in the Narcotics Register, "the most complete file of its type available anywhere in the United States." Which of these three categories of juvenile offenders was most likely to turn up in the heroin files later? The data appeared to confirm the progression hypothesis: ". . . while half of the male adolescent heroin users had a heroin record five or ten years later, about forty percent of the marijuana users also acquired a heroin record in this follow-up period. . . . *marijuana use is almost as portentous of adult heroin use as is actual use of heroin as an adolescent.*"

The authors strongly qualify the report's findings in their conclusions; they are in no way guilty of an attempt at an overextension of the applicability of their results. Of the four groups which the authors point out as most likely to use marijuana—the slum dweller, the bohemian, the college student, and the high school student—it is only among the first (and last) of these that the study's data was likely to be drawn. *And it is in this group that the transition to heroin is most likely.* In the other three groups, the use of heroin is certainly far lower than for the urban slum dweller, so that had the study covered all of the marijuana-using groups, the likelihood of later heroin use, and therefore of the transition taking place, would have been much smaller.

In fact, the findings are even more narrowly applicable than that. The marijuana smoker whose use is so *conspicuous* as to come to the attention of the authorities in no way represents users as a whole. To come to the attention of *any* agency of law enforcement is to be a part of a highly special and unrepresentative kind of social group. Such users are far more likely to be more highly involved with the drug, to be implicated in some of the more heavily sanctioned marijuana-related activities, such as selling, and to be incautious.*

The Blumer study emphasizes the importance of the cool style in one sector of marijuana users. This kind of user is inclined to denigrate the delinquency-oriented rowdy, who is both more likely to become arrested and to move to later addiction. The cool user is likely to do neither of these. It is almost a certainty that among this conspicuous group, progression to later heroin use is far more likely than among users as a whole.

The adolescents included in the NACC study are far from representative because they generally reflect the very highest levels of use. And it is among these levels of use that later heroin involvement is most likely. It is not unreasonable to assume that less and more cautious use, lower involvement in the marijuana subculture, and participation in a greater variety of social groups, will be far less likely to precipitate heroin use and addiction. In fact, the Narcotics Addiction Control Commission has probably selected the segment of users which has the *very highest* likelihood of later heroin use. The progression hypothesis holds up best in the very group where the commission gathered data.

Lower-class adolescent slum dwellers are far more likely to come to the attention of formal legal agencies of social control than the middle-class suburban teenager. For the latter, informal, nonrecord, nonarrest implementation is more likely than for the former, if caught. Again, it is a certainty that this progression to heroin is most likely among the slum dwellers, which the authors themselves state, and least likely at the top of the class structure, which is distinctly underrepresented in official records. The process of officially recording an individual's illegal behavior is highly *contingent* on social class, neighborhood, race, and education, among other contingencies. Official notice, in fact, is immersed in the very process the authors are trying to explain. The problem is not with differentials of law enforcement involvement, as the authors imply (i.e.,

---

* In the chapter on "Marijuana and the Law," we show that the large majority of arrests that occur are a result of accidental patrol enforcement. The statement on the incaution of arrested users does not contradict this fact. It is the incautious user who is most likely to be in situations where the police may accidentally discover his possession, use, and sale.

For a description of these various styles of drug use, see Herbert Blumer, Alan Sutter, Samir Ahmed, and Roger Smith, *The World of Youthful Drug Use* (Berkeley: School of Criminology, University of California, January 1967), pp. 13–47.

with the New York Youth Council files as opposed to incarcerated drug users), but with involvement with the law *at all* as opposed to *no* involvement. In my study only seven respondents were arrested on marijuana charges, and none was incarcerated. To reason from this handful of cases concerning the characteristics of the 200 users in my sample would have led to erroneous conclusions.

The Narcotics Addiction Control Commission survey at least implied that its validity was stronger in some groups and weaker in others. Another study[7] often cited by law enforcement officers to support their pot-to-heroin claim was conducted among the admissions to the Lexington and Fort Worth addiction centers' inmates in 1965. Of the addicts studied, 70 percent had used marijuana prior to their addiction, that is, had progressed to the narcotics from cannabis. This is quoted as definitive proof that the stepping-stone hypothesis is valid. Giordano, for instance, quotes the Lexington study to support his antipot propaganda. Haslip, too, uses the Ball Lexington research report as support for the progression thesis. Further, both pieces claim that the addict survey documents the pharmacological "effects" explanation for the transition to heroin.

What does the Ball article really say? Actually, its argument and presentation of fact is much more subtle than the law officers admit. The findings do not support the pharmacological explanation: they refute it. And they do not even document the progression theory; they qualify it. The main point of the Ball-Chambers-Ball article was not that 70 percent of all addicts once used pot. It is that where there is an illicit drug-using subculture, marijuana and heroin will be found as mutual components, making the link more likely; where there is no illicit drug subculture, the progression is unlikely, because there is no group to sustain the transmission. It is the subculture that makes for the pot-to-heroin connection, not the drug itself. The central concept in the Ball piece is "differential association—becoming part of a drug-taking group." Needless to say, the propagandists hold the article to support their own "effects" argument; the findings actually refute this contention. (Actually, in his conclusions, Ball also mentions the effects-reason as one of the various possible explanations for the link: "marijuana is taken for its euphoric effects.")

However, another caveat is necessary. The Lexington study, like most studies of drug progressions, was made up entirely of addicts, incarcerated ones at that. It was not done with a cross-section of marijuana users. Therefore, we have no idea of how typical their experience with drugs was. The relevant statistic should not be a retrospective percentage of narcotic addicts who have ever used pot, but a percentage of the total universe of all those who have ever used marijuana who also ever became addicted to heroin. The whole reasoning process in studies of addicts is backwards. By all indications, the percentage of marijuana users who ever become narcotics addicts is quite small; the relevant question here is whether this miniscule minority forms a larger percentage than the total universe of those who have never smoked marijuana.

Out of this seemingly innocent source, gallons of ink have gushed forth in fatuous debate. The progressionists claim that the percentage of addicts who have ever tried marijuana—70 percent in the Ball study, as high as over 90 percent in others—indicates that pot leads to heroin. The pro-pot propagandists claim that this figure is meaningless, because 100 percent of all addicts drank milk, so that milk is more predictive of later heroin use than marijuana. The antiprogression position is correct on one level, but erroneous on another. In theory, it is always improper to cite the percentage of addicts who ever used marijuana to demonstrate the validity of the stepping-stone hypothesis, because other progressions (milk to heroin) are even stronger. But empirically, we have to assume that the percentage of addicts who have ever used marijuana is higher than for the population at large. Since the percentage of addicts and nonaddicts who once used milk—100 percent—*is the same*, this factor provides no differentiating power. But the addict-retrospective argument is also improper, because (1) we do not know whether the percentage of addicts who once used pot is any different for addicts and nonaddicts (we have to assume it, though it is probably a correct assumption); (2) we do not know how much more the addict figure is; (3) and we do not know why it should be more. So the Lexington data does not really tell us very much about drug progression until we have more data, most particularly, a representative sample of the total universe of all marijuana smokers, not merely the ones who became narcotics addicts.

The theories explaining the progression from pot to heroin (assuming that it exists) boil down to two: the psychological-pharmacological, and the social. The former is espoused by the police; the latter, by nearly everyone else. The psychological-pharmacological interpretation holds that there is an actual property of achieving the high that impels the user from marijuana to heroin; basically it is the effect of the drug which dictates the link. The user, who is "kicks" or "thrill" oriented (otherwise he wouldn't smoke marijuana), seeks an increasingly bigger thrill. Gradually the excitement of marijuana begins to pale; he ceases to achieve the charge he first got; and he searches around for a greater kick. This, as we know, is heroin, the "boss kick," the ultimate high.[8] As Giordano has informed us, "Those seeking personal well-being and exhilaration through the stimuli of drugs ultimately discover that the opiates have more to offer." [9]

This combination psychological and pharmacological, or "effects," conception of the reason for the progression is that "the use of marihuana develops [in the user] a taste for drug intoxication which, in turn, leads many people to the use of more potent drugs—even heroin." [10] One problem with this view centers around the imputation of causality. Admitting that marijuana fails to provide the kick provided by heroin is in reality saying that marijuana is discarded for heroin. It is not that marijuana leads to heroin, according to this hypothesis, but that marijuana *fails* to lead to heroin. Marijuana is not a path, but a dead end: it even slowed down the search for the ultimate kick. If it hadn't been for marijuana, the user would have found heroin sooner.[11] Obviously, we need a different explanation.

Another problem with this conception involves the mechanism by which heroin is perceived as delivering the thrill claimed for it. The effects of a drug are not uniformly grasped by all who happen to come into contact with it; a drug has to be socially defined as delivering a boss kick. The lack of this social dimension weakens the simple effects argument. Were the social dimension taken into account, it would destroy the argument altogether, because the social perceptions of the various drugs vary considerably by user.

One of the problems with a theory that tends to equate all drugs as existing in the same social and phenomenological category is that those who use drugs illicitly do not perceive them as similar. Some classes of drugs will be thought of as opposites. The effects of the various drugs are extremely different, and their social definitions are even more heterogeneous. Drug users often make the distinction between "head" or "mind" drugs and "body" drugs. Head drugs include LSD, DMT, and DET, mescaline and peyote, and usually hashish and marijuana; these are referred to by drug propagandists, such as Timothy Leary, as the "psychedelics," a term coined by the physician Humphrey Osmond, and taken from the Greek, meaning "the mind is made manifest." The clinical professions often call these drugs "hallucinogens" or "psychotomimetics." (However, they rarely produce hallucinations, and they very rarely mimic a madness-like state, although this is dependent on one's definition of madness.) The body drugs encompass a wide range of substances: the amphetamines, cocaine, the barbiturates, the narcotics (including heroin), and alcohol. One of our respondents, a thirty-two-year-old actor, and a daily smoker of marijuana, spells out the differences between body and mind drugs by citing the irrelevance of heroin to the psychedelicist:

Heroin is a drag, I think, for anybody who is into mind drugs, because it's like being very, very drunk, and it tends to take one *out* of everything, as, I think, as Cocteau said,[12] it's just like getting off the express train that's going to death, and just sort of being nowhere for a while. The only pleasant aspect of heroin is the peculiar sensation of consciousness and unconsciousness at the same time, so that you can actually perceive what it's like to be asleep because part of your brain is still awake, digging it, digging the groovy feeling of being asleep. But other than that, I don't have anything to recommend it.

Cocaine, of course, and the other stimulants are what I call body drugs, which tend to accelerate your behavior, but which don't give you, particularly, any insights.

The miraculous thing about the psychedelics is that things just pop into your mind, and if you can just listen to what you're saying inside there, you can learn a lot. It seems to me that one of the great things about LSD is that any insights you happen to get behind it are reinforced at the same moment by an emotional response that is so total that you tend to accept the insight because you believe it intellectually and emotionally at the same time, and it stays with you later.

The single similarity between marijuana and heroin is that both seem to give, or are reported as giving, a kind of relaxing euphoria, a sense of floating well-being. Beyond that, their effects are almost diametrically opposed and are categorized as such. Marijuana seems to generate a speeded-up, irrational, and seemingly disconnected thought, while heroin slows down, dulls, and deadens the mental processes. Marijuana smokers are far more sensually inclined than heroin addicts; marijuana is closely linked with sex, with orgiastic eating practices, and with an appreciation of loud, vigorous and frenetic hard rock music, while heroin tends to produce a lack of interest in sex—even impotence—and food (junkies often eat just enough to keep themselves alive).

We are not claiming that the effects of one drug have nothing to do with whether a user will later use another drug whose effects are similar. But what we are saying is that *if* the effects-hypothesis holds up at all, it cannot explain the marijuana-heroin link. If anything, it casts doubt on it. A sociologist might say that it is possible for a subculture to define the effects as similar, and users will think that they are similar, isolate similar characteristics such as the feeling of euphoria, but then we have to move to an altogether new level of explanation, which the proponents of the pharmacological theory of the escalation are unwilling to do.

The social theory of the progressive drug use underplays the pharmacological characteristics of the two drugs. It is not so much that *getting high* pushes the drug user from marijuana to heroin, as Henry Brill claims: ". . . the association is not a direct pharmacological association, which means that if you take marijuana *ipso facto* you become physically vulnerable to the opiate. It isn't that way." [13] Furthermore, "there is no pharmacological relation between the two drugs in the laboratory, but it is far from certain that there is no association in the street." [14] Rather, it is that a specific social group defines both as acceptable and pleasurable, offering opportunities for members to use both. As the New York State Narcotics Control Commission data show, it is entirely possible that in slum and ghetto milieu, marijuana use leads to, or, in a very broad sense, potentiates, heroin use. But it is not marijuana, specifically, that provides the impelling force. Marijuana and heroin use in the slum are mutual components in a subculture. Marijuana is experienced sooner in the encounter with this subculture; it is on the periphery of this quasi-criminal subculture. Yet the involvement with marijuana is obviously a matter of degree. Taking a few puffs of a marijuana cigarette during a school lunch period may not implicate one in any heroin-linked activities or associations. But daily use has a far higher chance of doing just that. In the ghetto milieu, progressive involvement with marijuana is likely to precipitate encounters with heroin users. The more that one uses marijuana in the lower-class slum, the greater is the likelihood that one will later use heroin; the two exist in the same subcultural context. Interactions, friendships, associations, which are carried out as a result of marijuana use are likely to precipitate heroin-using involvements, particularly if they are frequent and intimate. In this sense, and in this sense only, marijuana use leads to heroin use.

One subcase of this line of reasoning is the "supplier" theory of drug progression. By smoking marijuana, one is to some degree forced to interact with the criminal underworld. The seller of marijuana is also invariably a narcotics supplier, or so the theory has it. By buying marijuana, one often interacts with, forms friendships with, comes to respect the opinions of, the seller of the drug, who is generally older, more experienced and sophisticated, involved in a daring and dangerous life, and is respected and eagerly sought after by many members of one subcommunity. This interaction can be seen as having a hook attached to it: the seller does not make as much profit from the bulky, low-priced, sporadically used marijuana as he would selling heroin, so that he is, therefore, anxious to have his customers use the more profitable drug. The neophyte drug user gradually acquires the seller's favorable definition of, and accepts opportunities for, heroin use.[15]

In large part, the association of the two drugs is seen as an unintended consequence of their mutual illegality. If marijuana were readily available, it would not be necessary to go to the underworld drug supplier, and the impelling thrust behind this relationship would be removed. This argument holds that the agent most responsible for the progression from marijuana to heroin is the police, that is, law enforcement agencies from the Federal Bureau of Narcotics to the local authorities. It is the fact that marijuana users, are, willy-nilly, involved in criminal activity and in criminal associations that makes for this drug progression.

The fact that those who use marijuana, a nonaddicting stimulant, are also required to see themselves as furtive criminals could in some part also account for the presumed tendency of the majority of, if not all, drug addicts to start out by using marijuana. It is a reasonable hypothesis that the movement from the nonaddicting drugs or stimulants to the addictive is made more natural because both are forced to belong to the same marginal, quasi-criminal culture.[16]

If the social theory of drug progression has any validity, then further thought yields the realization that marijuana has relatively little to do with the actual mechanics of the link. We must make a clear distinction between a simple association or correlation and actual cause. We are a long way from the description of a fact (marijuana and heroin exist, in some drug-using groups, in mutual association) to the attribution of causality (marijuana use causes heroin addiction). In this case, both marijuana use and heroin use are part of the same basic syndrome, only in one specific social environment. In other words, marijuana use does not cause heroin addiction, but both are caused by a third outside condition. The automatic attribution of causality here is classified as a *post hoc, ergo propter hoc* fallacy. Something that happens in association with, and after, something else is not necessarily *caused by* that earlier event. The link may exist elsewhere; in this case, the social environment. The simple-minded impute causality to time-ordered association. The sophisticated withhold such judgments. Naturally, this whole argument is dependent on the empirical fact of the mutuality of marijuana and heroin in "quasi-criminal" contexts which vary considerably from one group, class, and community to another.

A recent work on multiple drug use among college students shows the relative absence of the opiates on campus. According to Richard Blum,[17] the total number who used any of the opiates in each of the schools was always under five, or about 1 percent of his five campus samples. (Actually, most of those who had tried one of the opiates had tried opium, not heroin, which is far weaker in effect and very, very infrequently leads to addiction in America, although obviously, quite often in the Orient.) The marijuana use ranged from about a third of the students to a tenth, depending on the campus. The degree of the use of marijuana, as opposed to *any* opiate, including heroin, on the college campus, is of a wholly different magnitude. Even if heroin use on the college campus in the past two years has doubled or tripled, the numbers are still miniscule.

Does marijuana precipitate or lead to heroin on the college campus? Obviously not, if the heroin users are microscopic in number. Actually, this notion cannot be dismissed so lightly; it deserves some exploration. Even though the opiate users may be insignificant in number, it is entirely possible that the marijuana user is more likely to use one of the opiates than the person who does not use marijuana. Blum correlated figures for the use of each of the various drugs. These figures show that users of any given drug are more likely to use (or to have tried) any other drug. However, for each drug, the degree of increasing the likelihood varies from one drug to another. The users of LSD, say, are more likely to have taken at least one of the tranquilizers or barbiturates to get high than those who have never tried LSD; however, the difference between the two figures is small. On the other hand, using heroin considerably increases the chances of having taken, say, dolophine or dilaudid. Rather than looking to see whether there is a simple increase over the nonuser, it is more profitable to look at differences among various categories of drug users, as well as the degree of increase.

On the surface, this evidence will appear to support the anti-marijuana, progression hypothesis. In a very narrow statistical sense, marijuana does lead to heroin, even on the college campus. Of course, most pot users never even try any of the opiates, but at the very least, having smoked pot increases one's chances of ever trying (and possibly becoming deeply involved with) the addicting drugs. Or so it would seem. Blum's data, however, are more complex than that. The correlation between marijuana and the opiates is not substantial; however, it is statistically significant. But the correlation between tobacco and marijuana, and alcohol and marijuana, is as large, and even larger than, the marijuana-opiates correlation.

> tobacco-marijuana correlation: r = .31
> alcohol-marijuana correlation: r = .22
> marijuana-opiates correlation: r = .24

This means that if the argument that marijuana leads to the opiates is meaningful, so is the claim that alcohol or cigarettes lead to the use of marijuana.[18] Alcohol and cigarettes lead to marijuana in the same degree that marijuana leads to the opiates. If the former argument is absurd, then so is the latter. They make the same degree of empirical sense. These data, however valid, will be of no interest to the propagandists. The cliché that marijuana leads to heroin will be repeated without realizing that the argument that cigarettes lead to marijuana is equally valid and equally absurd. Thus, although alcohol and marijuana are often seen as competitors and are to some degree mutually exclusive, in fact, drinkers are more likely to smoke (at least, to try) marijuana than nondrinkers are. The few very heavy drinkers are unlikely to use pot regularly and if these near-alcoholics begin using marijuana, their alcoholic consumption typically drops. But on the gross overall levels, drinking liquor increases one's chances of trying marijuana. Individuals who drink more than occasionally have a much higher likelihood of ever trying marijuana than those who drink only occasionally. The Simon-Gagnon college youth survey [19] cited in Chapter 2 uncovered the dense and close relationship between the consumption of these two intoxicants. Only 4 percent of the male and 2 percent of the female nondrinkers had ever tried marijuana, but 22 percent of the male and 13 percent of the female moderate-or-more drinkers had done so. Moreover, only 6 percent of the men and 7 percent of the women nondrinkers who had never smoked marijuana said that they might like to try; while of the moderate or more drinkers, almost a third said they would like to try.

In a statewide representative study of the high school students in the state of Michigan conducted in 1968, a powerful relationship between drinking alcohol and smoking marijuana was found.[20] Only 2 percent of the students who said that they did not drink claimed ever to have smoked marijuana. The figure was nearly ten times higher, 17 percent, for the youths who drank alcohol. And almost 20 percent of these high school students who drank said that if they were offered pot in a congenial setting by a friend, they would accept; only 3 percent of the nondrinkers said that they would. On the other hand, only 8 percent of the drinkers said that if offered, they would tell officials about the offer, but a quarter of the nondrinkers would inform the police or a high school official representative. About twice the percentage of drinkers as nondrinkers thought that marijuana was basically harmless or beneficial. High school and college students who drink alcoholic beverages are clearly far more likely to progress to the use of marijuana than their peers who do not drink liquor.

This means that the claim that heroin addicts started with marijuana turns out to be false. The drug that nearly all addicts started started with is, of course, alcohol, and not marijuana. The adolescent's first experiences with a psychoactive drug are invariably with alcohol, and not marijuana. And the alcohol-drinking adolescent is statistically more likely to "go on" to use marijuana, just as the marijuana smoker is statistically more likely to go on to use heroin —or any other drug—than the adolescent who never drinks alcohol or smokes pot. Obviously, much of the causality in the relationship must be laid at the doorstep of experiences tracing back before the young adult's first marijuana experience.

In other words, it is not *only* the friendships and associations that the young marijuana user makes in the process of smoking pot which makes it more likely that he will experiment with more powerful drugs. It is also necessary to explore early family experiences. I do not refer to the classic psychoanalytic variables, but to cultural and style of life variables. Parents who drink are more likely to raise children who have a more tolerant attitude toward drugs in general, and who have a higher chance of experimenting with drugs.[21] The example of parents is a powerful factor in unwittingly generating the adolescent's deviant behavior. Parents who drink and smoke react hostilely to their children's drug use without realizing that they had a hand in it.

Some Recent Trends

Many journalists think that since about 1967 heroin is increasingly used in social groups which had shunned it previously. College students, suburban residents, white middle-class youths of all kinds are beginning to experiment with heroin and the other narcotics, some eventually becoming addicted. A newspaper story announces, "Heroin Invades Middle Class." [22] Another intones, "Use of Heroin Said to Grow in Colleges." [23]

No serious observer doubts that the use of heroin has increased in the past few years, and, moreover, is now used in social and economic groups which previously had shunned it altogether. College and even high school students with upper-middle-class backgrounds seem to be experimenting with, and even becoming addicted to, heroin in numbers which were totally unknown in 1967 or 1968. The suburban addict has become a reality. And of course, addiction to heroin seems to be rising among all groups, not merely the affluent, and especially among teenagers. (It is unfortunate that widespread public attention to this problem did not come about until it became a problem among white middle-class youth, and not when it was mainly concentrated in the slums.) For instance, teenage deaths from heroin overdosages in New York City have risen about five times since 1965. Arrests on "opiates" charges in California tripled between 1967 and 1968 for juveniles (see Table 8–8 for these figures.)[24] Schools in which heroin use was previously unknown find themselves with noticeable numbers of users; schools in which heroin use was rare but noticeable now have a thriving colony of users.

TABLE 8–8

Drug Arrests in California, 1960 to 1968 [a]

	ADULTS			JUVENILES		
	Marijuana	Opiates [b]	Dangerous Drugs [c]	Marijuana	Opiates [b]	Dangerous Drugs [c]
1960	4,245	9,135	3,533	910	160	515
1961	3,386	8,171	4,530	408	136	709
1962	3,433	5,939	5,865	310	83	906
1963	4,883	5,962	4,768	635	92	675
1964	6,323	7,597	4,577	1,237	104	639
1965	8,383	6,104	5,930	1,619	60	951
1966	14,209	6,364	6,064	4,034	118	1,007
1967	26,527	8,197	9,558	10,987	272	2,809
1968	33,573	10,411	13,459	16,754	838	8,240

[a] Does not include the category "other offenses."

[b] Not all "opiate" arrests are on the basis of heroin charges, although most are. In 1968, the California Bureau of Criminal Statistics combined the categories "heroin and other narcotics" and "narcotic addict or user" into the single category "opiates." Thus, for the previous years, I have combined these two categories to make them consistent with the 1968 designation.

[c] The main drugs included in the category "dangerous drugs" are the amphetamines and LSD; however, LSD was not added to the "dangerous drugs" category until 1965.

There is, then, no question that this process is taking place. But there is some question as to its extent. It is an easy matter to exaggerate the depth of a problem and to declare that a previously absent problem is reaching epidemic proportions. The question of whether a given condition should exist at all is completely separate from the issue of how widespread it is. It is necessary to place the problem in perspective. First of all, recall from earlier chapters that a minority of America's youth has tried marijuana once—about a quarter of college youth, and fewer younger adolescents and young adults who do not attend college. And the marijuana experimenters who progress to use marijuana regularly are only a small minority of this small minority. Further, the regular marijuana users who progress to heroin are still a smaller proportion of this tiny segment. Actual addiction is less likely still. Of course, in some milieu, such as in and near large cities, especially New York, far more adolescents will take heroin than in rural areas; but even in New York, it is a minority phenomenon.

In early 1970, I conducted a brief study of drug use among the students of a deviance and delinquency class in a large suburban university. Some tentative generalizations relevant to multiple drug use may be made, using this study. About a quarter of the over 500 students in the sample had not tried any drug, including marijuana, even once, to get high. (Medical uses were not considered.) About a third had tried marijuana at least once, but had not used any other drugs. Thus, slightly under half had smoked marijuana and, in addition, had used some other drug at least once: they were multiple drug users. Ranking the drugs according to what proportion of the students in the sample had ever used them produces a rank-order almost identical to my 1967 New York marijuana smokers study, cited in the beginning of this chapter, and the EVO study, also done in New York in 1967. The drugs most often used are the amphetamines and the psychedelics; one of the drugs *least* often used, aside from a variety of miscellaneous drugs, is heroin. Heroin does not appear among the first half-dozen drugs most often used among young adults. About a third of the students had taken at least one of the amphetamines at least once (although for exactly what purposes I was not able to determine due to the questionnaire's brevity—many used pills to study for examinations at night). The next most popular drug was mescaline; slightly fewer than a third had taken mescaline at least once. About a quarter of the sample had taken LSD. The next most frequent drugs used were the barbiturates and tranquilizers—about half as many as had tried LSD took "downs" at least once. The remaining drugs, in order of the number of students who had taken them, were: opium, cocaine, methedrine, and DMT. Heroin was sampled by about 5 percent of the students. Of these, about six students admitted to regular use (more than a dozen times); this is about 1 percent of the sample.

An exploratory study such as this cannot be regarded as precise or infallible; it is, for instance, possible for students to avoid admitting to drug use, even in an anonymous questionnaire distributed to a class of 500 students. (Some students hinted at exaggeration rather than understatement.) And the students in this particular class may not represent the entire university, and the experiences of this university may not be duplicated at other ones, and so on. But as a scrap of evidence, it may be useful to help piece together the whole picture. But bringing evidence to bear on the heroin question is not in any way an effort to minimize the problem. The use of this dangerous narcotic is engaging a larger and larger number of our youth today. The situation that exists in 1970 may not be valid in 1975. At the same time, it is necessary to examine the facts. And the facts indicate that there appears to be no cause for the cry epidemic. It is possible that in some neighborhoods or schools the problem is that extensive. But looking at the broader picture, such a situation has not materialized. A rational and sober assault on the heroin problem is called for, and not sensational cries of a mythical epidemic.

Although it in no way minimizes the heroin issue, a related point has tended to become lost in the public outcry against heroin. The heavy use of methedrine ("meth" or "speed") is actually far more dangerous than heroin addiction. The physically debilitating long-term effects of heroin—overdosing aside—are relatively trivial.* Methedrine, on the other hand, is debilitating and toxic. The nervous system is progressively destroyed by heavy continued dosages of this drug. Moreover, the use of this drug is extremely widespread; although exact figures are impossible to obtain, there may be more chronic users of methedrine than heroin addicts. This does not even count the millions of housewives, truckdrivers, and businessmen, who use smaller doses of the amphetamines over long periods of time. Although there has been some recent attention paid to the amphetamine and methedrine problem,[25] the public is generally completely ignorant about the degree of its seriousness, as well as its extent of use. As long as marijuana continues to be socially defined as a serious social problem, it is unlikely that any progress will be made toward a solution of the problem of the use of really potent drugs. There is no indication that any such awareness is emerging, so that American society will continue to have its heroin and methedrine problems for some time to come.

---

* This point illustrates the fact that addiction, in and of itself, is not an adequate measure of the degree of harm of a drug. Methedrine, which is not addicting technically, is more dangerous than heroin, which is.

NOTES

1. Elmer James Rollings, "Marihuana—the Weed of Woe" (Wichita, Kan.: Defender Tract Club, n.d. [circa 1938]).

2. Federal Bureau of Narcotics, "Living Death: The Truth about Drug Addiction" (Washington: U.S. Government Printing Office, 1965).

3. Gene R. Haslip, "Current Issues in the Prevention and Control of Marihuana Abuse" (Paper presented to the First National Conference on Student Drug Involvement sponsored by the United States National Student Association at the University of Maryland, August 16, 1967). See also, Henry L. Giordano, "The Prevention of Drug Abuse," *Humanist*, March–April 1968, pp. 20–23. Word for word, Giordano duplicates Haslip's sentence on drug progression.

4. Theo Wilson, "I am a Drug Addict: An Autobiography," New York *Daily News*, February 14, 1968, p. C6.

5. See *The East Village Other*, January 1–15, p. 6. Consider only the following possibilities of sampling bias: EVO readers do not represent marijuana smokers in general; EVO readers do not represent even New York area marijuana smokers; the EVO reader who is sufficiently motivated to fill out the questionnaire doesn't represent all EVO readers; all EVO purchasers do not represent all EVO readers; some EVO readers (none of which sent in the questionnaire) do not use drugs; and so forth. We use this survey only as rough corroborative evidence.

6. Daniel Glaser, James A. Inciardi, and Dean V. Babst, "Later Heroin Use by Marijuana-Using, Heroin-Using, and Non-Drug-Using Adolescent Offenders in New York City," *The International Journal of the Addictions* 4 (June 1969): 145–155.

7. John C. Ball, Carl D. Chambers, and Marion J. Ball. "The Association of Marihuana Smoking with Opiate Addiction in the United States," *Journal of Criminal Law, Criminology, and Police Science* 59 (June 1968): 171–182.

8. The best description of social definitions of heroin as the ultimate kick may still be found in "Cats. Kicks and Color," by Harold Finestone, in the anthology edited by Howard S. Becker, *The Other Side* (New York: The Free Press, 1964), pp. 281–297.

9. Giordano, *op. cit.*, p. 21.

10. Henry L. Giordano, "Marihuana—A Calling Card to Addiction," *FBI Law Enforcement Bulletin* 37, no. 11 (November 1968): 5. See also Giordano, "The Dangers of Marihuana, Facts You Should Know" (Washington: U.S. Government Printing Office, 1968).

11. I am grateful to Professor John Kaplan for this insight. See his *Marijuana: The New Prohibition*, forthcoming.

12. Jean Cocteau, French artist, writer, and filmmaker, 1891–1963, was addicted to opium in the 1920s; he wrote a book about his experiences, translated into English as *Opium: Diary of a Cure* (New York: Grove Press, 1958). The bodily effects of opium are superficially similar to heroin in some respects, although considerably weaker. Heroin is, of course, a derivative of opium.

13. Henry Brill, "Drugs and Drug Users: Some Perspectives," in New York State Narcotic Addiction Control Commision, *Drugs on the Campus: An Assessment* (The Saratoga Springs Conference on Colleges and Universities of New York State, Saratoga Springs, N.Y., October 25–27, 1967), p. 59.

14. Brill, "Why Not Pot Now? Some Questions and Answers," *Psychiatric Opinion* 5, no. 5 (October 1968): 18.

15. For an example of this line of reasoning, see Alfred R. Lindesmith and John H. Gagnon, "Anomie and Drug Addiction," in Marshall B. Clinard, ed., *Anomie and Deviant Behavior* (New York: The Free Press, 1964), pp. 171–174.

16. Kenneth B. Clark, *Dark Ghetto* (New York: Harper & Row, 1965), p. 90.

17. Richard H. Blum et al., *Students and Drugs* (San Francisco: Jossey-Bass, 1969), pp. 101–109.

18. I am making the empirically valid assumption that the first instance of alcohol and cigarette use generally precedes rather than follows the use of marijuana, and that the use of marijuana precedes the initial use of the opiates.

19. William Simon and John H. Gagnon, *The End of Adolescence* (New York: Harper & Row, 1970).

20. Richard A. Bogg, Roy G. Smith, and Susan Russell, *Drugs and Michigan High School Students* (Lansing: Michigan House of Representatives, Special Committee on on Narcotics, December 9, 1968). The figures I present were not calculated in this study. Mr. Bogg kindly lent me a copy of the IBM cards which stored this study's data, and I calculated the percentages myself. I would like to thank Mr. Bogg for his generosity.

21. See the study by the Addiction Research Foundation of Toronto, Canada, *A Preliminary Report on the Attitudes and Behaviour of Toronto Students in Relation to Drugs* (Toronto: Addiction Research Foundation, January 1969), p. 66 and Tables 18 and 19. Recently, Mayor Lindsay of New York City claimed that television was one of the causes of tolerance in attitudes toward drugs among today's youth, and partly responsible for drug use. Actually, as the Toronto study shows, drug users are more skeptical toward the mass media as a source of information about drugs than nonusers are. See pp. 56–57 and Table 45.

22. Philip D. Carter, "Heroin Invades the World of the White Middle Class," *The Washington Post*, February 16, 1969, pp. A1, A8.

23. Peter Kihss, "Use of Heroin Said to Grow in Colleges, but Number of Addicts is Still Small," *The New York Times*, March 11, 1969, p. 35.

24. State of California, Department of Justice, Bureau of Criminal Statistics, *Drug Arrests and Dispositions in California: 1968* (Sacramento: State of California, 1969), *1968 Drug Arrests in California: Advance Report* (Sacramento: State of California, April 1969), and *Drug Arrests and Dispositions in California: 1967* (Sacramento: State of California, 1968).

The same trends are noticeable in Great Britain. The number of cannabis offences and heroin addicts seem to be increasing almost identically. See Nicholas Wade, "Pot and Heroin," *New Society*, January 23, 1969, p. 117.

25. For a frightening, although sensationalistic, journalistic account of the lives of several chronic amphetamine users, see Gail Sheehy, "The Amphetamine Explosion," *New York*, July 21, 1969, pp. 26–42. Earlier journalistic articles include John Kifner, "Methedrine Use Is Growing," *The New York Times*, October 17, 1967, pp. 1, 40, and Don McNeill, "The A-Heads: An Amphetamine Apple in Psychedelic Eden," *The Village Voice*, February 2, 1967, pp. 11, 31. Blumer's study also contains some material on the use of the amphetamines.

: *Chapter 9* :

Marijuana, Crime, and Violence[*]

Introduction

If cannabis could be shown to have a criminogenic and violence-inducing effect, the argument would shift from an issue of civil liberties to the question of the protection of society. It would no longer be a matter of the condemnation and criminalization of a certain style of life, of preventing the user from "harming" himself and prohibiting him from enjoying his own particular "vice" in the privacy of his home, much like pornography. The issue of the criminogenics of marijuana takes the debate out of the murky habitat of the user. Everybody is affected if the drug produces the will to do harm to another. This deserves investigation.

The classic presentation of the position that marijuana unleashes violence in the user came out of the 1920s and 1930s. One such testimony details this position:

Police officials told us that the underworld has been quick to realize the possibilities of using this drug to prey upon human derelicts. It is used to sweep away all restraint. They have found that before undertaking a desperate crime, many a criminal indulges in marihuana cigarettes in order to do away with fear and to get the "courage" necessary for his crime. The

---

[*] I would like to thank Professor John Kaplan for giving me the idea for writing this chapter, which is heavily indebted to his "Marijuana and Aggression," a chapter in *Marijuana: The New Prohibition*, forthcoming.

marihuana addict may run amuck, and wreak havoc. Amnesia often occurs during this advanced stage, in which the subjects commit antisocial acts. . . .

Perhaps the most marked effects of marijuana can be observed in its attack upon the moral standards of the user. In this respect it goes farther than alcohol. Alcohol will lower the standards and release the inhibitions, allowing the individual to follow his base and secret desires. Marihuana destroys the inhibitions much more effectively and completely, abolishing the power of censoring one's acts, and doing away with the conception of right and wrong. It not only destroys the true conception, but sets up in its place a totally false conception. Whereas liquor breaks down moral standards, marihuana not only breaks them down, but sets up in their place standards diametrically opposed. Under alcohol it is all right to disregard that which is moral and right; under marijuana *it is not only right to do wrong, but it would be wrong not to do wrong.* . . .

. . . immediately upon the loss of moral control, the subject becomes convinced that a certain act, from pickpocketing and theft to rape and murder, is necessary, and is seized by an overwhelming desire to perform that act because to him it becomes a deed born of necessity. . . .

Intoxicated by liquor, a crime may be committed because moral restraint is not functioning; under the spell of marihuana, the crime *must* be committed because it is the right thing to do, and it would be wrong not to do it. . . .

A remarkable difference between opium derivatives and marijuana lies in the strange fact that while *under the influence* of marihuana the addict is frenzied and may do anything; it is only *when he is deprived of his drug* that the morphinist or the heroinist becomes frenzied and commits crimes.

Marihuana, while giving the hallucinations of cocaine, adds delusions of impending physical attack by one's best friend or close relatives. In addition, marihuana is intrinsically and inherently crime exciting. It has led to some of the most revolting cases of sadistic rape and murder of modern times. . . .[1]

This is the issue in its purest form. Although few participants of the debate would accept this version literally, some do accept its basic premise—that marijuana is inherently criminogenic. Thus, the question of marijuana's impact on crime needs exploration.

Doctors, Policemen, and Sociologists

The position that marijuana causes crime and violence does not have full support today. In fact, only the police and some segments of the public are solidly behind the contention that marijuana actually causes crime[2] and violence. The official stance of federal,[3] state, and most local law enforcement agents is that marijuana, at the very least, plays a significant role in the commission of crimes of violence. "Marihuana is not only an extremely dangerous drug, it is a menace to public health, safety and welfare" said the ex-Commissioner of the Bureau of Narcotics and Dangerous Drugs, Henry L. Giordano.[4] "Every user is a potential danger to the general public," Director of the New York State Bureau of Narcotic Control, and Executive Secretary of the International Narcotic Enforcement Officer's Association, John J. Bellizzi, is quoted as saying,[5] referring to a federally sponsored study to be discussed shortly. The Los Angeles Police Department, in conjunction with the Narcotic Education Foundation of America, has written, assembled, printed, and distributed a pamphlet entitled "Facts about Marijuana," which asserts the criminogenic power of cannabis.

There seems little doubt that probably a majority of all law enforcement officers believe that marijuana is instrumental in the precipitation of criminal behavior. There are, of course, exceptions. Thorvald T. Brown, for instance, in a textbook on drugs for policemen wrote:

. . . there is no more criminality in a tin of marijuana than there is in a fifth of whiskey, gin or vodka.

Bizarre criminal cases attributable to marihuana and other drugs, while common in newspaper stories, are rather rare in official police files. Crimes of violence such as murder, rape, mayhem, shootings, stabbings, pistol-whipping robberies and inane street beatings of innocent victims, occur every day in most American cities. Seldom is there any connection with these offenses and drugs.[6]

Most of Brown's fellow officers would disagree. Speeches published in the annual Conference Reports of the International Narcotic Enforcement Officer Association are representative of the official police ideology, and they invariably present the "hard line" on the criminogenics of marijuana. Published statements by the police taking anything but the hard line are extremely rare, and are, without any doubt, exceptional.

The medical profession is almost universal in its rejection of this position, a considerable change since the 1930s when many doctors writing about marijuana attributed to it a distinctly felonious character. Even today, however, we will find some physicians taking this view. In summing up, after reviewing over a dozen studies and opinions, Bloomquist explains the position this way:

What seems clear is that marijuana *per se* does not cause crime, in the sense that anyone taking it will of necessity commit criminal acts. But what is just as clear is that cannabis releases inhibitions and impairs judgment with such regular predictability that a user with criminal tendencies will readily commit crimes under the influence of marijuana. And it is documented that many already confirmed criminals use cannabis to buoy them [selves] up for the commission of criminal acts. The intent, or at least the disposition, to engage in criminal activity must exist in the user before using cannabis. But there seems to be a high incidence of what, at best, we must call unstable personalities who are attracted to cannabis, and the combination no doubt results in the frequently high correlation that law enforcement authorities have noted between cannabis and crime.[7]

From my review of the medical writings on marijuana, however, the majority of physicians diverge from this moderately hardline view. Louria, for instance, writes that "there is no statistical evidence associating marijuana with violence in the United States. . . . It would be fair to say that for the most part marijuana increases passivity, not aggression, but it does release inhibitions, it can produce panic or confusion and because of these effects can on occasion indeed lead to aggressive or violent behavior."[8] Roswell Johnson, Director of Health Services of Brown University, qualifies his position even less: "There is a widespread misconception that marijuana predisposes to crimes of violence. The *exact opposite* is probably closer to the facts. . . . reduction of work drive leads to a negative correlation with criminality rather than a positive one."[9]

In a testimony before the California Public Health and Safety Committee, Thomas Ciesla, a psychiatrist, was engaged in the following dialogue:

Question: Have you ever come across a single case where somebody has undergone, perhaps, some personality change, perhaps one of

having less personal restraint and has committed crimes because
of this? Any kind of minor crimes, even, because of his habitual
use of marijuana?

Ciesla: I have not.

Question: Do you know anyone who has?

Ciesla: No, I don't.[10]

Duke Fisher, at the UCLA Neuropsychiatric Institute, in an unpublished study is quoted as saying: "I have never seen an example
of an aggressive reaction to marijuana. In fact, I have found that
quite the opposite seems to be true."

It is reasonably safe to assume that of all the commentators on
marijuana, the police are likeliest to take the most stubborn position
on the drug's criminal dangers. Bloomquist suggests a situational
reason for this:

When the police hear that "only a few" users become involved with crime
they wonder how they keep meeting that few so constantly. And in
truth there is a considerable gap between the experiences of the sociologist
in his university office, or the psychiatrist in his handsomely appointed quarters on the one hand, and the police on the street on the other hand. It
may not be so much that one or the other is wrong as that they just move
in different circles.[11]

To a large degree, Bloomquist is misstating the sociologist's role.
As a student of deviant or criminal behavior, the sociologist should
be *at least* as acquainted as the policeman with street-level crimes,
since he has access to crimes that the policeman discovers only by
accident. In fact, the sociologist is in a far better position to see an
accurate picture of the criminogenic effects of marijuana than the
policeman, because he is around marijuana users (or should be, if
he is engaged in doing research on marijuana use) all the time,
when they are engaged in activities of *all* types—including crime.

The policeman, on the other hand is *only* concerned with the
criminal aspect of marijuana use, and this fact alone would necessarily exaggerate its importance. That is, after all, the only thing he
sees; that is what he is *supposed* to see. The policeman sees a visible
tip of a very deep iceberg, most of which is hidden from view—at
least, hidden from the view of the policeman. He is privileged to see
only a highly biased segment of a highly complex phenomenon.
Crimes, and especially violent crimes, are much more visible than
noncriminal activity, and the policeman sees that segment which is

most visible. They would therefore think that crime occurs among users much more than it actually does.

In addition, those users who happen to get themselves arrested for marijuana crimes (as well as for other crimes that accidentally happen to reveal marijuana possession) are more likely to be involved in other criminal activity as well. They are individuals who are likely to be less discreet about their use. They attract public attention and sanction, making them more likely to be the kind of person who attracts the attention and suspicion of the police about all kinds of activities, including nondrug crimes. Thus, the policeman, as we would suspect, thinks that the crime rate among users is much higher than it is, because he simply isn't in a position to see its true extent. His view is highly partial and unrepresentative, while the sociologist, who invades the privacy of the user and delves into any and all aspects of his life, has the chance to develop a more balanced view.

The Blumer report, still the definitive study of drug use in the ghetto slum, is highly skeptical of the marijuana-crime link. The project's researchers were engaged as participants and managed to observe every aspect of their subjects' social life. They found that drug users in the ghetto slum fell into four more or less distinct types: the "rowdy dude," the "pothead," the "mellow dude," and the "player." The first is a delinquent type, violent and criminal with or without the use of marijuana; the last is oriented to a life of professional criminality, marijuana use being one of his most harmless activites. The pothead and the mellow dude, basically, are hedonists, engaged in drug use, marijuana smoking almost exclusively, as an adjunct for pleasurable activities.

Far from discovering a violent influence on marijuana users, the Blumer research revealed quite the opposite. In fact, the use of marijuana was part of a socializing process that simultaneously initiated the neophyte into the ritual of use and a "cool," non-rowdy way of life. As the youthful nonmarijuana user makes contacts in the user world, and is accepted as a potential participant, he realizes that a violent, rowdy way of life is looked down upon, or "ranked." The "cool" nonviolent style accompanies regular use. The "rowdy," on the other hand, uses marijuana only rarely (the "cools" are unwilling to accept the rowdy socially and to sell marijuana to him), more often using such substances as alcohol, glue, gasoline, lighter fluid, and sometimes the amphetamines and barbiturates. As he learns to use marijuana, he realizes that those who are initiating him frown on his violent style. The weed, in short, is associated, the researchers found out, with nonviolence and a distinctly cool style.

See, people I know, after they got hip to weed, they just climbed out of that rowdy trip. They squared off completely, you know, wanted to jump sharp, enjoy themselves and be mellow instead of getting all brutalized. You don't hear much about gang fights any more. People getting hip to weed.

I can get loaded but there's a dude sitting right there I don't like, I hate his motherfucking guts, man, and if he says anything wrong, man, I can get up and hit him and think nothin' about it. But mostly people don't fight when they're loaded on weed. Weed slows you down and you don't think about fighting. You think about tripping. It's a big hassle to you, it's a big hangup.

What happened to me was I was sniffing glue and got to smoking weed, you know. I got busted in tenth grade behind sniffing glue. Sitting in back of the drugstore with big old bags. Glue messes you up, man, jerked my mind and I didn't want to sniff glue, you know. Then I got loaded [on marijuana] and this guy started getting me loaded and I dropped glue, see. But you know, if I were to have met somebody else that didn't smoke weed, maybe some rowdy cat, maybe I would have went somewhere else. I don't know what would have happened . . . took another course.[12]

These quotes from three users illustrate that marijuana is associated in this particular subculture with the movement away from a violent way of life. As to whether this is a property of the drug, or simply the way of life of the people who use it, is impossible to tell. As a sociologist, my inclination is to say the latter. It is possible that there is a certain amount of pacific potential in marijuana, but the characteristics of the users has far more to do with their behavior under the influence of the drug than the pharmacological action of the drug itself. (In fact, because of this, the term "under the influence" is misleading.) Whichever it is, however, the Blumer study definitely pointed to a disassociation of marijuana with serious crime, especially violence.

Issues, Meaning, and Method

As I see it, there are a number of separate yet interpenetrating problems associated with marijuana and crimes, all of which have to be solved before the issue can make sense in the first place:

1) What does it *mean*, logically and empirically, to ask: Does marijuana "cause" crime?
2) What *kind* of crimes are we talking about?
3) What are the various *reasons* for the causal connection, if any?
4) Does this causal connection vary from one social group to another, or is it the same for all?
5) Does any empirical *evidence* exist supporting or refuting this causal connection?

To get a meaningful understanding of the pot-crime issue, we must break down the various kinds of arguments and modes of reasoning. We encounter at least five methods of establishing the connection. The presentation of evidence gives a clue to the soundness of the argument. Some modes of presentation are crude, and the argument may be dismissed out of hand; others are more sophisticated and are more worthy of our attention. I will discuss the five types of arguments in order of their level of sophistication.

ENUMERATIVE METHOD: ACCIDENTAL PSEUDO-ASSOCIATION

While many attempts have been made to show that marijuana "causes" crime, the evidence presented to shore up the argument often only shows that *some* marijuana smokers commit crimes, or that it is *possible* to commit a crime under the influence of marijuana. Not even marijuana's staunchest supporter would argue that a crime has never been committed by a user while high. Yet, incredible as it seems, the burden of many "proofs" of marijuana's criminal effects has been precisely the simple fact that *it is possible to locate* crimes committed in conjunction with smoking marijuana. "Proof" by enumeration is no proof at all. By examining an enumeration of crimes which were committed under the influence of marijuana (even were this definitely known), it is impossible to determine the "cause" of the event taking place, in this case the crime

—or, indeed, that marijuana has anything whatsoever to do with its commission. Yet "proof" by enumeration is the most common method of "demonstrating" the causal connection between marijuana and crime. Countless works written today rely on this method of demonstration.[13]

In its field manual, the Federal Bureau of Narcotics and Dangerous Drugs requested district supervisors to obtain from state and local officials "reports in all cases . . . wherein crimes were committed under the influence of marihuana." To illustrate the selective process involved in this request, imagine the impressive dossier that would result from a request that reports be conveyed on anyone *wearing a hat* while committing a crime. A case could then be made for the criminogenic effect of hat wearing. In fact, we might very well collect not only more cases, but also even more gruesomely violent ones, since hat wearing is more common than marijuana smoking in connection with crime (as well as in conjunction with noncriminal activities).

The enumerative method is the most primitive technique of proof. It putatively links two items causally that are, in fact, sometimes found together. No effort is made to determine whether they are actually associated in any way other than would occur by chance. We all use the enumerative method, at least to illustrate an argument. Examples often dramatically pin down a stand which we take. It is impossible to bring systematic data to bear on every point we make. However, it is surprising that in this crucial issue, long debated, little attention has been given to the rigor of the method of analysis.

One thing that the enumerative method proves is that it is possible to commit a crime under the influence of marijuana, just as it is possible to commit crimes without marijuana. Most crimes, in fact, are committed without drugs in a normal mental and physical state; no one has yet submitted this as proof that being "normal" is criminogenic. Since we "know" that being normal doesn't induce crimes, we dismiss that argument and rightly so. But if this method of reasoning is absurd and invalid, then equally so is the attempt to link marijuana with crime by a case presentation, because both were documented in precisely the same manner. It is only because we have decided beforehand, before we have seen the evidence, that such a method of argumentation is convincing, because we have already been convinced. We search for a confirmation of our views. That marijuana causes crime *makes sense*—even when demonstrated by such shoddy and fallacious arguments—because we already "know" it to be true. Because our mind is already decided on the issue, we take the argument seriously. The same argument, presented in the same way, relying on the same methods, producing the same kind of evidence, taking the opposite point of view, will be rejected. Wielding evidence is only a political gambit to confirm our prejudices; we aren't too concerned about whether arguments make any sense—only that we are proven "right," however absurd the method of doing so.

DESCRIPTIVE ASSOCIATION

There is a basic question involved with a simple person-for-person, crime-for-crime relationship to marijuana use: Are marijuana users any more criminal than the rest of the population? Now, instead of a "sometimes" connection, which is vague and meaningless in the extreme, we have a comparison of the crime rate of one population with another. We might reason that, if users are more likely to commit crimes, the use of marijuana might very well have something to do with it. We are on firmer and more legitimate grounds, to be sure, but unfortunately, there is a considerable difference between association and causality. Two items, such as marijuana and crime, might very well be linked because of accidental reasons. In the above type of argument, we have no idea what the nature of the link actually is. In this type, we know that there is a link but we don't know if it means anything. The link might have occurred because of factors external to the two items. For instance, crime is committed most in the fifteen to twenty-five age range; marijuana is also used most by this group. If marijuana users are more often lawbreakers, it is possible that it can be accounted for simply because more users are in the most criminal age category; it might have nothing to do with the action of the drug itself.

Blind faith in a simple descriptive association between marijuana and crime (were it to exist) would lead us to accept many related associations which are absurd a priori in a causal sense, but true descriptively. For instance, we would probably find that users of aftershave lotion are more criminal, statistically and descriptively, than those who do not use it, simply because users of aftershave lotion are men, and men are more likely to break the law than women. Does perfume inhibit crime? Users of perfume are less likely to commit crime than individuals who do not use perfume, again, simply because perfume-users are women, a group wherein crime is less likely. If this logic holds up for these universally agreed-upon innocuous substances, then it would violate the logical method to deny the same procedure to marijuana.

ANALYTIC ASSOCIATION

We wish to know if, with all of the extraneous factors held constant—age, sex, urbanness, class background, etc.—whether marijuana smokers are any more criminal than the rest of the population. We wish to isolate out, or control, those variables that could enter into the relationship which would make it look as if an association exists, but which are actually outside the causal chain. That they *contribute* to the result, but have nothing intrinsically to do with the actual relationship between the two items we are interested in, means that we have a much more difficult task. We can't just look at marijuana and crime, even if we do have a reasonable comparison between the using and nonusing populations. We must also understand the nature of the composition of the two populations. People in cities have a higher crime rate than people in small towns—at least it is more often detected. This is true (at the very least) of homocide, rape, larceny, assault, burglary, and motor vehicle theft.[14] It is almost universally agreed that people in cities are far more likely to smoke marijuana. Men are more criminal than women; men are more likely to smoke marijuana. This list could be expanded *ad infinitum.*

Do marijuana users have a higher crime rate than nonusers? Because after we have gathered together all of the factors which could have an impact on the relationship, we would probably have more which strengthen than weaken it. What does this mean? It means that we can have an artificial relationship show up on paper, but not in the real world. The fact that men, city people, young adults, are more attracted to marijuana means that users may commit more crimes, not necessarily because marijuana has anything to do with it, but because of the accident of who it is that uses it.

What we want to know is do male marijuana users commit more crimes (or less) than male nonusers? Do female users commit crimes any more than female nonusers? Do middle-class, male urban dwellers, ages fifteen to twenty-five who *use* marijuana, commit crimes more frequently than middle-class, male urban dwellers, fifteen to twenty-five, who do *not* smoke marijuana? (We would then have to ask the same question of females, other age groups, other class categories, and dwellers of communities of a different size.)

We are still, of course, nowhere near the level of *cause*. We remain in the realm of association, but a higher level to be sure. Even after we have made this extremely complex comparison and control, we really do not know if marijuana actually "causes" crime or not. It could very well be that even after all of these extraneous factors are held constant, marijuana users are still more likely to commit crimes. And yet marijuana *itself* might very well have nothing to do with it. That a person is willing to try marijuana indicates something about the person, about his characteristics, his way of life, attitudes, notions of right and wrong, and so on. Marijuana users are of course, a vast and diverse tribe, but they are not identical to nonusers. They are more likely to have certain kinds of traits. Or, to put it a different way, people with certain kinds of traits are more likely to try marijuana. In a sense, some people are more predisposed to use marijuana. Now, at the same time, we cannot ignore the role of accident, propinquity, fortuitousness, ecology, location, and situational features of every description that tell us very little about the person himself. And, too, at the same time, we need not wallow about in the morass of personality theories of "ego inadequacy," "compensatory mechanisms," "adolescent rebellion," "rejection of adult authority," and so on, which obfuscate more than they clarify.

But it is difficult to deny this fundamental fact: marijuana users are *different*. They are a different social animal from the nonuser, and in specific ways. It is probably permissible to say that the marijuana smoker is less attached to the legal structure than is the nonuser. He is less authoritarian, less likely to follow the rule for the rule's sake, more likely to see many laws as being unjust. He is more experimental, more adventurous, more daring, at least vis-à-vis the law. He is not as concerned about the fact of legality or illegality. He is more likely to have a code of ethics which, he feels, transcends technical law, claiming allegiance to a "higher order." We would predict that he would be more likely to break the law than nonusers. Among my respondents, I asked the broad question, "How do you feel about having broken the law?" Only five respondents (2.5 percent) said that they were bothered, that they felt guilty about breaking the law; 6 percent said that they had mixed feelings about their infractions. The rest, 91 percent of the sample, said that it didn't bother them, that they didn't think about it, that they didn't consider it against the law (i.e., in their own personal creed), that it was a stupid law and ought to be ignored, etc.[15] The simple fact of "obeying the law," in and of itself, meant little or nothing, apparently, to most of them.

Now, many will condemn this point of view; some will applaud it. The psychologically inclined will see in it the germ of a self-destructive motive. Others will take it as proof that users are thrill and kicks oriented. Believers in the "letter of the law" will castigate; defenders of its "spirit" will withhold judgment. Regardless of our feelings concerning the less strict adherence to the rule of law and authority among marijuana users, the fact remains, this is likely to *predispose* them toward a higher crime rate, other things being equal.

It is entirely possible, then, that marijuana smokers *are* more criminal than their nonusing peers, even for the same age, sex, social class and educational groups, etc. It is possible that they are more "predisposed" toward crime. The fact that they are willing to break the marijuana laws might very well be an *indication* of their willingness to break laws in general. (In a moment, we will qualify this and explain *which* laws are more likely to be broken.) Yet, this would be true of *any* example of lawbreaking we select and may very well have little or nothing to do with the drug that they use. Suppose we ask the question: Are underage drinkers more likely to commit crimes than their peers who don't drink? Or is someone who engages in premarital intercourse (in states which have a law against it) more likely to engage in other illegal activities, on the whole, than someone who does not? My answer would have to be, probably. Not so much because of the nature of the activity, but because such breaches probably are a rough indicator of a greater willingness to deviate from the letter of the law, to be less concerned with public disapproval (or to accept deviant peer definitions of what is "right"), to explore the somewhat remote, to move away from parental and community standards. It could even be that *not* to partake in such activities indicates more about the abstainer than doing so does. That is, by now, premarital intercourse has become a "subterranean" norm among the young. Thus, the person who does not engage in sexual intercourse before marriage is likely to be more authoritarian, more religious, more tied to the conventional normative structure, less willing to stray from the well-known, the familiar, and to have great respect for rules. And, of course, less likely to commit crimes of any sort.

Now, what does our analysis tell us about the criminal effect of marijuana? Nothing really. We can know definitively that users are more likely to commit crimes than their age, sex, etc., cohorts, and yet know absolutely nothing about whether marijuana itself has anything to do with crime. (Any more than premarital sex does.) For this kind of statement, we have to move our analysis up to another level of sophistication.

PSEUDO-CAUSAL RELATIONSHIP

Marijuana is often cited as an agent, or a catalyst, in the commission of crimes, without raising the issue as to whether it is actually a direct cause. It is often attributed with an indirect role in the breach of laws. Thus, such an argument might be crystallized in the following kinds of questions: If those who now smoke had never smoked marijuana, would their crime rate be lower? Here we are moving closer to true cause. A comparison with heroin might prove to be instructive. Heroin *itself* doesn't cause crime—the drug, that is, doesn't induce a state of body and mind which induces violence and crime in those who take it—otherwise physician-narcotic addicts, whose drug of choice, meperidine (sometimes morphine), has effects similar to those of heroin, would be just as "criminal" as street junkies. But no one doubts that heroin is densely *implicated* in crime. Heroin itself has a soothing, soporific effect; if we knew nothing about the kinds of people who used the drug, we would predict that the drug would tend to reduce the likelihood of committing a crime. We would be right about the causal effect of the drug, but wrong about its indirect effect, and therefore, wrong about the actual crime rates of heroin users. The notion that marijuana "causes" crime could mean many different things, some of which would be acceptable by one definition, but not another, and vice versa. For instance, a pharmacologist is likely to have a very strict definition of cause; he is talking about the physiological action of the drug. A policeman would have a broader definition, since he wants to know whether or not, if there were no marijuana, the crime rate would go down. Thus, a pharmacologist would say that heroin does not "cause" crime, but a policeman would say that it does. It is not that one is wrong and the other right, they just have a different concept of what consititutes cause.

This type of argument assumes a number of guises. There are at least two subvarieties of the "indirect" or "pseudocausal" kind of connection between marijuana and crime. The one most acceptable to sociologists, at least theoretically, is a version of the "differential association" theory. By smoking marijuana, one is, willy-nilly, forced into intimate personal association with "real" criminals. In order to buy marijuana, it is necessary to interact with others who habitually break the law. Over time, the user, who was not criminal to begin with, has acquired a set of criminal associates and friends; one becomes implicated in a lawbreaking environment. Gradually, one comes to think of breaking the law as acceptable, and eventually leads a "criminal" life.

. . . The youthful narcotics user, even one who "takes a trip" only sporadically, is almost certain to make contact with some part of the criminal community that inevitably evolves around traffic in illegal merchandise. The boy or girl smoking marijuana in high school, for example, isn't just running the physiological and psychological risks, whatever they may be, attendant upon using the drug. There's the much greater risk of becoming inextricably tangled in an environment where regular criminal behavior is the accepted norm.

The prospects are particularly alarming for that large segment of the nation's juvenile society already stamped "delinquent" because of its wayward conduct. The potential in these young people's lives for serious encounters with the law is greatly intensified when they turn to narcotics; they've paid some of their dues to the criminal community. And it is in this group of youth that patterns of narcotics use develop earliest and become most firmly fixed.[16]

Another variety of the indirect relationship between marijuana and crime that is often invoked is that "one crime begets another," theme. By seeing that it is possible to get away with breaking the law, one becomes emboldened and goes on to other, more serious crimes. Marijuana use initiates the user into a "morass" of lawbreaking. The habit has a way of spreading. Eventually all laws become equally breakable, equally irrelevant. If drug laws do not command one's respect and compliance, then, eventually, no law does. (But, if the marijuana laws did not exist, then neither would this problem nor the escalation.) A difficulty with this point of view empirically is the fact that marijuana users who do *not* become arrested for marijuana use are probably *less* likely to commit other crimes later on, and eventually become arrested for them. Users who *are* arrested on marijuana charges are probably *more* likely to become arrested later on for something else more serious. Unless these facts are explained, the "emboldened" arguments will have to be revised.

TRUE CAUSAL RELATIONSHIP

The question here is: Does the pharmacological action of marijuana directly incite criminal and violent acts? An empirical test of this proposition is extremely difficult. In fact, there are few adequately controlled studies on the *general* effects of marijuana, none of which touch on crime or violence. A test of this sort in connection with crime is at least twenty years distant. Moreover, *no* chemical dictates to the human body so complex a behavior-syndrome as crime (or even violence). The organs of the human body may be affected by a chemical in a specific way—or more commonly, in a variety of ways—but what the mind tells the body to do as a result is not a chemical matter. The chemical imperative becomes filtered through an individual's personality, and his group's collective experiences, and his behavior is affected by them. The group translates what these vague bodily sensations mean, and what kinds of activities they may represent behaviorally. A drug may offer a bodily and behavioral potential for crime and violence, but it cannot dictate or determine that they will inevitably take place. Other elements must be present. Even Bloomquist admits that marijuana's positive impact on the commission of crime is partly dependent on whether or not the individual in question has "criminal tendencies," whatever that might mean.

In one of the more widely circulated works putting forth the claim of marijuana's crime-inducing effects, the following mechanisms are asserted as the "cause" of the crimes: "(1) use by criminals to fortify their courage prior to committing crimes; (2) chronic use resulting in general derangement and demoralization; (3) use resulting in the lowering of inhibition and bringing out suppressed criminal tendencies; and (4) use resulting in panic, confusion or anger induced in otherwise normal persons who have not been previous users." [17] Let us examine some of these undocumented claims.

One of the more direct criminogenic effects claimed for mari-juana has to do with the generation of courage in the commission of crimes. Many criminals supposedly use marijuana as a means of either becoming relaxed or hopped up—depending on who is offering this theory and his image of what marijuana does.

The claim is that it is the professional criminals who consciously employ the drug to commit crimes more effectively. If it is true that marijuana is used to become hopped up and to more quickly throw oneself into a kind of frenzied, maniacal state, this would obviously lower one's rational ability to commit crimes competently with a minimum of risk. Most professional crimes require stealth, skill, deftness, and controlled courage. It would seem peculiar indeed that the criminal would employ an agent that is reputed by those who attribute the criminal with employing it to have both an unre-liable and a kind of exciting, even deranging effect. If this is one of the many consequences of smoking marijuana, professional crim-inals would be among the last people on earth who would use the drug in conjunction with their "work." In my research, I have found strong indications that this supposed "hopping up" effect of mari-juana is simply a myth.

The other accusation (a mirror image, completely contradicting the first) is that the criminal uses pot to gain "controlled courage." Supposedly marijuana will be used by the lawbreaker on the verge of carrying out his crime because the drug has a calming effect; it reduces his panicky, irrational tendencies. It lowers his chances of "blowing" a job. It makes him cool and rational. If this is what happens (and it is closer to reality than the first claim), then mari-juana's effect is anything but criminogenic. It could help to calm nerves in any situation; it could aid rationality under all crisis con-ditions. It could aid the racing car driver, the nervous student tak-ing an exam, the job interviewee, the adolescent on his first date, the stage-struck actor. If it is the generation of a rational courage that gives marijuana its criminal thrust, then we discover that this effect has nothing specifically to do with crime. Criminals wear shoes, drive to the site of their crimes in cars, communicate with one another by means of the English language, but no one has thought of outlawing these crime-related agents.

Marijuana is said to "lower inhibitions." This leads to the com-mission of crime. It is taken for granted in a civilization that does not trust its innermost self that the lowering of inhibitions (or the loss of control) will necessarily have a violent and criminal countenance. Man, the theory goes, is protected from his animal nature by a thin veneer of culture; when this veneer is pierced or weakened, he becomes destructive. Man's inner being is savage, primitive, and inherently antisocial. This model of man, given its greatest impetus by Freud, had influenced popular criminology for almost a century. It is completely inadequate to explain anything, and blatantly false as a description of man and what makes him tick.

I will conclude this topic by asking a set of questions that any theory of lawbreaking must answer, which cast doubt on the theory of the lowering of inhibitions as a cause of crime (and as a reason why marijuana, specifically, is inherently criminogenic). No one has adequately explained why or how it is that a "loss of control" or a "release of inhibitions" will necessarily—or ever—result in violent crimes, or crimes of any sort. Why violence? Why crime? Why, if man becomes less inhibited, does he do harm to his fellow man? Is the internal life of man intrinsically antisocial? Do we really have such a gloomy image of who man "really" is, what he "really" wants to do? Are man's most fundamental and well-hidden desires really of such a destructive nature? How are these desires generated? Are they intrinsic in the nature of man? Or are they socially generated? Or do they exist at all? Why isn't man's internal life more creative, more directed toward the good of society (however that might be interpreted)? What, specifically, is the *mechanism* that translates a "loss of control" into acts of violence and crime? Could it be that man fears doing charitable acts toward his fellow man because he will be thought a dupe and a fool? Perhaps any "liberating" mechanism will bring out these philanthropic tendencies. Are charitable acts rewarded in our society? Perhaps "inhibitions" serve to restrain man from being generous and socially constructive. Are acts of creativity and imagination rewarded by us? Perhaps a release of inhibitions really serves to bring out man's inner being—which is more creative, not more violent, than is apparent in public. (The Timothy Leary camp, too, asserts that the psychedelic drugs release inhibitions, but their image of man's essential being is different from the antipot lobby's.)

The "fact" that marijuana releases inhibitions and, therefore, is criminogenic, is a common accusation. But it is built on a theory and an image of man that is essentially outdated today. There is no evidence to support the contention that man, disinhibited, is any more dangerous than man with his protective cultural shield around him. He who makes the accusation assumes automatically that inhibitions are a wholesome and protective device that no society can do without. Man, after all, the theory goes, is *essentially evil.* Therefore inhibitions are good, because they restrain man's essential nature. This is an assumption that many informed students of man are not willing to make. Before we can take seriously the accusation that marijuana releases inhibitions and therefore causes man to be violent, we will have to clear up the validity of many fundamental and essential theoretical questions which remain, at this time, speculative and unfounded.

Consider that the great majority of the most widespread and devastating violence in the world's history has stemmed not from aggressiveness, but from passivity and compliance. Most of the fighting personnel of nearly all armies of the modern world has been made up of only semiwilling young men who, basically, do not wish to kill or be killed, but who fear the social reprisals attendant upon their refusal to fight. The *passive* reaction is to go along with acceptable social definitions and pressures (often from those who do not themselves have to make such a decision) and commit acts of violence on one's fellow man. The aggressive and self-assertive reactions are to refuse to fight and kill in warfare. Thus, acceptable social and cultural responses, that thin layer of protective civilization, supposedly keeping man's destructive impulses in check, often lead to violence, while to be "released from inhibitions" sometimes means to be nonviolent. Often, by following one's inner bent, one's selfish desires, removed from society's pressures, one is less violent and less destructive.

The final accusation concerning marijuana's criminogenic impact has to do with "panic reactions." Marijuana causes crime, especially violence, because the drug has a psychotomimetic effect that deranges the mind, causing the user to run amok, wreaking incalculable damage to his fellow man. I have never seen a reaction of this type, and a number of physicians who specialize in psychoactive drugs have never seen it either with marijuana. (This does not mean that they do not exist; it probably means, however, that they are rare.) Panic reactions are more common with some other drugs, LSD, for instance. During the interviewing I gained the confidence of a number of users to such an extent that two called me while they were experiencing such a panic state under the influence of LSD. It took no psychiatrist to see that the reaction was fear and helplessness, not violence. The drug panic state is more generative of passive fright, withdrawn incapacity—a desire to flee threats and danger from others. If this occurs with any frequency with marijuana (I have never seen evidence that it does), it is without a doubt *not* a cause for violence and crime among users. We will have to search elsewhere for marijuana's criminogenics.

Studies and Surveys

We commonly read that a "study" has "proven" a causal connection between marijuana use and crime, particularly violent crime. Giordano, the former Associate Director of the Bureau of Narcotics and Dangerous Drugs, wrote as follows: "The Bureau of Narcotics and Dangerous Drugs recently conducted its own study. It revealed a definite pattern between marihuana usage and crime. City and state police agencies were surveyed to gather and assemble a volume of well-documented instances where criminal behavior was directly related to the use of marihuana." [18]

As no statistics were cited in this particular article wherein the claim was made—only isolated cases were enumerated—I wrote to the Bureau of Narcotics asking about this "study." Louise G. Richards, research social psychologist for the Division of Drug Sciences of the Bureau, replied: "The study mentioned by Mr. Giordano . . . was not a research project of this Division. I have never seen it referred to except in the cited article. As far as I know, it did not result in either a published or an unpublished report" (personal communication, June 3, 1969). In fact, no such systematic study was actually done by the Bureau—nor has there ever been a study that adequately and definitively demonstrated the reputed link between marijuana and crime. Systematic data have never been brought to bear on the question.

In 1968 (no date appears on the publication), the Los Angeles Police Department distributed a pamphlet, "Facts About Marijuana," which included sections entitled, "Does Marijuana Incite

Crimes of Violence?" and "Marijuana Crimes." The latter enumerated fourteen cases where marijuana was presumed to have been
causal in the commission of crimes. It contains the introductory
remarks: "In 1966 the Los Angeles Police Department conducted a
survey into the relationship between marijuana and criminal behavior. Hundreds of cases were documented during a one-year
period in which marijuana was involved as a factor of criminal
behavior. The next several pages contain a few criminal cases
selected from the survey to illustrate this relationship." [19]

I wrote to the Los Angeles Police Department about this study
made on the relationship between marijuana and criminal behavior.
I received a reply from Clifford J. Shannon, Captain, and Com-
mander of the LAPD's Public Affairs Division, which stated: "All
available information from the 1966 survey on the relationship between marijuana and criminal behavior is contained in . . . the
Los Angeles Police Department booklet, 'Facts About Marijuana.'
The survey has not been published as a separate document." In
other words, what was called a "survey" and a "study" was the
collection of scattered cases wherein marijuana was supposedly connected in some way or another with the commission of crime. Needless to say, as a descriptive or scientific document, this "survey" is
worthless. All "studies" which claim to establish the causal link,
upon close scrutiny, simply do not observe even the most elemen-
tary rules of rigorous empirical proof. All the restrictions of logic
and adequate documentation seem to be magically dissolved when
it comes to this question; emotion, rather than disinterested inquiry,
reigns supreme. The "proofs" which have been submitted on this
issue are perfect illustrations of our earlier axiom concerning the
need to shore up propaganda with pseudoscientific accoutréments.
Probably no area of endeavor better illustrates our principle concerning the "politics of reality" than this, the connection between
marijuana and crime. The causal connection between marijuana
and crime exists only in the minds of men. Paper, as Stalin so
cynically observed—and, indeed, put into practice—can be made to
print anything.

The studies most often cited to prove that marijuana causes crime
are those by Munch ("Marihuana and Crime"), Wolff (*Marihuana
in Latin America)*, Gardikas ("Hashish and Crime"), an unpublished
manuscript by Victor Vogel, and several works by the Indian Chopras.
We will examine these reports.

Half of Munch's eight-page article on marijuana and crime [20] is taken up with enumeration of crimes committed, supposedly, under the influence of marijuana. (Or so the caption indicates. There is no indication of how the police detected marijuana intoxication. During the entire period when all of the enumerated crimes were committed, there was no known method for detecting the presence of marijuana in the human body. In some of the cases, clues were mentioned, but most of them omit references to the drug.) Sixty-nine cases are included, going back to the 1930s (in one case, back to 1921, before the existence of marijuana laws). A typical case might be "Smoked marijuana for years; held up three taxi-cabs," or "Negro, shot and killed while attempting to holdup grocer in Harlem; plea guilty." Only a glance back at the discussion of the enumerative method of reasoning illuminates the worth of this procedure.

Another section of Munch's article is an enumeration of "references" which lists works, most of which assert the connection between marijuana and crime without empirical documentation. A table presents, supposedly, effects of marijuana on the human mind and body. Several of these effects have been empirically demonstrated to be false: hypoglycemia (decrease in blood sugar), a decrease in the rate of respiration, and mydriasis (marked dilation of the pupils), for instance. Other effects are merely asserted and are, by all known accounts, highly improbable: "chronic exposure produces brain lesions," "death by cardiac failure some individuals after 100 to 200 times therapeutic dose," [21] "hypersensitivity sensation of ants running over skin" (not one of my 200 respondents described this particular sensation), "diarrhea or constipation," etc. One wonders, after this inventory of effects, why anyone would ever try the drug; if one believed that these effects ever took place, the fact that millions of people in this country have tried it would be puzzling.

Another study commonly cited by police in an effort to demonstrate the criminal tendencies inherent in marijuana is Pablo Osvaldo Wolff's *Marihuana in Latin America: The Threat It Constitutes.* [22] Although this opus was published over two decades ago, it is still cited with approval by the antimarijuana propagandists. Rather than a study, it is another enumeration of crimes supposedly caused by marijuana, along with extravagant declarations as to marijuana's baleful effect: "With every reason, marihuana . . . has been closely associated since the most remote time with insanity, with crime, with violence, and with brutality." Again, one searches in vain for a systematic analysis of the criminogenic effect of this supposedly deadly drug. Instead, we are greeted with a barrage of rumor, distortions, blatant falsehoods, and dogmatic assertions. Although we have been assured by Anslinger in the foreword that the author is "impartial," and the monograph, "painstaking . . . erudite, well-documented . . . comprehensive . . . accurate . . . extensive . . . well-rounded . . . convincing," we are perplexed by the bombastic and otiose language which casts considerable doubt on its author as a reliable, impartial observer. We are assured that "this weed . . . changes thousands of persons into nothing more than human scum," and that "this vice . . . should be suppressed at any cost." Marijuana is labelled "weed of the brutal crime and of the burning hell," an "exterminating demon which is now attacking our country"; users are referred to as "addicts" (passim) whose "motive belongs to a strain which is pure viciousness." [23]

Wolff's work should be considered a relic of a benighted age, but it is taken seriously today by those who require confirmation of the dangers of this drug, as well as for the fact that this slim volume has provided a fertile seedbed of concepts, ideas, and distinctions which are very much alive today. Although it will be the job of later intellectual historians to trace the elaborate interconnections and influences of today's drug ideologists, both pro and con, many antecedents (on the contra side) may be discerned in Pablo Osvaldo Wolff; some may not have originated with him, but he gave them all propulsion. For instance, this work is very clear on the distinction between "an addiction in the classic sense of morphinism" and what Wolff (and physicians today) call "psychic addiction," or "habituation." [24] Needless to say, this distinction is crucial in today's medical writings; the similarity between the two use-syndromes is emphasized rather than their differences. (See the chapter on the physician's point of view toward marijuana for an elaboration of this distinction.) Second, Wolff distinctly presaged another dominant current theme:

. . . the use of marihuana is always an abuse and a vice in the strictest sense of the word. So far as this drug is concerned, there is no medical indication whatsoever that will justify its use in the present day and age. . . . at the present time there is no scientific therapeutic indication whatever still recognized in which cannabis has any part. . . . marijuana . . .

230

has no sublime characteristics, but only inflicts blows upon its addicts, renders them depraved, degrades them physically and morally. I repeat my initial warning: there is not, as is the case with the opiates, any reason, any excuse, any indication for its use. It is always abuse, dangerous to the individual and to the race.[25]

This definition of "abuse" forms the cornerstone of contemporary medical thinking concerning intoxicating drugs, especially marijuana. Aside from these two powerful and much used concepts, the evidence of Wolff's handiwork may be seen in dozens of conceptual and supposedly factual edifices. "All civilized countries have included in their protective legislation a prohibition of the use of cannabis for enjoyment purposes . . ." [26] Wolff intones; the echo of this pontification is heard today: ". . . why is it that marijuana is the *only* drug that is outlawed in every civilized country in the world?" [27] (It is difficult to fathom what is meant by "civilized," however; America, it is to be assumed, is civilized, while less enlightened countries are not.) Wolff's assertion that marijuana, with prolonged and "excessive" use, tends to produce an "irreparable brain lesion" [28] has its contemporary reverberation today in Munch's "chronic exposure produces brain lesions." [29] Naturally, we find in Wolff that marijuana influences violence, as for example, in the followers of Hasan and Pancho Villa; produces automobile accidents ("especially of buses"!); incites the "aggressive instinct"; activates "delinquency and criminality"; causes "episodic states of mental confusion, psychoses of short duration . . . , and chronic prolonged psychoses"; marijuana, we are told, is especially dangerous because "the effect that will be produced on each individual cannot be forseen," and because the drug seems to stimulate a proselytization among its habitués.[30] In short, the complete anti-marijuana propagandist's litany is present, intact, in Wolff. Many of us have learned nothing in the past generation.

Law-enforcement officers in an effort to document the crimino-genic impact of marijuana also cite Victor H. Vogel's "Excerpts from Statements Regarding Marihuana Use Made by One-Hundred Consecutive Heroin Addicts Interviewed by Dr. Victor H. Vogel at the California Rehabilitation Center During Release Hearings Beginning August 18, 1967." It is an unpublished manuscript of six·pages containing a collection of statements by 100 addicts in one or two-sentence form; statements such as: "We used to get into gang fights when we were high on marihuana"; "Makes me silly; everything I do or say or hear is funny"; "It exaggerates all feelings, including sex"; "It slowed me down so much I had to drop out of school."[31]

Since these statements were made before a release hearing, it is apparent that the addict knew that any indication of remorse on his part would be judged favorably, and would, therefore, make statements which he knew would help to secure his release. This alone makes these statements suspect. We would *expect* statements of conventional morality under these circumstances, expressions the judge wanted to hear. In a sense, then, these statements make up a kind of miniature *morality play*, where we learn not so much the nature of reality, but what the society staging it thinks about the nature of reality. Any addict knows that he will be treated more leniently if he expresses a conventional view of the dangers of marijuana, so that his statements correspond more to his perceptions of what the judge wants to hear rather than what the drug actually did for or to him.

In addition, heroin addicts are extremely atypical marijuana users. They are far more criminal than any other single group of drug users. The kind of person who becomes an addict is likely to have had committed a number of crimes (although addiction, obviously, increases their seriousness and extent) and therefore to have smoked marijuana at some time or another during the commission of a given crime. But this tells us nothing about whether marijuana had anything to do with the crime committed. It certainly tells us nothing about the effects of marijuana on crime, in general, on the nonaddict population. These statements simply do not apply beyond the addict population who uttered them.

It seems peculiar that antimarijuana ideologists will accept the statements of addicts in a situation where it is to their advantage to present the criminogenic argument, and will reject the statements of marijuana smokers made in a situation where no such advantage accrues to them. Nonincarcerated marijuana users, when interviewed in their living room by a stranger they will never see again, are far more likely to express a favorable view of the effects of the drug and to deny most of its negative effects. Their motives for lying are certainly far less powerful than those which faced Vogel's addicts.

In an effort to forge a link between crime and marijuana, some commentators have used the research of the Chopras, three physicians who have written on cannabis use in India for over thirty years. To use the Chopras in support of the criminal impact of this drug, one must be extremely selective, because they not only underplay this aspect, they often deny it altogether. Bloomquist, Miller, Munch, and Haslip,[32] all cite the Chopras' research as confirming marijuana's criminogenic effect. Most of these quotes use the statement that sometimes users are subject to "fits of aggressive mania." Yet the Chopras' most recent statement, largely a summary of their previous work, asserts that, "With regard to premeditated crime, in some cases, the drugs [bhang, ganja and charas] not only do not lead to it, but actually act as deterrents. One of the most important actions of cannabis is to quiet and stupify the individual so that there is no tendency to violence . . ."[33] A Canadian physician, H. B. M. Murphy, is quoted by Chopra as a summary on marijuana and crime, saying, "Most serious observers agree that cannabis does not, per se, induce aggressive or criminal activities, and that the reduction of the work drive leads to a negative correlation with criminality rather than a positive one."[34] The Chopras seem to provide thin fodder for the argument of the criminal inducement of cannabis.

The same cannot be said for the work of Gardikas ("Hashish and Crime").[35] A police officer and head of the Greek Criminal Service in Athens, Gardikas reviewed 379 cases of individuals who were arrested for publicly using cannabis between 1919 and 1950. In the sample, 117 cases were first arrested for cannabis offenses and, after their release, became "confirmed criminals," having been arrested for a total of 420 offenses in the period studied. The fact that they became criminal only *after* their involvement with hashish demonstrates to Gardikas as well as to law enforcement officers and to various other commentators that hashish *causes* crime. Over 200 cases in the sample were already criminal prior to starting the use of hashish, and the remaining fifty-three, after their arrest for cannabis, did not commit any nonhashish crimes later.

We are not told how these cases were selected. Are they the only cannabis offense cases that came to Gardikas' attention? Were they gathered more or less by accident? Were they a result of random selection? Or were they selected for the very fact that their crime rate was so high? We have no way of knowing. And what social universe does this group represent: All hashish smokers in Greece? Not having this information, the methodology seems dubious.

It is a certainty that *arrested* cannabis smokers are different from nonarrested ones, just as arrested violators of any law are radically different from those who also commit the same crimes, but who do not get arrested. The class factor operates here powerfully, just to mention a single source of variation. The middle-class violator is far more able to avoid detection through a combination of bias and caution, as well as a number of other factors, such as police saturation in poorer areas. Working-class patterns of crime, particularly certain kinds of crime, such as violent ones, are very different from those of the middle-class user. To use *arrested* hashish smokers as an indication of the criminal potential inherent in the *drug* is fallacious.

Also, it might very well be necessary to raise the question of the criminogenic effect of the Greek penal system. Anyone arrested once becomes subject to greater scrutiny, and therefore, almost of necessity, his crime rate will be higher. The police simply "being around" accounts for much of the differential in crime rates. A crime undetected is, from an official point of view, a crime uncommitted. In addition, many criminologists think that having been exposed to prison gives a person criminal tendencies.[36] Prisons are the most effective spawning grounds of criminals known to man. Anyone who has served some time in prison is more likely to come out a potential professional criminal than he is to be "rehabilitated."

In addition, Gardikas assumes that the crimes for which the 117 offenders were arrested were the result of having been involved with hashish, since they followed the hashish arrest. This is a good example of the post hoc fallacy. We have no idea why these 420 offenses were committed, let alone can we be sure that they were caused by the hashish. Nor do we know that the arrested individuals were not involved in a life of crime *before* the hashish arrest. Merely because they had not been arrested until then is no indication that they did not commit nonhashish crimes. They might very well have been criminals all along and picked up hashish along the way, and been merely unfortunate enough to get arrested first for the hashish.

All we really know from the Gardikas study is that arrested hashish smokers are involved in a good deal of crime. We have no idea whether hashish "causes" the violations, or was associated with them in any way. We know nothing about whether the nonarrested smoker is also as criminal, or whether he ever commits crimes. We do not know how representative the sample even is of arrested users, let alone users in general. As a demonstration of the criminogenic effect of cannabis, this study is of extremely dubious value at best.

Our Two Hundred Interviews

In our interview study, we asked the respondents to enumerate any and all arrests which they might have experienced. It is almost impossible to make a systematic, rigorous, and meaningful comparison with the general population with the aim of determining whether marijuana users are "more criminal" or "less criminal" than nonusers. Our sample is not representative. (But no sample of lawbreakers ever is a true cross-section.) It is a different average age than the American population—a median of twenty-two as opposed to twenty-seven, with almost no very young or very old. It is entirely urban—nearly all reside in New York City. It is more middle-class than the nation as a whole. We know that all of the sample, to be included in the study, have engaged in criminal behavior—marijuana use, possession, and sale—and on that basis alone, be expected to be arrested more times than the average member of American society. We might isolate out at least a dozen such factors which make the two "populations" incomparable. Some of these factors would tend to inflate our sample's lawbreaking tendencies, while others might decrease them. Taken together, the methodological problems with such a comparison are insurmountable, if we wish to test this question scrupulously and definitively.

However, if we wish to use our sample's arrest data as a very loose indication of their degree of criminal involvement and make a casual comparsion with the overall arrest figures for the United States, not as an attempt at a conclusive demonstration, but as a crude approximation which at least poses this question, then perhaps light might be shed on the issue. One qualification we must keep in mind concerns the adequacy of arrest figures to measure criminal activity. Recall that all of the marijuana-related activity of our sample resulted in a total of only nine marijuana arrests. Most of these were the consequence of an accident of some sort. Thus, people who are not arrested are not necessarily noncriminal but often merely lucky or evasive enough to be undetected. Is the non-apprehended population less criminal than the arrestees? We have no way of knowing. We do know that nonarrestees commit a very large number of crimes. Of course, it varies by the nature of the crime; murder is very often detected, and the offender arrested, while crimes without victims usually go undetected.

At any rate, our 204 respondents admitted arrest a total of fifty-five times, for all nontraffic, nonmarijuana offenses. As a parallel, keep in mind that in 1965, the arrest rate for the American population was 3.7 arrests per 100 in the population.[37] One difficulty we have in comparing these two figures is that our figure is the number of arrests which *ever* took place, while the U.S. figure is the recorded rate for that one year only. Since the median age of our respondents is twenty-two, let us assume that the age range during which an arrest is possible and likely is seven years—age fifteen to twenty-two, even though the earliest arrest in our sample took place at age ten. Therefore, we might divide the fifty-five arrests figure by seven, yielding a yearly rate of about 3.9 arrests per 100 individuals. (Even if we include the nine marijuana arrests, the figure is 4.5 per 100.) The fact that this is almost identical with the national rate is surprising.

If we examine the *types* of crimes our respondents were arrested for, however, we find ourselves looking at a pattern totally unlike the national picture. Drunkeness accounts for by far the most arrests nationally; in fact *one-third* of all the arrests recorded in the United States in 1965 were for the single infraction of public drunkenness. Disorderly conduct, a vague rubric, garnered about a tenth of all arrests. Larceny, driving under the influence of alcohol, simple assault, burglary, violation of the liquor laws, vagrancy, gambling, and motor vehicle theft, constituted the eight next most frequent offenses.[38] No single crime among my respondents on the other hand attracted more than a few scattered arrests, except for participation in political demonstrations. Over a third of their arrests (nineteen out of fifty-five) were for protesting, picketing, or demonstrating—nonviolently. We only reveal our political biases if we conceive of these "crimes" as criminal in the conventional sense. If we wish to hold that by smoking marijuana, our sense of ideological involvement will be heightened, we will please the proclivities of the marijuana-smoking subculture, and probably proponents of the "far right" as well, who oppose both marijuana and political demonstrations. But to call this activity a crime in any but the formal sense makes us a part of the ideological machinery which structures the "politics of reality" by giving a discrediting label to anything that opposes its definition of the truth.

If we search the remaining arrests, a few do not fall within our conception of a "conventional" crime. One interviewee, an artist, dancer, jewelry designer, and mime performer, was arrested for wearing a painted mime face, illegal under an obscure local ordinance. Thus, a "crime" was committed, and an arrest made. Can we say, therefore, that the marijuana subculture had anything to do with this particular respondent's "criminal tendencies"? Twelve of the fifty-five arrests took place before the respondent was "turned on" to marijuana. (A policeman scrutinizing this would conclude that it is a "criminal type" who eventually turns to drugs.)

In view of the police supposition that marijuana causes crime, particularly crimes of violence, it might be instructive to look at the relationship, if any, that exists between the rate of crime and the *amount* of marijuana the respondent smokes. The reasoning would be that, if it is true that the drug stimulates a physical and mental state which is dangerous and criminogenic, then the more the person experiences this state, the greater his likelihood of committing crimes, and the greater his chances of being arrested. We would expect the *daily* smoker, who is high from two to possibly eighteen hours every day, highly likely to be arrested, because he is in a "criminal" state of mind for such long periods of time. To test this proposition (an informal test, neither rigorous nor conclusive) we excluded all the "political" crimes (arrests for nonviolent demonstrations). (Interestingly enough, these were by far most common among the *least* frequent smokers, and least common among the most frequent smokers.) We are then left with twenty-one arrests for "serious" crimes committed by fifteen respondents. These crimes include nonmarijuana narcotics possession, disorderly conduct, drunkenness, burglary, assault, auto theft, serving liquor to a minor, and larceny. Do heavy marijuana smokers commit these crimes more frequently than infrequent smokers? We are surprised to discover that according to our study, they do not commit crimes any more frequently. Furthermore, there appears to be no relationship whatsoever between the amount the respondent smokes and his likelihood of arrest. Three of our daily smokers had been arrested for "serious" crimes; three of those who smoked three to six times a week were arrested for these crimes; three of our one to two times weekly smokers were so arrested, three of the respondents who smoked one to four times monthly were arrested, and three of the less than monthly users were arrested for these crimes. Although these numbers are extremely small, the fact of their perfect dispersal is perhaps indicative of the lack of a crime-inducing effect of the drug. It is, at any rate, a proposition which ought to be tested more systematically in the future with more complete data. For the moment, there are indications that point to the fact that the marijuana smoker is no more criminal than the rest of the population.

A Note on the Sociology of Crime

The typical smoker's attitude toward the law cannot be thought of simply as a general "disrespect for law," that is, any and all laws. Law is not thought of as evil by users simply because it is law. Certain laws are thought of as good and others as evil. Obviously, the marijuana laws are rejected as unjust. (Among our respondents, 95 percent wanted to do away with the marijuana laws.) But simply because "the law is the law" does not make it just. There is a *selectivity* accorded to laws. Therefore, this inclination toward greater deviance in general actually predisposes users to disobey only *certain* laws. Users do not question the justice of many laws, particularly laws connected with violence—armed robbery, rape, mayhem, murder, assault. Others of a *political* character will be more readily rejected. As I pointed out, my interviewees *were far more likely* to commit and be arrested for crimes connected with political demonstrations than any other type of crime. Marijuana users are also probably more likely to commit sex crimes than nonusers. Not sex crimes connected with violence or coercion, such as rape, child molestation, or exhibitionism; probably not even sexual crimes that result in arrest. But many sexual activities are criminal: fellatio, cunnilingus, premarital intercourse, adultery, pornography, abortion, sodomy, homosexuality. There is no doubt in my mind that users are far more likely to commit these "harmless" sex crimes than nonusers. Their greater willingness to deviate,

238

to experiment, to disregard conventional sexual mores, probably indicates a more general unconcern for norms that, they think, are obsolete.

The word "criminal" conjures up in the mind a definite stereotype. When we think of crime, we generally think of *violent* crimes. If I had to hazard a guess, I would say that marijuana users probably commit violent crimes no more than, and possibly less than, the population at large. But violent crimes are only a small fraction of all crimes. Many activities have become criminalized. The designation "criminal" is social, not legal. A person who has technically breached the law is technically a "criminal." Yet society has decided which of these breaches will qualify its transgressor for the title of criminal, and which will not. Our conception of what is criminal is not governed by the laws, but by the norms.

The conventionally inclined will bridle at the thought of the tendency of so many marijuana users picking and choosing which laws they will obey and which they will ignore. Actually, we all do this. We are all lawbreakers in one way or another. The landlord with inspection violations, the dubious and illegal business practices of many ghetto merchants, the monopolistic and price-fixing tendencies of some large corporations, the employer who pays wages under the minimum wage—all are breaking the law (although these laws are not generally covered by the umbrella of "criminal" law). But when we think of "law and order," we do not include these infractions; we think of them merely as sharp business practices. The policeman who uses illegal and overly violent methods to arrest a suspect [39] is violating the law, but our very selective perception of this phenomenon—what is law and order, and what is illegal and disorderly—excludes the violent policeman. If any of the perpetrators of such acts is ever prosecuted for their infractions and actually serves a prison sentence—such as happened with General Electric's executives a few years ago—many of us are outraged, because the price-fixing executive does not conform to our stereotype of a criminal and his crime does not fit our notion of what crime is.

Thus, in the strict sense, the question of the greater "criminal" activity of marijuana users is meaningless. "Crime" is not a unitary phenomenon. We would not expect anything to have a systematic relationship with all kinds of crime, since some types of crime will be found to vary inversely with other types. For instance, violators of price-fixing statutes will certainly have a lower crime rate compared with other types of crime—violent crime, for instance—than the population at large.

Thus, it is impossible to give a meaningful answer to the simple question as to the greater criminality of marijuana smokers, because the concept of crime is so vague. It would, of course, be possible to devise an overall crime rate for both groups, or for user and nonuser matched samples. But such a figure would not be very useful or indicative of anything in general; because in order to answer the question intelligibly, it would be necessary to know the reasons for which the question was asked. Crimes vary in nature. What is it that we are trying to determine by asking the question? The overall fact of having technically breached this or that law? This might be useful for propaganda purposes—to say that users are a highly "criminal" population, if that is true, in order to cast doubt on them, as well as on the use of marijuana—but not if we are trying to understand the nature of society and what makes it work as it does. At the very least, we would have to separate out the various kinds of crimes which we are interested in.

NOTES

1. Earle Albert Rowell and Robert Rowell, *On the Trail of Marihuana: The Weed of Madness* (Mountain View, Calif.: Pacific Press Publishing Association, 1939), pp. 13, 46, 48, 67.

2. We must keep in mind the fact that possession of marijuana is *itself* a crime, so that by definition any marijuana user is a "criminal." Obviously, we must exclude marijuana use from our concept of crime, otherwise our discussion would be a tautology —it would be true by definition. Thus, when we refer to crime, we assume that it means nonmarijuana crimes.

3. The federal position may in flux. Under Henry L. Giordano, Harry Anslinger's hand-picked successor, the Bureau of Narcotics took the position that marijuana caused crime. The present director, John E. Ingersoll, appears to be in the process of re-evaluating the Bureau's past policies. In a recent speech to the National Academy of Science, he said that "established positions, where no longer valid, will no longer be maintained." It is too early to discern what direction this policy will take. However, the fact that Ingersoll has asked Congress recently to lower the federal penalties on marijuana possession may very well indicate that the Bureau's position on the criminogenics of marijuana has softened considerably.

4. Henry L. Giordano, "Marihuana—A Calling Card to Narcotic Addiction," *FBI Law Enforcement Bulletin* 37, no. 11 (November 1968): 2.

5. New York State Department of Health, "Violence Direct Result of Marijuana,

Says Bellizzi; State Health Official Cites 27 Murders by Drug Users," *New York State Department of Health Weekly Bulletin* 20, no. 26 (June 26, 1967): 101.

6. Thorvald T. Brown, *The Enigma of Drug Addiction* (Springfield, Ill.: Charles C Thomas, 1961), pp. 61, 62.

7. Edward R. Bloomquist, *Marijuana* (Beverly Hills, Calif.: Glencoe Press, 1968), p. 97.

8. Louria, *The Drug Scene,* (New York: McGraw-Hill, 1968), p. 110.

9. Roswell D. Johnson, "Medico-Social Aspects of Marijuana," *The Rhode Island Medical Journal* 51 (March 1968): 176, 177.

10. Thomas Ciesla, Testimony, in *Hearings on Marijuana Laws Before the California Public Health and Safety Committee* (Los Angeles, October 18, 1967, morning session), transcript, pp. 110–111.

11. Bloomquist, *op. cit.,* p. 93.

12. Herbert Blumer et al., *The World of Youthful Drug Use* (Berkeley: University of California, School of Criminology, January 1967), p. 30.

13. James C. Munch, "Marihuana and Crime," United Nations *Bulletin on Narcotics* 18, no. 2 (April–June 1966): 15–22; Bloomquist, *op. cit.,* pp. 4–5; New York Department of Health, *op. cit.,* p. 101; Giordano, *op. cit.,* pp. 4–5; Donald E. Miller, "Marihuana: The Law and Its Enforcement," *Suffolk University Law Review* 3 (Fall 1968): 86–87; Los Angeles Police Department, "Facts About Marijuana," pamphlet (Los Angeles: Narcotic Educational Foundation of America, n.d. [circa 1968]), pp. 7–8; Martin Lordi, "The Truth about Marijuana: Stepping Stone to Destruction," leaflet 1, No. 5 (Newark, New Jersey: The Essex County Youth and Economic Rehabilitation Commission, June 1967), n.p.

14. The President's Commission on Law Enforcement and Administration of Justice, "Crime in America," in *The Challenge of Crime in a Free Society* (Washington: U.S. Government Printing Office, 1967), Table 8.

15. This fact does not contradict the fact that users often fear arrest. But they typically think in terms of "don't get caught"—i.e., in largely *tactical* terms. They do not feel guilty about having broken the law because they do not feel that the law is just. But regardless of whether it is just or not, users cannot ignore it.

16. Robert Osterman, *A Report in Depth on Crime in America* (Silver Spring, Md.: The National Observer, 1966), p. 94.

It is a curious irony of this position that the most effective means of reducing the putative link between marijuana and crime is to decriminalize marijuana. If it were not illegal to use, own, buy, and sell marijuana, then not only criminals would use it, and one need not associate with criminals to buy it. So that the user is not seduced into a life of crime. No adherent of this position, however, would be willing to accept its conclusions.

17. Gene R. Haslip, "Current Issues in the Prevention and Control of the Marihuana Abuse" (Paper presented to the First National Conference on Student Drug Involvement sponsored by the United States National Student Association at the University of Maryland, August 16, 1967), pp. 4–6.

18. Giordano, *op. cit.,* p. 4. Some of the crimes gathered in this pseudo-study are presented in Louis C. Wyman, "Examples of Marihuana and Crime," *Congressional Record,* April 4, 1968, pp. E2753–E2754. I would like to thank Dr. Richards for her assistance on these facts, in spite of my disagreement with the Bureau's policies.

19. Los Angeles Police Department, *op. cit.,* pp. 6–8.

20. Munch, *op. cit.*

21. The question of a "lethal dose" is debatable. Since marijuana is not toxic in the same way that alcohol is, there is no known lethal dosage. However, any agent, including water, has some level at which it may be fatal, if only for the fact that it obstructs normal and vital bodily processes. It is probably impossible to *smoke* a lethal dose of marijuana—the smoker would have passed out long before his intake reached a level of danger to his body—but one can probably ingest a fatal amount by eating, simply because the effects will be felt long after intake occurs; the same could be said for any substance, however inert.

22. Published by the Linacre Press, in Washington, in 1949.

23. Wolff, *op. cit.*, pp. 52, 53, 50, 45.

24. *Ibid.*, pp. 46, 47.

25. *Ibid.*, p. 53.

26. *Ibid.*, p. 49.

27. Martin Lordi, "The Truth about Marijuana" Letter to the Editor, *Playboy*, June 1968, p. 163.

28. Wolff, *op. cit.*, p. 22.

29. Munch, *op. cit.*, p. 17.

30. Wolff, *op. cit.*, pp. 13, 23–27, 31, 33–36, 37, 39.

31. Vogel, *op. cit.*, pp. 1, 3, 5, 6.

32. Bloomquist, *Marijuana*, p. 95; Miller, *op. cit.*, p. 85; Munch, *op. cit.*, pp. 15, 22; Haslip, *op. cit.*, p. 5.

33. Gurbakhsh Singh Chopra, "Man and Marijuana," *The International Journal of the Addictions* 4 (June 1969): 240.

34. H. B. M. Murphy, "The Cannabis Habit," United Nations *Bulletin on Narcotics* 15, no. 1 (January–March 1963): 13–23; cited at Chopra, *op. cit.*, p. 240.

35. C. G. Gardikas, "Hashish and Crime," *Enkephalos* 2, no. 3 (1950): 201–211.

36. For a first-person account of the horrors of Greek prisons written by an American arrested and sentenced for selling hashish in Greece, see the essay by Neal Phillips, "Notes Fom Tartaros," in George Andrews and Simon Vinkenoog, eds., *The Book of Grass* (London: Peter Owen, 1967), pp. 230–234.

37. The President's Commission, *op. cit.*, Table 2, p. 20.

38. *Ibid.*

39. For three excellent essays discussing illegal police practices—most of which are generally considered within the profession good police work and are never viewed by society as "criminal", see Paul Chevigny, *Police Power* (New York: Pantheon, 1969); Jerome Skolnick, *Justice Without Trial* (New York: Wiley, 1966), and *The Politics of Protest* (New York: Ballantine, 1969).

: *Chapter* 10 :

Using, Selling, and Dealing Marijuana

Introduction

It could be that 100 times as much marijuana, in bulk, is consumed now in comparison with ten years ago. But whether our estimate is considerably larger or smaller than this, tons of this drug move about the country in some sort of orderly fashion. It is grown, imported, distributed, and consumed according to a pattern. Our understanding of this complex, controversial drug must include an investigation of its distribution.

One item in the marijuana controversy is the attempt to legitimate one or another conception of marijuana selling. The drug's opponents, as a strategy of discrediting marijuana use, promulgate the position that it is imported, distributed, and sold by professional gangsters for profit to unsuspecting youths who have been duped by the gangsters' tricky techniques. The cannabis advocates, on the other hand, maintain that selling (and especially giving away) marijuana is an act of love representing a desire to "turn on" the whole world to beauty and euphoria. Although both views adumbrate value-tinted conceptions of its use, marijuana nonetheless continues to be grown, brought, sold, and consumed. By investigating the empirical phenomenon of marijuana distribution, we may aid and abet one or another ideological view, but the empirical substratum will remain unchanged. The pattern by which the drug moves, however, can be determined, and it is our task to shed some light on it.

The classic antimarijuana stance with regard to marijuana selling has existed at least since the 1930s,[1] though it has undergone some modification since then. For instance, even the police realize that drug sellers need not proselytize potential users, that friends introduce friends to a drug. The essential features of the marijuana opponent's position on selling are (1) selling marijuana is a highly profitable activity; therefore, pot sellers are either linked to, or part of, the criminal underworld; (2) the personnel of marijuana selling and heroin selling overlap considerably; (3) potselling is typically a career, continued over a long period of time, with a high degree of commitment, as a means of livelihood; (4) if relatively uncommitted individuals (such as college students) who are only marginally involved with the criminal underworld are selling marijuana, they act as a kind of front for the real criminals, who use them for contact, distribution, and respectability purposes.[2]

The police are convinced of the dominant role of profit in marijuana selling. One indication of this is the news releases given by the police to the media citing the value of their drug seizures. In order to emphasize the role of profit and inflate the importance of the job that they are doing, the police extravagantly exaggerate the monetary worth of the drugs that they have confiscated is a given raid. One of the most spectacular examples occurred in the fall of 1968, when the New York Police Department, with agents of the Federal Bureau of Narcotics and Dangerous Drugs, seized, in a psychedelic "church": 4,500 doses of LSD, 1,500 of STP, fifty of mescaline, ten pounds of hashish, and ten pounds of marijuana. The cache was valued by the police at six to ten million dollars.[3] About a week after the raid, *The New York Times* printed a letter from "an irate marijuana smoker"[4] who calculated the value of the seizure, at current prices, at $50,000, less than 1 percent of the police estimate. The enormity of the disjunction calls for a look at the patterns of marijuana selling. When there are systematic patterns in the versions of reality espoused by individuals variously located in the social structure of an activity or institution, we are forced to understand how location influences perception.

The student of a deviant or illegal activity struggles with the subterranean character of his data. His area of investigation is half-hidden, usually fully accessible only to the participants. Facts are discovered in a patchy and unsystematic manner, revealing one facet of a reality, while others that might tell a very different story remain obscured. The more inaccessible a phenomenon, the broader the latitude for delineating totally contradictory portraits of it. Add to this the saturation of that phenomenon in emotional and ideological arenas, and the stage is set for every conceivable version describing it to run rampant. This is extravagantly the case with marijuana selling. In the past two or three years, journalistic accounts of marijuana selling from the inside have become public knowledge.[5] Although necessarily partial, these accounts reflect a previously unexplored source of information which must be taken into account before we can claim to understand the phenomenon in question.

To know anything about a deviant activity, it is necessary to interview the participant. For some inexplicable reason, this maxim has rarely been followed in marijuana dealing. During the course of the research, I saw dozens of transactions, ranging from several pounds to the smallest purchase. In addition, I requested several dealers to prepare written statements of their selling activities. Third, so many of my 200 interviewees had sold at least once that the formal interview captured a greal deal of information on buying and selling. From these various sources, I was able to piece together something of a consistent picture of marijuana selling.

Levels of Selling

The most striking source of the discrepancy between the police image of the marijuana market and that of the insider—i.e., the dealer—is a lack of specification of the level at which deals customarily take place. The police tend to identify one aspect with the whole, that aspect most clearly spelled out by the stereotype of the dealer conducting deals of large volume and high profit. Yet, this comprises a small percentage of all transactions which take place and, indeed, transactions at that level need not take place at all.

The metaphor which best describes the heroin distribution system is that of two funnels, one inverted, with their ends meeting. The raw opium is harvested at the production end by thousands of small and medium-sized farmers, mainly in Turkey, Southeast Asia, and Mexico, and sold at the consumption end to thousands of addicts, with a small number of highly organized criminals in between, who buy, process, and distribute the drug, earning immense profits. Although recent indications point to the fact that non-Mafia criminals are being allowed to distribute heroin,[6] the newcomers are nonetheless organized professional criminals. There are no amateurs at the upper levels of the heroin scene.

The two funnels model does not work quite so well with marijuana. Although it is possible that organized crime may import, distribute, and sell some of the marijuana consumed in America (no definitive or systematic evidence has yet been presented which supports this contention), it is certain that enormous quantities of marijuana never pass through the hands of professional criminals at all. The leakage from these funnels is sufficient to invalidate the funnel model altogether. To begin with, there is the factor of growing one's own marijuana. "Plant your seeds," advises a cartoon Mary Jane figure in the October 1968 issue of *Other Scenes,* a staunchly promarijuana underground newspaper; "keep prices down." About six of my interviewees were actually growing marijuana in New York apartments at the time of the interview.[7] One had set up an elaborate greenhouse, with fluorescent lighting, in a closet. Another grew it in a bathtub on his terrace until it was harvested and stolen by an observant thief. A recent publication, *Home Grown Happiness,*[8] distributed by *The East Village Other,* sells thousands of copies. It gives a detailed account of the most effective methods of growing and harvesting high-quality marijuana, including sections on "Selecting The Seed," "Transplanting," "Artificial Light," and so on. The last page contains the injunction, in capital letters, "Remember, every time you throw away a teaspoon of seeds you have destroyed a potential 100 or more ounces of marijuana!" Across the front page of the April 9, 1969, issue of EVO ran the headline, "This is the Week to Plant Your Pot Seeds." A letter to the editor in the same issue announced: "The time is ripe for planting marijuana. Spring has sprung. . . . Beautify America. . . . Trees of grass in every park, vacant lot, roadside, tree box. . . . free marijuana for all next fall." It was signed by Ed Grassplanter.

As late as the early 1950s, huge quantities of marijuana were growing wild in empty lots in New York City; in one sortie in 1951, the New York Sanitation Department destroyed over 30,000 pounds of marijuana pulled up in these lots.[9] Although rumors are often circulated concerning marijuana's growth in New York,[10] it is unlikely that any plant could survive today growing wild in any urban area; it risks decimation from friend and foe alike.[11] However, this is not the case in sparsely settled areas. Numerous cases exist of college students earning handsome profits by gathering wild marijuana spotted from cruising cars.[12] According to one account, the "major sources of marijuana for Midwest students are the surrounding corn fields." [13] (This is less likely to be true today than in 1965.)

Although *most* of the marijuana consumed, both in terms of bulk and in terms of the number of transactions, will not be homegrown or gathered wild—the majority of all marijuana smoked still comes from Mexico—a sizeable minority of it is, and these sources should not be discounted in delineating the marijuana distribution system. (In addition, it must be kept in mind that American-grown marijuana is considerably less potent than Mexican-grown cannabis.)

Far more users planted their seeds (which many keep around for just such contingencies) during the drought year of 1969 than any in recent years. In addition, a great deal more hashish became available in 1969, possibly only part of a general trend toward greater hashish use—which is on the rise much faster than the use of leaf marijuana—or, possibly, partly as a response to this lack of availability of Mexican marijuana. In any case, most of the time, most of the marijuana consumed in America originates from Mexico.

A reasonable price for a ton of marijuana, purchased from a middleman in Mexico, is between $10,000 and $20,000, which means that it costs about five or ten dollars per pound, or less than fifty cents per ounce. A typical wholesale price in New York, buying in a bulk lot of several kilograms, is about $120 per kilo, or about $3.50 per ounce. (California prices are generally about half New York prices.) Most characteristically, ounces are sold at the retail street price of twenty or twenty-five dollars.* If the smoker wishes to purchase joints (individual marijuana cigarettes) already rolled, he pays between fifty cents and a dollar apiece. Employing simple arithmetic, we find that the mark-up from field to joint can be considerably higher than 100 times in price, that is, buying at two

---

* These prices were current *before* the Mexican border blockade and increased vigilance of 1969 and 1970. At the present time (February 1970), prices are about one and a third to one and a half more than what they were a year earlier, even assuming the availability of marijuana, which is often problematic.

joints per penny at the ton price, and selling at one dollar per joint at the joint price. Thus, the enterprising dealer might see in marijuana sales a source of enormous profits. This is, however, a naive inference. The novice might make the same mistake about the workings of the marijuana market as do the police.

The joint price, a dollar per joint, is a ghostly abstraction. Few purchase individual joints, pre-rolled. Almost every smoker beyond the level of rawest novice rolls his own. (Except, I am told, in Vietnam, where large joints of excellent quality may be purchased in emptied American cigarette packs.) Even when he buys the smallest bulk quantity, the "nickel bag," for five dollars, he must strain out the twigs and seeds, buy cigarette papers (the same as for tobacco roll-your-owns), and learn the technology involved in manufacturing a smokable joint. The nickel bag is a common quantity for a smoker only moderately involved with the drug and its subculture. In New York, this is between one-fourth and one-eighth of an ounce, enough marijuana to make between eight to fifteen marijuana cigarettes, depending on the size of the joints, the dealer's generosity, and the purchaser's willingness to be short-changed.

As both the market and the subculture of marijuana use expand, purchases become increasingly larger in bulk. In the 1930s and 1940s, purchasing individual joints was common. A few years ago the nickel bag purchase was characteristic. Now the smoker buys an ounce, enough marijuana for fifty to seventy joints. This means that each cigarette costs him somewhere between twenty-five and forty cents—not a dollar. Economy is part of the motivation; obviously, the larger the size of the purchase, the lower the unit cost. It is also to the advantage of the purchaser to minimize the number of transactions in which he is involved: the greater the number of purchases he makes, the greater the chance of coming into contact with an undercover agent and getting arrested. As the user becomes increasingly sophisticated about the workings of the market and the activities of law enforcement agencies, the size of his purchase increase correspondingly. Thus, the recent appearance of the typical ounce purchase. Since the ounce is the most characteristic purchase, it comes closest to being what corresponds, in the purchase of legal goods, to the "retail" price.

A given bulk quantity of marijuana in a dealer's living room or garage automatically is worth less than if it is split up and distributed among his customers. Selling marijuana, at least at the dealer-to-user level, is hard work; each deal involves a certain amount of moving about and a lot of socializing. No farmer would reckon the value of his tomato crop in the field on the basis of its total sale at the supermarket. The final product is saturated with the value of labor. Thus, a dealer's cache of several kilograms is worth the kilogram price—in New York, about $120 per kilo. If sold to the customer, that cache might eventually earn twenty dollars per ounce instead, but the point is, it *hasn't* been sold to the customer, and it is, therefore, worth correspondingly less.

In addition, the multi-kilo purchaser rarely earns twenty dollars per ounce, because he doesn't generally sell in ounces. At that level, two or three stages below the original source, he is most likely to break up what he has into pounds, and sell pounds for $100 or $120. He usually does not want to be bothered with ounce purchases, except as a favor to friends, because it involves a great many discrete transactions. Even though the margin of profit is higher if he buys several kilos and sells 100 or 200 ounces, the profit on each transaction is much smaller, and each transaction represents work, time, and danger. He leaves the ounce sales to the man below him, who has bought his pound. A 20-year-old male college student-dealer explains his usual marketing procedure with a kilo (a "ki" or "key" in the jargon):

Well, let's say I pick a ki or something like that, instead of breaking it up into nickels (laughs) and dimes, you know, and trying to squeeze every penny out of it, I'll probably just break it in half and sell it in pounds, or something like that, and I might make $100 off it, and that'll keep me going for three or four weeks.

Yet, even this qualification simplifies the actual situation because unlike legally sold products, a great percentage of the marijuana that finally reaches the user is not sold at the retail or consumer level. A given kilogram may be cut into at many different levels. Since all (or nearly all) sellers smoke, a given proportion will be diverted for the dealer's own use at wholesale prices with no profit. Depending on how much he smokes, a purchase of a kilogram will typically involve a diversion of, say, half a pound for his own private use. Another chunk will be given or sold at cost to close friends, offered to guests, girl friends, used to cancel debts, so that marijuana may be thought of as a kind of tribal barter currency.

Out from the center (the dealer) are less intimate friends and acquaintances who might pay less than the standard prices—in New York, probably ten dollars per ounce. Further out will be the near-stranger transactions, which will entail payment of the full retail price. It is obvious, therefore, that the leakage from the wholesale to the retail price is considerable. A marijuana purchase occurs at nearly any link in the producer-to-consumer chain, depending on one's intimacy with the dealer and one's knowledge of the current market price.

Max Weber maintained that one of the triumphs of Western civilization was the introduction of the universalistic price system. Products are held to be worth a given fixed quantity. As with time, the universe is segmentalized into uniform units of equal size, infinitely reproducible. Any and all products are held to be translatable into a standard measure, easily arranged into an unambiguous hierarchy of clearly gradable value. How much a man is "worth" is how much money he has. The marijuana subculture is a kind of island of tribalism within a sea of commercial ethic. Value, like time, is relative. How much a given quantity of marijuana is worth depends less on an abstract quality inherent in the product than on a variety of concrete and personal indices. While the junkie mentality in many ways is a ruthless exaggeration of the spirit of capitalism, the committed marijuana smoker's subculture represents its very opposite.

If this is so as a general guiding principle, it is especially so when marijuana itself is at issue. This is not to say that money has no meaning for smokers, even in marijuana exchanges, nor that all heads are idealistic flower children. Representatives of the bourgeois spirit may be found everywhere, even among the most seemingly uncommitted. Capitalists of the drug underground abound, and mimeographed demands are circulated from time to time in various drug-using communities that the local dealers should try to curb their avarice, lower their prices and hand out more free grass. Where there is demand for something, money, goods, or services will be exchanged for it, whatever it is, wherever it is. Nor does it mean that marijuana is not felt to be "worth" anything. But what is so strange about the attitude of heads toward marijuana is that its value seems to be so curiously *elastic*. A dealer who would not hesitate to hand out dozens of free nickel bags to friends couldn't imagine giving away the same value in real money—either what the substance is supposed to be worth, or even what it cost him. It is as if marijuana isn't quite real, as if it exists in some sort of other world, where the rules of the game are different. The closest thing that comes to it in the "straight" world is food. It is an act of hospitality to feed one's guests; a breach of common good manners to allow them to go hungry. Smoking marijuana, like eating together, binds its participants in a primitive sense of fellowship.

Using and Selling

The police commonly express the view that the real target of their efforts is the dealer, not the user. Their imagery is commonly borrowed from the world of heroin addiction, where, it is asserted, the narcotics peddler makes a profit from human degradation and misery. Marijuana use, too, supposedly typifies this clear-cut distinction between user and seller.

The problem with this view is that selling takes place on many levels, among many kinds of participants. Selling is often a matter of convenience; it may be an arbitrary decision as to who is the buyer and who the seller on a specific transaction. Knowledge of current deals being transacted, or simply having requisite cash, often defines who is to play the role of the dealer on a given occasion. Among our informants, nearly half (44 percent) said that they had sold at least once. Moreover, there was a continuum from the user who had sold only once (12 percent of those who admitted ever selling) to the one who sold frequently, say, more than fifty times (18 percent of all sellers), with shades of variation between. One is struck by the evenness of the range of selling, while if one took the classic pattern of pushing seriously, one would expect to see very few sellers, with nearly all of those that sold to have done so innumerable times in gigantic quantities. Rather, what we actually find is that many marijuana smokers sell, characteristically in very small quantities. Over a third of those who had sold (36 percent) reported that they most commonly sold in ounces, and about 5 percent said that selling in quantities of a pound or more was usual. The typical seller sold a median of eight times in an average quantity of two ounces.

However, far more important than the mere incidence of selling —since our sample is not "representative"—is the systematic variation in selling according to certain key variables. The most important variable influencing whether the smoker sold or not is how much he uses: the more one smokes, the greater is the likelihood that he sold. Among our respondents, the relationship between these two variables could hardly have been more striking (see Table 10–1).

TABLE 10–1

Selling by the Amount One Smokes

"Have you ever sold marijuana?"
Percent saying "yes"

The Amount One Smokes	Percent	N
Daily	92	26
3 to 6 times weekly	80	42
1 to 2 times weekly	40	55
1 to 4 times monthly	14	36
Less than monthly	11	45

The logistics of continued heavy use implies, and even demands, selling. The heavy marijuana user invariably keeps a supply, and many only occasional smokers do as well. The more that one smokes, the greater is the likelihood that one will have a supply. Not one of the twenty-six daily smokers said that they did not have a supply of marijuana (see Table 10–2).

TABLE 10–2

*Keeping a Supply of Marijuana by
Marijuana Use*

"Do you generally keep a supply of marijuana around your house?" [a]

Marijuana Use	(percent) Yes	No	N
Daily	85	0	26
3 to 6 times weekly	64	21	42
1 to 2 times weekly	54	28	54
1 to 4 times monthly	29	41	34
Less than monthly	11	79	38

[a]All other replies aside from "yes" and "no" eliminated from table.

It is characteristically the case that even heavy marijuana smokers will not be able to use up, within a brief space of time, the quantities that they purchase. Often a sale will be on a basis of "take it or leave it." An available quantity might be an ounce, in which case none of it will be sold, or a pound, or a kilogram, in which case most of it will be sold. The only way the marijuana user can limit his transactions and his exposure to arrest is to purchase large amounts. By buying a pound at the near-wholesale price of $120, and selling twelve ounces to twelve friends at ten dollars for each ounce, one thereby has four ounces free. "Free grass" is an inducement for selling.

On the surface, the parallel with the heroin addict might seem striking: each sells to support the habit, getting nothing else out of it. Yet, even if the marijuana seller smokes five joints a day, an enormous quantity, he would consume a pound every six months, which means that his habit costs about fifty cents a day, at the most. We are forced, therefore, to discard the "support the habit" explanation for selling.

Every marijuana user is not only a marijuana user, he is invariably also a friend, and his friends also smoke. There is a positive and linear relation between the amount one smokes and the percentage of one's friends who also smoke (see Table 10–3).

TABLE 10–3

Percent of Closest Friends Who Are Regular Marijuana Smokers [a]

Marijuana Use	0–29	30–59	60–100	N
Daily	4	35	62	26
3 to 6 times weekly	14	36	50	42
1 to 2 times weekly	35	24	41	54
1 to 4 times monthly	42	31	28	36
Less than monthly	72	19	9	43

[a] Designated as at least once per week.

This would create, therefore, a certain amount of pressure to sell. The more that one smokes marijuana, the higher the proportion of one's friends who are marijuana smokers; the higher the proportion of one's friends who are marijuana smokers, the greater is the probability that they will buy and sell from one another, particularly as their turnover in supply is so much greater (see Table 10–4).

TABLE 10–4

*Selling by Closest Friends Who Are
Regular Marijuana Smokers*

"Have you ever sold marijuana?" Percent
saying "yes"

Percent of One's Friends Who are Regular Marijuana Smokers	Percent	N
60–100	68	73
30–59	43	56
0–29	21	72

Moreover, not only is a higher proportion of the heavy smoker's friendship network more likely to smoke, but he is also more likely to have access to information concerning the availability of periodically appearing quantities of marijuana on the market. He is more likely to know others who buy and sell and who are higher up in the distribution ladder. He is more acquainted with the price system, which fluctuates even in the short run. He knows more about some of the rules and precautions to take to avoid arrest, thefts, "burns" and being short-changed, as well as buying adulterated goods. He can buy and sell successfully and with confidence. Anyone arriving on the marijuana scene in a complete-stranger situation would encounter great difficulty in making a large purchase.

There is a two-way process at work here. On the one hand, one must be implicated in a web of social relations to be able to purchase the drug. In this sense, friendship patterns are a necessary condition for selling to take place. But one's friendship network is not merely a passive requirement for selling and buying; it is also an active force which insures one's involvement in selling as an activity, since friends who smoke make requests and demands that often relate to marijuana sales. In addition, selling further implicates one in social relations that are marijuana-based. By buying and selling, one extends one's network of acquaintances, almost all of whom are marijuana users. In short, friendships and sales intersect with one another; they are inseparable elements of a single dimension. Their relationship with one another must be seen in dialectical terms, rather than simple cause and effect.

Generally, selling must be considered as part of the syndrome of use. It is not simply that the user must purchase his drug supply from the seller to consume the drug (this symbiotic relationship exists with heroin as well), but that the user and the seller are largely indistinguishable; there is no clear-cut boundary between them. A large percentage of users sell, and nearly all sellers use. In fact, the determining force behind selling is use: heavy users are very likely to sell, while infrequent users are unlikely to do so. The fact that a given individual sells—whether it be done once, occasionally, or frequently, specifically for a profit—is determined mainly by his involvement in the drug, in its subculture, with others who smoke. Selling marijuana, then, to some degree presupposes involvement with the marijuana subculture which, in turn, implies at least a moderate degree of use. Selling and using involve parallel activities and associations; the seller and the user inhabit the same social universe. The difference between them is simply a matter of degree, since selling is a surer indicator of one's involvement with the drug subculture than is buying or, even more so, using. To think of the dealer as preying on his hapless victim, the marijuana smoker, as profiting on his misery, is to possess a ludicrously incorrect view of the state of affairs.

It is necessary, therefore, to abandon the conspiratorial view of the relationship between the marijuana user and the seller—a primitive model borrowed from the world of addiction. Rather, selling must be looked at as an index of involvement with the marijuana subculture. At the peripheries of the marijuana scene, we find the experimenter, the extremely infrequent user, the dabbler, the once, twice, or dozen-time user. He has few marijuana-smoking friends, is rarely presented with opportunities for use, is curious about its effects, and usually discontinues its use after his curiosity is satisfied. It is possible that he is the most frequent representative of the total universe of all individuals who have ever used the drug; if not, at any rate, he forms a sizeable minority of all users.

At the lowest levels of use, the smoker does not even buy marijuana; close to three-quarters of our less than monthly smokers (71 percent) said that they never bought the drug. He is dependent on friends who are involved with marijuana to offer him the drug when he visits. In fact, when the drug is extended, it is not thought of as one person giving another a material object. Generally, a joint is passed around to all present in a kind of communal fellowship. Hence, giving marijuana away, in this specific sense, is more common than selling. In volume, of course, marijuana is far more often sold than given away. But more individuals have given marijuana away than have sold, since nearly every smoker who owns any amount of the drug has smoked socially, and has passed a communally smoked joint around to his guests.

The infrequent user generally does not seek out the drug, but accepts it when offered. This pattern is most characteristic of women. If the experimenter is unlikely to buy, it holds, *a fortiori*, that he is unlikely to sell. At the middle levels of use, the smoker will generally buy his own marijuana, keep a small supply for occasions when the mood strikes him, and only occasionally sell to others when he happens to have some extra, or when asked by a friend who finds other channels unavailable. At the highest levels of use, the smoker will not only buy and have his own supply, but also sometimes sell in fairly sizeable quantities, and explicitly for a profit, although this may be only one among a variety of motives. (Not all, or even most, heavy users are large-scale dealers, but the dealer is most *likely* to be found among the heavy users.) Each of these activities can be thought of as an index of one's involvement with the marijuana-using subculture. Each represents a kind of subtle step into another social world.

There are, it would seem, two types of marijuana exchanges. One type is "dealing," which may be defined as selling explicity for a profit at current street prices to anyone one trusts. A dealer (*not* a "peddler" nor a "pusher," although, sometimes, a "connection") is the person who sells a certain quantity in high volume for a profit. (He will always, in addition, *also* sell to friends at little or no profit.) Often someone who sells regularly to friends and acquaintances for minimal profit will be requested by a near-stranger to sell some of his supply. His answer will often be, "I'm not a dealer," meaning, not that he is averse to selling *per se*, but that he sells only to certain people, and only as a favor to them; he does not deal for a profit. At one end of the spectrum, then, we have transactions involving little or no profit (at the extreme, giving marijuana away, either in bulk, or, in the form of individual joints, in one's home, as a gesture of hospitality like a glass of sherry). At the other end, "dealing" means many transactions, usually in sizeable quantities (although the "nickels and dimes" street hustler must be considered), always for a profit, and often to near-strangers. Although the law treats these two types of exchanges as being in the same category, entailing the same penalties, they are distinct sociologically. Legal categories are often meaningless as social descriptions of the acts they penalize, although often accurate, even simultaneously, as a description of how these acts are viewed by the rest of society. Naturally, there is an entire *continuum* between these two types, with mixed characteristics. But in terms of the sheer number of transactions—because the product is finally fanning out to the consumer, and is, therefore, small in bulk and large in number—the friendship end of the spectrum is far more common than the profit end.

Motives for Selling

The motives underlying marijuana dealing are complex. Although at the top of the hierarchy of selling, profit is likely to dominate more than is true at the bottom, there is no level in the distribution system (on the American side of the transaction at least) where profit is the sole reason for dealing. In contrast, the expressed motives for selling heroin might be reduced to two: profit (at the top), and the use of heroin (at the bottom). With marijuana, the picture is considerably more intricate. Certainly the free use of marijuana predominates—at least in frequency, if not in the strength of motivation.

But beyond "free grass" and some profit, the reasons for selling vary. Some dealers enjoy the cloak and dagger intrigue, at least in the beginning:

The dealer commands a certain mystique in the East Village. He is playing a far more dangerous game than the customer, and he is respected for it. For himself, the excitement surrounding a "big deal" and the ritual and accoutrements of the trade act as an antidote for the growing plague of boredom. Most dealers are proud of their fine scales, and enjoy the ritual of sifting and weighing their stock. The exchange, sometimes involving large amounts of cash and drugs, is the climax of the business and may have an "007" sort of intrigue.[14]

The fact that one is a sometimes central figure in a subcommunity whose values and evaluations of others revolve,[15] in part, around drug use and especially "inside dopester" information concerning drug prices and sources acts as an attraction for many users to sell and deal. The dealer is acquainted with a scene from which the nondealer is to some degree excluded. The dealer simply knows more about what is happening in a sphere of some importance to the smoker; moreover, he distributes a valued object, which the smoker could obtain with a little more difficulty from others. A twenty-seven-year-old high school teacher only sporadically involved in selling explains the reasons for his involvement.

It's this: being in on something that's important to others. Other people are dependent on you. They have to rely on you. You are, in a minor sense, controlling their destiny. You are important—you have a source and they don't, and that shows how "in" you are, how others trust you and maybe even like you. You are a big man. Others come to you needing something, and you dispense largesse. It's kind of an ego boost, I guess. Like, after copping a quarter of a pound of grass, the guy I copped from said, man, I want to get some DMT. I was in debt to this guy for getting the grass, see, so I said, I can get you some DMT, man. It shows how much you know, how you are in the middle of things, how you are hip.

The dealer, a respected figure on the drug scene, commands a kind of low-level charisma. Often relations spill onto one another, his dealer role and activities becoming translated into access to, and demands for, activities in other valued spheres. "As a dealer," said one heavy drug user, "it was easy to become a witch doctor, soul counselor, elder brother." [16]

Every drug seller is a political man as well as an economic and social man, so that satisfactions with their drug activities often include motives having a somewhat *civic* character. A twenty-two-year-old college student dealer delineates his involvement with marijuana:

I'm spreading drugs around, and turning people onto drugs, and thereby they're meeting people who are, you know, involved politically, or involved in the revolution in its many facets, and they're just becoming involved with other people. I consider it, you know, kind of humanitarian, getting people away from plastic and steel, and getting them back toward the funk of life, you know, digging people as just being people.

It seems clear, then, that for some dealers a variety of expressed motives are of at least some degree of importance in their involvement in the drug selling scene; they must be counted as impelling reasons for participation in dealing. All of this does not deny the role of profit in selling. What it does do, however, is affirm that in most transactions, pure profit never rules supreme; it is always alloyed with motives that make a mercenary image of the dealer empirically suspect. The bulk, if not nearly all, of marijuana buying and selling transactions that take place entail some profit, generally modest, and of secondary consideration. Of course, even if profit were a potent motive in dealing, the question remains: why deal in preference to anything else? Why deal marijuana in preference to any other drug? There are endless number of ways of making a living. Why sell pot?

Selling, Dealing, and the Law

When we attempt an appraisal of the role of the organized criminal in marijuana dealing, we encounter a number of logical and methodological obstacles. A given quantity of marijuana bought by a dozen members of a criminal ring from a middleman in Mexico, imported to this country and sold for a considerable profit to hundreds of American dealers, will be broken down into increasingly smaller quantities, eventually sold among friends for little or no profit. What will be bought at the top in one transaction will be sold at the bottom in thousands of transactions, so that if we take as our basic unit of analysis the transaction, typically marijuana is sold for no profit, in an unorganized fashion, among friends. On the other hand, an immense quantity of marijuana does pass through the hands of individuals who earn their living from selling drugs and nothing else. In *bulk*, then, most marijuana was sold at one time among professional criminals for profit. How we characterize marijuana selling depends on what level the transaction takes place. This might lend sustenance to the ideologically involved contestants, since they may, without distortion, portray dealing in a fashion which pleases their biases.

Just how involved the large-scale dealer is in marijuana selling is obliquely determined by the size of the seizures of imports from Mexico. In terms of the number of these smuggling attempts, clearly the overwhelming majority are of relatively insignificant quantities—under a pound. The largest recent border seizure was about a ton of marijuana. An operation of this size obviously requires organization: a micro-bus, middlemen in Mexico, drivers and high-level dealers for distribution. This is not Cosa Nostra organization, but it is organization. If we mean by "organized crime," a syndicate involving thousands of tightly knit, lifelong committed gangsters whose entire livelihood derives from illegal activities, then marijuana probably is not sold, never has been sold, and never will be sold by professional criminals. If, however, we mean an independent operation involving a score of individuals whose activities are coordinated, and who will earn their living for a few years from marijuana sales, then it is true that marijuana is often sold by professional criminals. Just how much of the total of marijuana consumed derives from this kind of source is impossible to determine.

This is why a consideration of the level at which a deal takes place is important. The importer *is* often a criminal: his livelihood is importing grass; he is a capitalist who sells an illegal product with no particular committment to marijuana as an agent of mind-transformation, an element in a subculture, or a catalyst in social change. He probably does not smoke marijuana. The unsystematic business practices of "head" dealers created a vacuum into which he stepped. The multi-kilogram top-level dealers to whom he sells are also primarily profit seekers. The crucial difference between the importer and his deal-customers is that the dealer sells to consumers as well as to other dealers and is very likely to be a consumer himself. Next to the consumer, friendship transactions are common. Thus, to say that marijuana is a business is both true and false. At some levels it is; at some, it is not. To say that it is big business is misleading. A monthly take of a quarter of a million dollars, split twenty ways, might represent the very top of the profession. Lower down, even dedicated hustling brings in what an unskilled factory worker might make. Below that, the profit motive breaks down entirely.

A commonly encountered argument against the use of marijuana employs the differential association theory: by using the drug, one is thrown into association with the criminal underworld and, therefore, attitudes toward, and opportunities for, committing extremely serious crimes, and for using heroin, will become increasingly favorable. This statement is made in complete ignorance of how the market works. The average American user never comes into contact with the underworld, even if every gram he smokes were the handi-work of a tightly organized network of full-time professional gang-sters. The typical marijuana smoker has no idea where his grass comes from. It has been filtered down through so many levels, has exchanged hands so many times, that the world of top-level selling and of the average user are as alien to one another, and about as likely to associate with one another, as the tobacco auctioneer and the cigarette smoker. The average user buys his pot from a friend, even though it may originally have been derived from someone whose livelihood is dealing.

In New York State, the line dividing a misdemeanor from a felony in marijuana possession is either twenty-five cigarettes or an ounce; the reasoning is that anyone with such a quantity may be pre-sumed to intend to sell, even if no actual sale is detected. On one level, this distinction is absurd and erroneous; on another, it indirect-ly captures something of the flavor of the actual situation. To suppose that anyone who purchases and possesses one ounce—or who hap-pens to have an ounce lying around, remaining from a possibly even larger purchase—is necessarily going to sell anything from that ounce, is to adopt a peculiar conception of what is actually happen-ing. But to think that anyone who has as much as an ounce is sufficiently integrated into the marijuana community as to render it likely that he has participated in a number of marijuana-related activities—*selling among them*—is an accurate supposition. The smoker who purchases (and possesses) only an ounce is unlikely to split it up for the purpose of selling it to others.

The law, moreover, makes no distinction between the act of sell-ing or giving away small quantities to friends or acquaintances for little or no profit, and dealing on a large-scale professional basis. In September 1969, a twenty-one-year-old man was sentenced to *fifty* years in prison by the state of Texas for the act of selling two marijuana cigarettes.[17] Although the legal implications of petty selling and professional dealing are identical, the social worlds of these activities are radically disjunctive.

So there is the question of what the penalties are designed to deter. Is it the technical fact that the literal act of an exchange of money for marijuana took place? Or is it designed to eradicate the source of the drug? Can a user who has only an ounce or two in his possession where distribution sources must be measured in kilo-grams, not ounces, possibly be the original source for anyone's drug use, aside from his own and a few friends? In fact, it is probably safe to say that the user who possesses only an ounce is almost certainly not a large-scale dealer.

There is the argument that the penalties for marijuana possession (and use) should be reduced, but not for selling. This distinction violates empirical reality; it implies the existence of two relatively separated social and moral spheres that articulate on a superficial basis—profit. If the seller is guilty, the user is, too, because the user is the seller, and the seller the user. The technical exchange of contraband goods for money takes place at every conceivable level and by nearly everyone above the minimally involved. Labelling all selling heinous and use only moderately reprehensible, is to display ignorance of how the market works. The present law, as well as the moderate reforms currently being proposed, puts use in one legal, logical category, and all levels of selling in another. We find use and most selling transactions to be logically and socially indistinguishable while high level, high volume, and high profit selling transactions exist in a disjunctive social and moral universe. If we believed in "natural" social categories, the present confusion would represent as great an intellectual blunder as classifying whales as fish and bats as a species of bird.

NOTES

1. It is interesting that the most vigorous of the antimarijuana propagandists of the 1930s, Harry Anslinger, denied that marijuana was sold by professional gangsters in 1937: ". . . the control and sale of marijuana has not yet passed into the hands of the big gangster syndicates. The supply is so vast, and grows in so many places, that gangsters perhaps have found it difficult to dominate the source. . . . gangdom has been hampered in its efforts to corner the profits of what has now become an enormous business." See Harry J. Anslinger, with Courtney Ryley Cooper, "Marijuana—Assassin of Youth," *American Magazine* 124 (July 18, 1937): 152–153.

2. The clearest recent statement of this position may be found in Will Oursler, *Marijuana: The Facts, the Truth* (New York: Paul S. Eriksson, 1968), pp. 113–120. Oursler seems to think these college student distributors are gangland fronts, and are called "beavers" in the underworld.

3. *The New York Times*, September 27, 1968.

4. *Ibid.*, October 6, 1968.

5. The most informative of recent accounts must include: James T. Carey, *The College Drug Scene* (Englewood Cliffs, N. J.: Prentice-Hall, 1968), esp. chs. 2, 4, 5; Jerry Mandel, "Myths and Realities of Marijuana Pushing," in J. L. Simmons, ed.,

Marijuana: Myths and Realities (North Hollywood, Calif.: Brandon House, 1967), pp. 58–110; Don McNeill, "Green Grows the Grass on the Lower East Side," *The Village Voice*, December 1, 1966, pp. 3, 21; "Ric," "I Turned on 200 Fellow Students at the University of Michigan," *Esquire*, September 1967, pp. 101, 190–193; Anonymous, "On Selling Marijuana," in Erich Goode, ed., *Marijuana* (New York: Atherton Press, 1969), pp. 92–102; Jaakov Kohn, "Superdealer," *The East Village Other*, January 10, 1969, pp. 3, 14–15 and "Midipusher," *The East Village Other*, January 24, 1969, pp. 6–7, 21; Nicholas von Hoffman, *We Are the People Our Parents Warned Us Against* (Chicago: Quadrangle, 1968).

6. Charles Grutzner, "Mafia is Giving Up Heroin Monopoly," *The New York Times*, September 2, 1968, pp. 1, 49.

7. This raises uncomfortable and intriguing constitutional questions that we do not have the space to elaborate on. The parallels between growing one's own marijuana and consuming it in the privacy of one's own home, and pornography consumed in private, are striking. Since the Supreme Court has ruled that owning privately consumed pornography is legal, the same demand could be made for marijuana consumption. See the article by Michael A. Town on the constitutionality of marijuana use as being protected by the right to privacy: "The California Marijuana Possession Statute: An Infringement on the Right of Privacy or Other Peripheral Constitutional Rights?" *The Hastings Law Journal* 19 (March 1968): 758–782. Now that growing one's own has become so important among many users, this consideration is especially crucial. ·

8. Michael W. Morier, *Home Grown Happiness* (New York: Mikus Book, 1967). See also Robert G. Barbour, ed., *Turn on Book: Synthesis and Extractions of Organic Psychedelics* (BarNel Enterprises, 1967); this latter volume includes instructions on preparing and growing a dozen psychedelic drugs, including marijuana, mescaline, DMT, LSD, peyote, and psilocybin.

9. "Saw Toothed," *New Yorker*, August 11, 1951, pp. 18–19; however, probably only one-tenth or less of this bulk would be useable marijuana.

10. Unquestionably the most fantastic of these rumors is the story, in the January 30, 1965, issue of *The Marijuana Newsletter*, a short-lived mimeographed publication whose purpose was to "disseminate information toward the legalization of marijuana," about a form of marijuana called "Manhattan Silver," marijuana grown inadvertently in sewers by the seeds having been flushed into the sewage system and growing untended (silver because of the lack of light). The story was a hoax. It was, nonetheless, believed, picked up, and passed on both by advocates and opponents of marijuana use. See John Rosevear, *Pot: A Handbook of Marijuana* (New Hyde Park, N. Y.: University Books, 1967), pp. 42–43, and Edward R. Bloomquist, *Marijuana* (Beverly Hills, Calif.: Glencoe Press, 1968), pp. 5, 14, for two contestants—the first pro- and the second antimarijuana use—taken in by the hoax.

11. However, at least one account quoted an informant who claimed that "over a hundred pot smokers, himself included, are growing hidden little marijuana gardens in Manhattan's Central Park." See James Sterba, "The Politics of Pot," *Esquire*, August 1968, p. 59.

12. As a rough indication of the extent of growth of the marijuana plant in the Midwest, consider that a botanist recently stated that 17 percent of the seasonal pollen in the air in Nebraska originates from the marijuana plant. Cited in Sterba, *op. cit.*, p. 118. See Julian Steyermark, *Flora of Missouri* (Ames: Iowa State University, 1963).

13. Richard Goldstein, *1 in 7: Drugs on the Campus* (New York: Walker, 1966), p. 115.

14. McNeill, *op. cit.*, p. 21.

15. I depart from Mandel, *op. cit.*, p. 93, on this point; Mandel underplays the prestige motive among sellers.

16. Anonymous, in "A Note From the Underground," in J. L. Simmons, ed., *Marijuana: Myths and Realities* (North Hollywood, Calif.: Brandon House, 1967), p. 19.

17. Jack Rosenthal, "A Fresh Look at Those Harsh Marijuana Penalties," *The New York Times*, Sunday, October 19, 1969, Section 4, The Week in Review, p. E8.

: *Chapter* 11 :

Marijuana and
the Law

The Federal Marihuana Tax Act: 1937–1969

In 1937, the "Marihuana Tax Act" was passed by Congress at the insistence of Harry Anslinger, then the Commissioner of the Federal Bureau of Narcotics. There was little debate on the measure, and the chief witness in support of the bill was Anslinger himself. It was signed into law by President Roosevelt with little public notice. While Howard Becker's "moral entrepreneur" argument takes us a long way in explaining the passage of the bill,[1] it is really only a partial explanation. As Becker tells us, moral crusades are launched against every conceivable issue; often a seemingly apathetic public will become outraged over an issue under the fervent tutelage of a resourceful crusader. Sometimes, however, statutes can even be passed without public support or knowledge. In the case of the Marihuana Tax Act, most of the hysterical and exaggerated antimarijuana articles seem to have appeared *after* the federal law was passed, ostensibly to justify it.[2] But whether the act was passed for purely ideological reasons, or as a calculated measure to expand the operations and budget of the Federal Bureau of Narcotics,[3] it had been preceded by a marijuana statute in every state of the union. In a sense, then, the federal law was redundant and unnecessary, as all states had a law prohibiting marijuana, and many of them were more rigorous than the federal law.

Moreover, the design of the federal act was peculiar. It did not outlaw the possession of marijuana. Rather, it penalized the failure to pay the prohibitive excise tax of $100 per ounce on the transfer of marijuana. However, if anyone attempted to comply with the law and filed the necessary form with the Internal Revenue Service declaring his intention to purchase a quantity of the drug along with the details of where, when, from whom, and how much, he would automatically have incriminated himself under the state law. Actually, the federal law was designed as a prohibitive measure. It was presumed that nobody would ever comply, file the forms, and pay the tax. No illicit user of marijuana could ever acquire the necessary license, even if he were willing to pay the tax. Because of the double jeopardy feature of the act, the Supreme Court, in *Leary v. United States,* nullified it. It was impossible to comply with the law without facing sanction from the state laws because federal officials passed on the intention-to-purchase information to state officials.

The law was not struck down because the Supreme Court justices thought that marijuana should be legalized. Indeed, it is entirely possible (and even probable) that the Marihuana Tax Act will be replaced by another federal statute outlawing the use, possession, and sale of marijuana which is not marred by the self-incrimination feature. It is only because there are effective state laws that the federal statute was nullified, and the state laws will likely remain in force for some time to come.

The State Laws

It is, of course, impossible to detail the provisions of each state law within the space of a few pages. Occasionally crossing the state line can make a dramatic difference. Until 1969, South Dakota imposed a ninety-day sentence for marijuana possession, while North Dakota had a ninety-nine-year penalty. However, South Dakota stiffened its penalty, bringing it in line with that of the other, more punitive states.[4] Many of the states have adopted the model Uniform Narcotic Drug Act, and thus, there is now a large degree of uniformity of state marijuana laws.

Not only is California the most populous state in the union, it is also a trend-setting state: much of what is fashionable in California later spreads to other states. There is no question about the state's dominance in marijuana use. In terms of the sheer numbers, as well as percentage, California has more marijuana users by far than does any other state. (In addition, the most reliable arrest statistics come from California's Bureau of Criminal Statistics.)

We will now examine California's laws pertaining to marijuana. Section 11530 of the Health and Safety Code prohibits the possession of marijuana, which is defined as a narcotic. A recent District Court decision limited the amount possessed to a useable amount. What amount is "useable" is not clear: it varies from one narcotic drug to the next, but a 1966 decision held that fifty milligrams of marijuana was *not* a useable amount. Judges usually dismiss possession cases based on a single "roach." A first violation of Section 11530 calls for a one-to-ten-year prison sentence; a second-time offender will be punished by a two-to-ten-year sentence, and any subsequent violation calls for a five-year to life penalty.

Section 11530.5 of the Health and Safety Code penalizes the possessor of marijuana for the purpose of selling it. No fixed amount is stipulated that defines the amount necessary to constitute a violation, although if the marijuana is packaged, presumably the intention to sell is evident. A two-to-ten-year first offense sentence is imposed, while there is a five-to-fifteen-year sentence (with a three-year minimum) for the second offense. The third and subsequent offenses are punished by ten-years-to-life imprisonment with a six-year minimum. Section 11531 of the California Code covers selling (and giving away) marijuana. The first offense provides for a five-years-to-life penalty; the offender is ineligible for parole before three years. A second offense calls for a minimum penalty of five years, and a third-time offender must serve at least ten years before being considered for parole. Section 11532 stipulates that if an adult "hires, employs, or uses a minor in unlawfully transporting, carrying, selling, giving away, preparing for sale . . . any marijuana or who unlawfully sells, furnishes, administers, gives, or offers to sell, furnish, administer, or give any marijuana to a minor, or who induces a minor to use marijuana" is subject to ten years to life imprisonment.

The above offenses are felonies. The California statutes also provide for a variety of less serious misdemeanor penalties, for less serious offenses. For instance, marijuana use in California, or being under the influence of marijuana, is penalized by a ninety-day-to-one-year sanction (Section 11721). Another section (11556) rules it illegal to visit or be in a room or any place wherein marijuana is being used "with knowledge that such activity is occurring." The harshness of these penalties is mitigated by the fact that Section 1202b of the California Penal Code grants discretion to the judge if the felon is under the age of twenty-three. Thus, many mandatory minimum sentences may be reduced to six months.

In 1962, Rhode Island stiffened its marijuana penalties. Possession of marijuana calls for a three-to-fifteen-year penalty; possession with the intent to sell, a ten-to-thirty-year penalty; the gift or sale of marijuana, a twenty-to-forty-year sentence; and the sale to anyone under twenty-one, a thirty-year-to-life penalty. Only first degree murder and treason carry such harsh penalties. Second degree murder, armed robbery, and rape are considered less serious under Rhode Island law than the sale of marijuana.[5] Section 220.05 of the New York State Narcotics Laws holds the possession of any amount of marijuana to be a misdemeanor: a one-year penalty in prison. Section 220.15 rules that the possession of twenty-five or more marijuana cigarettes, or one ounce or more, is a felony: a four-year jail term. This section is comparable to California's Section 11530.5, possession with the intent to sell, and presumes that anyone with the stipulated quantities intends to sell. Actual sale is a seven-year penalty in New York, and sale to a minor, under twenty-one-years old, is a twenty-five-year felony. Several states (Georgia and Colorado) have the death penalty for selling marijuana to a minor.

Strategies of Enforcement: Arrest

In view of the extraordinarily high incidence of marijuana use and possession, these penalties might seem harsh, even barbaric. Let us look to see whether the provisions contained in the laws are carried out. If, as we pointed out earlier, one-fifth or one-quarter of America's college students have tried marijuana[6] and if more will do so by the time they graduate, we are criminalizing the activities of several million human beings. The prisons of this country are insufficient to hold such immense numbers of inmates. What, then, are the patterns of enforcement of the marijuana laws?

It is a common belief in the marijuana subculture that the big-time, high-volume, large-scale profit dealer is protected by the police, largely because of pay-offs, and that the nondealing user and the petty low-volume dealers are arrested and convicted in order to give the police a respectable record. Rumors were rife after the massive raid at Stony Brook in February 1968, involving 200 policemen ("Operation Stony Brook") and two or three dozen college students, that the biggest dealers on the campus were not arrested, while all of those arrested were users or petty dealers.

The user often feels that arrests are motivated by personal or political reasons. A college student elaborates:

The police don't bust Mafia dealers. The cops are too busy playing games with little people who just, like, go home and smoke a joint. But I guess these people are a threat. They look pretty scary in their long hair and nasty clothes and things like that (laughs). And besides a cop can't understand, when you get some dumb cop—even some smart cop, they're still dumb—but they can't understand how these longhaired faggot commie pinkos can, like, can even get *laid*. What could a girl see in a cat that's so fucked up? I think this has a lot to do with it. Because the drug movement is so sexual. These people, they just can't understand how this happens. And this really insults this cop. Seriously, 'cuz he's probably having trouble getting it from his *wife* once a week. And this whole thing—jealousy, man, is an animal instinct. It's all an extension, man, a sexual extension. The cops are a strange phenomenon. They go after the people that *look* weird, because they figure that probably, well, this is my guess, they figure that these are the kids that are into the revolution, they're obviously revolting in some way.

Many observers of the American drug scene disagree with this characterization and maintain that, on the whole, the actual implementation of the harsh penalties for marijuana possession are very rarely carried out, especially for small quantities obviously intended for one's own use. Former Commissioner Giordano has been quoted as saying that the chance that an apprehended college student with a single marijuana cigarette will actually be jailed "is absolutely nil."

In fact, the police will often express disinterest in arresting the marijuana dabbler, the once, twice or a dozen-time user. They say that their real target is the supplier, the dealer, the narcotics peddler who makes a profit on misery:

Our Bureau is not interested in arresting the young student user especially those who become innocently involved. We are not interested in giving these youngsters a prison record which will hamper them throughout life, which will deny them, and society, professional careers. We are interested in getting at the source, the supplier, the pusher, the drugiteer, the rackiteer who is behind the distribution. . . . We are not interested in arresting students; we are interestd in preventing . . . drugs from invading our campuses and student population; we are interested in apprehending the outside distributor who is working making the drugs available to our students; we are interested in protecting the bulk of the student population from being exposed to . . . drugs and from being innocently arrested or raided concerning violations or narcotics laws. . . .[7]

Doubtless most police officers do not take so tolerant and lenient a stand on marijuana use. (In fact, Bellizzi himself also stated, in the same paper just cited, "Every user is a potential danger to the general public.") The level at which the clearest distinction is made between the dealer (especially the large-scale dealer) and the user is at the federal level; even before the nullification of the "Marihuana Tax Act," most arrests at the federal level were for dealing, not for simple possession. At the *local* level, however, the officer is more likely to see a grave threat even in the occasional user, and will arrest anyone whose use is detected on whom he can make a reasonable case. However, as we will make clear shortly, a great deal is determined by the *strategies* chosen for detection.

TABLE 11-1

Marijuana Arrests, State of California, 1960–1968

	1960	1961	1962	1963	1964	1965	1966	1967	1968
Adult	4,245	3,386	3,433	4,883	6,323	8,383	14,209	26,527	33,573
Juvenile	910	408	310	635	1,237	1,619	4,034	10,987	16,754

Source: State of California, *Drug Arrests and Dispositions in California, 1967* (Sacramento: Department of Justice, Bureau of Criminal Statistics, 1968), pp. 4, 5, and *1968 Drug Arrests in California, Advance Report,* April 1969, pp. 4, 6.

In order to make the scope of the arrest picture clear, I present a table from California's official *Drug Arrests and Dispositions in California, 1968* (the most recent year available). It is the total number of arrests for the years 1960–1968 on marijuana charges. We use California's data because they are the most reliable, complete and detailed. (In fact, this chapter could not have been written without this excellent set of yearly statistics.) We are struck at once by the massive increases in the number of arrests in the past few years— increases which, by all indications, will continue for the forseeable future. The increase from 1960 to 1968 was about eight times for the adults and more than eighteen times for juveniles. The rise did not begin until 1964 or 1965, and in 1965–1966 and 1966–1967 the rises were enormous. In fact, so recent is the expansion of marijuana arrests that in a book published in 1965, Alfred R. Lindesmith, whose data on marijuana arrests ended in 1962, claimed that on the federal level, ". . . the number of marihuana arrests has steadily declined and by 1960 it was close to the vanishing point. . . ." [8] In a table enumerating an admittedly incomplete count of marijuana arrests, federal, state, and local, for 1954, a grand total of 3,918 in the United States was listed. In 1967, in the county of Los Angeles alone, there were over four times as many marijuana arrests. In December 1967, there were almost as many California arrests on marijuana charges in one month as there were in the entire country for any entire year prior to 1960.

By any criterion, the number of arrests is enormous—except when compared with the number of users who are not arrested. The official who claims that marijuana use is generally tolerated and ignored by law enforcement agents does not have the facts. The claim that only dealers are arrested, too, is patently false. Included in the arrests are users of every "size." With these massive arrest figures, let us look at how users and sellers get arrested and what happens to their cases in court. Keep in mind that we are using California's data because they are the only useable ones available. We assume, however, that the California situation pertains in some degree (and in general, to an explicit degree) to what is valid in other states. California differs principally in the *size* of arrest figures, and the close acquaintance of its judges with marijuana arrestees since they see so many of them. But the way most users and sellers are arrested, the trend of arrests, and their disposition, should not be radically different from that of the other states.

Detection of marijuana violations is typically extremely difficult. There is no victim and no complainant, so that systematic surveillance techniques inherently involve a certain loss of civil liberties. The success of any police venture is determined by various *stituational* features having to do with the kinds of crimes that they are attempting to detect and prevent. For instance, it is obvious that

See p. 272

acts conducted by two consenting adults who have a long-term relationship with one another, and who have no incentive to punish or discredit one another, conducted in privacy, are highly unlikely to be detected and sanctioned. On the other hand, acts perpetrated on many people by one person, previously unknown to them, in public, which they define as harmful, are highly likely to be detected, and the perpetrator punished for his act. Marijuana use, for instance, is clearly of the former type. It is generally conducted among intimates or semiintimates, all of whom are compliant, in private; moreover, it rarely incurs negative consequences, at least in the microcosm of the single act of smoking during a single evening.

We would expect the ratio of undetected to detected acts relating to marijuana violations to be extremely high. Among our 204 respondents, we have a total of literally hundreds of thousands of instances of use, several thousand cases of sale and purchase, and tens of thousands of days of possession. That seven cases were brought to the attention of the law enforcement authorities indicates the low degree of access the police have to marijuana crimes. If we compare marijuana infractions with a high-access and high-victimization crime, such as murder, the contrast is dramatically clear. A tiny fraction of marijuana crimes, probably less than one one-hundredth of 1 percent, are detected with the violator arrested. With murder, probably over 90 percent of all violators are arrested and brought to trial.[9] Even if we compare marijuana with another crime without a victim, narcotics possession and sale, the incidence of detection is extremely low. The narcotics addict must purchase heroin several times a day, in public. Even the heavy user of marijuana who does not sell for a profit will make a purchase once a month or so—one one-hundredth as often as the junkie—probably from a close friend, in an apartment, in a calm emotional atmosphere. He is, therefore, far less likely to be detected, and far less likely to be arrested.

It is therefore apparent that the police face serious logistic problems in apprehending the marijuana seller and user. To transcend the limitations and restrictions surrounding them, special efforts at detection must be made. Generally, the police have three methods at their disposal: informants, undercover agents, and patrol. The most common type of informant, in spite of frequent police denials, is the "arrestee informant." They cooperate with the police because they have themselves been arrested and promised lenience if they supply the names of marijuana violators known to them, usually their own dealers. The more names, and the bigger the names given to the police, the more lenient the police are. However, since most sellers known to the average marijuana user are probably his friends, this procedure is likely to bring conflicting pressures to bear on the suspect. It is not unknown for the informant to select the names not on the basis of the volume of sales, which is what the police are interested in, but on the basis of his attitude toward the person he is about to incriminate. The list of names often reaches down the distribution ladder, rather than up.

The use of the undercover agent is designed to allow the police to observe a criminal scene from inside. The agent poses as a user, seller, artist, poet, or student, and takes part in marijuana use and selling transactions himself. Often the agent will attempt to purchase progressively larger amounts from progressively bigger dealers to reach and eradicate the source, in which case, he will often ignore the petty dealers.

Another procedure is simply to arrest anyone on whom incriminating evidence has been gathered, as occurred with the Stony Brook arrests of 1968 and 1969. The agent will frequently use the technique of entrapment—i.e., request a purchase or sale himself, thus "creating" the crime *de novo*, although it is illegal. Often, instead of trying to make a case for selling, an extremely difficult proposition involving solid evidence, the agent will collect names on whom "probable cause" will be exercised—that is, their premises will be searched on the presumption that a quantity of marijuana will be found.

Actually, although these two methods, the use of informants and undercover agents, are dramatic and infamous in marijuana storytelling lore, they result in a small minority of arrests. A 100-page monograph published in the *UCLA Law Review* in 1968, based on 1966 data, attempted a complete exploration of marijuana arrests, carrying the cases down to their complete post-arrest disposition.[10] I will rely heavily on this report, which I will call the Los Angeles study, in the following exposition. Much valuable information, not available anywhere else, is presented in this document. For instance, the Los Angeles study revealed that very few marijuana arrests are the result of preplanned strategy on the part of the police. In the sample of arrestees in the study, only 3 percent of the adult arrestees and 7 percent of the juveniles were the work of undercover agents, while 23 percent and 15 percent of the adult and juvenile arrests, respectively, resulted from information supplied by an informant. Thus, in three-quarters of the cases (74 percent of the adults and 79 percent of the juveniles) neither an informant nor an undercover agent was used. The overwhelming bulk of these cases, nearly all in fact, resulted from patrol enforcement, in general, by far the most common source of marijuana arrests. All indications point to the fact that the vast majority of all marijuana arrests are not the result of a systematic search, but accident. No arrest warrant was used in 92 percent of the Los Angeles adult cases, and no search warrant in 97 percent of the adult cases; in only four out of almost 200 juvenile cases was either used.

Another indication of the accidental and unplanned character of most marijuana arrests, in the Los Angeles study at least, is the fact that more arrests were made in the arrestee's *automobile* than anywhere else (45 percent for adults, and 36 percent for juveniles). Nearly all of these arrests were, obviously, fortuitous.

A person is driving an automobile, and he goes through a red light. The police give him a ticket, and they notice a marijuana cigarette in an ash tray. . . .[11]

. . . in the routine case, what happens is an automobile is stopped because the tail light is out, or something is wrong and there is a traffic violation, and, as a result of the accident, a small quantity of marijuana is discovered, and the people that are in the car are then arrested. . . .[12]

Often the marijuana in the car is visible. Often it is not. Many automobiles are stopped because the occupants look like candidates for a marijuana arrest; if no marijuana is visible, the automobile will be searched. The line between "probable cause" for an automobile search, and no probable cause, and an illegal search, is thin. The smell of marijuana smoke may constitute probable cause. A hand motion may be interpreted by the patrolman as a "furtive gesture," perhaps to throw a joint out of the car window. Or shoulder-length hair on a teenaged boy may inform the policeman that he is unconventional enough to smoke pot. Many of the signs interpreted by the arresting officer as probable cause will be rejected by the judge. Often automobile searches will be an instrument in systematic harassment, rather than motivated by the desire to make a case that will hold up in court. At any rate, hundreds of such illegal automobile searches are made routinely in New York's Greenwich Village and East Village. By the law of chance, a sizeable number inevitably turn up a quantity of marijuana. Since the searches are done on those who are likely to be marijuana smokers as well as the young and unconventional, a legitimate protest against such harassment would be ineffective. It does, after all, secure a great many arrests. The New York police automatically search all parts of impounded and towed-away, illegally parked cars for drugs, any area of the car, in fact, that they don't have to break into. This routinely gathers a large number of arrests, but the American Civil Liberties Union claims illegal search and seizure on all of these arrests and most are actually dismissed because of their illegal character.[13]

Another large proportion of the arrestees were apprehended in a public place—21 percent of the adults and 35 percent of the juveniles. Public arrests are often the consequence of "stop and frisk" procedures, the suspect supposedly having given the arresting officer "probable cause" to be searched. Obviously, much of the same police conduct occurs with public arrests as those which take place in the automobile of the suspect. The remaining third or so (35 percent for adults; 29 percent for juveniles) of the arrests took place in a private place, most likely a house or apartment.[14] Most of the "systematic" arrests, i.e., those which result from the work of an undercover agent or an informer, take place in a private establishment. However, probably most of these "private" arrests are also a result of accident. A common sequence of events is as follows: ". . . a person gets in bad company, or ends up at an address where they (the police) have some information about a loud party, and they go there and they smell marijuana smoke, and four or five, six, perhaps seven, people are arrested and complaints are issued and these people are charged with the crime of marijuana."[15]

Obviously, the tactic used in law enforcement will influence the kind of suspect arrested; a change in methods will result in the capture of a different sort of person. Who gets arrested and who doesn't when arrests take place by accident or patrol harassment? It seems clear that because of their sheer numbers, these methods are likely to result in the arrest of a great many mere users. The frequent user-petty seller is vulnerable to arrest, simply because he is around marijuana most of the time, and any random moment he is approached by the police will find him possessing incriminating evidence. The large-scale dealer who does not use is highly unlikely to be arrested if random patrol methods are employed if he disposes of his goods quickly. In fact, since nearly all fairly regular marijuana smokers have a supply on hand for their own use, the prevailing arrest tactics are most likely to snare users; medium- to high-level dealers who have marijuana on hand continuously are only slightly more likely to be arrested than the regular user—who also has marijuana on hand most of the time, although generally, a smaller amount.

The present enforcement methods, not being designed to arrest the dealer, are unlikely to make a dent in the source of the drug and will only result in feelings of injustice among users who are arrested, since the seriousness of the crime bears a scant relationship to detection and arrest. In fact, since the ratio of undetected to detected crimes is so high with marijuana violations, the relatively few (which is large in absolute numbers) who are arrested will always ask, "Why me?" In California alone in 1968 there were 50,000 arrests on marijuana charges. What proportion of this figure could possibly have been large-scale dealers? How many were dabblers, teenagers who had tried the drug a few times and possessed a few joints for experimentation? (Over 16,000 of these arrests were under 18 years of age.) More felons are arrested on marijuana charges than for any other felony. At the same time, a lower proportion of marijuana felonies and felons are detected and arrested than possibly for any other felony. And probably in no other crime is there so loose a relationship between seriousness and likelihood of arrest. It is unlikely that the present tactics will do anything about eradicating the marijuana traffic, but at least by arresting so many users, the police will create an illusion that an effective enforcement job is being done.

Arrestees, remember, do not represent all users. We do not have a cross-section of users when we look at arrest statistics. There are certainly systematic differences between them. It is no contradiction to say that most arrests are accidental and, at the same time, to say that arrestees do not form a random sample of all users. To begin with, "accidental" is not the same thing as "random." When an automobile is stopped for some trivial reason, marijuana is stumbled upon, and the occupants are arrested—this is an accident. But it is not a random event. Over one-third of all marijuana arrests took place in an automobile. What about the users who never drive, or never drive when they are in possession of marijuana? Obviously they will be underrepresented in arrest figures. Or those that never, or almost never, carry marijuana in public—these users are also less likely to be arrested, appearing only infrequently in the composition of arrestees.

Most state and local marijuana violation arrests are for simple possession—83 percent of the adults and 87 percent of the juveniles in the Los Angeles study. Only 9 percent of all marijuana arrests, both adult and juvenile, were for sale, regardless of quantity.[16] This is partly a reflection of the unsystematic character of patrol enforcement and partly a matter of a desire to make a case stick. In order to make a case for selling, actual undercover work must be done, which is rare. Often a known seller will be arrested simply for possession because that is far easier to prove.

Only seven of my respondents were arrested on marijuana charges, so that we do not have a complete picture of how arrests are made and cases disposed of. However, we can examine their experiences as a reflection of general law enforcement processes. In addition to the seven who were formally arrested, one was apprehended, but not arrested, possibly because of the illegal nature of the apprehension. One individual (arrested twice) involved in smuggling was not arrested in the United States. One of the arrestees was judged at his trial not to be in technical possession of the marijuana (one roach!), and the charges were dismissed.[17] Of the five remaining cases, one was arrested twice. None of the five was incarcerated for his crime; four received suspended sentences, and one was still awaiting trial at the time of the interview.

With all of our cases, the detection of the crime was fortuitous; in no case did an undercover agent seek out use and selling. We cite three typical examples of the police accidentally stumbling upon marijuana crimes:

A friend of mine whom I turned on felt guilty and told his father about it. His father told the police, and the police followed him to my house. At four a.m., the police rang my doorbell, and, when I answered, beat me up, and then called my parents. I was adjudged a youthful offender, and placed on probation for 14 months.

twenty-year-old college student

I was playing pool with another guy, and two cops walked in, took us outside, and searched us, me and my friend, and then they searched our car. One joint was in the car. We were searched illegally; we were handcuffed before they even found anything. The charge is going to be dropped because I'm getting a recommendation from a youth counsellor.

twenty-one-year-old clerk in a gift shop

I was sent one joint from Mexico through the mail. The customs officials delivered the letter to my apartment in person—they had a search warrant —and said that they were going to search my apartment. But I went and got my supply, and gave it to them. They said that they were going to arrest me, but they were willing to cooperate if I did. I supplied them with a name of a dealer—knowing that he was leaving for Canada that day. I wasn't arrested.

nineteen-year-old female clerk in a bookstore

Post-Arrest Disposition

Arrest is only the first step in a long legal process. The questions involved in the post-arrest disposition are often extremely complex and technical. The policeman, who operates on the basis of simple guilt or innocence, is frustrated and angered to see one of his cases dismissed on a minor technicality, feeling that the lawyers and judges are trying to abort law and order. However, these formalities were designed to protect the possibly innocent suspect, and they usually err on the side of being overly generous in letting many probably guilty suspects go free, rather than making the mistake of jailing a few possibly innocent suspects. That this happens to such a degree with marijuana charges points to the fact that many judges, district attorneys, and lawyers have lost faith in the justice of the marijuana statutes. A certain degree of leeway is allowed the public officials after arrest; where many decisions are resolved in favor of the suspect, we are forced to accept the conclusion that the prosecuting officials do not support the laws as they stand.

By making the arrest, the policeman is registering his presumption as to the guilt of the arrested party. Actually, in the overwhelming majority of the cases, he will be correct. The suspects he arrests are almost certainly guilty of some marijuana-related crime, if not at that instance, then probably at some other time. Anyone around a quantity of marijuana, who associates with marijuana smokers, who is arrested along with others who use, possess, and sell the stuff, is highly likely to have used, possessed, and sold at some time or another. The innocent suspect in the typical marijuana arrest is extremely rare; the suspect who, by some outlandish accident, happens to find himself, at the time of the arrest, for the first time in his life, among users, and is suddenly arrested, is almost nonexistent. Each arrest has a history of use behind it. Each arrest has built into it a past of marijuana crimes which carry with them heavy penalties. The arresting officer is dead right in his assumptions, and is consistent in his actions. The technicalities of court law obstruct his design. If guilt is certain, why not prosecute? If the law is on the books, why not back it up? If they are not firmly supported by the actors involved in the post-arrest procedures, then why have them in the books?

Post-arrest disposition consists of procedural steps leading from the arrest of the marijuana pusher or user to his imprisonment. At any one of these stages, the arrestee may be freed from having to proceed to the next step. The attorney may refuse to file a complaint against him; the judge at the preliminary hearing may refuse to "hold the defendant to answer" a complaint that has been filed; the trial judge (or jury) may find the defendant innocent; and finally, the defendant may be released on probation.

There are two types of factors which influence the district attorney and the judge in deciding whether to release the arrestee at any of the above stages. The first type of factors are those which the law requires the trier of fact to consider in determining guilt. . . . In marijuana offenses these include the legality of a search, sufficiency of the evidence, and knowledge on the part of the arrestee that he possessed marijuana. . . .

[The] other factors which either the judge or district attorney may consider in making his decision to release . . . include the defendant's age, his attitude, his previous contact with the law, his family situation, and what the judge or district attorney believes to be his moral culpability.[18]

Great discretion, then, is permitted judges in marijuana cases. Some who believe that marijuana use and sale are antisocial acts rarely initiate dismissal procedures; others are known for being lenient. Generally, small-town judges will dismiss less often than those in urban centers. There is probably a positive relationship between the frequency of marijuana cases brought before a judge and the likelihood of dismissal. In the Los Angeles study, 12 percent of the cases brought before the district attorney for filing were rejected, and the arrestee freed; in addition, 14 percent were rejected at the preliminary hearings.[19] Half of the cases wherein the judge dismissed the disposition before him and refused to hold the defendant to answer the complaint were because the police searched the defendant's person or apartment on no "probable cause," i.e., the search was random and unprovoked; the defendant was doing nothing which could have aroused the arresting officer's suspicion, and the search was illegal. About one-third of the dismissals were for insufficient evidence, a handful were dismissed on the basis of entrapment, and a few were dismissed because the amount possessed was insufficient (a few seeds, traces, or a roach). (Judges usually have an informal "one joint" rule on the sufficiency of the amount; a roach is technically useable, but few urban judges prosecute on that amount.)

Very few cases go before a jury; over 95 percent of the adult Los Angeles cases were tried before a judge. Defendants rightly feel that a judge who sees marijuana cases daily takes the seriousness of the offense more lightly than do members of a jury, who are far more likely to be ignorant of the immensity and extent of use today among the young. About two-thirds of the adult Los Angeles cases which finally reached the trial stage were adjudged guilty. This represents slightly under one-third of all arrests.

Of all the California adult marijuana dispositions registered in the official state statistics—in other words all of the dispositions which took place in the entire state of California—handled in 1967 (some of which were arrested that year, and some earlier), slightly over half, 56 percent, were released, dismissed, or acquitted, and one third (35 percent) were convicted.[20] Marijuana arrestees received much more lenient treatment at the hands of California judges than heroin suspects, 40 percent of whom had their cases dropped while 44 percent were convicted.

Of the adult convictees, 59 percent of those who were arrested on possession charges were "convicted as charged," while 41 percent were convicted on a lesser drug charge. For those charged with sale, 48 percent were convicted as charged, and 52 percent were convicted on a lesser charge. (Sale is more difficult to prove.) Of these almost 4,000 possession convictions, 44 percent received "straight probation," and 34 percent received a combination of probation and a minor jail sentence. Those convicted of marijuana sale were not quite so fortunate; 23 percent received probation, and 46 percent got probation and jail. Only 10 percent of the possession convictees received a straight jail or prison sentence; and 20 percent of the sale convictees got the same.[21]

Looking at the yearly trend, we see clearly that probation is becoming increasingly common. In 1961, under 50 percent of the adult convictees got either straight probation or a combination of probation and a light jail sentence; in 1967, the figure was almost 80 percent.[22] It seems apparent that judges are gradually losing faith in jail sentences in rehabilitating marijuana users; they are increasingly thinking of marijuana infractions, particularly simple possession and use, as trivial offenses not worthy of a prison sentence. Of the variables which most strongly influence the granting of probation, probably the convictee's prior arrest record influences judges the most. Of all the adults convicted for marijuana possession, with *no* prior sentences, 65 percent received straight probation, with no jail sentence; for those with a record as a minor, 49 percent got only probation; for those with an adult record, only 25 percent received probation; and for those who actually had a prior prison record, 16 percent got probation.[23] The percentage getting a prison or jail sentence was 2 percent, 6 percent, 17 percent, and 41 percent for each of these categories, respectively.

Even a consideration of the incarceration sentences reveals more leniency than would be assumed from the length of sentences that are called for in the law books. Well over a third (39 percent) of the adult marijuana possession convictees who received a jail sentence served *less than three months*. (Most of these received these light sentences in conjunction with probation.) Only 13 percent received jail sentences lasting more than nine months. However, those convicted on *sale* charges received sentences comparable to heroin possession sentences; about one-quarter of both got the less than three-month sentences, and about the same amount received sentences of more than nine months.[24]

Many judges take an arrestee's attitude of remorse seriously, even though users are likely to adopt a cynical and mocking attitude toward their own rehabilitation, which they consider a cruel joke. Since very few users think of marijuana use as a problem, they may adopt a pose of penitence for utilitarian purposes. During the months after the 1968 raid on the Stony Brook campus, which netted two dozen student users, a program was set up which resembled Synanon, and was designed to rehabilitate and "redeem" the marijuana user. The program was viewed by users and nonusers alike as a pathetic farce, but the arrestees participated in it because they believed that their presiding judge would be merciful as a result. It is this kind of thinking that led one lawyer-observer of the pot scene to write:

It is important for the defendant to have a cooperative attitude with the probation officer. . . . Stable employment, conforming dress and sincere remorse for having broken the law, combined with a positive plan for future rehabilitation must be presented. . . . One who stands convicted of a crime cannot expect lenient treatment if he goes before those who are about to sentence him with the attitude that his actions are acceptable and the law is wrong. Such an expression would probably encourage any judge, otherwise disposed to grant probation, to allow the offender to spend a substantial amount of time in jail to think about, and possibly modify, his attitude. It is better to play it cool.[25]

Arrest as a Status Transformation

Legal agencies have the power to define legal reality. They can, of course, create laws and criminals *de novo*. But in a narrower sense, the legal process is successful to the extent that it either (1) compels the individual to accept society's version of himself as *in fact* criminal, i.e., criminal in more than a technical sense, a person deserving of society's scorn and punishment, or (2) discredits the individual in important areas of his life, impugning his trustworthiness, moral rectitude, and integrity for many members of society. An arrest is able to do at least the latter. There are, of course, those for whom an arrest is a mark of honor, or at least has no moral significance. But public exposure is often unavoidable in an arrest. Consequently, one's private life is subject to public scrutiny. Surveillance involves encroachments of privacy.[26] Policemen rarely make the fine distinctions between uncovering necessary evidence and a wholesale invasion of privacy.

Being suspected of committing a crime, being under surveillance, having one's dwelling and/or person searched, being arrested, booked, brought to trial, and (if it comes to that) convicted, not to mention the nature of one's experiences in a penitentiary, all serve as *public degradation ceremonies*.[27]

The legal apparatus has immense power to determine the nature of a felon's *public and private presentation*. Although this is a variable and not a constant, in all likelihood he sees himself as a man who has done something which is technically against the law, but which in no way qualifies him for a criminal status, for "true" criminality. He may not see himself as being "a criminal." Nor does society, not knowing about his crimes. Marijuana users often state that they "don't think of marijuana use as a crime." But going through the procedure of being arrested impresses in the mind of the offender the view that one powerful segment of society (and perhaps, by extension, society in general) has of his activity's legality.

In other words, the elaborate legal procedure, and its attendant social implications, serve as a kind of *dramaturgic rite de passage*, which serves to transform the transgressor publicly into a criminal, into "the kind of person who would do such a thing." Although many going through the ritual will reject the definition of them imposed by the process, it nonetheless leaves its impress.

Formal Law, Substantive Law, and Law Enforcement

A common argument against marijuana use involves its legal status. Aside from the debate concerning its dangers, or lack thereof, to the human mind and body, the single irreducible fact regarding marijuana which is universally agreed upon is that its use, possession, and sale are illegal. The opponents of marijuana use this as an effective weapon in their dialogue with the drug's advocates. Regardless of one's point of view on marijuana, it is outlawed. Everyone who uses it is a criminal, someone subject to the risk of arrest and imprisonment who should expect to be punished.

Actually, this argument fails under close scrutiny. Many laws— perhaps *most* laws—are not enforced. Formal law, law as it exists on the books, is very different from substantive law, law as it is actually enforced. The breach of some laws engenders widespread moral outrage, while the *enforcement* of other laws incurs that same public wrath. "It's the law" can never be an excuse for sanctioning an act, because "the law" is a hodge-podge of archaic long-forgotten, and ignored statutes that are never executed, along with those that are respected and daily enforced. Masturbation is illegal in a number of states (Pennsylvania, for instance), and in Indiana and Wyoming, it is criminal to encourage a person to masturbate. In forty-five states, adultery is illegal; Connecticut calls for five-year imprisonment upon prosecution. Mere fornication is a crime in thirty-eight states, and a breach of this law theoretically carries a fine of $500 or two-years imprisonment, or both.[28] Many states dictate the manner in which one may make love to one's spouse; cunnilingus and fellatio, for instance, are against the law in many legal jurisdictions.[29] In view of the near-universality of masturbation among men and the fact that a majority of all couples marrying today engaged in premarital intercourse, the virtual absence of any prosecution for these crimes is remarkable. Although sanctioning all crimes without victims entails severe problems of logistical detection, with adultery at least, divorce suits constitute a fertile field. In New York state, where until recently adultery was the only legitimate grounds for divorce, thousands of divorces have been filed and granted in the past few years, yet almost no one is ever prosecuted for this crime.[30]

The enforcement of certain laws, therefore, cannot be taken for granted. Enforcement is problematic. Thus, when a law is enforced, it is necessary to ask why. What is it that differentiates those laws that are enforced and those that are not enforced? The argument that a man should refrain from performing certain kinds of sexual acts with his wife, because "it's the law," is never invoked. Yet this same argument holds up in marijuana debates. Surely, it is not the formal status of the marijuana laws that dictates their enforcement, but attitudes toward its use prevailing among the public, law enforcement officers, and agents which make leniency improbable. Rather than a matter of formal laws, marijuana enforcement is a matter of morality.

The marijuana laws are an example of the many "crimes without victims," an effort to legislate morality. There is no victim, no complainant. The use of marijuana harms no one except the user. (And there is question whether the user is harmed.) The marijuana laws represent an example of the criminalization of deviance. The legal machinery creates, by fiat, a class of criminals. If a law is annulled, criminals magically become law-abiders. Prior to 1961, homosexual acts were a crime in Illinois; after that, they were legal. It is the law that creates the crime.

Yet, someone who violates a law is not necessarily a criminal, at least, he is not viewed so by society. He must violate a law which is more than formally illegal. Public attitudes toward the law must be supportive, and toward its violators, condemnatory. Arrest reinforces society's negative attitudes toward illegalized behavior, and arrest is facilitated, and made more likely, if society condemns, as well as illegalizes, the behavior in question.

Every society is in varying degrees made up of disparate subcultures with competing versions of reality; the larger and more complex the society, the greater the corresponding diversity of subcultures in that society. Yet power is never distributed in any society randomly; members of some subcultures will always have more than members of others. And, although power over someone is by definition linear and hierarchical, subcultures are mosaic and incommensurable. Given the diversity of subcultures, some sort of effort has to be made in effectively neutralizing power challenges from members of another group not in power, or legitimating the validity of one special definition of reality. Differential power and its exercise represents attempts at moral hegemony, rather than simply protection and extension of economic interests. Society is rent by large groups of individuals who simply see right and wrong in radically different ways. And many individuals have a powerful emotional investment in the dominance of one particular subcultural point of view. These are the moral entrepreneurs, the cultural imperialists who wish to extend their way of life to all members of society, regardless of the validity of that way of life for the individual or group in question.

Although laws exist merely as a potentiality for sanctioning, the mere fact that a norm, regardless of whether it has any general community support, has been formally crystallized into law, makes a great deal of difference as to whether any given individual will be penalized for an activity condemned by the dominant culture. Since each subculture has differential access to the formal agencies of social control, a norm can have lost legitimacy for a majority of the citizenry, and yet there will be some individuals who continue to regard the law as just and legitimate, who happen to be in a position of determining and defining the legal process, and are therefore able to sanction in the absence of general societal licitness. Laws and formal agencies of social control may be thought of as a resource in the hands of one subculture to enforce their beliefs on other, dissident subcultures. So powerfully is this the case that members of a group may be punished, ostensibly for an act which is in fact illegal, but in reality for another act which is not formally illegal, but which the wielders of social control find repugnant. Known political radicals are often arrested for marijuana possession by evangelistic law enforcement officers, frustrated because most forms of politically radical activity are not formally illegal.[31]

Clearly, however, most of the laws that are enforced have a high degree of moral legitimacy. But legitimacy is a matter of degree; the more widespread and deeply held a given norm is, the greater the likelihood that its transgression will be effectively sanctioned. The moral legitimacy of a given norm can be looked at as another resource in the hands of moral entrepreneurs to punish dissident groups.

It is, of course, highly relevant *who* accepts the norm. The ability to translate infractions into sanctions is differentially distributed throughout the social structure. Among some subgroups in a given society there will be a closer correspondence between their own norms and the law. Norms apply more heavily to subgroup and subculture members, but laws generally apply to all. It is likely that those groups which exhibit the greatest identity between norms (their own) and the laws are specifically those groups that have the greatest power to effect sanctions.

Moral entrepreneurs, of course, think of their work as protective in nature. They see their task as protecting society from the damaging effects of the criminal behavior, and the individual committing the criminal acts from damaging himself. There is the attempt, then, to extend beyond a simple prohibition of an act because it is "immoral," within the confines of a specific moral code; there is the further assertion that the act causes objectively agreed-upon damage to the individual transgressor himself, as well as to the society at large. Yet the very perception of the act as immoral structures one's perceptions concerning the actual occurrence of the "objectively agreed-upon" damage.

The Law and the Question of Legalization

The question is often raised as to the justness of the marijuana statutes, arrests, and sentences. A legal advisor to the Bureau of Narcotics wrote, in a prepared speech before the National Student Association: "With the exception of fringe elements in society, represented by confessed users, few authorities take issue with the present prohibitory scheme." [32] This charge was absurd in 1967; today it is even more so. In fact, aside from employees of the Federal Bureau of Narcotics, as well as other law enforcement agencies, the present legal structure has the support of very few. Many of the drug's toughest critics such as Donald B. Louria, advocate a considerable reduction in penalties on use and possession ("so that a minor crime is punished by a minor penalty"), an absolute elimination of the penalties for being in a place where marijuana is smoked, but a retention of the existing penalties for sale and importation.[33] (Louria calls his suggestions "the middle road.") And in a recent government publication, the appropriateness of the federal penalties on marijuana and the basic antimarijuana arguments were seriously called into question; this federal scrutiny of marijuana was made specifically because "the law has come under attack on all counts." [34]

Huge segments of the American population feel that the legal ban on marijuana use and possession should be lifted. There is not a majority in any geographical locale, but this sentiment has powerful support among many social segments—the young, for instance. There are probably age categories where close to a majority support some version of legalization. Certainly a referendum of college students, if effected, would call for a considerable reduction in the existing penalties; probably at least a sizeable minority of all college students in a national survey would endorse outright legalization. However, a clear majority of college students support legalization in some form or another in a great many schools, especially those in or near urban centers—UCLA,[35] California Institute of Technology[36] and Stony Brook, for instance. A recent referendum at the last of these schools, showed the following degree of support for various legalization alternatives: (see Table 11–2).[37]

It is necessary to consider some fundamental questions. What do we want the laws to do? What is the purpose of the existing penalty structure? What are we trying to achieve by punishing the use, possession, and sale of marijuana? These questions are neither rhetorical nor scornful. By asking them, I am calling for a sincere, hard look at the laws and their basic underlying assumptions. If we have been deluded about how they work, perhaps it is time for a reassessment of their status.

As I see it, the laws against marijuana have at least the following five functions (which bear with them correlative assumptions about criteria of effectiveness): (1) deterrence, (2) rehabilitation, (3) public safety, (4) vengeance, and (5) symbolic representation.

The first three of these functions are what might be called "instrumental" goals, and the last two are "expressive." Deterrence, public safety, and rehabilitation are goals whose attainment can, within the very severe limitations of bias and differential perception —which influence everyone at all times—at least *ideally* be determined. Of course, the public image of a given reality may be wildly different from the image that a panel of disinterested experts would have (were it possible to find them). Who determines whether and to what extent goals have been attained? Thus, the criteria for

TABLE 11–2

Support for Legalization at Stony Brook (percent)

"What changes in state and federal marijuana laws would you make?"

Increase penalties for sale and possession	7
No change	14
Decrease only penalties for possession	12
Abolish penalties for possession, and retain some penalty for sale	9
Restricted legalization (state licensing of distributors, sale only to adults, etc.)	38
Complete unrestricted legalization	21
	N = 2,435

effectiveness, and the determination of whether the goals have been reached, although ideally perceptible, in practice become somewhat muddied. But we should be able to see, in theory, at least, that the first three of these goals are tangible. The last two are not tangible. We can establish whether punishment rehabilitates the user, but it is impossible to determine the effectiveness of the vengeance or the symbolism criterion. It is not that the task would be too imposing; it is that they are ends in themselves, given in the nature of things— for some observers—and they must be either accepted or rejected outright. Their rightness or wrongness depends entirely on intangibles, on emotion, sentiment, predisposition.

At first glance, a consideration of the first goal, deterrence, might seem a vain issue, after even the most cursory glance at the enormity of the arrest statistics. To the 50,000 California marijuana arrests in

1968, we have those of every state—none so great in number, singly, as California, but altogether at least doubling and possibly tripling the figure for the whole country.

What of 1969 and 1970? Deterrence? Who, indeed, is being deterred? But consider the question of whether the use of marijuana would not actually be even higher were the drug legalized. The assumption about use being stimulated by the thrill of breaking the law—the "forbidden fruit" hypothesis—has no validity. Most users are not attracted by the risk of incarceration, on the contrary, most use marijuana in spite of the risks. Some psychiatrists feel that lawbreakers feel guilty about imagined past transgressions and seek a means to be punished. Such psychiatric judgments can often be used as an instrument to attack any and all protests of the existing legal structure. By giving scientific legitimation to such psychiatric claims concerning deviants, a case is made for slavish conformity to the law. Perhaps some psychiatrists' patients fit this description, but as a general characterization of marijuana users, it is clearly in error. Not only would the number who try the drug once or a dozen times be much greater were it legal and readily available, but regular (or "chronic") use would claim far more participants as well.

Concerning our deterrence criterion, we are impelled to ask: Are the laws "working"? The answer does not come easily; how we answer it depends on our notion of what constitutes the criteria of effectiveness. The marijuana laws probably work more ineffectively than laws against any activity which is taken seriously enough to draw a penalty regularly. That does not mean that some, or many, potential users are not deterred. In a classic work written over three-quarters of a century ago, _The Division of Labor in Society,_ Emile Durkheim wrote that society's enforcement of the law has an effect on those who are punished less than on those who are not—that is, those who might violate the law otherwise. In a sense, those who go to jail are "sacrifices" in order to serve the function of deterring their peers. And potential marijuana users are deterred in massive numbers by the example of arrests and punishment meted out to the less cautious. Exactly how many are deterred, and how many the law fails to deter, is impossible to determine. We can safely say, however, that the deterrence function is breaking down yearly. I suspect that marijuana's appeal is greater to the young than that of alcohol. Therefore, I would say that were all restrictions removed, the under-twenty-five-years of age range would use cannabis more than liquor today. Furthermore, I would guess that a significant proportion would continue to use it into their 30s and 40s. In other words, I think that marijuana would eventually partly supplant liquor as an intoxicant, were it legal and as available. Seen in this light, the laws have a *powerful* deterrent impact.

Marijuana users, as we might expect, do not want to be rehabilitated. This is not true of many lawbreakers who are caught. Narcotics addicts are extremely ambivalent about their addiction; many have a sincere desire to kick the habit—although very few do. Not so with marijuana smokers. They feel that they have no "habit" to begin with. They will claim that they can give it up any time. It is not a problem with most users. They will simply not see the *point* of "rehabilitation." It would be like suddenly defining sexual activity as a dependency, and attempting to rehabilitate those who wish to indulge in sex; they would ask, "What for?"

Arrestees are likely to be puzzled or angered by a marijuana sentence. They are, to a considerable degree, isolated from the dominant American ideology on pot and deeply involved in their own subculture's conception of it as harmless and beneficial. Moreover, the relatively few (but absolutely, many) users who are arrested gives them cause for the accusation of distributive injustice. Rehabilitation is predicated on the notion that the transgressor thinks of his transgression as wrong. Users often give up use of the weed after arrest but for practical reasons, not out of a desire to rid themselves of a nasty habit. To demonstrate these assertions, a study of arrestees would have to be made. In the absence of such a study, two users who were arrested or who are serving prison sentences for violation of the marijuana statutes voice reactions to their legal experiences:

It's rather discouraging to spend time in jail for the "crime" of possessing a weed. I haven't hurt anybody, I haven't stolen from anybody, I haven't raped anybody's daughter. Why am I in jail? I don't feel like a criminal.

I committed a charitable act. . . . I agreed to turn this poor cat onto some grass at his request. He promptly turned me in.

This silly grass law is only one small reflection of the mentality that rules America and dictates what we can read, what we can think and what position we must use when we make love.

My love to all the gentle people. Our day is coming.[38]

Having been convicted of selling five dollars' worth of seeds and stems to an informer, I am currently serving a twenty-to-thirty year sentence. . . .

. . . my bail was set at $45,000—an impossible sum for me to raise. So I sat in jail for four months before being tried. There were twenty-five other marijuana arrests in [the] . . . County in the past two years, but I am the only one who has been sent to the penitentiary. Why this special treatment for me? [39]

Law enforcement officers, however, often feel rehabilitation to be a worthy goal. Often a judge's sentence will hinge on his feeling that a jail sentence actually serves a rehabilitation function. We are reminded of Lindesmith's description of one such case:

. . . an occasional judge, ignorant of the nature of marihuana, sends a marihuana user to prison to cure him of his nonexistent addiction. The writer was once in court when a middle-aged Negro defendant appeared before the judge charged with having used and had in his possession one marihuana cigarette during the noon hour at the place where he had worked for a number of years. This man had no previous record and this fact was stated before the court. Nevertheless, a two-year sentence was imposed to "dry up his habit." [40]

What, in fact, are the effects of arrests, convictions, and jail sentences on users? Are they as likely to use again as they would if they were never arrested? This is, obviously, impossible to answer. Nor can we compare their later arrest figures with the arrest figures of a comparable group which was not arrested when they were. (We don't know the base figure—i.e., the total number of users we are making the comparison with.) Since a small percentage of marijuana arrests were arrested before—two-thirds of the 1967 California arrestees had no prior arrest record and a fifth had a "minor" record—we are not struck at once by any evidence of obvious recidivism. Over a third of the heroin arrestees in California and almost two-thirds of the "narcotic addict or user" arrests had either a major record or a prison sentence in his past. We know then that an immense percentage of heroin users are not "rehabilitated." We cannot draw such an obvious inference with marijuana users, since recidivistic arrests are so much lower for them.

In the absence of proper data, some guessing here may be justified. I would suspect that they use marijuana less after their arrest than they would have had they not been arrested. How much less? Two-thirds? Half? Enough to make it worthwhile? If rehabilitation is an absolute goal, then any degree of reduction is a positive gain. Viewed in this light, the laws are effective, merely because they bring about *some* degree of reduction in use. In this special sense, the judges may be right.

Some penologists are of the opinion that incarceration may have a subtle criminogenic effect. By being sent to prison along with professional criminals, drug addicts, and the violent, a lawbreaker with little or no commitment to crime as a "way of life" will absorb many attitudes, practices, and skills which will contribute to their post-release criminality. In a sense, prisons train people to become criminals. There is no doubt that this process occurs with juvenile delinquents. I suspect that marijuana users are well-insulated and sufficiently emotionally involved in their own subculture, which basically frowns on professional and violent forms of criminality, to be to some degree immune from such influences. Perhaps, however, this applies only to the middle-class, college-educated marijuana smoker who finds himself in prison. Blumer, in a study of marijuana in the ghetto, claims that a prison term is decisive in turning an ordinary pothead to a life of "hustling" criminality.

The player is to be seen . . . as an enterprising member of the adolescent drug world, alive to opportunities to get money by small-time dealing in drugs, ready to engage in a variety of other illicit sources of monetary profit, and strongly attracted toward moving into a full time job of hustling by associating with hustlers and learning of their hustling practices. It should be noted here that the most effective way of getting such practical work knowledge is through prison experience. If he is incarcerated he is likely to be thrown into contact with older and more experienced hustlers who, if they identify him as safe and acceptable, are almost certain to pass on accounts of their experience.

We suspect that prison incarceration is more decisive than any other happening in riveting the player in the direction of a hustling career.[41]

However, whether this process occurs at all, and it is certain to do so in some degree, it occurs with breakers of all laws, not only those concerned with marijuana.

Consideration of the public-safety issue is even more complex and unanswerable than the deterrence effect of the laws. Suppose marijuana were legalized: would society experience more damage than it does now? As stated in earlier chapters, this depends entirely on one's notions of what constitutes "damage." There are effects that some members of society would consider favorable which others would consider society's downfall. We need not go into this argument here. But what about those effects which all or nearly all members of society would consider damaging? Certain effects are nonpolitical; for instance, death, insanity, automobile accidents, lung cancer, violence, and brain and tissue damage. Are we contributing to public safety by outlawing pot? To begin with, the addition of another intoxicant to liquor would not be additive. (See Louria's argument on this.) [42] The evidence suggests that, although the user is more likely to drink liquor than the nonuser, he cuts down on consumption of liquor after his use of marijuana. Schoenfeld writes: "The incoherent vomit-covered drunk was a common sight in college infirmaries a few years ago. He is now rarely seen on campuses where students have switched to marijuana." [43] Seymour Halleck, another physician, comes up with the same answer:

Perhaps the one major effect of the drug is to cut down on the use of alcohol. In the last few years it is rare for our student infirmary to encounter a student who has become aggressive, disoriented, or physically ill because of excessive use of alcohol. Alcoholism has almost ceased to become a problem on our campuses. [44]

Tod Mikuriya, a physician, has recommended (not supplied) marijuana to his alcoholic patients, and claims improvement for them when the substitution is made. And Blum's data suggest that regular marijuana smokers have decreased their alcohol consumption markedly, and the more they smoke, the more they cut down on liquor.

It would, therefore, be improper to add the damaging effects that (we know) result from alcohol to those which (we suppose) will result from pot. Were marijuana legal, a great percentage of liquor drinkers, possibly some alcoholics, would desert their liquid intoxicant for the burning weed. In one sense, though, the result would be additive: we would have a greater total number than presently who become intoxicated. That is, the number who become high on marijuana (whether once, twice, occasionally, or regularly) plus the number who become drunk, would be greater than the two figures now. There are certainly many who would like to get high from time to time who do not now because of the laws, but who do not like to drink. Thus, the figure who use some intoxicant would increase were pot legalized, but it would be far lower than the additive effect of all those who now use liquor added to all those who might use pot.

If we want to consider the effect of the marijuana laws on public safety, we are therefore faced with the prospect of comparing the relative merits of alcohol and marijuana. As stated earlier, marijuana users cite the comparison as a powerful argument in the drug's favor, while physicians dismiss the argument. Where does that leave us?

In terms of tissue damage, the evidence is clear; no sane observer of the American drug use scene would claim for marijuana the ravaging effect that alcohol has. Daily moderately heavy usage of American or Mexican cannabis, say, six joints a day, produces no known bodily harm. (But we must remember that we have no valid studies of potsmokers which span any length of time.) Daily moderately heavy use of alcohol—the quantity comparable to the amount of marijuana which would intoxicate the user for an equal length of time, i.e., the whole day, would be about half a quart a day—will destroy, threaten or damage most of the body's vital organs over a long period of time. In terms of auto accidents, the evidence we have suggests a gain. The drunk driver behind the wheel is far more of a threat and a danger than the high pothead. Empirical tests show that alcohol discoordinates the driver far more than marijuana—if it occurs with marijuana at all.[45] Decrease in aggression, violence, and crime, too, would be only a positive gain. Alcohol moreover is often directly linked with the commission of crime; far from inciting crime, marijuana, contrastingly, possibly inhibits it. Our speculations on insanity would have to be even less firmly grounded in known fact than those for tissue damage, automobile accidents, and violence, but marijuana would have to strive to catch up with alcohol's record; one of four admissions to a mental hospital is an alcoholic. Here, too, I think, the use of pot would be a clear gain.

The members of the antipot contingent who claim that alcohol is preferable to marijuana, and that legalization would be nothing but a disaster for this or any nation, do have a single telling point, as I see it. This is that marijuana is *always* used to become intoxicated, or high, and alcohol is *often*, indeed, perhaps most of the time, used for nonintoxicatory purposes. Alcoholic substances are frequently consumed on many occasions where the drinker does not become drunk or intoxicated. For instance, at many sporting events—football and baseball games—several bottles of beer may be drunk by a spectator without effect. The same may be said for wine at a meal, cocktails (sometimes) at a party, or sherry as a nightcap. Of course, many marijuana smokers do drink liquor, beer, and wine, on those very occasions in which the drinker also drinks them; drinking alcohol and smoking pot are not disjunctive and mutually exclusive activities. The very people who use one often use the other as well on those occasions when it may seem more appropriate. In fact, marijuana smokers are more likely to drink alcoholic beverages than nonsmokers are.* It is entirely possible that the legalization and widespread availability of marijuana will not necessarily result in a greater number of total events in which people wish to become intoxicated simply because users will continue to use pot selectively as they presently do. They become high when they feel that the occasion calls for it and use the same (potentially intoxicating) substances that the rest of society does, in moderation, when they feel that the occasion calls for that as well. However, it is an empirical question which can not be answered beforehand as to whether those specific *occasions* where alcohol is now consumed without intoxication will eventually call for marijuana use. I suspect that potsmokers will continue to follow the same sorts of patterns in liquor consumption that their nonsmoking peers do, drinking their beer, wine, and sherry as a pleasant companion to other pleasant activities. The appropriateness of one's agent of choice is defined by the social group that uses it, and many occasions do not call for getting high.

But what of the other side? What social costs do we have to consider when examining the damages the present policy is causing? To begin with an issue most Americans assume that they are hard-headed and pragmatic about—money and resources—we would have to admit that the present policies are extremely costly. The deployment of huge numbers of law enforcement officers in the effort to stop pot use and sales necessarily takes resources away from heroin and amphetamine traffic. In this sense, the present laws encourage the use of truly dangerous drugs. And the court costs of processing a single marijuana case can be, and often are, staggering, and the number of cases handled every year in this country are beginning to run over 100,000. How many millions of dollars do we feel is worth spending? In addition, the laws contribute to a great deal of

---

* It is no contradiction to say that marijuana users are more likely to drink, or to have drunk alcohol, than nonusers are, and drinkers typically cut down on their alcohol consumption when they begin to smoke marijuana regularly; in fact, both statements are true empirically.

resentment on both sides. The police realize that they are enforcing a law without ideological support from large segments of the public. The murderer never questions the right of the police to arrest him; the marijuana user questions the legitimacy of the law, and thus, the police and the entire legal process. By multiplying the areas in which the police are expected to enforce the law, a variety of paranoia develops among the police—in Jerome Skolnick's terms,[46] they begin to see "symbolic assailants" in the populace. In the sense that they would be able to concentrate on truly dangerous crimes, as well as crimes on which there is public support for their prohibition, the police would score a clear gain were marijuana use to be relegalized.[47]

The damages to an individual traceable to the effects of marijuana are minimal when compared with the damages he sustains at the hands of the legal system.[48] Marijuana use and possession probably represents—next to numerous sex crimes without victims, such as cunnilingus—the clearest case where the penalty is incommensurate with the seriousness of the crime. In most cases, the user suffers no damage whatsoever from the use of this weed. In the typical case, it is a harmless activity. Arguments will often be made, particularly by the police, that, of course, in the typical case, marijuana use is relatively innocuous, but that is only because of the relative innocuousness of currently available marijuana. *If* the user were to get his hands on really potent cannabis—North African hashish, for instance—some serious damage would manifest itself.[49] Thus, what is being done is to punish someone for something which is essentially harmless because if he weren't punished, he might do something which is harmful. (Even assuming that there are such great differences in harm to users due to the varying potency different of cannabis preparations.) To my knowledge, this principle is not applied to any other area of law.

Moreover, no solid case has been made for the prohibition. In 1937, not a scrap of evidence existed for justifying the passage of the federal law. Today, over a generation later, the fairest statement that could be made is that adequate systematic evidence definitively testing the relative harm of this drug has simply not been gathered. And if a deprivation of liberties is to be imposed, a conclusive case has to be made, as Justice Goldberg declared in *Griswold v. Connecticut*. The burden of proof is clearly on he who would deprive liberties, not he who would exercise them.[50]

It should be realized that although these "empirical" issues of public safety, rehabilitation, and deterrence are useful for *rhetorical* purposes, they are not the most powerful motives underlying the administration of the laws. The emotional and "expressive" goals of symbolism and vengeance are far more important, in my opinion. To someone who feels that marijuana use is evil, the laws are just no matter what their practical result. They are an expression of a moral stance, and are beyond criticism on that level. The question of "evil" is intrinsically unanswerable. Merely because crime is widespread is no indication that the laws attempting to prevent it (and failing, in a sense, to do so) are invalid and ought to be abolished. Over 10,000 murders occur in the United States every year; should laws against murder be nullified? There are about a half-million auto thefts yearly in this country, and over a million burglaries. Should laws outlawing these activities be done away with? The fact that the laws are relatively ineffective in deterring an activity is no argument for their abolition. If we feel the activity to be damaging to society—everyone has his own personal definition of what constitutes damage—we resent efforts to evaluate the law in terms of "effectiveness."

I feel that, essentially, pot is a bogus issue. The present hostility in some quarters toward its use and its users cannot be accounted for by a consideration of the pros and cons of its effects. The degree of emotion generated by the marijuana issue, on both sides, leads an observer to conclude that marijuana must be a symbol for other issues and problems. Psychoanalysts will often venture the opinion that marijuana use represents a symbolic rebellion against authority. But, curiously, the irrational motivation of their parents have never been entertained seriously by psychiatrists who devise such theories about the young—possibly because the psychiatrists who devise such theories are largely themselves parents with adolescent children. Is the present ferment of the young an attempt to kill the father? It might more plausibly be argued that the reactions of the adult generation to the activities of the young is an attempt to kill their sons. Marijuana merely serves to crystallize a number of other issues, none of which bear any relation to empirical and rational issues connected with public safety. A rejection of the young for being young, for being different from the older generation, for having long hair, for being radical, for being uninterested in a plastic civilization, for being too sexually permissive, essentially, for having a different style of life, for drifting beyond parental control, for having different tastes and values—these issues, rather than the concrete issues of public safety, generate the conflict.

The United States is a cosigner of the 1961 Single Convention on Narcotic Drugs, which constrains its signees, among other things, to prevent the "abuse" of cannabis. The antimarijuana lobby is firm in emphasizing the obligation of the United States to respect this international treaty, perhaps one of the few cases on record where political conservatives urge compliance to an international law in preference to the hypothetical federal and state legalization which the liberal pro-pot forces urge. The argument is that when the American government became a partner to the SCND, it became legally impossible to change the federal or state laws to make marijuana possession legal. Harry Anslinger writes: ". . . the United States became a party to the 1961 Single Convention on the control of narcotic drugs which obligates the signatories to prevent the misuse of marihuana. Accordingly, it will be utterly impossible for the proponents to legalize marihuana to do so." [51]

Actually, the Single Convention is so worded that it would actually be possible to remove the legal sanctions against cannabis without violating the conditions of the treaty. Article 36 of the Convention states that the signing nations shall devise sanctions for the possession and sale of cannabis "subject to its constitutional limitations," and that "the offense to which it refers shall be defined, prosecuted, and punished in conformity with the domestic law of a Party." In other words, a signing nation may decide, after signing, that the stipulations of the treaty violate its internal laws, and may nullify those portions which do so. Certain states of India, for instance, have retained the legalization of many cannabis products, deeming a prohibition in violation of local custom and law. In addition, the Single Convention only refers to the pressed resin preparations of the cannabis plant—that is, hashish—and not the leaf substances. The substance customarily used in the United States is not covered by the restriction. Thus, in most cases, the Single Convention would simply be irrelevant. [52]

NOTES

1. Howard S. Becker, *Outsiders* (New York: Free Press, 1963), pp. 135–146.

2. Donald T. Dickson, "Bureaucracy and Morality: An Organizational Perspective on a Moral Crusade," *Socal Problems* 16 (Fall 1968): 143–156.

3. *Ibid.*, pp. 151–156.

4. For the lament of one user, snared after the change in the marijuana law in South Dakota, see the letter to the editor, "Marijuana Law," in the July 1969 issue of *Playboy*.

5. Roswell D. Johnson, "Medico-Social Aspects of Marijuana," *The Rhode Island Medical Journal* 51 (March 1968): 175.

6. American Institute of Public Opinion (Gallup Poll), *Special Report on the Attitudes of College Students*, no. 48 (Princeton, N.J.: AIPO, June 1969), p. 30.

7. John J. Bellizzi, "Stonybrook Could Have Been Avoided" (Albany: International Narcotic Enforcement Officers Association, 1968), pp. 2, 7.

8. Alfred R. Lindesmith, "The Marihuana Problem—Myth or Reality?" in *The Addict and the Law* (Bloomington: Indiana University Press, 1965), p. 237.

9. J. Edgar Hoover, *Crime in the United States* (Boston: Beacon Press, 1965), p. 21. Murder is more likely to take place among intimates than among strangers. Where there is a complainant or an obvious victim—a body, in this case—enforcement is facilitated; where there is no complainant, it is rendered more difficult, because the police have far less access.

10. Allan Morton, Joel Ohlgren, John Mueller, Roger W. Pearson, and Sheldon Weisel, "Marijuana Laws: An Empirical Study of Enforcement and Administration in Los Angeles County," *UCLA Law Review* 15 (September 1968): 1499–1585.

It should be kept in mind that the data on which the Los Angeles study are based are state and local arrests. *Federal* arrests include a much higher proportion of dealers, while state and local arrests are mainly of users and petty sellers. Federal law enforcement officers utilize different techniques—undercover agents principally—while state and local arrests are primarily the product of accidental patrol procedures.

11. Joe Reichmann, Testimony, in *Hearings on Marijuana Laws Before the California Public Health and Safety Committee* (Los Angeles, October 18, 1967, morning session), transcript, p. 6.

12. Luke McKissick, Testimony, in *ibid.*, p. 62.

13. Howard Smith, "Scenes," *The Village Voice*, August 1, 1969, p. 20.

14. Morton et al., *op. cit.*, pp. 1533–1539, 1579, 1584.

15. McKissick, *op. cit.*, p. 63.

16. Morton et al., *op. cit.*, pp. 1579, 1581.

17. Erich Goode, ed., *Marijuana* (New York: Atherton Press, 1969), p. 97.

18. Morton et al., *op. cit.*, p. 1543.

19. *Ibid.*

20. State of California, Department of Justice, Bureau of Criminal Statistics, *Drug Arrests and Dispositions in California: 1967* (Sacramento: State of California, 1968), p. 76.

21. *Ibid.*, p. 82.

22. *Ibid.*, p. 85.

23. *Ibid.*, p. 87.

24. *Ibid.*, p. 89.

25. Marvin Cahn, "The User and the Law," in J. L. Simmons, ed., *Marijuana: Myths and Realities* (North Hollywood, Calif.: Brandon House, 1967), pp. 56–57.

26. In "On Being Busted at Fifty," Leslie Fiedler describes electronic surveillance

devices being used to detect the possession of hashish during the ceremony of his Passover Seder. See *The New York Review*, July 13, 1967, p. 13.

27. Harold Garfinkle, "Conditions of Successful Degradation Ceremonies," *The American Journal of Sociology* 61 (March 1956): 420–424.

28. Samuel G. Kling, *Sexual Behavior and the Law* (New York: Bernard Geis and Random House, 1965).

29. In partial contradiction to the general point concerning differential enforcement, *Playboy* magazine prints large numbers of letters from men in prison who were convicted for these crimes; our surprise at their legal status is surpassed only by our discovery that anyone is ever sanctioned for them.

30. Even the occasional exception illustrates the point. A case in a rural area of Vermont involving alleged adultery between a married black man and a divorced white woman demonstrates the need of a community to punish an activity which is legal (interracial intercourse) in the guise of an illegal activity (adultery). For a description of the events, see *Life*, April 4, 1969, pp. 62–74.

31. The "yippie" ideologue, Jerry Rubin, recently arrested on a marijuana possession charge by officers who emphatically acknowledged their solely political concern in the arrest, reconstructs questions directed at him by the policemen: "Why do you hate America?" "Why did you go to Cuba when your government told you not to?" "Hey don't you have any patriotic magazines, any American magazines?" In concluding his article, Rubin writes, "My case will show cops whether or not it is easy to get away with political persecution disguised as drug busts," Cf. Jerry Rubin, "The Yippies Are Going to Chicago," *The Realist*, no. 82 (September 1968): pp. 1, 21–23. See also Don McNeill, "LBJ's Narco Plan: Lining Up the Big Guns: Crackdown on the Way?" *Village Voice*, March 14, 1968, pp. 11ff., and Irving Shushnick, "Never Trust a Man with a Beard," *The East Village Other*, January 12–19, 1968, p. 4. All of these journals favor legalizing marijuana.

32. Gene R. Haslip, "Current Issues in the Prevention and Control of Marihuana Abuse" (Paper presented to the First National Conference on Student Drug Involvement sponsored by the United States National Student Association at the University of Maryland, August 19, 1967), pp. 11–12.

The Bureau of Narcotics seems curiously cut off from communication with other government agencies. In addition to Haslip's charge—so wildly different from the view presented by the President's Commission survey of the literature—another Bureau lawyer, Donald Miller, in an article published in the fall of 1968, argued that the Marihuana Tax Act does *not* constitute self-incrimination, and that its operation was "critically different" from the gambling and firearms statutes, recently ruled upon by the Supreme Court; a few months later the Court, in an *unanimous* decision, ruled *precisely* that the Marihuana Tax Act constituted self-incrimination, as it had in the gambling and firearms statutes. See Miller, "Marihuana: The Law and Its Enforcement," *Suffolk University Law Review* 3 (Fall 1968): 80–100.

33. Louria, *op. cit.*, p. 120.

34. The President's Commission on Law Enforcement and Administration of Justice, "Marihuana," in *Task Force Report: Narcotics and Drug Abuse* (Washington: U.S. Government Printing Office, 1967), pp. 12–14.

35. "Referendum," Student Legislative Council, November 29 and 30, 1967 (unpublished), p. 1.

36. Kenneth Eells, *A Survey of Student Practices and Attitudes with Respect to Marijuana and LSD* (Pasadena, Calif.: California Institute of Technology, 1967).

37. "Election Results," *Statesman*, State University of New York, Stony Brook (October 1968). The Ns for "other" responses and "abstain" were eliminated from the computation. There is, of course, the methodological problem that students who are interested enough to respond to the survey are those who most favor legalization. That does not vitiate the notion that prolegalization is a common sentiment on college campuses however.

38. Trod Runyon "Marijuana Blues," Letter to the Editor, *Playboy*, April 1968. Partly as a result of this letter's publication in *Playboy*, its author was freed after a

liberalization of Alaska's marijuana laws. See Runyon's letter in the September 1968 issue of *Playboy*.

39. Larry L. Belcher, "Marijuana Martyr," Letter to the Editor, *Playboy*, June 1968.

40. Lindesmith, *op. cit.*, p. 239.

41. Herbert Blumer et al., *The World of Youthful Drug Use* (Berkeley: University of California, School of Criminology, January 1967), p. 71.

42. Louria, *op. cit.*, pp. 115–116.

43. Eugene Schoenfeld, "Hip-pocrates," *The East Village Other*, August 9, 1968, p. 6.

44. Seymour L. Halleck, "Marijuana and LSD on the Campus" (Madison: Health Services, University of Wisconsin, 1968).

45. Alfred Crancer, Jr., et al., "Comparison of the Effects of Marihuana and Alcohol on Simulated Driving Performance," *Science* 164 (May 16, 1969): 851–854.

46. Jerome H. Skolnick, *Justice without Trial* (New York: John Wiley, 1966), pp. 45–48, 105–109, 217–218.

47. See the letter to the Editor of *Playboy*, published in the March 1970 issue, written by a former police officer, Richard R. Bergess, who retired from the San Francisco police force after twelve years, in part as a result of his feeling that the marijuana laws were unjust and unenforceable. Bergess writes: ". . . police efforts to enforce these laws only increases the disrespect and hatred of large numbers of young people. This loss of public respect is no small problem: It concretely hampers police efficiency in dealing with real crimes against people. *The true crisis in law enforcement today is police alienation from the public they are sworn to serve*" (Bergess' emphasis).

48. Even some critics of marijuana use admit this. See Stanley F. Yolles, "Pot is Painted Too Black," *The Washington Post*, Sunday, September 21, 1969, p. C4. Yolles states: "I know of no clearer instance in which the punishment for an infraction of the law is more harmful than the crime." At the same time, Yolles feels that the legal restrictions against use and possession of marijuana should not be removed.

49. See Miller, *op. cit.*, and Malachi L. Harney, "Discussion on Marihuana: Moderator's Remarks," International Narcotic Enforcement Officers Association, *Eighth Annual Conference Report* (Louisville, Ky., October 22–26, 1967), pp. 50–51.

50. These points, and others as well, are brilliantly and passionately argued by J. W. Spellman, in "Marijuana and the Laws: A Brief Submitted to the Committee of Inquiry into the Non-Medical Use of Drugs—Government of Canada" (Buffalo: LEMAR, 1969).

51. From a letter, dated August 21, 1967, cited in Goode, *op. cit.*, p. 137.

52. Michael R. Aldrich, "United Nations Single Convention Can't Stop Legalized Marijuana," *The Marijuana Review* 1, no. 2 (January–March 1969): 11. For the full record of the SCND, see United Nations Conference for the Adoption of a Single Convention on Narcotic Drugs, Official Records, vols. 1 & 2 (E/Conf. 34/24 and E. Conf. 34/24/ Add 1). These volumes were published by the United Nations in 1964.

: *Chapter* 12 :

Epilogue: Models of Marijuana Use

Every scientific discipline employs conceptual and theoretical constructs that help its practitioners to organize and make sense out of the often confusing facts before them. An event does not simply occur; it is noticed and classified. These constructs generally cohere into models: detailed generalizations, each element of which contributes to the central theme, or thesis. Models structure our attitudes and responses toward a given phenomenon; they tell us what to see and what to ignore. Models represent archetypical patterns built into our minds as a way of understanding events around us. Some models are more useful than others, organizing facts more faithfully. By equipping ourselves with one model, we may distort the essential reality of a phenomenon—although, at the same time, clarify a small segment of the same phenomenon—while using a different one will immediately introduce clarity where a swirling fog-bank of obfuscation and confusion previously prevailed.

Of all arenas of human behavior, illicit nonmedical drug use provides one of the best examples of the tyranny of models of man. In few spheres are facts perceived more selectively—by experts and the public alike—and with less correspondence to the real world. At least two factors account for the mythical character of contemporary drug models. The subterranean nature of illegal drug use renders direct confrontation with a wide range of users, as well as a broad spectrum of the many aspects and manifestations of use, unlikely even for the dedicated researcher. What takes place in the laboratory may not take place in the street; what takes place in the slum may not happen on the college campus. We are all at the mercy of culturally (and historically) generated models to explain the few, highly selective facts which filter through to us. In addition, the emotional involvement of every member of society in the drug issue reduces his objectivity and detachment.

What, then, is to be done? It depends on whether we are deductive or inductive in our method. A common cry today is that we need less prejudice and more fact. This statement ignores man's powerful ability to perceive facts selectively. Presenting the same set of facts to two different observers, each with his own set of ideological and theoretical perspectives or models, will produce reports whose conclusions differ fundamentally on every conceivable important question. Facts are not perceived in the abstract; they are linked to a general scheme. They are manifestations of larger processes. By themselves, facts are chaotic assortments of trivia. At the same time, an iron-clad adherence to a meaningless model, an ignorance of the facts in preference to an outworn but elegant scheme, is equally as sterile and misleading. It is at the general level that we must begin.

What are these obsolete drug models? They range from the ludicrous to the nearly plausible. The least useful and most erroneous of these models—and the one most densely woven into historical and cultural folklore—is what might be called the "Dr. Jekyll and Mr. Hyde" model of marijuana use. The essential elements of this notion are that: (1) there is a germ of evil in even the best of men; (2) some potion, or external chemical agent, may release this evil; and (3) once the agent is ingested, the evil will express itself in aggressive and destructive acts under any and all circumstances. However, this belief that a normal person, upon ingestion of marijuana, will instantly become a dangerous and violent maniac is not entertained very seriously in many quarters today. A perusal of the antimarijuana propaganda of the 1930s would yield full-blown expressions of this tribal mythology; even today, the police commonly propagate the notion that there is a direct causal association between the use of marijuana and the commission of violent crimes. Not only is this belief held by a minority among all groups in American society, it is slowly a dying belief, even among the police. The "Dr. Jekyll and Mr. Hyde" model of marijuana use is interesting mainly for antiquarian purposes.

A newer and somewhat more realistic model of marijuana use, taken seriously by medical and lay figures alike, in part reflects the shift from a punitive to a rehabilitative approach to the drug question (a shift not yet institutionalized among law enforcement agencies). This model could be called the "pathology" or "medical" model. According to this model, marijuana use, particularly at its more extreme levels of frequent use and high dosages, has features resembling a medical disease; therefore, physicians have special competence in dealing with it. In both its cause and consequence, marijuana use is viewed as a kind of pathology. Marijuana appeals predominantly to the neurotic and the troubled young. Although some essentially normal youths will wander in and out of a marijuana-smoking crowd, the frequent and fairly long-term, or chronic user, is far more likely to manifest psychiatric disturbances.

In addition, the marijuana experience is itself seen as pathological. Being high, under the influence of the drug, is thought to be by definition abnormal. This view holds that marijuana intoxication is such that reality is distorted: the subject feels euphoric (in clinical terms, "where there is no objective basis for euphoria"); he often emits unmotivated laughter; his sense of time is elongated (that is, he judges time "incorrectly," or his sense of time is "distorted"); he thinks he hears music more acutely; he thinks food tastes better; he has illusions of a superior aesthetic sense; and so on. In other words, according to the pathology model, what is felt and perceived under the influence of a drug which differs from the normal or nondrug state is *in and of itself* abnormal and pathological. In addition, it is an essential tenet of the pathology model that marijuana tends to induce temporary insanity, "psychotic episodes," in some users.

Moral positions are often justified on rational grounds. To admit that one or another point of view is merely a matter of taste is rarely sufficient, particularly to someone who struggles for moral and ideological dominance. A common strategy to discredit other points of view is to adopt a health-pathology model of justification. One's own ideology represents mental or physical health, while that of one's opponents is pathological. Some of the best examples of this variety of rationalization may be found in the area of sexual behavior. To the sexually permissive, indulgence is normal, and abstinence is sick. To the supporters of abstinence, it is precisely the reverse:

What is the right thing for the young unmarried woman? The physician is not a religious teacher and he does not speak on grounds of morality. He speaks from the standpoint of health, which includes emotional health. From this standpoint I submit that the desirable ideal is premarital chastity.[1]

The physician stands in excellent relation to society to make such judgments. He has sufficient scientific credentials in the public eye, as well as great prestige, to command credibility. Moreover, his views are not markedly out of line with those of the majority, so that he may be useful as a means to justify and rationalize many traditional values, employing a rhetorical or scientific rationality.

The sociology of medicine is one of the more fascinating the field has to offer. The illness and health of the human body are social definitions, not simply natural categories. Even death has a social dimension; it is not only a physiological fact. What is conceived of as a matter for appropriate medical attention is decided by doctors, not by the human body. What the body is thought to do, and what is thought to be the cause of what it does, varies from society to society, from epoch to epoch. What attracts a physician's attention at one time may be of no concern at another—either because of a change in moral climate or because of new discoveries in medical science. For example, masturbation was once thought to be "medically" harmful. Nineteenth-century physicians, from Krafft-Ebing[2] to the local general practitioner, attempted to dissuade adolescents from practicing masturbation for *medical* reasons; a moral evaluation was framed in health terms. What was disapproved of inevitably had to be thought of as physically harmful as well. The sinner had to bear the bodily signs—*stigmata*—of his transgressions. William Acton, the famous Victorian physician, describes the ravages of masturbation:

The frame is stunted and weak, the muscles undeveloped, the eye is sunken and heavy, the complexion is sallow, pasty, or covered with spots of acne, the hands are damp and cold, and the skin moist. The boy shuns the society of others, creeps about alone, joins with repugnance in the amusements of his schoolfellows. He cannot look any one in the face, and becomes careless in dress and uncleanly in person. His intellect has become sluggish and enfeebled, and if his evil habits are persisted in, he may end in becoming a drivelling idiot. . . . Such boys are to be seen in all stages of degeneration, but what we have described is but the result towards which *they all* are tending.[3]

The parallels between society's condemnation of masturbation in the Victorian period, and its condemnation of marijuana use today, extend beyond the claim that both activities ruin the health of the participant. More specifically, insanity was often viewed as a likely outcome of both. Both were seen as an indulgence, a form of moral flabbiness, selfish and unrestrained pleasure-seeking. And both have earned the label "abuse;" in fact, even today "to abuse oneself" specifically means to masturbate, a relic of an earlier moral stance. In both cases, society's moral attitude toward the activity has elicited from the medical profession a condemnatory justification cast in the form of medical objectivity. Social control and the preservation of the status quo become functions of physicians. When society no longer holds a morally castigating point of view toward marijuana use, the physician's services will be withdrawn and called for in a new area.

Popular sociology, as practiced by physicians as well as journalists, policemen as well as educators, has traditionally conceived of human activity in *zero-sum* terms. That is, it was thought that participation in one kind of human endeavor naturally and inevitably cancelled out another; the more time, emotion, and effort invested in one activity, the less left over for another. Recent research in many areas of human life has more often given support to precisely the opposite perspective: generally, the hypothesis of "the more, the more" holds up. As John Gagnon put it, the imagery describing human activities has shifted from Adam Smith to John Maynard Keynes. Wisely withholding one's time and energy from one activity often results not in more time and energy for other activities, but no activity at all. And participation in certain kinds of activities often means involvement in many others as well. "Spending" one's time and energy in one sphere often implies spending more, not less, in other spheres as well.

In fact, extending our Victorian sexual analogy a step further, it was not uncommon in the nineteenth century to employ economic imagery to describe sexual activity; having an orgasm, for instance, was labelled "spending." And it is in the realm of economics that the Victorian zero-sum model seems to operate best. One has a fixed amount of money, and "spending" it leads to its depletion. Analogously, engaging in sexual activity depleted one's energy; by conserving it, one had more left over for nonsexual spheres. Sex, in short, was seen as diminishing one's everyday, socially approved life.

Few areas of social life reflect this thinking more than the question of marijuana use. The traditional view holds that smoking marijuana automatically means the deterioration of one's "normal" socially approved life, that deterioration is a cause of marijuana use in the first place, and that further use contributes to deterioration. Antidrug campaigns often base their appeals on this assumption. During 1969 and 1970, the National Institute of Mental Health has engaged in a propaganda effort to dissuade young people from using drugs. In one of its commercials, a short film, sequences of pot-smoking youths (who, the commentator informs us, have copped out) are alternated and contrasted with shots of several clean-cut, energetic college-age young adults who are engaged in community and social work efforts. In fact, the basic assumption underlying nearly all antidrug propaganda compaigns is that marijuana use and all of the things normally valued by our society are mutually exclusive and incompatible. One chooses drugs *or* political activism.

Closely related to the zero sum model is the "escape from reality" conception of marijuana use. The central axiom of this thesis is that the user is a troubled individual, who finds life threatening and frightening, and seeks to alleviate his difficulties by drifting off into a never-never land of euphoria. The state of intoxication associated with the marijuana high is viewed as intrinsically outside the orbit of the normal and the real and, therefore, by definition, the user seeks an unreal and abnormal state. It necessarily follows that anyone who smokes marijuana seeks to escape from reality, since reality is defined as what is socially acceptable. Thus, marijuana smokers are seen as truants from life, drop-outs, dwellers in a fantasy world, spinners of illusions—all living in hallucinations.

Another model currently applied to marijuana use is the "stoned" view of marijuana use. Many arguments which attempt to discredit its use and individuals who use it are based on the assumption that the typical smoker is high a substantial portion of his waking hours, if not the entire day. There is the feeling that if someone finds marijuana pleasurable, he will want to become high all the time. If anyone can justify the use of the drug occasionally, then why not frequently? The use of marijuana conjures in the mind of the uninformed an image of the frequent or "chronic" user. Partly, this attitude is based on the fear of the unknown, fear that anything which is threatening will become dominant, overwhelming and destroying that which one values. Part of the image of the stoned model stems from the world of narcotics addiction where, it is true, a huge proportion of users eventually become chronic users.

An essential element in all of the traditional and conventional models of marijuana use is the view that it is *radically discontinuous* with everyday life. Drug use is seen as existing in a moral and empirical realm wherein all of the taken-for-granted rules of life are suspended. What governs the law-abiding citizen is not thought to apply to the drug user, since he is, the thinking goes, removed from the pale of the law.

I propose to substitute for these models that depend on the disjunction of the marijuana user from everyday life two more useful models which, instead, rely on a linear continuum between the user and the rest of society. In each of these classic models—the Dr. Jekyll and Mr. Hyde, the pathology, the zero-sum, the escape from reality, and the stoned models of marijuana use—there is an either/or assumption. One is a user, or he is not; marijuana leads to heroin addiction, or it does not; marijuana causes psychotic episodes, or it does not; marijuana use is a neurotic acting out, or it is not. I suggest that the assumptions on which these models rest are empirically and conceptually inadequate; they are simply erroneous.

If we look at the facts, we see not a discontinuity separating the marijuana smoker from the rest of society, but a spectrum ranging from the nonuser, through the potential convert, the experimenter, the occasional user, on up to the daily committed smoker who consumes ten or twelve joints a day, and who is high most of the time. In a sense, it is improper to speak of *the* marijuana user, since there are so many styles of use and degrees of involvement. Generalizations which apply to the daily user may be completely erroneous when applied to the experimenter, and so on. We can only say that one or another statement is more or less likely to hold up for one or another group.

The idea that marijuana use could not only not detract from, but actually be associated with, an improvement in the volume and quality of those very things that are generally considered desirable, is heresy to the committed antimarijuana lobby, as well as to an entire tradition in marijuana commentary. Yet such a conclusion is difficult to avoid. The marijuana user appears to be more active socially than the nonuser. He has more friends and socializes more. He is engaged in a larger number and a greater variety of activities than the nonuser—aesthetic appreciation and creation, political activism, and social welfare, for instance. (Of course, some other human endeavors, such as traditional and formal religious participation, are less often the object of marijuana users' interests.)

The zero-sum notion assumes that the two realms, the straight and the stoned, are antagonistic and incompatible, enjoyed by a wholly different and distinct personnel. In reality, most potsmokers do not rob their straight life to pay their stoned existence. More commonly, the two enrich each other. Thus, any model based on the assumption that by using marijuana those activities which society values will typically or necessarily deteriorate in the lives of users has to be faulty. In the average user, no such process takes place. (It will, of course, be a relatively simple matter to uncover exceptions.) The average marijuana smoker utilizes his drug of choice as an adjunct and an enhancer of many of the activities that the ordinary law-abiding citizen participates in.

The dire predictions of what happens when someone takes to the weed do not seem to happen. It is said that although marijuana is not technically addicting, it does generate a kind of psychological addiction (thus, the stoned model), and that once legal restrictions are relaxed, huge numbers of persons will be stupefied most of their waking hours. When we look at the facts, this argument evaporates. Most marijuana users smoke the weed occasionally. The truly committed "head," the smoker who is high the whole day, day in and day out, is a relative rarity, perhaps comprising 1 or 2 percent of everyone who has ever smoked marijuana. And yet it is from this rarefied upper reaches of the world of potsmoking that society's model of marijuana use is borrowed.

We will, of course, be able to locate specific individuals who are, in fact, high a great proportion of their waking hours. But the difference between marijuana and any of the physiologically addicting drugs—including alcohol—in this respect is so great as to be a difference of kind, and not simply a matter of degree. It is only because the medical profession views marijuana use by definition pathological and abnormal ("abuse" is defined as taking a drug outside a medical context) that any use of marijuana has to be viewed, medically, as a kind of habituation, or psychological addiction. Something anomalous, puzzling, and disturbing must be labelled pathological. But in less moralistic terms—and it is only on moral grounds that the medical label makes any sense at all—it is necessary to face the fact that the study of a cross-section of all individuals who have tried marijuana, or even who smoke it regularly, however regularly might be defined, will yield very few who are high all of the time, or even more than a few hours each evening. The facts do not support the stoned model. When the user smokes marijuana he does, indeed, become high, or stoned. And if one observed his behavior during this period, he is often measurably less active than normally. But to say that it is the ultimate goal of a large proportion of users to seek this state most of the time is to distort the facts. It is only because researchers cannot understand why anyone would want to become high in the first place that they find it necessary to attach the label "psychological addiction" or "habituation" to his behavior and motives. If they found use of the substance acceptable, they would not emit this labelling behavior.

It is clear that another model is necessary. And this model, I propose, is the recreational model. It fits the facts more faithfully than any of the previously mentioned models. And it contains none of the moral judgments that the others are clearly guilty of. The recreational model takes issue with these perspectives. Essential to the recreational conception of marijuana use are the following elements: (1) it is used freely, noncompulsively; (2) it is smoked episodically—once or several times a week or so on the average; (3) it is experienced as pleasurable by the participants; (4) it is used in conjunction with (and not a replacement for) other enjoyable activities; (5) its impact on one's life is relatively superficial; (6) its use results in relatively little harm to the individual; and (7) its use is highly social. By adopting the recreational perspective toward marijuana use, I do not wish to imply that everyone who has ever smoked marijuana may be described in terms of this model, nor even that a majority of all users are typified by all of these principles. It is, however, to say that this model presents a relatively accurate summarization of the experiences of the characteristic user, that these traits are typically found in marijuana use. In any case, the issue is an empirical one; if the model is ineffective, then it must be discarded. In my own research, however, the recreational model yielded far more insights and more accurately described the reality I investigated than did any of the traditional models. I found that *most* users smoke marijuana recreationally, and I believe that any study investigating a fairly representative group of smokers will support the same generalization. It is possible, of course, to uncover some individuals who are motivated by compulsive forces and experience overwhelmingly unpleasant reactions. A study based on users who visit psychiatrists will, naturally, be far more likely to be composed of users whose experiences differ from the normal everyday user's, and therefore cannot be taken as typical. In the open air of the user's habitat, the recreational model will be found to be more fruitful.

A second model which, in my opinion, yields more mileage than the traditional and conventional images of use is the *subcultural* or *life-style* conception of the user. Marijuana use is the product of the same essentially normal values and beliefs of large groups of people that guide other kinds of everyday activities and choices. Voting for a political candidate, making a purchase, reading a magazine or newspaper, listening to music, playing and watching sports—all of these are influenced by the social groups to which we belong. No one questions the fact that Jews are more likely to vote Democratic than Protestants, that a heavier proportion of working-class men read the New York *Daily News* than read *The New York Times*, while among professional workers, it is the reverse, that residents of large cities spend proportionally more of their time and money on "serious" art and music than do residents of more rural areas. These sorts of subcultural appeals are well-known and entreat our common sense.

But if our attention turns to less common and more condemned activities, we find it necessary to ignore these broad and essentially normal appeals and to search out pathological motives. If it is the young to whom marijuana appeals, we must assume that they are rebelling against authority, or trying to kill their fathers, or escaping from boredom or reality, or whatever. If it is the urban dweller who is more likely to use marijuana, we point to an anomic, disintegrating urban society. If it is the affluent, then we complain about how the affluent are overindulging their young, and intone darkly about the hazards of affluence.

Different social groups in society have somewhat different marijuana potentials. Greater or lesser proportions of their ranks are likely to try and use the weed because of characteristics relating to that group. Patterns of use are not accidental, and they are not pathological. They emerge out of the social fabric of the values and the circumstances of a segment of society. They do not typically occur as a result of some dark, unconscious motive. The subcultural attitudes and values of some groups support such an action as marijuana use, while those of other groups oppose it. In addition, opportunities for use are differentially dispersed throughout society. Simply by being around the stuff ecologically, groups differ in their likelihood of taking it.

Thus, when we say that men are more likely to smoke marijuana than women, it is not permissible to say that men are more likely to be psychiatrically disturbed than women. Rather, it makes more sense to say that there is something about the role of men in this society that is related to marijuana use—a greater emphasis on experimentation, adventure, masculine daring, a greater influence of youth peer groups, and so on. And when we say that marijuana use is more likely to take place on the left of the American political spectrum than on the right, we cannot say that the left is in need of medical and psychiatric attention. Although it would serve a useful ideological function to any existing regime to pin a pathology label on its radical critics, it would not serve a scientific function. Such a position represents an attempt to discredit an opposing point of view by crystallizing one's own ideology into a pseudoscientific reality. Marijuana experimentation is woven into the life style of the political left (except, as we pointed out earlier, at the very extreme left), and not of the political right; is it then possible to say that the left is wrong, or bad, and the right good, or right? When two-thirds of the students of Columbia Law school say that they have tried marijuana, and nearly 100 percent say that marijuana use and possession should be legalized, do we then attempt to uncover pathologies in the members of Columbia Law School? Do we really wish to pathologize the activities and beliefs which separate one generation from another? Do we wish to stigmatize our future?

NOTES

1. Max Levin, "The Meaning of Sex and Marriage," *Bride and Home*, Autumn 1968, p. 103.

2. Recall that the subtitle of Richard von Krafft-Ebing's study, *Psychopathia Sexualis* first published in 1886, was "A Medico-Forensic Study," which means that he was presenting cases in a court in an effort to demonstrate that they should be treated

medically, not punitively; he had, therefore, to present moral outrage at the practices he described to gain the confidence of the court. This merely emphasizes my point, however.

3. Quoted in Steven Marcus, *The Other Victorians* (New York: Basic Books, 1966), p. 19.

: *Appendix* :

Research Experience

As Howard Becker pointed out almost two decades ago, drawing a random sample of marijuana users is an impossibility. No list of all users, or even a large number of users, exists. There are several organizations concerned with marijuana. LEMAR, for instance, as its name implies, has as its goal the legalization of marijuana. The "Jade Companions" offer legal assistance to those arrested for the possession of psychedelic drugs. It would seem that these organizations provide a starting point for the collection of an informal sample of marijuana smokers. One problem with approaching an organization of this kind is that each one, for good reason, fears publicity, police surveillance, and harassment. LEMAR, for instance, would certainly attempt to keep a listing of their membership from falling into the hands of anyone outside its organization. Since the existence of the organization is a matter of public record, they are, even without notoriety, open to the possibility of harassment. If it were known that a sociologist had interviewed their members, the further likelihood of their attracting incriminating attention would be multiplied several times. In fact, at the first organizational meeting of the Stony Brook campus chapter of LEMAR, potential members were dissuaded from joining if they were presently users of the drug; "If you smoke, don't join," they were urged. This advice protects both the individual in that his membership, if known, would automatically cast suspicion on the legality of much of his behavior, as well as the organization, since a large number of members who are vulnerable to arrest threatens its stability and existence. In any case, none of the individuals associated in a leadership capacity with the drug-related organizations whom I contacted was willing to cooperate with the study. Not wanting to threaten their already dubious relationship to the law and law enforcement agencies, I respected their unwillingness. It was apparent that a less formal means of sample recruitment had to be found.

One of the main channels of access that I used to collect respondents was through acquaintance with individuals who occupied positions in organizations which, although in no way formally drug-related, included marijuana users. This segment of the sample was generally gathered by going with the "gate keeper" individual to the place of employment and getting the names of users willing to be interviewed. Many interviews were conducted on the job, either during the lunch hour or a lull in work; others were carried out after working hours, usually at the residence of the interviewee. These organizations included two large New York universities, a large publishing house, and a market research firm.

The second source of my sample was through friends and their acquaintances. A kind of "snowball" method of gathering names was adopted, whereby each interviewee would supply me with one or two names of people who also used marijuana. Often the original person would contact his acquaintance and ask if he would consent to an interview; in this case, he received the refusal or the acceptance, not I. Frequently, I initiated the contact. Considering the illegal nature of the activities I questioned them about, the number of refusals was negligible. In fact, when I contacted the individual directly, only four refused. As to the rate of refusal through the indirect route, I cannot estimate.

The main concern was that I might be a policeman. It is puzzling to me as to why this was so, but their initial fears were fairly easily quelled; after all, were I actually a policeman, I would reassure them that I was not in the same soothing tones. Perhaps, like everyone else, marijuana smokers often react to stereotypes, and I certainly do not *look* like a policeman. The second worry was that their names would be kept and used, that it would be known publicly that they were lawbreakers. I was careful to assure them of anonymity, and to explain my procedure as to the use of names, which invariably eased their doubts. It seems strange, but these two worries, that I was a policeman and that their names would be taken down, were articulated in a minority of cases; in about two-thirds of the cases, this was not necessary. It seemed that my original contact had vouched for my veracity, and that was apparently sufficient.

It should be emphasized that this is *not* a representative sample, and is *in no way* a cross-section of all marijuana users. At this point, the collection of such a sample is impossible. Therefore, to use the composition of this sample as an accurate description of marijuana smokers in general would be completely fallacious and misleading. To reason, for instance, that since 47 percent of my respondents were female, the same percentage of all users are female, would be to distort the meaning of this study. I am not presenting a profile of marijuana smokers, but an analysis of the social structure of marijuana use. This unstructured manner of collecting interviewees for a study of a deviant and illegal activity has both advantages and drawbacks. The potential interviewee in a complete stranger situation will normally fear detection by law-enforcement agencies, and will be unwilling to be interviewed in the first place, or, if willing, would be evasive and even dishonest. Cooperation, then, would, have been problematic had more formal techniques, such as neighborhood sampling, or drawing from a complete listing of individuals working in an organization known to include high proportions of individuals who smoke marijuana. What was necessary for me to be able to approach my interviewees was that someone in the network of social relations be able to vouch for my veracity and basic harmlessness. Only in this way was the cooperation of my interviewees assured. Moreover, this method avoids the oft-trod route of studying individuals who have come to some sort of official notice— incarcerated criminals, for instance, or those who have made some sort of court appearance. As we now know, deviants who have attracted some form of official notice present a systematically biased view of any group under study, unless, of course, that group under study is individuals who have attracted public notice.

The severe and restricting drawback to this casual and informal technique of gathering respondents is, of course, that the interviewees were certainly not representative of marijuana smokers in general; moreover, just how unrepresentative they were, is unknown. The specific individuals known to me reflect my personal associations; another researcher with a different set of acquaintances would have drawn a somewhat different set of respondents. And the organizations to which I had informal access do not necessarily house a cross-section of the marijuana-using population.

Moreover, the persons whom the original contact designates as a potential interviewee will be distinctive in crucial ways. For one thing, he must be willing. For another, those who are so designated are likely to be obvious and conspicuous enough users (to their friends, at least) for the designator to think of him off-hand specifically as a marijuana smoker. (In spite of the fact that I requested users of every level of use.) In all, the sources of bias were strong and have many ramifications. For this reason, we must consider this study exploratory, and its findings tentative. We hope that the guesses and hypotheses suggested by our data will be tested subsequently by more careful instruments.

Since our sample is unrepresentative, it is important to describe its composition. The respondents were slightly more than half (53 percent) male, relatively young (the median age was twenty-two, and three-quarters of the respondents were in their 20s), and overwhelmingly white (8 percent were black, and five respondents, or 2.5 percent, were Puerto Rican.) Slightly over a quarter (27 percent) had parents with a Protestant background, 44 percent were Jewish, and about a seventh had Catholic parents (14 percent) or had parents with different religions (15 percent). Not quite four-fifths (78 percent) were single, and a tenth were divorced. A high proportion were students; 4 percent were high school or grade school students, a quarter (27 percent) were college students, and about a tenth (11 percent) were graduate students. The occupations of the remaining respondents were professional, technical, or kindred, 26 percent; managerial, official or proprietor, 4 percent; sales or clerical, 16 percent; manual laborer, 5 percent; unemployed, 5 percent; housewife, 3 respondents. A third of the fathers of the respondents (34 percent) were professional, between a third and a quarter (29 percent) were managerial, officials or proprietors, and a quarter (24 percent) were manual laborers; the remainder (14 percent) was made up of salesmen or clerical workers.

Of the respondents who were not at the time of the interview in school (or, if the interview was conducted in the summer, who did not plan to attend school in the fall), not quite half had dropped out either of college (4/5 of this group) or of high school. In fact, about 25 percent of the total sample was a college drop-out. (It is, of course, impossible to estimate the likelihood of these respondents returning to college. It should be kept in mind that only about half of all those *in general* who enter college actually receive a bachelor's degree.) About 10 percent of those not presently attending school had a graduate degree, and about twice this number either attended some graduate school without receiving any degree, or had received a B.A. without attending graduate school. All of the respondents were residing in New York or its suburbs at the time of the interview (although a few were in transit); our findings, then, will apply most directly to the New York subset of marijuana smokers, and only by inference to users elsewhere in the country. The data are probably without application outside the United States.

An estimate as to the degree to which my sample varies from the large and unknown universe of all users would be sheer speculation, of course. I suspect, however, that the following differences would be observed between a random sample and mine:

1) A random sample of all marijuana users would be overwhelmingly male—probably about three-quarters.
2) It would be more heavily black.
3) It might be slightly younger, possibly at a median age of about nineteen.
4) It would contain a lower proportion of individuals with any contact with college.
5) It might include a lower proportion with a middle-class background.
6) Fewer would be Jewish, more would be Catholic and Protestant, and very few would have a mixed religious background.

The interviews took place between February and September 1967. Rapport with the interviewees was, on the whole, excellent. Not one interview was terminated by the interviewee. (I terminated two; one received too many telephone calls for me to finish the interview, and later attempts at scheduling proved fruitless, and the second was a psychotic whose answers bore no relation to the questions.) Many interviewees reported that the interview was interesting; my rapid pace kept their interest from flagging. More important, of course, is that I believe that I received honest answers, although more than a casual check is impossible. I was careful to point out inconsistencies when they did occur, and I rarely allowed vague answers to pass unclarified. Most of the individuals interviewed were supplying information about felonious acts. Although relatively few reported serious crimes beyond drug use, the few that did appeared to be candid about it, although wary. When I asked one chronic user of amphetamine how he was able to pay for such heavy drug use he thought for a moment, turned to the tape recorder, which was running, and said, "Could you turn that thing off?" He then proceeded to divulge the nature and frequency of the crimes which he did commit. When I asked a former heroin addict the same question, she responded shyly, "I was a prostitute." Undoubtedly, there were some evasive replies; some probably lied. But I believe that, given the nature of the enterprise which they were describing, this was minimal and exceptional, and certainly not characteristic.

The author conducted all of the interviews (except two). About half were conducted at the interviewee's place of domicile (or, rarely, at that of a friend), a quarter were conducted at his place of employment, and perhaps another quarter was done at the author's residence. A scattered few were done in public places—a coffee house, a restaurant, a bar. The first fifty were tape-recorded, and the remaining one hundred-fifty were transcribed almost verbatim.

There is, of course, the matter of variables which influence interview rapport. It is possible that the rapport is greatest when the characteristics of the interviewer are the same as those of the interviewee, although there are important exceptions to this, especially for certain kinds of information. During the period of the interviewing, I was twenty-eight years old, while the median age of the respondents was about twenty-two. I was in fact told frankly by a half-dozen respondents that had I been noticeably older, they would not have been willing to be interviewed. Another important factor was attire. To have done the interviews in a suit, white shirt and a tie would have threatened rapport; at the very least, it would have placed a chasm of distance between myself and the respondents. My dress was always informal, usually no different from that of the interviewees. In general, dress may be considered a part of the "hip-straight" continuum. (The word "hip" is both an adjective and a noun. It is permissible to speak of "having hip." "Hip" is also used as a verb: "I hipped him to the scene.") To the users who did think of themselves as "hip," hair style played an important role in their identification, as well as in the identification of others. During the period of the interviewing, I had very long and shaggy hair. Although I did not grow my hair long for the study, it had a peculiar relevancy for many respondents which I had not anticipated. Since the "hip" style is itself so variable, or, at least, there are degrees of "hip," many participants in this subculture might have thought that my innocuous style was exceedingly "square." As I was walking into an East Village artist's loft, two members of a motorcycle cult walked out, claiming that they felt "bad vibrations." It should be noted that among many "hippies," the mere fact of wanting to conduct an interview is "square." It is possible that this does not indicate the success of my unintended disguise, but I was approached several times on the street in the "East Village": "You want to cop some grass, man?" (Sometimes hashish as well.) It is possible, however, that anyone who appeared to have any money would have been approached. Other indicators of my ability to blend into the marijuana scenery were several tribal greetings which I received from people unknown to me on the East Village streets, as I went to and from interviews: the extension of an open palm (which calls for slap into the palm), spoken tokens of phatic communion ("Like, what's happening, man?"), and similar examples of communication. Once, while sitting in a coffee shop, three young girls in their middle 'teens, in "hippie" garb sat across the counter. (I quote from my field notes):

They smile and wave. To me? I look around. It looks like me. One says, "How's your trip?" Stupidly, I ask: "What trip?" "You know," one says, giggling, with her hand over her mouth, "LSD." Slowly realizing what's going on, I ask "How did you know?" "Oh, we can tell—it's the glint in your eyes." Oh, yeah. Anyway, here's the scene: they took me for a hippie. Why? What are the status cues?

Another indicator by which respondents, actual or potential, may have sensed my lack of connection with law-enforcement agencies and were, therefore, willing to confide in me, was in my understanding and occasional use of slang terms. Although some are in current use everywhere, such as "pot" and "grass," others are somewhat more esoteric: "spaced," "zonked," "blind," "wiped," to mention only a few for the notion of being "high." It is interesting that many of the respondents used these terms freely—none ever gratuitously explained them to me—assuming that I understood them.

It should be noted that any of these indicators of one's "purity"— i.e., lack of affiliation with the police—could be faked. Undercover agents (such as the ones planted on Stony Brook's campus) learn the argot, the manner of dress, the style of life, tonsorial cut (or lack thereof), and so on. In fact, I interviewed an undercover agent, a policeman who possessed all of the necessary appurtenances. The user's naive faith in style leads him to believe that he is able to sense a threat to him, when in fact, I doubt very seriously if this is the case. When asked how he knows something, a "hip" marijuana-using resident of the East Village will often reply, "Vibrations, man."

It must be remembered that at least half of my respondents thought of themselves as in no way involved in the "hip" way of life. I interviewed Wall Street lawyers and corporation executives as well as "hippies," dealers, and unemployed wanderers who remained high most of their waking hours. For many, marijuana did not change their basic style of life. Had the lawyers and executives who smoked wandered into the habitat of the "hippies," they would have been thought of as "freaks." (For some strange reason, the term "freak'" has a dual usage. It refers to a "square" who would be egregiously out of place in a "hip" environment, and a "hippie" who would be equally unfit for a place in "square" society. Both would be "freaks" in the opposite setting. When asked why he wore a silver lamé jacket on the stage when it was so hot, a rock performer replied "Because I'm so freaky." It was, of course, a boast. Usually, however, the term "freak" has negative connotations.)

Therefore, these comments on "hip" only apply to a segment, certainly less than half of the sample in full degree, since "hip" is a matter of degree. But as a qualifier to this qualifier, it should be noted that the more one was involved in the drug scene, and with drug use, the more that one was likely to display a "hip" style of life.

Perhaps in one respect, my rapport with the respondents may have reduced the amount of information which I received, at least before I began to probe and ask for elaboration. It was often assumed that I *knew* what the respondent was describing. I received the response, in the middle of a description: "Oh, I don't have to go on—you *know* what I mean!" A pose of complete innocence was not possible in many cases, although it is possible that this approach would have yielded more information.

In addition to the responses to the formal interview, I observed a great deal of drug-related behavior casually; I was a "participant observer." In addition to the interview situation, I interacted informally with many of my interviewees. Knowing that I was doing the study, as well as for more personal reasons, they often invited me to observe and take part in various drug-related social events, such as parties, the "turning on" of a curious potential marijuana smoker, the baking and eating of various foods in which marijuana was cooked, feasts and dinners eaten while high, LSD trips, "be-ins," "smoke ins," concerts (listened to while high), drug sales and transactions, and so on; I was called twice to calm frightened LSD "trippers," so that I spent two evenings doing just that (which taught me both that LSD is not the harmless drug it is sometimes portrayed by drug users to be, and the difference between temporary panic, and hospitalization is often an understanding guide). I would estimate that I observed about two or three thousand man-hours of marijuana use in the eight months of the field research. That is, the number of people times the number of hours I spent observing; I spent about five hundred of my own hours in the company of someone who was high.

One problem which *any* sociologist of deviant behavior faces is that he has access to information concerning illegal activities of his respondents which, if publicity and conviction ensued, could result in long prison sentences for those so generously supplying the information. In order to secure this information in the first place, the researcher must assure his subjects of complete confidentiality, that their names will be revealed to no one. A betrayal of trust would be suicidal. This is both a matter of professional ethics, as well as a question of sheer practicality: if it became known that sociologists were unable to keep their word concerning confidentiality, that, by revealing compromising information about oneself, one thereby was placed in serious trouble, the student of criminal behavior would not long be in business. Adhering to the rule of confidentiality is absolute, a rule that must not be broken.

No serious researcher of crime questions the maxim. But alas, it is not so clear-cut. The sociologist is often called upon not only to find out about illegal activities, but, as I said, to observe them as well, and occasionally to participate in them. The journalist-writer of a recent book, *The Seekers*, Jess Stearn, refused even to be present when drugs were present in the same room: "It was against the law to knowingly stay where marijuana was smoked." As the book testifies, Stearn learned nothing about drug use. There is no handy rule of thumb here. My colleague, Ned Polsky, admits that he has been unwilling to witness a number of illegal acts which were morally repugnant to him (beatings, for instance), and, in so doing, slightly compromised his role as a sociologist.

In my case, then, I witnessed hundreds of cases of drug use,

possession, and/or sale. As I said about one hundred of the interviews were conducted in the place of residence of the respondent,
or a friend of his. In about half of these cases, or about fifty interviews, the respondent used marijuana *during the interview*. The
likelihood of that many respondents smoking during the interview
was far greater than would have been expected randomly, judging
from the fact that the overwhelming bulk of the sample claimed to
smoke less than daily, and even the daily smokers did not typically
remain high during the whole day. My chances of hitting the respondent while he was smoking, then, was far smaller than the 50
percent of the at-home interviews I did, or even the 25 percent of
the total. This was a most curious tendency. Possibly talking about
the drug stimulated the respondents to smoke. When I asked one
respondent to describe the marijuana high, he said, "I'll have to get
high first," and lit up a pipeful of hashish.

There is, of course, the issue of criminality of the author's behavior. It was witnessing crimes "taking place," i.e., I knew that the
respondent possessed and used marijuana. In addition, I was present during several purchases, which is also a criminal offense. By
law, one must report felonies of which one has knowledge. And in
this sense, in not reporting criminal acts, my behavior was criminal.
Obviously, I share this trait with every other criminologist or researcher of deviant behavior who does his research "in the field,"
i.e., in the open air outside the jail cell or correction house. (And
any criminologist who does all of his work within the confines of an
institution of incarceration itself cannot be taken very seriously as a
criminologist.)

I felt it to be of great importance to protect my respondents'
identity in any way that I could. I followed a number of procedures
to assure them of a relative degree of protection. When a subject
was contacted, I wrote his name on a small slip of paper. After the
interview was complete, I destroyed the slip, and I no longer had
either the name or any way of contacting the individual. At no time
did I have a list of any more than twenty individuals (who were
potential interviewees); at no time did I have a list of any of the
respondents who had already been interviewed. Moreover, since I
have gradually allowed myself to forget the names of all the
respondents whom I interviewed, I am not at this time able to get
in touch with any but a tiny handful of the subjects of my study.
Truman Capote claims to have cultivated the ability of almost total

recall after an interview, an ability which he employed in the writing of *In Cold Blood*. With regard to names at any rate, I cultivated precisely the opposite skill: that of forgetfulness.

This precaution was a way of making sure that the fact that I had written down names and telephone numbers of respondents and potential interviewees did not place any of them in jeopardy. They were assured anonymity, and I felt that it was necessary to do whatever I could to protect that. If, for some reason or in some way, the research became known to law-enforcement officers who saw me as a route to the names of users and, possibly, suppliers, I would be able to at any given time to be of as little use to them as possible, even in the case that they confiscated the names. After the interviews were completed, of course, I became of no use to them whatsoever.

Glossary

A: the amphetamines; any amphetamine; methedrine

A-head: frequent or regular user of the amphetamines or methedrine

Acapulco gold: a superior and powerful form of marijuana, said to grow in the Acapulco region of Mexico; often, any strong marijuana

acid: LSD

acid freak: chronic and frequent user of LSD

acid head: more or less regular user of LSD *but not both*

acid rock: music influenced by the psychedelic experience or thinking process

amys: vials of amyl nitrite, a vasodilator

bag: (1) a quantity of drugs: for marijuana users, a "nickel bag"; for heroin addicts, a quantity of heroin; for amphetamine users, a quantity of methedrine; (2) a mood, a direction, an emphasis, style or taste

bang: (1) a sudden, sensual flush of pleasure as an intravenously injected drug—heroin or methedrine, usually—begins to take effect; (2) to have sexual intercourse

barbs: barbiturates

behind: (1) under the influence of a drug, as in: "I hallucinated behind acid"; (2) to be addicted to a drug: "That cat's strung out behind H."

bennies: benzedrine, an amphetamine

blast: to smoke marijuana (an obsolete term)

blind: to be under the influence of a drug, often marijuana, to such an extent that one is unable to function normally

boo: marijuana; although generally obsolete, sometimes used humorously

brick: a block of marijuana, compressed and packaged; usually a kilogram in weight, although sometimes slightly less bring down: to lose one's high; anything which causes one to lose one's high; that which causes one to lose any positive euphoric feeling; anything which is depressing

bum trip, bummer: a negative or unpleasant experience with a psychedelic drug; generally, any unpleasant experience

burn: to sell someone else a quantity of drugs, and not deliver them, or give adulterated drugs

bust: to arrest

buzz: a slight tingle of a drug feeling, used especially with marijuana; "I just got a buzz from that joint."

can: a quantity of marijuana, slightly more than an ounce; more often used in some geographical locales than others—Chicago, for instance (see "lid")

cap: a capsule of a drug, usually LSD

carrying: to be in possession of a drug

chippy: to use an addicting drug, usually heroin, sporadically, so that one does not become addicted

clean: (1) to prepare marijuana for smoking by removing stems, twigs, and seeds; (2) not to be in legal possession of any drug, so that when the police search one's dwelling or person, no drugs will be found; (3) among addicts: abstention from an addicting drug

cocktail: a "roach" or a small amount of marijuana or hashish twisted into a regular tobacco cigarette

coke: cocaine

come down: see "bring down"

connection: drug supplier or source

cop: to obtain or buy a quantity of drugs—see "score"; generally, to obtain anything

crash: to "come down" from the long-term effects of the amphetamines

crutch: a device, often a folded matchbook, used for holding a burned-down marijuana cigarette butt (see "roach") to prevent one's fingers from being burned; a "roach holder"

crystal, crystals: methedrine

deal: to sell drugs

dealer: a seller of drugs, usually on a large scale commercial basis

dex, dexies: dexedrine, an amphetamine

dime, dime bag: Ten dollars worth of a drug

do: to take a drug; see "make"

dope: humorous term used by drug users for drugs, usually marijuana: "I smoke dope"; often heroin

downs, downies: barbiturates or tranquillizers

down: anything depressing

dynamite: an exceptionally powerful and pure quantity of a drug:
"That's dynamite grass"; often denotes anything exceptionally
good

fall out: to go to sleep, often after taking a drug

Fed: a federal narcotics agent

fiend: see "freak"

flash: see "rush"

freak: a chronic and heavy user of a drug, never marijuana; the
term has a distinctly negative connotation

freak out, flip out: to have a psychotic experience with a psychedelic drug

fuzz: the police

gage: obsolete (sometimes humorously used) term for marijuana

G.B.: goofballs; barbiturates

gold: see "Acapulco gold."

goofballs: barbiturates

grass: marijuana

guide: someone who accompanies a person taking an LSD "trip"

H: heroin

hash: hashish

head: (1) user of a drug; contains no negative connotation; (2)
mood, thoughts, opinion, taste: "Where's your head at?"

heat: the police

high: to be under the influence of a drug

joint: a marijuana cigarette

joy pop: see "chippy"

key, ki: a kilogram, usually of marijuana (or sometimes hashish)

kif: North African cannabis

lay on: to give someone something, often a quantity of drugs: "I
laid some grass on the cat"; could also mean to tell someone
something

lid: a quantity of marijuana, generally slightly more than an ounce;
usually regionally distinctive for California and the West Coast

make: (1) to take a certain drug, to have experience with a specific
drug, as in: "Did you ever make acid?" (2) to have sexual intercourse

man: (1) the police; (2) occasionally, a dealer

manicure: to take the twigs, stems, and seeds out of a bulk quantity of marijuana to prepare it for smoking

Mary Jane: an obsolete term for marijuana; sometimes used in jest

meth: methedrine, a powerful stimulant closely related to the amphetamines

micro, mike: microgram, a measure for LSD; generally, anything having to do with LSD

nark, narco: narcotics agent

nickel, nickel bag: five dollars worth of a drug, often marijuana

nod, nod out, go on the nod: to become extremely lethargic and sleepy under the influence of a narcotic drug, usually heroin

O: opium

O.D.: to take an overdose of a drug (never marijuana), usually heroin

O.Z.: an ounce, usually marijuana

Panama Red: powerful form of marijuana, usually coming from Panama

panic: the general unavailability of a drug in a given area

pod: obsolete term for marijuana

poke: (1) a puff of marijuana; (2) the jab of a needle into one's skin

poppers: vials of amyl nitrite

pot: marijuana

Prince Albert: a quantity of marijuana, or a "can," so-called because it was once put into an empty Prince Albert pipe tobacco can

psychedelic: having the quality of "expanding" the mind

pusher: obsolete term for a seller of drugs

quill: see "crutch"

reefer: a quantity of marijuana; as applied to a single marijuana cigarette, or "joint," it is generally obsolete

roach: the butt of a marijuana cigarette

rush: the sensuous feeling of an injected drug

scag: heroin

scoff: (1) to swallow a drug orally; (2) to eat

score: (1) to obtain a quantity of a drug; see "cop"; (2) the quantity of drugs that one obtains; (3) to have sexual intercourse

shit: any drug, but usually heroin; occasionally, marijuana

skin pop: to inject a drug subcutaneously, rather than intravenously, usually to avoid addiction smoke: marijuana

snappers: vials of amyl nitrite

snort: to inhale a drug sharply through one's nostril; used with heroin and methedrine among the less frequent users (the heavier users more often inject the drug), and almost always with cocaine

snow: often heroin, sometimes cocaine

spaced, spaced out: to be high

speed: usually methedrine, but can be any of the amphetamines

spike: a hypodermic needle

spoon: (1) a level teaspoon of a drug, usually methedrine; (2) the device used to hold heroin or methedrine while it is being heated and liquified in preparation for intravenous hypodermic injection

stash: a quantity of any drug that is hidden; generally, an amount of a drug

stoned: to be very high

stone: superlative, completely, absolutely, the ultimate

stick: obsolete term for "joint"

tab: a tablet of a drug, usually LSD *also called "hit" (of acid)*

taste: a small amount of a drug, often given in exchange for a favor, or as a sample

take off: (1) see "get off"; (2) to steal a quantity of drugs

tea: somewhat lighthearted term for marijuana

toke: a puff of marijuana (sometimes opium)

toke pipe: a small pipe used especially for smoking marijuana or hashish

trey: a three dollar quantity of a drug

trip: a psychedelic drug experience; generally any involved and dramatic experience

turn on: (1) to take a drug; (2) to take a drug for the first time, almost always marijuana; (3) to become high for the first time, usually on marijuana; (4) generally, to introduce or sensitize someone to something

ups, uppies: stimulants, almost always the amphetamines

wasted: to be under the influence of a drug to such an extent that one is able to do little else but rest or sleep

weed: marijuana

weight: a large quantity of a drug, usually marijuana, often for selling purposes: "I'm looking to cop weight."

wiped out: see "wasted"

wig: an insane person

wig, wig out: to have a psychotic episode under the influence of a psychedelic drug; see "freak out," "flip out"

works: the equipment used to inject drugs intravenously, the needle, especially

yard: $100

zonked, zonked out: see "wasted"; generally, also, to be tired

INDEX

Index

Index

Index

marijuana *(cont'd.)*
marijuana-opiates correlation, 200; methedrine vs. heroin, 20, 205; other drugs used, 183–184; police, 229; psychological-pharmacological argument, 194–195; salience of marijuana, 186, 187; social theory, 194, 197–198; studies of addicts, 191–194; supplier theory, 198; tobacco-marijuana corelation, 200

marijuana and the law: arrests, 35, 269–270, 275, 276, 287–288, 290; arrest as status transformation, 281–282; California, 265–267; Colorado, 267; Connecticut, 282–283; convictions and sentences, 279; as criminalization of deviance, 283; dealers, 266, 267, 268, 270, 275; detection of violations, 270–275; deterrence, 287, 288, 296; dismissal of complaints, 278–279; distribution, 261–262; effectiveness of laws, 196; enforcement officers, 283, 290; federal Marihuana Tax Act, 264–265, 295; formal vs. substantive law, 282–285; Georgia, 267; Illinois, 283; incarceration, 279, 280; Indiana, 282; informants, 271–272, 273; judges' attitudes, 277, 278, 279, 283, 290, 291; legalization of marijuana use, 285–286, 288—289, 291–292, 293, 294; legitimacy of laws, 284–285; Los Angeles study, 272, 276, 278, 279; marijuana vs. alcohol, 292–294; New York, 261, 267; North Dakota, 265; Pennsylvania, 282; police, 268, 269, 295, 302; post-arrest disposition, 277–281; private arrests, 274; probation, 229–280; public arrests, 274; public degradation ceremonies, 281; public safety issue, 291, 292–294, 296, 297; rehabilitation, 289–291, 296; Rhode Island, 267; social costs, 294–295; South Dakota, 265; systematic arrests, 274; Texas, 261; undercover agents, 271, 272–273; Wyoming, 282

Marijuana Newsletter, 71

marijuana, use of: addiction, 114; as adolescent *rite de passage,* 131–132; by adolescents, 103, 111–112, 222; and the arts, 54–55; Assassins, 12; authoritarian views, 62; cigarette-marijuana-heroin progression, 181–182; civil libertarian view, 87, 89, 96; in colleges, 3, 27, 103, 267, 268, 286; as crutch, 139; as cultogenic, 21; and cultural values, 97; curiosity as motive, 134; as deviance, 62–63; 88–90; dimensionalist

terms of, 27; as discontinuous with real life, 307–309; as drug abuse, 61, 100, 231; educational programs on, 66–67; empirical reality concerning, 57–60; epistemological hegemony, 96; etiology of, 62; family influence, 296–297; as fictitious necessity, 83; as fun, 73, 74, 84, 86, 132, 133; as group activity, 123–124, 133–134; habitation, 230, 309; hedonism, 73, 74; human empathy, 83–85; governing factors, for beginning, 127–128, 130–131; illegality as lure, 228; increase in, 3–4; and inhibitions, 82; initiation to, by friends, 124–126; innocence of, 69–71; insanity, 114, 229–293; labelling, as argument, 60–66, 308, 309; legalization of, 58, 65, 73–74, 87–88, 104, 109, 111, 113–114, 117, 173, 238, 243, 285–286, 288–289, 291–292, 293, 294; medical views of, 56, 61–62, 66–67, 87, 94–118, 172, 231, 293; and moral standards, 208–209; motives for, 7–8; mythology of, 8–9, 12–13, 23, 89–90, 137; as neurotic, 101; in Orient, 11, 18, 65, 142–143; as pathological, 61–62, 73, 98, 99, 100, 101, 117, 310; peace and love, 11, 12, 59, 85; and personal inadequacy, 102; psychiatric views, 78–79, 97, 101, 104, 106, 107, 288, 296; as psychological abnormality, 62–63; psychological addiction, 230, 308, 309; and psychological dependency, 61, 72, 100, 104–106, 114, 230, 308; psychological views, 56, 101; psychotomimetic, 60, 76, 106, 107, 134, 137, 196, 226; vs. Puritan ethic, 97–98; as a rational choice, 7; and reality, 51–53, 56, 59, 86–87, 112, 139, 167, 232, 303, 310; as rebellion of youth, 38, 103, 219, 296, 310; recreational, 24–25, 62, 83, 100; and social values, 53–57; as sociogenic, 21–25; sociology of, 8, 11–12, 22, 50, 98, 101, 212, 213, 222; as subculture, 22–23, 33, 61, 72, 80, 91, 110, 111, 112, 123, 134, 135, 142, 160, 173–175, 189, 190, 192, 193, 195, 197, 237, 248, 250, 255, 257, 260, 268, 284, 289, 291, 318; and tribal mind, 54; turn-on defined, 122–123; values vs. fact, 53, 57; and violence, 115

marijuana users: vs. addict, 29–30; age range, 30–32, 235; among artists and writers, 41; authoritarianism, 46, 47, 62, 221; among blacks, 36; as buyers and sellers, 33–34; characteristics of,

Index